Fodor's

SAN DIEGO

28th Edition

Fodor's Travel Publications   New York, Toronto, London, Sydney, Auckland

www.fodors.com

Eugene Fodor:
The Spy Who Loved Travel

As Fodor's celebrates our 75th anniversary, we are honoring the colorful and adventurous life of Eugene Fodor, who revolutionized guidebook publishing in 1936 with his first book, *On the Continent: The Entertaining Travel Annual.*

Eugene Fodor's life seemed to leap off the pages of a great spy novel. Born in Hungary, he spoke six languages and graduated from the Sorbonne and the London School of Economics. During World War II he joined the Office of Strategic Services, the budding spy agency for the United States. He commanded the team that went behind enemy lines to liberate Prague, and recommended to Generals Eisenhower, Bradley, and Patton that Allied troops move to the capital city. After the war, Fodor worked as a spy in Austria, posing as a U.S. diplomat.

In 1949 Eugene Fodor—with the help of the CIA—established Fodor's Modern Guides. He was passionate about travel and wanted to bring his insider's knowledge of Europe to a new generation of sophisticated Americans who wanted to explore and seek out experiences beyond their borders. Among his innovations were annual updates, consulting local experts, and including cultural and historical perspectives and an emphasis on people—not just sites. As Fodor described it, "The main interest and enjoyment of foreign travel lies not only in 'the sites,' . . . but in contact with people whose customs, habits, and general outlook are different from your own."

Eugene Fodor died in 1991, but his legacy, Fodor's Travel, continues. It is now one of the world's largest and most trusted brands in travel information, covering more than 600 destinations worldwide in guidebooks, on Fodors.com, and in ebooks and iPhone apps. Technology and the accessibility of travel may be changing, but Eugene Fodor's unique storytelling skills and reporting style are behind every word of today's Fodor's guides.

Our editors and writers continue to embrace Eugene Fodor's vision of building personal relationships through travel. We invite you to join the Fodor's community at fodors.com/community and share your experiences with like-minded travelers. Tell us when we're right. Tell us when we're wrong. And share fantastic travel secrets that aren't yet in Fodor's. Together, we will continue to deepen our understanding of our world.

Happy 75th Anniversary, Fodor's! Here's to many more.

Tim Jarrell, Publisher

FODOR'S SAN DIEGO
Editors: Salwa C. Jabado, lead editor; Jennifer DePrima

Writers: Maren Dougherty, Maria Hunt, Amanda Knoles, Christine Pae, AnnaMaria Stephens, Claire Deeks van der Lee, Bobbi Zane

Production Editor: Jennifer DePrima
Maps & Illustrations: David Lindroth and Mark Stroud, *cartographers;* Bob Blake, Rebecca Baer, *map editors;* William Wu, *information graphics*
Design: Fabrizio La Rocca, *creative director*; Guido Caroti, *art director*; Tina Malaney, Nora Rosansky, Chie Ushio, *designers*; Melanie Marin, *associate director of photography*
Cover Photo: (Brown Pelican): Tim Laman/National Geographic/age fotostock
Production Manager: Angela L. McLean

28th Edition

ISBN 978-0-679-00972-6

ISSN 1053-5950

SPECIAL SALES
This book is available at special discounts for bulk purchases for sales promotions or premiums. Special editions, including personalized covers, excerpts of existing books, and corporate imprints, can be created in large quantities for special needs. For more information, write to Special Markets/Premium Sales, 1745 Broadway, MD 3-1, New York, NY 10019, or e-mail specialmarkets@randomhouse.com.

AN IMPORTANT TIP & AN INVITATION
Although all prices, opening times, and other details in this book are based on information supplied to us at press time, changes occur all the time in the travel world, and Fodor's cannot accept responsibility for facts that become outdated or for inadvertent errors or omissions. So **always confirm information when it matters,** especially if you're making a detour to visit a specific place. Your experiences—positive and negative—matter to us. If we have missed or misstated something, **please write to us.** Share your opinion instantly through our online feedback center at fodors.com/contact-us.

PRINTED IN SINGAPORE

10 9 8 7 6 5 4 3 2 1

CONTENTS

Fodor's Features

CONTENTS

ABOUT THIS BOOK

Our Ratings

As travelers we've all discovered a place so wonderful that its worthiness is obvious. And sometimes that place is so unique that superlatives don't do it justice: you just have to be there to know. These sights, properties, and experiences get our highest rating, **Fodor's Choice,** indicated by orange stars throughout this book. Black stars highlight sights and properties we deem **Highly Recommended.** By default, there's another category: any place we include in this book is by definition worth your time, unless we say otherwise. And we will. Disagree with any of our choices? Care to nominate a place or suggest that we rate one more highly? Visit our feedback center at www.fodors.com/feedback.

> For expanded hotel reviews, visit **Fodors.com**

Hotels

Hotels have private bath, phone, TV, and air-conditioning, and do not offer meals unless we specify that in the review. We always list facilities but not whether you'll be charged an extra fee to use them.

Restaurants

Unless we state otherwise, restaurants are open for lunch and dinner daily. We mention dress only when there's a specific requirement and reservations only when they're essential or not accepted—it's always best to book ahead.

Credit Cards

We assume that restaurants and hotels accept credit cards. If not, we'll note it in the review.

Budget Well

Hotel and restaurant price categories from ¢ to $$$$ are defined in the opening pages of the respective chapters. For attractions, we always give standard adult admission fees; reductions are usually available for children, students, and senior citizens.

Listings
★ Fodor's Choice
★ Highly recommended
✉ Physical address
✛ Directions or Map coordinates
🕮 Mailing address
☎ Telephone
🖷 Fax
⊕ On the Web

✍ E-mail
🎟 Admission fee
☉ Open/closed times
Ⓜ Metro stations
▭ No credit cards

Hotels & Restaurants
🏨 Hotel
🛏 Number of rooms
△ Facilities
🍽 Meal plans
✕ Restaurant
🕭 Reservations
🏛 Dress code
🚭 Smoking

Outdoors
⛳ Golf
△ Camping

Other
🎪 Family-friendly
⇨ See also
✉ Branch address
☞ Take note

Experience San Diego

SAN DIEGO TODAY

Like every city, San Diego has issues that unite—and divide—its 3 million denizens. We'd just as soon forget the local government scandals that rocked national attention in recent years (Randy "Duke" Cunningham, anyone?), while playing up our strong suits (like fun in the sun). But certain civic subjects are always up for discussion. ■TIP→ Want to read up on the local news before your visit? Check out www.voiceofsandiego.org, a nonprofit news blog that's earned kudos from the New York Times for its regional reporting.

Today's San Diego:

. . . is conserving water. A popular topic around the water cooler is—ironically enough—the lack of water in San Diego. A persistent state of drought in Southern California has county residents conserving like never before. In some areas, restrictions are mandatory, and overuse is subject to steep fines—frustrating gardeners and those accustomed to green lawns. Experts disagree on long-term solutions, but nearly everyone has an opinion. How it affects you: many restaurants no longer bring water to the table unless you ask, and some hotels encourage guests to reuse towels and consume water responsibly. Eco-savvy locals go so far as to turn the shower off while shampooing and soaping.

. . . is building for the future. Along with water conservation, a big part of smart city planning is sustainable architecture—and attractiveness is nothing to scoff at either. Downtown's New Children's Museum is just one example of a gorgeously green building. Architecture in general is a buzzworthy local topic. San Diego has improved its cityscape immeasurably by preserving the old while fostering the new, especially in the Gaslamp Quarter and East Village. There's even a local annual architecture awards ceremony, Orchids & Onions, where honors are given to the best and boldest—and to the total stink bombs. The Starlite bar was a recent Orchid winner, while the planned Jamul Casino skulked away in Onion shame.

. . . is due for a natural disaster. Wildfires always pose a risk in San Diego County, especially in late summer and early fall, when dry Santa Ana winds sweep through with their devastating wrath. Out-of-control blazes have scorched huge swaths of San Diego County, including the wildfires of 2007, which burned nearly 300,000 acres, and the human-caused Cedar Fires

WHAT WE'RE TALKING ABOUT

Admittedly, we're not quite as celeb-obsessed as the Angelenos to the north, but our proximity to L.A.—and our showstopping natural surroundings—have turned San Diego into a popular spot for **moviemaking** and vacationing A-listers. And that's been the case since Wyatt Earp set up shop in the Gaslamp Quarter in 1885.

Southern California may be calorie-conscious, but foodies here are obsessed with the freshest flavors—and brownie points if produce and meats are from nearby farms. The West Coast obsession with all things **locavore** may be feeding the fervor for haute, healthy cuisine, but we're still hungry for more. We're also eager to get our kids involved, and local schools like High Tech High have planted interest with community gardens.

in 2003, which killed 15 people. These firestorms were visible from space!

Like hurricanes and tornados, wildfires get locals talking—you'll know if they're headed your way. If you do hear talk of wildfires during your visit, keep in mind that they burn hot and fast, so if you're staying beyond the urban center, familiarize yourself with evacuation routes. And, if you're playing in the great outdoors, don't forget Smokey the Bear's advice: only you can prevent wildfires.

Earthquakes, on the other hand—talk about no warning. All you need to know is that San Diego's overdue for a big one, which scientists and regional media seem to enjoy reminding us. Our advice: make sure your family knows how to respond, just in case.

. . . is in a state over real estate. Want to rouse a rabble? Talk to locals about real estate and you'll get a lot of opinions, some logical and some bordering on conspiracy theory. The truth is that for years, the city's infamously high median home prices (a half million to buy a starter home) climbed as if they were on an endless ladder up, but then the market went bust and a lot of people were stuck with $600K downtown lofts that

were worth about $300K to new buyers. Housing costs have fallen to a more reasonable range now—unless you look at the luxury listings, where a few hundred thousand barely makes a dint in the asking price.

. . . has to build to keep the Bolts. The fate of the NFL's San Diego Chargers is a topic that gets sports' fans' blood boiling. Locals want the Bolts to stay in San Diego, a fact that the team's owner is fully aware of as he lobbies for a brand-new stadium to replace Qualcomm Stadium, which was built in the late '60s, can hold around 75,000 fans, and has hosted three Super Bowls. The Chargers have looked at potential sites from Oceanside to Chula Vista, shelling out a cool $10 million in their search. Residents are split on the idea of a new stadium, but few want to see their football team go. In 2009, an escape clause in the Chargers' contract became active, with a buyout penalty that decreases yearly. So the heat is on for the Bolts and their fans.

Sustainability is a growing—and greening—passion. More than ever before, area builders are striving for LEED certification, leading to a growing number of green resources for locals. UCSD's Sustainability 2.0 initiative bills itself as a "living laboratory" that integrates education, research, and application. We need the smartest on board as we step up our stewardship of San Diego—and the planet.

Every day in San Diego, scary stories about the **U.S.-Mexico border** surface, from drug-gang violence to people-smuggling coyotes. But for all the border woes, our proximity to Mexico has enriched our city in many ways, from the food (taco stands on every corner) to the music (who can resist norteño?).

WHAT'S WHERE

1 Downtown. Downtown used to be a real downer, a mix of bland office towers and seedy sidewalks after sundown. Preservationists and entrepreneurs saved the day, starting with Horton Plaza, a six-block shopping and dining complex. Now, the streets are lined with nightclubs, boutiques, and restaurants, from the glam Gaslamp Quarter (a former red-light district) to the edgier East Village (where Padres fans get their baseball fix at PETCO Park). Also nearby: Seaport Village, the Embarcadero, Little Italy, and harborside recreation areas.

2 Balboa Park. Smack in the center of the city, this 1,200-acre patch of greenery is home to world-class museums and performing arts, stunning Spanish colonial revival architecture, and the famous San Diego Zoo. Gentle pathways lead to gardens, fountains, and groves of shady trees, plus plenty of play area for pooches. It's like the Central Park of the West—a leafy urban getaway for locals and an absolute must-see for tourists.

3 Old Town. Before there was a sprawling city, there was an Old Town, where you'll find remnants of San Diego's—and California's—first permanent European settlement. The former pueblo is now a pedestrian-friendly state historic park, with original and reconstructed buildings and sites, along with a tourist bazaar of souvenir shops, art galleries, and Mexican eateries with margaritas and mariachi aplenty.

4 Uptown. Uptown is a handy catchall for a cluster of trendy neighborhoods near downtown and north of Balboa Park. Hillcrest, the heart of the city's gay and lesbian community, caters to a stylish, adventurous crowd. In North Park, a hip and edgy set keeps the boutiques, galleries, eateries, and bars hopping. The cool crowd has also converged on University Heights, where new dining and nightlife spots crop up constantly.

5 Mission Bay and the Beaches. Home to Sea-World, Mission Bay also boasts a 4,600-acre aquatic park perfect for boating, jet skiing, swimming, and fishing, plus land-based activities like biking, basketball, and kite flying. It's neighbored by the bustling Mission Beach and Pacific Beach communities, where streets are lined with surf shops, ice-cream stands, and beach bars.

6 La Jolla. La Jolla lands lavish praise for its picturesque cliffs and beaches, not to mention a bevy of the finest hotels, restaurants, art galleries, and shopping. From the cove's sunning sea lions and Windansea's locals-only surf scene to cocktails at a grand hotel where the Hollywood elite once retreated, there's something for everyone.

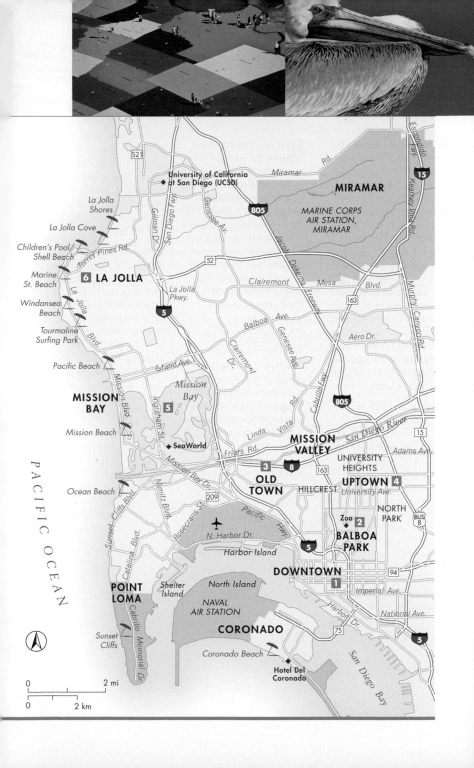

PACIFIC OCEAN

University of California
at San Diego (UCSD)

La Jolla
Shores

La Jolla Cove

Children's Pool/
Shell Beach

Marine
St. Beach

6 LA JOLLA

Windansea
Beach

Tourmaline
Surfing Park

Pacific Beach

**MISSION
BAY**

Mission Beach

Ocean Beach

**POINT
LOMA**

Sunset
Cliffs

MIRAMAR

**MARINE CORPS
AIR STATION,
MIRAMAR**

La Jolla
Pkwy.

Clairemont Mesa Blvd.

Balboa Ave.

Aero Dr.

La Jolla Blvd.

Torrey Pines Rd.

Gilman Dr.

San Diego Fwy.

Genesee Av.

Clairemont Dr.

Genesee Ave.

Jacob Dekema Freeway

Kearney Villa Rd.

Murphy Canyon Rd.

Espondido Fwy.

Grand Ave.

**Mission
Bay**

Ingraham St.

Mission Blvd.

SeaWorld

Linda Vista Rd.

Cabrillo Fwy.

San Diego River

Adams Ave.

**MISSION
VALLEY**

3 **8**

**OLD
TOWN**

HILLCREST

**UNIVERSITY
HEIGHTS**

UPTOWN **4**

University Ave.

**NORTH
PARK**

BUS
8

Mission Bay Dr.

Friars Rd.

Nimitz Blvd.

Sunset Cliffs Blvd.

Catalina Blvd.

Rosecrans St.

Pacific Hwy.

N. Harbor Dr.

Harbor Island

Shelter
Island

North Island

**NAVAL
AIR STATION**

Zoo **2**

**BALBOA
PARK**

DOWNTOWN

1

Imperial Ave.

National Ave.

94

75

CORONADO

Coronado Beach

Hotel Del
Coronado

Cabrillo Memorial Dr.

Harbor Dr.

San Diego Bay

5

S21

805

805

5

5

5

52

163

163

15

15

15

209

0   2 mi

0   2 km

WHAT'S WHERE

7 Point Loma. Point Loma curves crescentlike along the bay. Its main drags are cluttered with fast-food joints and budget motels, but farther back, grand old houses give way to ocean views. At the southern tip of the peninsula, the majestic Cabrillo Monument commemorates the landing of explorer Juan Rodríguez Cabrillo at San Diego Bay in 1542; the 360-degree vista sometimes includes glimpses of migrating gray whales. Farther north, make time for tide pools at Ocean Beach's Sunset Cliffs.

8 Harbor and Shelter Islands. Harbor Island is a man-made strip of land in the bay across from the airport, while to the west, Shelter Island is known for its yacht-building and sport-fishing industries. Both have a handful of hotels and restaurants, plus unsurpassed views of the downtown skyline in one direction and Coronado in the other.

9 Coronado. Historic Coronado, an islandlike peninsula across from the San Diego waterfront, came of age as a Victorian resort community. Its seaside centerpiece is the fabled (and gabled) Hotel Del Coronado, a favorite haunt of celebs, A-listers, and—well—ghosts, if you believe local lore. The upscale area, also home to a naval base, offers plenty of shopping, dining, and pleasant stretches of sand. Drive across the bridge or take the ferry to reach it.

10 Mission Valley. Every town needs an area like Mission Valley. It falls short on history and charm, but provides all the central necessities: chain lodging, soulless condos and office towers, big-box stores, shopping malls (including fancy Fashion Valley), and Qualcomm Stadium, home to the Chargers. Hotel Circle is hotel central in all price ranges.

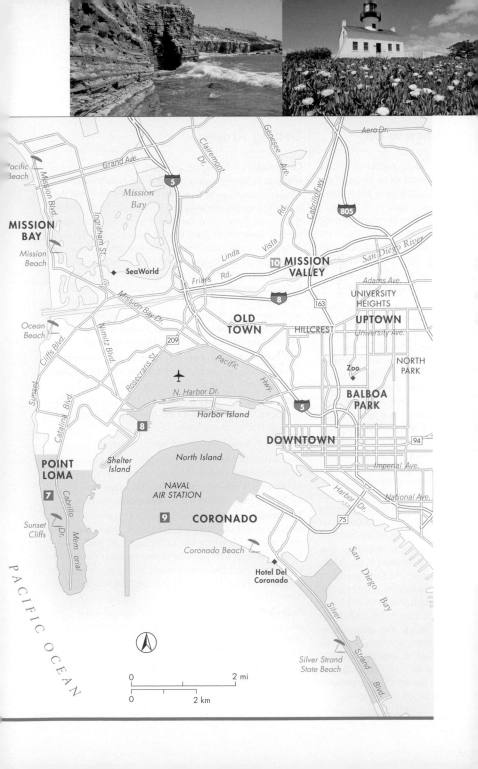

SAN DIEGO PLANNER

When to Go

San Diego's weather is so ideal that most locals shrug off the high cost of living and relatively lower wages as a "sunshine tax." Along the coast, average temperatures range from the mid 60s to the high 70s, with clear skies and low humidity. Annual rainfall is minimal, less than 10 inches per year.

The peak season for sun seekers is July through October. In July and August, the mercury spikes and everyone spills outside. Beaches are a popular daytime destination, as is Balboa Park, thanks to its shady groves and air-conditioned museums. Summer's nightlife scene thrives with the usual bars and clubs, plus outdoor concerts, theater, and movie screenings. Early fall is a pleasant time to visit, as many tourists have already left town and the temperature is nearly perfect. From mid-December to mid-March, whale-watchers can glimpse migrating gray whales frolicking in the Pacific. In spring and early summer, a marine layer hugs the coastline for much or all of the day (locals call it "June Gloom"), which can be dreary and disappointing for those who were expecting to bask in Southern California sunshine. However, wildflowers also blanket the mountainsides and desert in early spring.

Getting Around

Car Travel: To fully explore sprawling San Diego—especially with kids in tow—consider renting a car. Nearly everything of interest can be found off the I–5 or I–163, and the county's freeways are wide and easy to use. Traffic isn't a major issue if you avoid rush hour. Parking in urban areas is typically metered, Monday through Saturday, 8 to 6, unless otherwise marked. You may park for free outside those hours, and on Sunday and holidays. ■TIP→ Yellow commercial loading zones are fair game for parking after 6. During special downtown events, such as Padres games, you'll likely have to settle for one of the many paid parking structures—they cost around $20 close to the action. Parking at beaches is free for the most part, though tough to come by on sunny days unless you stake out a spot early.

Foot Travel: Walking is the way to go once you've reached a destination area. Balboa Park and the zoo are walkers' paradises, and all of downtown is pedestrian friendly.

Public Transportation: Visit ⊕ www.sdcommute.com, which lists routes and timetables for the Metropolitan Transit System and North County Transit District.

The "Trip Planner" section is a terrific resource.

Local/urban bus fare is $2.25 one way, but you can pick up an unlimited day pass for $5 (exact change only; pay when you board). A one-way ride on the city's iconic red trolleys is $2.50; get your ticket at any trolley vending machine.

Taxi Travel: Cabs are a fine choice for trips to and from the airport and short jaunts around town. The approximate rates are: $2.20 for the first 1/10 mi, $2.30 each additional mile, and $19 per hour of waiting time. You can find taxicab stands at the airport, hotels, major attractions, and shopping centers. Downtown, your best bet is to flag one down, New York City–style.

Pedicab Travel: These pedal-powered chariots are a great way to get around downtown. Just be sure to agree on a price before you start moving, or you could get taken for the wrong kind of ride. Many pedicab drivers offer up their own unique commentary on the sights, though take what they say with a grain of salt—fibbing is part of the fun.

1

What to Wear

You won't find a more casual big city. Flip-flops are the favored footwear, shorts and tiny skirts comprise the summer uniform, and designer jeans qualify as dressing up. Despite the city's easygoing vibe, San Diegans value labels—just look at Fashion Valley's lineup of high-end outposts like Jimmy Choo and Louis Vuitton. Dining out warrants a little research; some eateries barely toe the "no shirt, no shoes" rule, while others require more elegant attire.

Safety

San Diego has some sketchy areas, although tourists typically encounter few problems. Downtown can get a little rowdy at night, especially toward 2 am, when bars boot drunken patrons out on the sidewalks. The city also has a large homeless population, who often camp out on shadowy side streets not far from East Village. Most are harmless, aside from the occasional panhandling, but it's safest to stick to well-lighted, busy areas. Certain pockets of Balboa Park are frequented by drug dealers and prostitutes after hours; if you're attending a nighttime theater or art event, park nearby or use the valet. And if you plan to head south of the border, browse our Tijuana section for safety tips.

Where to WWW

Browse these online options for more about what's on.

⊕ *www.fodors.com*, check out the forums on our site for answers to your travel questions and tips.

⊕ *www.sandiego.org* for the San Diego visitor bureau.

⊕ *www.sandiegoreader.com* posts tons of event listings, from big concerts to little community to-dos.

⊕ *www.signonsandiego.com* is where the scaled-down *San Diego Union-Tribune* posts all its daily newspaper and original online content, including a searchable entertainment section.

⊕ *www.sdcitybeat.com* for the online version of the alternative weekly *San Diego CityBeat*, a guide to the city's edgier side, from regional politics to the hottest local bands.

⊕ *www.urbanistguide.com* is the ultimate how-to for hip urban explorers, including curated calendar picks, Q&As with local scene makers, and an interactive map feature.

Festivals

Pencil in these festivals when you're in town.

Winter: Drawing 100,000 visitors the first Friday and Saturday of December, **Balboa Park December Nights** offers festive carolers, food, music, and dance. The **San Diego Bay Parade of Lights,** also in December, lights up the harbor with boats decked out for the holidays.

February's **Farmers Insurance Open** is the Holy Grail for golf fans; the celeb-heavy tourney has been held at the scenic Torrey Pines Golf Course for decades. Later in the month, the **Mardi Gras** block party in the Gaslamp Quarter invites revelers to let the good times roll.

Spring: The **Adams Avenue Roots Fest** gives music fans a weekend of free blues, country, folk, and jazz, while Little Italy's annual **ArtWalk** showcases local art talent on tent-lined streets.

Summer: The **San Diego County Fair,** the Old Globe's **Summer Shakespeare Festival,** the city's huge **LGBT Pride Festival,** racing season at the **Del Mar Fairgrounds,** and outdoor classical concerts at the **Embarcadero** all take place in summer.

Fall: Music fans eagerly wait the **Adams Avenue Street Fair,** a weekend of concerts and a carnival.

SAN DIEGO TOP ATTRACTIONS

Balboa Park
(B) Oasis is hardly hyperbole when it comes to describing this 1,200-acre cultural heart of San Diego. Take a peaceful stroll or plan a full day of perusing Balboa Park's many museums, theater spaces, gardens, trails, and playing fields. And don't forget the park's famous San Diego Zoo.

Beaches
(D) San Diego boasts 70 mi of coastline, with beaches for everybody, from pail-and-shovel-toting toddlers to hard-bodied adventurous types—even nudists have their own sheltered spot at Black's Beach. Coronado is a family favorite, twenty-somethings soak up sun at Pacific Beach, and surfers swear by various stretches of shore. Life's a beach, here, literally.

Cabrillo National Monument
(C) On the southern tip of the Point Loma peninsula, this landmark commemorates the 1542 landing of explorer Juan Rodríguez Cabrillo in San Diego Bay. Unparalleled harbor and skyline views, a military history museum, tidal pools, and an old lighthouse are among the offerings. In winter, lucky visitors may even catch sight of migrating gray whales along the coast.

Carlsbad Flower Fields
(A) Fifty acres of flowers, mostly ranunculus, bloom in Technicolor hues every March on a hillside perched above the Pacific Ocean. Timing is everything, but if you visit in spring, don't miss this showy display of stunning natural beauty.

La Jolla
First things first: It's pronounced La Hoya. And it's one of the prettiest places in California, a wealthy enclave with a small-town feel and world-class scenic coastline. Visit the Children's Pool, populated by sunbathing seals, or watch locals ride waves at Windansea Beach. Then again, you could just shop and nosh the day away.

LEGOLAND California
(E) A whole universe of LEGO fun awaits the pint-size set and their chaperones in Carlsbad, including more than 60 rides and attractions. Especially cool is Miniland USA, scaled-down cities built entirely from LEGO bricks, as well as Dino Island and the Egyptian-theme Dune Raiders, a 30-foot racing slide.

San Diego Zoo
(G) One word: pandas. The San Diego Zoo has several of the roly-poly crowd pleasers. And yes, they're that cute. But the conservation-minded zoo offers much more, from Polar Bear Plunge, the arctic creature's recently revamped habitat, to oh-so-close encounters of lions, tigers, and bears. Explore the huge, hilly attraction by foot, or take advantage of the guided bus tours, aerial tram, and seated shows. Also a roaring good time: Escondido's Safari Park.

SeaWorld
(H) Awe-inspiring orcas and other cute sea critters perform splashy tricks at stage shows, but there's plenty else for families to enjoy, from the Journey of Atlantis water ride to feeding chum to bottlenose dolphins at Rocky Point Preserve. And don't miss SeaWorld's Penguin Encounter, one of two places in the world where emperor penguins are kept in captivity.

Torrey Pines State Natural Reserve
(F) The nation's rarest pine tree calls this area home, as do the last salt marshes and waterfowl refuges in Southern California. Hikers can wind their way down windswept trails that stretch from the high coastal bluffs to sandy Torrey Pines State Beach below. Panoramic views abound.

TOP EXPERIENCES

Did we mention the beach?

If stretching out on the sand with a sunscreen-stained paperback sounds like a snooze, there's always swimming, snorkeling, surfing, diving, and deep-sea fishing. And that's just in the water. On the sand, serve and spike in a friendly beach volleyball pickup or pal around with your pooch at a leash-free dog beach. The truly adventurous should sign up for Over-the-Line, a massive beach softball tourney that takes place every July—the title refers as much to blood alcohol levels as the rules of the game.

Sail away

So you don't own a historic tall ship. Who says you can't experience the thrill of sailing the seas in high style? Several times a year, the **San Diego Maritime Museum** offers public adventure sails aboard the *Star of India,* the *Californian,* and the HMS *Surprise.* And, on very rare occasions, the ships even stage cannon battle reenactments in the San Diego Bay. *Master and Commander* wannabes, consider it your shot at combat glory.

Culture vulture

San Diego's artistic scene gets short shrift compared to the city's outdoorsy offerings, which is a shame. Truly top-notch theater dominates the dance cards of local culturati, like **La Jolla Playhouse,** which routinely hosts Broadway-bound shows before they head east. The **Old Globe**—the oldest professional theater in the state—stages everything from Shakespeare to the avant-garde at its cluster of spaces, including the new state-of-the-art Conrad Prebys Theatre Center. Both locations (downtown and La Jolla) of the **Museum of Contemporary Art San Diego** showcase thought-provoking exhibitions, from regionally focused to international retrospectives, while niche galleries throughout the county cater to the visually curious. And no matter what the season, visitors will find something fetching from area performing-arts staples such as the **San Diego Symphony Orchestra, San Diego Opera,** and **San Diego Ballet.**

Bogey bliss

Whether you're timid at the tee or an aspiring golf pro, San Diego's wide-ranging golf options will wow you. Never mind the fact that water restrictions have left some greens a little less, er, green. Golfing in San Diego is an experience par none, no matter what your price range and ability. If you can swing the fees, splurge at Carlsbad's **Park Hyatt Resort Aviara** or at the **Rancho Bernardo Resort & Spa.** La Jolla's **Torrey Pines Golf Course,** home to the 2008 U.S. Open and every Buick Invitational (now the Farmers Insurance Open) since 1968, is one of the finest 18-hole public courses in the country, and a more affordable outing. Just be sure to book tee times well in advance.

Sky high

Sometimes, soaring above the earth is the best way to get a sense of its mind-blowing scale—to wit, the colorful hot-air balloons that dot the horizon at sunrise and sunset. Tiny and toylike from the ground, they offer big bird's-eye views to those who take flight. The annual **Temecula Balloon & Wine festival,** typically in June, is a favorite among fliers. If standing beneath an open flame makes you a basket case, perhaps tandem paragliding will put you in your proper airborne place. An instructor handles the hard work. All you have to do is shout in glee as the winged glider climbs and dips above cliff-bordered beaches.

Charge it

When your Visa bill reads like a vacation diary, you know you're a serious shopaholic. Jimmy Choo, Hermès, and Louis Vuitton? That was just an afternoon at **Fashion Valley!** San Diego has options to suit every style of shopper. For unique, edgy scores, scour boutiques in neighborhoods like **Hillcrest, Little Italy,** and **North Park.** Sleek storefronts in **La Jolla** and other well-heeled areas carry all variety of luxury goods, while downtown's **Westfield Horton Plaza** stocks standard mall fare. For souvenirs—seashells and such—try **Seaport Village,** or browse festive Mexican arts and crafts at Old Town's **Fiesta de Reyes.**

Hang loose, dude

Only a grom (a newbie) would say hang loose, but "dude" is definitely a prominent part of the local surfer's vocabulary (as in, duuuuude). If you have the courage to wriggle into a wetsuit and waddle into knee-deep white water with a big foam board, you might just catch a wave—or at least stand up for a few seconds. Learning to surf is hard work, so your best bet is to take lessons, either private instruction or group-based. Try La Jolla's **Surf Diva Surf School,** geared primarily toward ladies, or Carlsbad's **San Diego Surfing Academy** in North County.

Sample the fish tacos

The humble fish taco is a local foodie favorite. Beer-battered and fried or lightly grilled, topped with salsa or white sauce and cabbage, tacos around town appeal to every palate. Sample the different styles from simple storefront restaurants and mobile taco trucks, and be prepared for a heated discussion. The only thing most San Diegans agree on is that fish tacos taste even better with a cold beer.

Spa-tacular

Money may not buy happiness, but it can definitely purchase a day of pampering at one of San Diego's many upscale spas. There's no limit to the luxuriating, from youth-restoring facials to aromatherapy massages that unkink months' worth of muscle aches. If cost is no concern, book an afternoon at Carlsbad's idyllic **La Costa Resort and Spa,** or at the historic **Hotel Del Coronado,** a beauty-boosting seaside retreat since the Victorian days.

Skip town

San Diego's allure extends well beyond its famous coastline. To the east, visitors will find forested mountains and an otherworldly desert landscape. The tiny town of **Julian,** in the Cuyamaca Mountains, charms with olden-day bed-and-breakfasts and ample slices of apple pie. In winter, weather allowing, visitors can even take horse-drawn sleigh rides. One of San Diego's most underrated natural attractions is the vast **Anza-Borrego Desert State Park,** 600,000 jaw-dropping acres of protected land crisscrossed with hiking trails. Rough it at a campground or hole up at a hotel. Spring, which blankets the valleys with desert wildflowers, is peak season. Just steer clear of summer, when temperatures skyrocket into the 100s.

GREAT ITINERARIES

ONE DAY IN SAN DIEGO

If you've only got 24 hours to spare, start at **Balboa Park,** the cultural heart of San Diego. Stick to El Prado, the main promenade, where you'll pass by peaceful gardens and soaring Spanish colonial revival architecture (Balboa Park's unforgettable look and feel date to the 1914 Panama-California Exposition). Unless you're a serious museum junkie, pick whichever of the park's many offerings most piques your interest—choices range from photography to folk art. If you're with the family, don't even think of skipping the **San Diego Zoo.** You'll want to spend the better part of your day there, but make an early start of it so you can head for one of San Diego's **beaches** while there's still daylight. Kick back under the late afternoon sun and linger for sunset. Or, wander around **Seaport Village** and the **Embarcadero** before grabbing a bite to eat in the **Gaslamp Quarter,** which pulses with nightlife until last call (around 1:40 am).

Alternate plan: Start your day at **SeaWorld** and wrap it up with an ocean-view dinner in **La Jolla.**

FOUR DAYS IN SAN DIEGO

Day 1

The one-day itinerary above also works for the first day of an extended visit. If you're staying in North County, though, you may want to bypass the zoo and head for the **San Diego Safari Park,** a vast preserve with huge open enclosures. Here, you'll see herds of African and Asian animals acting as they would in the wild. It's the closest thing in the States to an exotic safari. Not included in the general admission—but worth the extra cost if it's in the budget—are the park's "special experiences": guided photo caravans, rolling Segway tours, mule rides, and the new Flightline, which sends harnessed guests soaring down a zip-line cable high above earthbound animals. Another North County option for families with little ones: **LEGOLAND** in Carlsbad. **Note:** the San Diego Zoo, the San Diego Safari Park, and LEGOLAND are all-day, wipe-those-kids-right-out kind of adventures.

Day 2

Your first day was a big one; ease into your second with a gut-busting breakfast (**Richard Walker's Pancake House** in downtown's East Village is a crowd pleaser), followed by a 90-minute tour aboard the **SEAL Amphibious Tour,** which departs from Seaport Village daily. The bus-boat hybrid explores picturesque San Diego neighborhoods before rolling right into the water for a cruise around the bay, all with fun-facts narration. Back on land, devote an hour or so to **Seaport Village,** a 14-acre waterfront entertainment complex with around 50 shops and more than a dozen restaurants. Meant to look like a harbor in the 19th century, Seaport features 4 mi of cobblestone pathways bordered by lush landscaping and water features. From there, stroll north to the **Embarcadero,** where you'll marvel at the historic maritime vessels, including the *Star of India* (the world's oldest active ship), *Berkeley*, *Californian*, *Medea*, and *Pilot* (in summer, a few of the ships stage cannon battles). Learn about local nautical history at the **Maritime Museum,** or explore San Diego's military might at the **San Diego Aircraft Carrier Museum** aboard the USS *Midway*, a permanently docked aircraft carrier with more than 60 exhibits and 25 restored aircraft. Spend the rest of your afternoon and evening in

Coronado, a quick jaunt by ferry or bridge, or walk a few blocks north to the **Gaslamp Quarter,** where the shopping and dining will keep you busy for hours.

Day 3

Set out early enough, and you might snag a parking spot near **La Jolla Cove,** where you can laugh at the sea lions lounging on the beach like lazy couch potatoes at the **Children's Pool.** Then head up one block to Prospect Street, where you'll find the vaunted **La Valencia** hotel (called the "Pink Lady" for its blush-hue exterior) and dozens of posh boutiques and galleries. Head east to the **Museum of Contemporary Art San Diego**'s La Jolla location, which impresses as much with its ocean views as it does with its world-class collection of artwork. MCASD's Museum Café is a casual but elegant spot for a light lunch. If you're with kids, skip the museum and head for **La Jolla Shores,** a good beach for swimming and making sand castles, followed by a visit to the **Birch Aquarium** and a fresh bite to eat at **El Pescador Fish Market** (⇨ *for this and other restaurant reviews, see Chapter 8: Where to Eat*), an always-crowded lunchtime favorite. Once you've refueled, head for **Torrey Pines State Natural Reserve.** Your reward for hiking down the cliffs to the state beach: breathtaking views in every direction. If you're with small children, the trek might prove too challenging, but you can still take in the views from the top. For dinner, swing north to **Del Mar**—during racing season, the evening scene is happening—or, for families, head down to **Ocean Beach** for a juicy burger at the surf-theme **Hodad's.**

Day 4

Begin with a morning visit to **Cabrillo National Monument,** a national park with a number of activities. Learn about 16th-century explorer Juan Rodríguez Cabrillo, take a gentle 2-mi hike on the beautiful Bayside Trail, look around the Old Point Loma Lighthouse, and peer at tide pools, which teem with sea life (remember: look but don't touch). ■ **TIP→** Find out if low tide is in the morning or afternoon before planning your itinerary. After Cabrillo, hop in your car and head to **Old Town,** where San Diego's early history comes to carefully reconstructed life. The Mexican food here isn't the city's best. Leading contenders for that honor are Las Cuatro Milpas in Barrio Logan and **Tacos El Gordo** in Chula Vista, both too out-of-the-way for most tourists. The Old Town restaurants aren't even particularly authentic, but they are bustling and kid-friendly, and frosty margaritas make an added incentive for grown-ups. After that, spend a few hours exploring whatever cluster of neighborhoods appeals to you most. If you like casual coastal neighborhoods with a youthful vibe, head to **Pacific, Mission,** or **Ocean Beach,** or venture up to **North County** for an afternoon in Encinitas, which epitomizes the old California surf town. If edgy and artsy are more your thing, explore the **Uptown** area, where you'll find super-hip shops, bars, and eateries.

ALTERNATIVES

If you're an **adventure junkie,** ignore all of the above suggestions and skip ahead to the Sports and the Outdoors chapter. You can easily fill four days or more with every imaginable outdoor activity, from swimming, surfing, and sailing to hiking, golfing, and paragliding. San Diego is an athletic enthusiast's heaven—unless you're a skier, that is.

TIPS

■ Sure, it's fun to dip those toes in the sand and saunter through one of the world's most incredible zoos. But don't overlook San Diego's somewhat underrated performing arts scene. It's extremely easy to add a theater performance or a concert to any of the four days described above. Some of the city's top performance venues are in Balboa Park (Day 1), downtown (Day 2), and La Jolla (Day 3).

■ If you plan to tour more than a couple of museums in Balboa Park, buy the **Passport to Balboa Park,** which gets you into 14 attractions for just $45, or the **Passport to Balboa Park Combo Pass,** which also gets you into the zoo (it costs $75). You can buy these at the **Balboa Park Visitor Center** (☎ *619/239–0512* ⊕ *www.balboapark.org*).

■ Locals complain about public transportation as often as they complain about the price of fuel, but the **trolleys** and the **Coaster** are a hassle-free way to get to foot-friendly neighborhoods up and down the coast. Public transportation saves you the headache of traffic and parking, and includes free sightseeing along the way. You can head almost anywhere from the historic **Santa Fe Depot** downtown (don't miss the cutting-edge Museum of Contemporary Art next door to the station).

In **winter,** adjust the itineraries to include more indoor activities—the museums are fantastic—as well as a whale-watching boat tour.

In **summer,** check local listings for outdoor concerts, theater, and movie screenings, all a wonderful way to while away a warm evening.

One last alternative plan is **Tijuana.** Though the Mexican border town is not for the anxious traveler—it's dirty and can be quite dangerous at times—there are attractions worth experiencing, from the garish but exuberant Avenida Revolución, a junk-filled shopping bazaar, to Centro Cultural Tijuana (CECUT), with its Omnimax Theater and excellent exhibits on Baja California's history, flora, and fauna. For the extra-emboldened, traditional bullfights at the Plaza Monumental are simultaneously violent and graceful, and quite beloved by locals.

LIKE A LOCAL

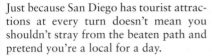

Just because San Diego has tourist attractions at every turn doesn't mean you shouldn't stray from the beaten path and pretend you're a local for a day.

A pared-down pace

Balboa Park is the city's preferred playground. Visitors with detailed agendas (Museums? Check. Zoo? Check.) often miss out on the sweet spots that keep locals coming back time and again. Grab a map from the visitor center and explore the park's nooks and crannies. Or throw down a blanket on the lawn and laugh at the other tourists with their impossibly long to-do lists.

The hoppiest place on Earth

Cold beer seems to suit San Diego's chill personality, which may be why our craft-brewing scene has been lauded as one of the most cutting-edge in the world. You could easily spend an entire day visiting breweries, from the tiny **Alpine Beer Company**—to Escondido's venerable **Stone Brewing**, which started off as a pet project and now ships nationwide. If a full-fledged beer tour is out of the question, try a bold double IPA—a San Diego specialty—at **O'Brien's**, a Kearny Mesa pub that's low on personality but high on hops, or head to **30th Street** in North Park, which is lined with so many brewpubs that it's been nicknamed the "Belgian Corridor" by in-the-know imbibers.

Fill your heart with art

MCASD-Downtown's **Thursday Night Thing**—aka TNT—is a boisterous quarterly museum party that puts to rest all notions of an artless art scene.

Sunrise, sunset

Our beaches can't be beat, but battling the crazy summer crowds for a spot on the sand is far from relaxing. Take a brisk stroll just after dawn, and savor the views without distraction. Or, find a secluded spot on the cliffs for a sunset happy hour. Booze is banned at beaches, but a little creativity will have you toasting in no time (hint: wash and save a couple of paper coffee cups).

Break for breakfast

Even fitness freaks—and San Diegans are among the country's fittest—will agree that a slow-paced morning meal is a lovely start to the weekend, which explains the long lines at any place worth the wait.

The **Mission** has locations in Mission Beach (⊠ *3795 Mission Blvd.* ☎ *858/488–9060*), North Park (⊠ *2801 University Ave.* ☎ *619/220–8992*), and the East Village (⊠ *1250 J St.* ☎ *619/232–7662*) plus a spot in La Jolla called the Coffee Cup. The café food is simple and hearty, ranging from traditional fare (eggs, pancakes) to the Latino-inspired (the Papas Locas or "crazy potatoes" will burn a hole in your tongue).

Big Kitchen (⊠ *3003 Grape St.* ☎ *619/234–5789*) is a misnomer—the Golden Hill eatery is tiny. But it is jam-packed with charm, from the photo-plastered walls (including autographed pics of Whoopi Goldberg, a former employee) to owner "Judy the Beauty," who greets every guest. Cash only.

Kono's Café (⊠ *704 Garnet Ave.* ☎ *858/483–1669*) in Pacific Beach lures locals with an outdoor patio and ocean views, but the last thing you'll want to do after eating one of Kono's massive breakfast burritos is slip into a bikini. There's a reason for the expression "burrito belly"—but it's a small price to pay for brazenly overindulgent pleasure.

SAN DIEGO WITH KIDS

Beach fun

A pail and shovel will keep your kids entertained for hours at the beach—**Coronado Beach** is especially family-friendly. Be liberal with the sunscreen, even if it's cloudy, and prepare for a car full of sand, a small trade-off for their satisfied smiles.

If you're visiting in summer, check out the **U.S. Open Sandcastle Competition** (⊕ *www. usopensandcastle.com*) at Imperial Beach, which usually takes place in late July or early August. There is even a kids' competition.

Drop off the tweens and teens for a morning **surf lesson** and enjoy some guilt-free grown-up time. Or rent bikes for a casual family ride along the **Mission Bay boardwalk.** If that's not enough of an adventure, take your daring offspring on the **Giant Dipper,** an old wooden roller coaster at Mission Bay's **Belmont Park,** also home to a huge arcade.

Top attractions

LEGOLAND California is a full day of thrills for kids 12 and under, while the **San Diego Zoo, SeaWorld,** and **San Diego Safari Park** satisfy all age groups and every kind of kid, from the curious (plenty of educational angles) to the boisterous (room to run around and lots of animals to imitate). They even offer family sleepover nights in summer.

Winter sightings

If you're visiting in winter, definitely try a **whale-watching** tour. Even if you don't see any migrating gray whales, the boat ride is fun. La Jolla's **Birch Aquarium** is one of the country's best, with enough glowing and tentacled creatures to send imaginations plummeting leagues under the sea.

Museums geared to kids

An afternoon at the museum might elicit yawns until they spy all the neat stuff. Balboa Park's **San Diego Air and Space Museum** celebrates aviation and flight history with exhibitions that include actual planes, while **Reuben H. Fleet Science Center** inspires budding scientists with interactive exhibits and its IMAX dome theater. The **San Diego Model Railroad Museum** features miles and miles of model trains and track, including an incredibly detailed reproduction of the Tehachapi railroad circa 1952.

Downtown's **New Children's Museum** appeals to all age groups; too-cool teens can even retreat to the edgy Teen Studio. With installations geared just to them and dry and wet art-making areas (less mess for you), kids can channel all that excess vacation energy into something productive. While they color and craft, you can admire the museum's ultracontemporary, sustainable architecture.

Take me out to the ball game

Baseball buffs will have a blast at **PETCO Park,** where the San Diego Padres play all spring and summer. PETCO's Park at the Park, a grassy elevated area outside the stadium, offers stellar center-field views—plus all the action on a big-screen—with a sandy play space if your kids get bored after a few innings. Plus, it's only $5.

Treating your tots

Ocean Beach's yummy **CupcakesSquared** (✉ *3772 Voltaire St.* ⊕ *cupcakessquared. com*) took first place in Martha Stewart's Southern California Cupcake Showdown. Also delish is Hillcrest's **Babycakes** (✉ *3766 5th Ave.* ⊕ *www.babycakessandiego.com*), a stylish spot nestled in an 1889 Craftsman near Balboa Park. Bonus: Babycakes serves beer and wine for weary moms and dads.

FREE (AND ALMOST FREE) IN SAN DIEGO

1

San Diego may levy an unofficial "sunshine tax," but it makes up for it with plenty of free stuff. Aside from the beaches, backcountry trails, and verdant city parks—all as free as the steadfast sun and endless blue skies—a little careful planning can land you cost-free (or very cheap) fun for the whole family.

Free in Balboa Park

Balboa Park hosts its one-hour **Twilight in the Park** concert series from June to August, Tuesday through Thursday at 6:15 pm. Sit under the stars and take in everything from Dixieland Jazz to Latin salsa. Also at the park, check out the **Spreckels International Organ Festival** concerts Monday at 7:30 pm, from June to August, as well as 2 pm Sunday matinee concerts throughout the year. Balboa Park's **Screen on the Green**, an outdoor movie screening, runs throughout summer. The **Timken Museum of Art** in Balboa Park is always free.

Free concerts

The Del Mar Fairgrounds' summertime **4 O'Clock Fridays** series features big-name local and national bands; it's technically free, though you still have to pay a few bucks for racetrack admission.

Also worth catching: Carlsbad's **TGIF Jazz in the Parks,** Friday at 6 pm; **Coronado Summer Concerts-in-the-Park,** Sunday at 6 pm, May–September; **La Jolla Concerts by the Sea,** Sunday at 2 pm, July and August; the **Del Mar Twilight Concert Series**, Tuesday at 5 pm, June–September; and Encinitas' **Sunday Summer Concerts by the Sea,** 3 pm, July and August.

The annual **Adams Avenue Roots Festival** in spring and **Adams Avenue Street Festival** in September both hit pay dirt: blues, folk, country, jazz, indie, world, and more—all for free.

Tastings

Beer aficionados can take a 45-minute tour of the 55,000-square-foot **Stone Brewing Company**—groups fill up fast, maybe because of the free tastings at the end. At **Alpine Beer Company,** four tasters are just $1.50. Wine lovers might pack a lunch and head for **Orfila Vineyards & Winery,** where picnic tables dot the pastoral landscape—the wine's not free, but the views are. Or spend an entire afternoon in **Temecula Wine Country.** Tastings typically aren't free, but you can find twofer coupons and other discounts at ⊕ *www.temeculawines.org.*

October freebies

October is Kids Free Month at the **San Diego Zoo** and the **San Diego Safari Park;** all children under 11 get in free.

Free museums

Both locations of **MCASD** are always free for patrons under 25, and for everyone else the third Thursday of the month from 5 to 7 pm.

In February, you can pick up a free **Museum Month Pass** at Macy's that offers half-off admission to 40 museums for the entire month.

Many of San Diego's museums offer a once-a-month free Tuesday, on a rotating schedule (*Fsee www.balboapark.org for the schedule*) to San Diego city and county residents, active military, and their families; special exhibitions often require separate admission.

Discounts and deals

Try **Just My Ticket** (⊕ *www.justmyticket. com*) for deals on last-minute theater, concert, and sporting event tickets, as well as restaurant coupons.

A WALK THROUGH SAN DIEGO'S PAST

Downtown San Diego is a living tribute to history and revitalization. The Gaslamp Quarter followed up its boisterous boomtown years—the late 1800s, when Wyatt Earp ran gambling halls and sailors frequented brothels lining 4th and 5th Avenues—with a long stint of seediness, emerging only recently as a glamorous place to live and play. Little Italy, once a bustling Italian fishing neighborhood, got a fresh start when the city took its cause to heart.

Where It All Started

Begin at the corner of 4th and Island. There you'll find the 150-year-old **William Heath Davis House,** a saltbox structure shipped around Cape Horn and assembled in the Gaslamp Quarter. Among its famous former residents: Alonzo Horton, the city's founder. Take a tour, keeping a lookout for the house's current resident: a lady ghost.

From there walk a block east to 5th Avenue and head north. Along the way, you'll see some of the 16½-block historic district's best-known Victorian-era commercial beauties, including the Italianate **Marston Building** (at F Street), the **Keating Building,** the **Spencer-Ogden Building,** and the **Old City Hall.** Architecture buffs should pick up a copy of *San Diego's Gaslamp Quarter,* a self-guided tour published by the Historical Society.

At E Street, head back over to 4th Avenue and you'll behold the **Balboa Theatre,** a striking Spanish Renaissance-style building that was constructed in 1923 and restored in 2007. Right next to it is **Westfield Horton Plaza** mall, which opened its doors in 1985. This multilevel mall played a huge role in downtown's revitalization, as entrepreneurs and preservationists realized the value of the Gaslamp Quarter. Pop across Broadway to check out the stately **U.S. Grant Hotel,** built in 1910 by the son of President Ulysses S. Grant.

Art Stop

Follow Broadway west to Kettner Boulevard, where the **Museum of Contemporary Art San Diego (MCASD)** makes a bold statement with its steel-and-glass lines. It's definitely worth a wander, as is MCASD's newest addition across the street, situated in the renovated baggage depot of the 1915 **Santa Fe Depot** (the station itself is also a stunner).

From Fishermen to Fashionistas

From there, head north on Kettner until you hit A Street, make a quick right, and then take a left on India Street. This is the heart of **Little Italy,** which at the turn of the 20th century was a bustling Italian fishing village. The area fell into disarray in the early 1970s due to a decline in the tuna industry and the construction of I–5, which destroyed 35% of the area. In 1996, a group of forward-thinking architects—commissioned by the city—created a cache of new residential, retail, and public areas that coexist beautifully with the neighborhood's historic charms. Now, it's a vibrant urban center with hip eateries, bars, and boutiques. You'll find remnants of retro Little Italy, from authentic cafés (check out **Pappalecco,** a popular gelateria) and boccie ball matches played by old-timers at **Amici Park.**

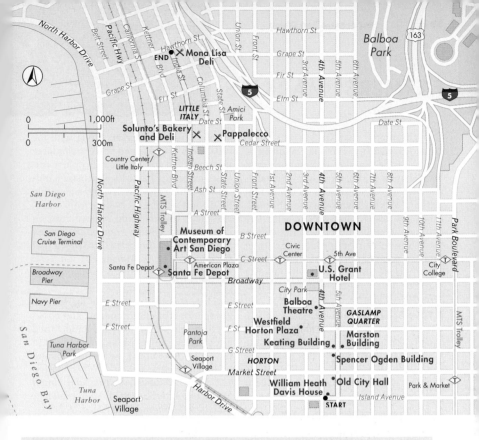

Highlights:	The restored gas lamps that give the Gaslamp its name; the juxtaposition of old and new architecture; Little Italy's sidewalk cafés.
Where to Start:	At the corner of 4th and Island avenues, at the William Heath Davis House. It's a short walk from most downtown hotels. If you drive, park in a paid lot or at nearby Horton Plaza, which offers three free hours with validation (get your ticket stamped by a store).
Length:	About 3 mi and three to four hours with stops round-trip. Take the Orange Line trolley from Santa Fe Depot back if you're tired.
Where to Stop:	From Little Italy follow the same path back or head down Laurel Street to Harbor Drive and wander along the waterfront until you hit Broadway.
Best Time to Go:	Morning or early afternoon.
Worst Time to Go:	In the evening, when it's just too crowded.
Where to Refuel:	If your stomach is growling, Little Italy is waiting for you like an Italian mamma: mangia, mangia! Try **Solunto's Bakery and Deli** (⊠ 1643 India St.) or **Mona Lisa** (⊠ 2061 India St.).

FARMERS' MARKETS

Take advantage of San Diego's year-round gorgeous weather and visit a farmers' market or flea market during your stay. You'll have a chance to mingle with locals and pick up some bargains on things that are hard to find downtown or at the mall. Enjoy the festive atmosphere with live entertainment as you browse the tempting selection of fresh produce, gourmet foods, arts and crafts, fresh flowers, and more. Below are a few of our favorite markets. You can find more on ⊕ *www. sdfarmbureau.org.*

■**TIP**➔ Before you head out, be sure you wear comfortable shoes and bring a tote bag to carry your purchases. Arrive early for the best selection, and assume that you'll have to pay with cash rather than plastic. A little haggling is expected, but be sure to do it politely, with a smile.

Cedros Avenue Farmers Market. Located at the south end of the Cedros Design District, this upscale market offers organic veggies and herbs, regionally grown fruit, healthy juices, California wines, smoked salmon, to-die-for chocolates, freshly baked bread loaves, and all-natural dog treats. ⊠ *410 Cedros Ave., at the corner of Cedros Ave. and Rosa St., Solana Beach* ☎ *858/755– 0444* ⊕ *www. cedrosdesigndistrict.net* ⊙ *Sun. 1–5.*

Coronado Farmers' Market. Located in the parking lot of Il Fornaio restaurant, this small market boasts a scenic bayside setting and more than a dozen vendors selling a variety of fresh produce and exotic flowers from local farms. Specialty foods include organic cheese, butter, and premium meats. ⊠ *Old Ferry Landing, First St. and B St., Coronado* ☎ *760/741–3763* ⊙ *Tues. 2:30–6.*

La Jolla Open Aire Market. Along with the usual fresh produce and flowers, this large market with a county fair atmosphere features paintings from local artists, handmade clothing and jewelry, and a tempting food court serving everything from crepes and tacos to gyros and roasted corn on the cob. ⊠ *La Jolla Elementary School playground, at the corner of Girard and Genter Sts. 1111 Marine St., La Jolla* ☎ *858/454–1699* ⊕ *www.lajollamarket. com* ⊙ *Sun. 9–1.*

Little Italy Mercato. This festive market has a stage for live entertainment and cooking demonstrations. Shop for handcrafted gifts, cheese, nuts, Mexican candy, and olive oil to take home, and enjoy a panino or Italian pastry as you stroll the aisles. ⊠ *Date St. (between Kettner and Union Sts.), Little Italy* ☎ *619/233–3769* ⊕ *www. littleitalysd.com/mercato* ⊙ *Sat. 9–1:30.*

North Park Farmers' Market. Held rain or shine, this market features more than 30 vendors, locally grown produce, fresh flowers, arts and crafts, and an impressive selection of gourmet foods. ⊠ *CVS parking lot, University Ave. and 32nd St., North Park* ☎ *619/233–3901* ⊙ *Thurs., spring and summer 3–dusk, fall and winter 2–dusk.*

Ocean Beach Farmers' Market. Voted "Best Farmers Market in California" by *Sunset* magazine, this popular midweek event features live music, crafts, fresh produce, samples from local restaurants and more. An adjacent parking lot offers handmade apparel and accessories, holistic products and llama rides for kids. ⊠ *Newport Ave. between Cable St. and Bacon St., Ocean Beach* ⊙ *Wed., summer 4–8, winter 4–7.*

Downtown

EAST VILLAGE, EMBARCADERO, GASLAMP QUARTER, AND LITTLE ITALY

WORD OF MOUTH

"We spent several enjoyable days in SD . . . Touring the [USS] *Midway* is very interesting and has the bonus of offering good views of Coronado Island. The Embarcadero is a nice opportunity to stroll along the water's edge."

—saige

GETTING ORIENTED

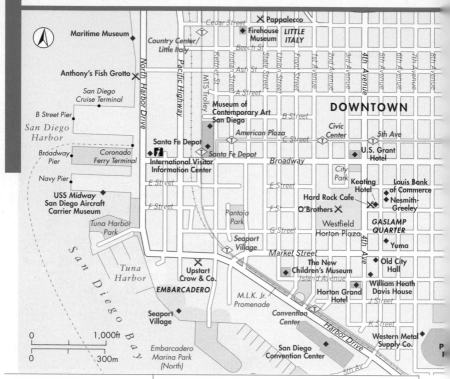

GETTING HERE	TOP REASONS TO GO

GETTING HERE

It's an easy drive into downtown, especially from the nearby airport. There are reasonably priced ($4–$7 per day) parking lots along Harbor Drive, Pacific Highway, and lower Broadway and Market Street. Most restaurants offer valet parking at night, but beware of fees of $15 and up.

If you tire of exploring downtown on foot, hop aboard a horse-drawn carriage, pedicab, San Diego Trolley, or a GoCar (three-wheel cars equipped with a GPS-guided audio tour).

TOP REASONS TO GO

Waterfront delights: Stroll along the Embarcadero, explore Seaport Village, or enjoy a harbor cruise.

Contemporary art for all ages: From the stunning galleries of the Museum of Contemporary Art to the clever incorporation of art and play at the New Children's Museum, downtown is the place for art.

Maritime history: Climb aboard and explore a wide array of vessels from sailing ships to submarines.

Delicious dining: Fresh seafood along the Embarcadero, authentic Italian cuisine in Little Italy, and the high-style restaurants of the Gaslamp make downtown San Diego a diner's delight.

Happening Gaslamp: It's hard to believe this hip neighborhood filled with street art, galleries, restaurants, and buzzing nightlife was once slated for the wrecking ball.

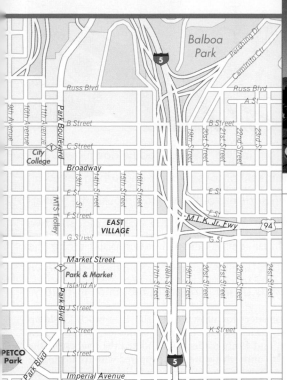

PLANNING YOUR TIME

Most of downtown's attractions are open daily, but the Museum of Contemporary Art, and the New Children's Museum are closed Wednesday, and the Firehouse Museum is only open Thursday through Sunday. For a guided tour of the Gaslamp Quarter Historic District, visit on a Saturday. A boat trip on the harbor, or at least a hop over to Coronado on the ferry, is a must at any time of year. From December through March, when the gray whales migrate between the Pacific Northwest and southern Baja, definitely consider booking a whale-watching excursion from the Broadway Pier.

VISITOR INFORMATION

International Visitor Information Center. Located across from Broadway Pier, this office is a great resource. ■TIP→ Need to feed the meter? A change machine is located inside the visitor center. ⊠ *1040 ⅓ W. Broadway, at Harbor Dr., Embarcadero* ☎ *619/236–1212* ⊕ *www.sandiego.org* ⊙ *June–Sept., daily 9–5; Oct.–May, daily 9–4.*

QUICK BITES

Upstart Crow & Co. This combination bookstore and coffeehouse serves good cappuccino and espresso with pastries and cakes. ⊠ *835 W. Harbor Dr., #C, Seaport Village, Central Plaza, Embarcadero* ☎ *619/232–4855.*

Anthony's Fish Grotto. Grab a fried shellfish plate or a fine variety of good, carefully grilled fish here before your bay cruise a few blocks north of Broadway Pier. ⊠ *1360 N. Harbor Dr., Embarcadero* ☎ *619/232–5103.*

You can get everything from cinnamon rolls to sushi at the informal eateries on **Westfield Horton Plaza's top level.** On level 1 of the mall, O'Brothers offers a completely organic menu including delicious burgers, salads, and wine.

Pappalecco. Kids and adults alike will swoon over the addictive gelato at Pappalecco, near the Firehouse Museum. ⊠ *1602 State St., Little Italy* ☎ *619/238-4590.*

Updated by
Claire Deeks
van der Lee

Nearly written off in the 1970s, today downtown San Diego is a testament to conservation and urban renewal. Once derelict Victorian storefronts now house the hottest restaurants, and the *Star of India,* the world's oldest active sailing ship, almost lost to scrap, floats regally along the Embarcadero. Like many modern U.S. cities, downtown San Diego's story is as much about its rebirth as its history.

Although many consider downtown to be the 16½-block **Gaslamp Quarter**, it's actually comprised of eight neighborhoods, including East Village, Little Italy, and Embarcadero. Considered the liveliest of the bunch, Gaslamp's 4th and 5th avenues are peppered with trendy night-clubs, swanky lounge bars, chic restaurants, and boisterous sports pubs.

Nearby, the most ambitious of the downtown projects is **East Village**, encompassing 130 blocks between the railroad tracks up to J Street, and from 6th Avenue east to around 10th Street. Sparking the rebirth of this former warehouse district was the 2004 construction of the San Diego Padres' baseball stadium, **PETCO Park**. As the city's largest downtown neighborhood, East Village is continually broadening its boundaries with its urban design of redbrick cafés, spacious galleries, rooftop bars, sleek hotels, and warehouse restaurants.

Unlike many tourist-driven communities, the charming neighborhood of **Little Italy** is authentic to its roots, from the Italian-speaking residents to the imported delicacies. The main thoroughfare—from India Street to Kettner Boulevard—is filled with lively cafés, gelato shops, baker-ies, and restaurants. Art lovers can browse gallery showrooms, while shoppers adore the Fir Street cottages. As if transplanted directly from a European village, Little Italy is marked by charming subtleties like the Catholic church bell that rings on the half hour, and Amici Park, where Italians gather daily to play boccie. After an afternoon of gelati and espressos, you may just forget that you're in Southern California.

Running along the San Diego harbor is downtown's **Embarcadero**, home to the **USS *Midway***, the **Maritime Museum**, and **Seaport Village**. The

Martin Luther King Jr. Promenade project put 14 acres of greenery, a pedestrian walkway, and artwork along Harbor Drive from Seaport Village to the **San Diego Convention Center.** The Embarcadero cuts a scenic swath along the harbor front and connects today's downtown San Diego to its maritime routes.

2

EXPLORING DOWNTOWN

GASLAMP QUARTER REVIVAL

The Gaslamp Quarter has the largest collection of commercial Victorian-style buildings in the country. Despite this, when the move for downtown redevelopment gained momentum in the 1970s, there was talk of bulldozing them and starting from scratch. In response, concerned history buffs, developers, architects, and artists formed the Gaslamp Quarter Council. The council gathered funds from the government and private benefactors to clean up and preserve the quarter, restoring the finest old buildings and attracting businesses and the public back to its heart. Their efforts have paid off. Former flophouses have become choice office buildings, and the area is filled with hundreds of trendy shops, restaurants, and nightclubs.

The majority of the quarter's landmark buildings are on 4th and 5th avenues, between Island Avenue and Broadway. If you don't have much time, stroll down 5th Avenue, where highlights include **Louis Bank of Commerce** (No. 835), **Old City Hall** (No. 664), **Nesmith-Greeley** (No. 825), and **Yuma** (No. 631) buildings. The Romanesque Revival **Keating Hotel** at 432 F Street was designed by the same firm that created the famous Hotel Del Coronado, the Victorian grande dame that presides over Coronado's beach. At the corner of 4th Avenue and F Street, peer into the **Hard Rock Cafe,** which occupies a restored turn-of-the-20th-century tavern with a 12-foot mahogany bar and a spectacular stained-glass domed ceiling.

The section of G Street between 6th and 9th avenues has become a haven for galleries; stop in one of them to pick up a map of the downtown arts district. Just to the north, on E and F streets from 6th to 12th avenues, the evolving **Urban Art Trail** has added pizzazz to drab city thoroughfares by transforming such things as trash cans and traffic controller boxes into works of art. During baseball season, the streets flood with Padres fans, and festivals, such as Mardi Gras in February, ShamROCK on St. Patrick's Day, Jazz Fest in June, and Monster Bash in October, bring in partygoers. To miss the Gaslamp Quarter would be to miss San Diego's most exciting neighborhood.

EMBARCADERO TOUR

The bustle of Embarcadero comes less these days from the activities of fishing folk than from the throngs of tourists, but this waterfront walkway—comprised of Seaport Village and the San Diego Convention Center—remains the nautical soul of the city. There are several seafood restaurants here, as well as sea vessels of every variety—cruise ships, ferries, tour boats, and Navy destroyers.

Docked off the Navy pier, the USS *Midway* aircraft carrier was once home to 4,500 crew members.

On the north end of the Embarcadero at Ash Street you'll find the **Maritime Museum.** South of it, the **B Street Pier** is used by ships from major cruise lines—San Diego has become a busy cruise-ship port, both a port of call and a departure point. Tickets for harbor tours and whale-watching trips are sold at the foot of **Broadway Pier.** The terminal for the Coronado Ferry lies just beyond, between Broadway Pier and B Street Pier. One block south of Broadway Pier at Tidelands Park is **Military Heritage Art,** a collection of works that commemorate the service of the U.S military.

Lining the pedestrian promenade between the Cruise Ship Terminal and Hawthorn Street are 30 "urban trees" sculpted by local artists. Docked at the Navy pier is the decommissioned **USS *Midway*,** now the home of the **San Diego Aircraft Carrier Museum. Tuna Harbor,** at the foot of G Street, was once the hub of one of San Diego's earliest and most successful industries, commercial tuna fishing. The industry has moved far away to the western Pacific, so these days there are more pleasure boats than tuna boats tied up at the G Street Pier. The pleasant Tuna Harbor Park offers a great view of boating on the bay and across to any aircraft carriers docked at the North Island naval base.

The next bit of seafront greenery is a few blocks south at **Embarcadero Marina Park North,** an 8-acre extension into the harbor from the center of Seaport Village. It's usually full of kite fliers, in-line skaters, and picnickers. Seasonal celebrations, including San Diego's Parade of Lights, the Port of San Diego Big Balloon Parade, the Sea and Air Parade, and the Big Bay July 4 Celebration, are held here and at the similar **Embarcadero Marina Park South.**

Providing a unique shopping experience, **Seaport Village** covers 14 acres of waterfront retail stores, restaurants, and cafés. Even window-shoppers are treated to a pleasant experience with 4 mi of cobblestone paths, trickling fountains, and beautiful gardens.

The **San Diego Convention Center,** on Harbor Drive between 1st and 6th avenues, is a waterfront landmark designed by Canadian architect Arthur Erickson. The backdrop of blue sky and sea complements the building's nautical lines. The center often holds trade shows that are open to the public, and tours of the building are available.

TOP ATTRACTIONS

Maritime Museum.

Fodor's Choice ★ ⇨ *See the highlighted listing in this chapter.*

Fodor's Choice ★ **Museum of Contemporary Art San Diego (MCASD).** At the downtown branch of the city's contemporary art museum, explore the works of international and regional artists in a modern, urban space that is easily accessible via San Diego's trolley system. In January 2007, the museum expanded its galleries across the street in a superb juxtaposition of old and new. The Jacobs Building—formerly the baggage building at the historic Santa Fe Depot—features large gallery spaces, high ceilings, and natural lighting, giving artists flexible spaces to create large-scale installations. MCASD showcases both established and emerging artists in rotating exhibitions, as well as permanent, site-specific commissions by Jenny Holzer and Richard Serra. Free cell-phone audio tours and Podcasts are available for most exhibits; if you don't have an iPod with you, the museum will lend you one. ■ TIP→ Admission is good for seven days, and includes both the downtown and La Jolla locations. ⊠ *1100 and 1001 Kettner Blvd., Embarcadero* ☎ *858/454–3541* ⊕ *www.mcasd.org* ⌨ *$10; ages 25 and under are free, free 3rd Thurs. of the month 5–7* ☺ *Thurs.–Tues. 11–5, 3rd Thurs. until 7. Closed Wed.*

Fodor's Choice ★ **The New Children's Museum (NCM).** Opened in May 2008, NCM blends contemporary art with unstructured play to create an environment that appeals to children as well as adults. As San Diego's largest public green building project, the 50,000-square-foot structure was constructed from recycled building materials, operates on solar energy, and is convection-cooled by an elevator shaft. It also features a nutritious and eco-conscious café. Interactive exhibits include designated areas for toddlers and teens, as well as plenty of activities for the entire family. Several art workshops are offered each day, as well as hands-on studios where visitors are encouraged to create their own art. The studio projects change frequently, and the entire museum changes exhibits every 18 months, so there is always something new to explore. The adjoining 1-acre park and playground is conveniently located across from the convention center trolley stop. ⊠ *200 W. Island Ave., Embarcadero* ☎ *619/233–8792* ⊕ *www.thinkplaycreate.org* ⌨ *$10; 2nd Sun. each month free 10–4* ☺ *Mon., Tues., Fri., Sat. 10–4, Thurs. 10–6, Sun. noon–4.*

Fodor's Choice ★ **San Diego Aircraft Carrier Museum.** After 47 years of worldwide service, the retired USS *Midway* began a new tour of duty on the south side of the Navy pier in 2004. Launched just after the end of World War

MARITIME MUSEUM

✉ *1492 N. Harbor Dr., Embarcadero* ☎ *619/234-9153* ⊕ *www.sdmaritime.org* 🎫 *$14 includes entry to all ships except the Californian* ⊙ *Daily 9–8, until 9 pm Memorial Day to Labor Day.*

TIPS

■ Sail the Pacific on the Californian. Weekend sails, typically from noon to 4, cost $42 for adults; buy tickets online for 10% off or at the museum on the day of sail. Arrive at least an hour early on sunny days for a spot onboard.

■ Cruise San Diego Bay for only $3 plus museum admission on the 1914 Pilot boat. The 45-minute narrated tours are offered at several times.

■ Partnering with the museum, the renowned yacht America also offers sails on the bay, and whale-watching excursions in winter. Times and prices vary. Parties of eight or more should call ahead for special group admission and a guided two-hour tour.

■ Exploring the submarines requires climbing through several midsize hatches; wear flat shoes and pants.

■ Keep an eye out for the workshop onboard the Berkley where volunteers build extraordinary model ships.

From sailing ships to submarines, the Maritime Museum is a must for anyone with an interest in nautical history. This collection of restored and replica ships affords a fascinating glimpse of San Diego during its heyday as a commercial seaport.

HIGHLIGHTS

The jewel of the collection, the *Star of India,* is often considered a symbol of the city. An iron windjammer built in 1863, the *Star of India* made 21 trips around the world in the late 1800s, when it traveled the East Indian trade route, shuttled immigrants from England to New Zealand, and served the Alaskan salmon trade. Saved from the scrap yard and painstakingly restored, the *Star of India* is the oldest active iron sailing ship in the world.

The popular HMS *Surprise,* purchased in 2004, is a replica of an 18th-century British Royal Navy frigate, and was used in the Academy Award–winning *Master and Commander: The Far Side of the World.*

The museum's headquarters are on the *Berkeley,* an 1898 steam-driven ferryboat, which served the Southern Pacific Railroad in San Francisco until 1958. Its ornate detailing carefully restored, the main deck serves as a floating museum, with permanent exhibits on West Coast maritime history and complementary rotating exhibits.

Two submarines are featured at the museum: a Soviet B-39 "Foxtrot" class submarine and the USS *Dolphin* research submarine. Take a peek at the harbor from a periscope, get up close with the engine control room, and wonder at the tight living quarters onboard.

II, the 1,001-foot-long ship was the largest in the world for the first 10 years of its existence. Now it serves as the most visible landmark on the north Embarcadero and as a floating interactive museum—an appropriate addition to the town that is home to one-third of the Pacific fleet and the birthplace of naval aviation. Starting on the hangar deck, a free audio tour guides you through the massive ship while offering insight from former sailors. Through passageways and up and down ladder wells, you'll get to see how the *Midway*'s 4,500 crew members lived and worked on this "city at sea." While the entire tour is impressive, you'll find yourself saying "wow" when you step out onto the 4-acre flight deck—not only the best place to get an idea of the ship's scale but also one of the most interesting vantage points for a view of the bay and the city skyline. An F-14 Tomcat jet fighter is just one of many incredible aircraft on display. There are free guided tours of the bridge and primary flight control, known as "the Island," departing every 10 minutes from the flight deck. Many of the docents stationed throughout the ship served in the Navy, some even on the *Midway*, and are eager to answer questions or share stories. The museum also offers multiple flight simulators for an additional fee, climb-aboard cockpits, and interactive exhibits focusing on naval aviation. There is a gift shop and a café with pleasant outdoor seating. This is a wildly popular stop, with most visits lasting several hours. ⚠ Despite significant efforts to provide accessibility throughout the ship, some areas can only be reached via fairly steep steps; a video tour of these areas is available on the hangar deck. ✉ *910 N. Harbor Dr., Embarcadero* ☎ *619/544–9600* ⊕ *www. midway.org* ✈ *$18* ⊙ *Daily 10–5, last admission 4 pm.*

🕙 **Seaport Village.** On a prime stretch of waterfront that spreads out across 14 acres connecting the harbor with hotel towers and the convention center, the three bustling shopping plazas of Seaport Village are designed to reflect the New England clapboard and Spanish Mission architectural styles of early California. A ¼-mi boardwalk that runs along the bay and 4 mi of paths lead to specialty shops—everything from a kite store and swing emporium to a shop devoted to hot sauces—as well as snack bars and restaurants, many with harbor views; there are more than 60 in all. Seaport Village's shops are open daily 10 to 9; a few eateries open early for breakfast, and many have extended nighttime hours, especially in summer. Restaurant prices here are high and the food is only average, so your best bet is to go elsewhere for a meal. Live music can be heard daily from noon to 4 at the main food court. Additional free concerts take place every Sunday from 1 to 4 at the East Plaza Gazebo. If you happen to visit San Diego in late November or early December, you might be lucky enough to catch Surfing Santa's Arrival and even have your picture taken with Santa on his wave. Every year in April catch the Seaport Buskers Fest, featuring a wide array of street performers.

The **Seaport Village Carousel** has 54 animals—lots of horses plus a giraffe, dragon, elephant, dog, and others—hand-carved and hand-painted by Charles Looff in 1895. (This is a replacement for Seaport Village's previous historic carousel, also a Looff, which was sold in 2004.) Tickets are $2. Strolling clowns, balloon sculptors, mimes, musicians, and magicians are also on hand throughout the village to entertain kids. ✉ *849 W. Harbor Dr., Embarcadero* ☎ *619/235–4014 office and events hotline* ⊕ *www.seaportvillage.com.*

Westfield Horton Plaza. This downtown shopping, dining, and entertainment mecca fronts Broadway and G Street from 1st to 4th avenues and covers more than six city blocks. Designed by Jon Jerde and completed in 1985, Westfield Horton Plaza is far from what one would imagine a shopping center—or city center—to be. A collage of colorful tile work, banners waving in the air, and modern sculptures, Westfield Horton Plaza rises in uneven, staggered levels to five floors; great views of downtown from the harbor to Balboa Park and beyond can be had here.

Macy's and Nordstrom department stores anchor the plaza, and an eclectic assortment of more than 130 clothing, sporting-goods, jewelry, book, and gift shops flank them. Other attractions include the country's largest Sam Goody music store, a movie complex, restaurants, and a long row of take-out ethnic food shops and dining patios on the uppermost tier—and the respected San Diego Repertory Theatre below ground level. In 2008 the **Balboa Theater,** contiguous with the shopping center, reopened its doors after a $26.5 million renovation. The historic 1920s theater seats 1,400 and offers live arts and cultural performances throughout the week.

The mall has a multilevel parking garage; even so, lines to find a space can be long. ■ TIP→ Entering the parking structure on G Street rather than 4th Avenue generally means less traffic and more parking space. Parking validation is complimentary whether you spend a bundle or just window-shop. Validation machines (open 7 am–9 pm) throughout the center allow for three hours' free parking; after that it's $8 per hour (or $2 per 15-minute increment). If you use this notoriously confusing fruit-and-vegetable–themed garage, be sure to remember at which produce level you've left your car. If you're staying downtown, the Old Town Trolley Tour will drop you directly in front of Westfield Horton Plaza. ✉ *324 Horton Plaza, Gaslamp Quarter* ☎ *619/238–1596* ⊕ *www.westfield.com/hortonplaza* ⊙ *Weekdays 10–9, Sat. 10–8, Sun. 11–7.*

WORTH NOTING

☾ **Firehouse Museum.** Firefighting artifacts of all sorts fill this converted fire station, which at one time also served as the repair shop for all of San Diego's firefighting equipment. Three large rooms contain everything from 19th-century horse- and hand-drawn fire engines to 20th-century motorized trucks, the latest dating from 1943. ✉ *1572 Columbia St., Little Italy* ☎ *619/232–3473* ⊕ *www.sandiegofirehousemuseum.com* ⊠ *$3; free 1st Thurs. of the month* ⊙ *Thurs. and Fri. 10–2, weekends 10–4.*

Horton Grand Hotel. This Victorian hotel was created in the mid-1980s by joining together two historic hotels, the Brooklyn Kahle Saddlery Hotel and the Grand Horton Hotel, built in the boom days of the 1880s; Wyatt Earp stayed at the Brooklyn Kahle Saddlery Hotel while he was in town speculating on real estate ventures and opening gambling halls. The two hotels were not originally located at this address; they were once about four blocks away, but were dismantled and reconstructed to make way for Horton Plaza. ✉ *311 Island Ave., Gaslamp Quarter* ☎ *619/544–1886.*

Home of the San Diego Padres, PETCO Park offers behind-the-scenes tours.

PETCO Park. Opened in 2004, PETCO Park is a state-of-the-art major league ballpark and home to the San Diego Padres. In 2007 the park also started hosting the Rugby Union USA Sevens. Built at a cost of $450 million, the stadium features a 30- x 53-foot LED video board and more than 1,000 televisions, and is strategically designed to give fans a view of San Diego Bay, the skyline, and Balboa Park. Reflecting San Diego's beauty, the stadium is clad in sandstone from India to evoke the area's cliffs and beaches; the 42,000 seats are dark blue, reminiscent of the ocean, and the exposed steel is painted white to reflect the sails of harbor boats on the bay. A main draw of PETCO is the family-friendly lawnlike berm, "Park at the Park," where fans can view the game for a $5 fee. Behind-the-scenes guided tours of PETCO, including the press box and the dugout, are offered throughout the year. ⊠ *100 Park Blvd., East Village* ☎ *619/795–5011 Tour hotline* ⊕ *www.padres.com* ⊠ *$11 tour* ☉ *Tours offered 7 days a week; times vary seasonally—call ahead.*

Santa Fe Depot. The Mission-style Santa Fe Depot, which replaced the original 1887 station on this site when it opened in 1915 for the Panama–California International Exposition, serves Amtrak and Coaster passengers. A booth here has bus schedules, maps, and tourist brochures. Formerly an easily spotted area landmark, the graceful, tile-dome depot is now overshadowed by **1 America Plaza,** the 34-story office tower across the street. At the base of this skyscraper, designed by architect Helmut Jahn, is a center linking the city's train, trolley, and bus systems. The building's signature crescent-shape, glass-and-steel canopy arches out over the trolley tracks. ⊠ *Broadway and Kettner Blvd., Embarcadero.*

U.S. Grant Hotel. Far more formal than most other hotels in San Diego and complete with a $56 million renovation in 2006, the doyenne of downtown lodgings has a marble lobby, glittering chandeliers, attentive doormen, and other touches that hark back to the more gracious era when it was built in 1910. Funded in part by the son of the president for whom it was named, the hotel was extremely opulent from the beginning; 350 of its 437 rooms had private baths, highly unusual for that time. Through the years it became noted for its famous guests—hosting several U.S. presidents and countless celebrities. The U.S. Grant recently discovered marble floors and alabaster railings that had been covered for more than 70 years. Below the main lobby, the historic lower level features photographs and exhibits detailing the hotel's history. Taking up a city block—it's bounded by 3rd and 4th avenues, C Street, and Broadway—the hotel occupies the site of San Diego's first hotel, constructed by Alonzo Horton in 1870. ⊠ *326 Broadway, Gaslamp Quarter* ☎ *619/232–3121.*

> ## WESTERN METAL SUPPLY
>
> Initially scheduled for demolition to make room for PETCO Park, the historic Western Metal Supply Co. was instead incorporated into the ballpark and supports the left-field foul pole, 334 feet from home plate. Great care was taken to retain the historic nature of the building's exterior despite the extensive interior renovations. Constructed in 1909, the four-story structure originally manufactured wagon wheels and war supplies, and today holds the Padres' Team Store, the Padres' Hall of Fame Bar and Grill, and rooftop seating.

William Heath Davis House. The oldest wooden house in San Diego houses the Gaslamp Quarter Historical Foundation, the district's curator. Before Alonzo Horton came to town, Davis, a prominent San Franciscan, had made an unsuccessful attempt to develop the waterfront area. In 1850 he had this prefab saltbox-style house, built in Maine, shipped around Cape Horn and assembled in San Diego (it originally stood at State and Market streets). Audio-guided or brochure-guided museum tours are available with museum admission. Regularly scheduled two-hour walking tours of the historic district leave from the house on Saturday at 11 and cost $10. If you can't time your visit with the weekly tour, a self-guided tour map is also available for purchase for $2. ⊠ *410 Island Ave., at 4th Ave., Gaslamp Quarter* ☎ *619/233–4692* ⊠ *$5* ☉ *Tues–Sat 10–5, Sun 12–4.*

3

Balboa Park and San Diego Zoo

WORD OF MOUTH

"To me, Balboa Park was a major highlight of our trip. When I think of it, I'll always think of golden sunlight. Sigh."

—April

GETTING ORIENTED

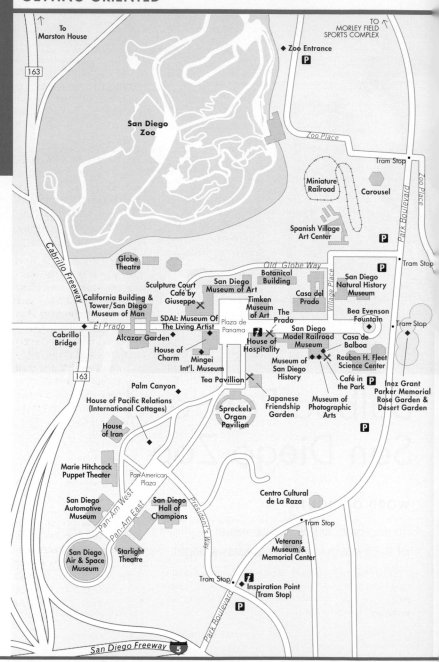

To Marston House

TO MORLEY FIELD SPORTS COMPLEX

Zoo Entrance

163

San Diego Zoo

Zoo Place

Tram Stop

Miniature Railroad

Carousel

Spanish Village Art Center

Park Boulevard

Zoo Place

Globe Theatre

Old Globe Way

Botanical Building

Casa del Prado

San Diego Natural History Museum

Tram Stop

Cabrillo Freeway

Sculpture Court Café by Giuseppe

San Diego Museum of Art

Timken Museum of Art

The Prado

Village Place

Bea Evenson Fountain

California Building & Tower/San Diego Museum of Man

SDAI: Museum Of The Living Artist

Plaza de Panama

San Diego Model Railroad Museum

Casa de Balboa

Tram Stop

Cabrillo Bridge

El Prado

House of Hospitality

Alcazar Garden

House of Charm

Mingei Int'l. Museum

Museum of San Diego History

Reuben H. Fleet Science Center

163

Palm Canyon

Tea Pavillion

Japanese Friendship Garden

Café in the Park

Inez Grant Parker Memorial Rose Garden & Desert Garden

House of Pacific Relations (International Cottages)

Spreckels Organ Pavilion

Museum of Photographic Arts

House of Iran

Marie Hitchcock Puppet Theater

Pan-American Plaza

Centro Cultural de La Raza

Pan-Am West

San Diego Automotive Museum

Pan-Am East

San Diego Hall of Champions

President's Way

Tram Stop

Veterans Museum & Memorial Center

San Diego Air & Space Museum

Starlight Theatre

Tram Stop

Inspiration Point (Tram Stop)

Park Boulevard

TOP REASONS TO GO

San Diego Zoo: San Diego's best-loved attraction, the world-renowned zoo is set amidst spectacular scenery in the heart of Balboa Park.

Museums galore: Automobiles and spacecraft, international folk art and Baroque masters, dinosaur fossils and mummified humans—there is something for everyone at Balboa Park's many museums.

The great outdoors: Escape down a hiking trail, try your hand at a new sport, or just soak in the sunshine from your own stretch of grass. You may even forget you are in the middle of the city.

Gorgeous gardens: From the lush tropical feel of the Botanical Building to the refined design of the Rose Garden, Balboa Park's intricate gardens and landscaping are sure to delight.

Free cultural events: The park is full of freebies, from weekly concerts at the organ pavilion to annual events like Earth Day and December Nights.

QUICK BITES

Quick snacking opportunities abound throughout the park, from cafés tucked in among the museums and grounds, to hot dog, tamale, or ice-cream carts along the walkways and plazas. Good bets include the sushi, noodles, and, of course, tea at the **Tea Pavilion** outside the Japanese Friendship Garden, or sandwiches, cookies, and espresso drinks at the **Café in the Park,** inside the Casa de Balboa.

The most formal, and favored, restaurant in the park,

The Prado. Enjoy inventive cuisine in a gracious setting inside the House of Hospitality. An extensive lunch and dinner menu is offered in the dining room; casual bites are served in the bar. ☎ 619/557-9441 ⊘ No dinner Mon.

GETTING HERE

Located just north of downtown, Balboa Park is easily reached from both Interstate 5 and Highway 163. The most spectacular approach is from 6th Avenue over the Cabrillo Bridge. There are also several entrances off Park Boulevard.

Balboa Park is served by public buses, particularly the No. 3, 7, and 120 lines. Taxis can sometimes be found inside the park close to the visitor center, and more often, lined up outside the zoo.

While Balboa Park as a whole is massive, many of its star attractions are located quite close to each other. That being said, exploring the park can lead to a lot of walking, particularly if you throw in a trip to the zoo or take on one of the many hiking trails. The park's free tram service stops at several spots around the park, and can give tired feet a welcome rest at the end of a long day.

VISITOR INFORMATION

House of Hospitality. The visitor center located here is an excellent resource for planning your visit to the park. Check the website before you go or spend a few minutes there when you arrive. There's usually a special event happening on the weekend, from festivals to fun runs. ⊠ 1549 El Prado, Balboa Park ☎ 619/239-0512 ⊕ www.balboapark.org ⊘ Daily 9:30–4:30.

Sightseeing
★★★★★
Nightlife
★☆☆☆☆
Dining
★★★☆☆
Lodging
☆☆☆☆☆
Shopping
★★★☆☆

Overlooking downtown and the Pacific Ocean, 1,200-acre Balboa Park is the cultural heart of San Diego. Ranked as one of the world's best parks by the Project for Public Spaces, it's also where you can find most of the city's museums, art galleries, the Tony Award–winning Old Globe Theatre, and the world-famous San Diego Zoo. Often referred to as the "Smithsonian of the West" for its concentration of museums, Balboa Park is also a series of botanical gardens, performance spaces, and outdoor playrooms endeared in the hearts of residents and visitors alike.

Updated by
Claire Deeks
van der Lee

Thanks to the "Mother of Balboa Park," Kate Sessions, who suggested hiring a landscape architect in 1889, wild and cultivated gardens are an integral part of the park, featuring 350 species of trees. What Balboa Park would have looked like had she left it alone can be seen at Florida Canyon (between the main park and Morley Field, along Park Boulevard)—an arid landscape of sagebrush, cactus, and a few small trees.

In addition, the captivating architecture of Balboa's buildings, fountains, and courtyards gives the park an enchanted feel. Historic buildings dating from San Diego's 1915 Panama–California International Exposition are strung along the park's main east–west thoroughfare, El Prado, which leads from 6th Avenue eastward over the Cabrillo Bridge (formerly the Laurel Street Bridge), the park's official gateway. If you're a cinema fan, many of the buildings may be familiar—Orson Welles used exteriors of several Balboa Park buildings to represent the Xanadu estate of Charles Foster Kane in his 1941 classic, *Citizen Kane*. Prominent among them was the California Building, whose 200-foot tower, housing a 100-carillon bell that tolls the hour, is El Prado's tallest structure. Missing from the black-and-white film, however, was the magnificent blue of its tiled dome shining in the sun.

The parkland across the Cabrillo Bridge, at the west end of El Prado, is set aside for picnics and athletics. Rollerbladers zip along Balboa Drive, which leads to the highest spot in the park, Marston Point, overlooking downtown. At the green beside the bridge, ladies and gents in all-white outfits meet regularly on summer afternoons for lawn-bowling tournaments—a throwback to an earlier era.

East of Plaza de Panama, El Prado becomes a pedestrian mall and ends at a footbridge that crosses over Park Boulevard, the park's main north–south thoroughfare, to the perfectly tended Rose Garden, which has more than 2,000 rosebushes. In the adjacent Desert Garden, trails wind around cacti and succulents from around the world. Palm Canyon, north of the Spreckels Organ Pavilion, has more than 50 varieties of palms along a shady bridge. Pepper Grove, along Park Boulevard south of the museums, has lots of picnic tables as well as play equipment.

San Diegans spend years exploring this local jewel. And even though you'll just be scratching the surface, a visit here is worth peeling yourself away from the beaches for at least one day. To visit San Diego and overlook Balboa Park would be to miss out on the city's most cherished treasure.

BALBOA PARK PLANNER

BEST TIMES TO VISIT
San Diego's ideal climate and sophisticated horticultural planning make visiting Balboa Park a year-round delight. However, summer brings longer opening hours, additional concerts at the Spreckels Organ Pavilion, and the beloved Shakespeare Festival at the Old Globe's outdoor stage.

OPEN HOURS
Most of the park's museums and attractions are open from 10 or 11 am until 4 or 5 pm, with the zoo opening earlier. Some offer extended hours during the summer. Many of the park's museums are closed on Monday. Balboa Park is beautiful by night, with the buildings along El Prado gorgeously illuminated. The Prado restaurant and the Old Globe Theatre keep this portion of the park from feeling deserted after dark.

PLANNING YOUR TIME
It's impossible to cover all Balboa Park's museums and attractions in one day, so choose your focus before you head out. If you plan on visiting the San Diego Zoo, expect to spend at least half the day there, leaving no more than a couple of hours to explore Balboa's other attractions afterward. ⇨ *See the highlighted listing for more information about the San Diego Zoo.* Otherwise, check out these itineraries.

Two Hours: To help maximize your time, rent one of the 60-minute audio headsets that guide you on a tour of the park's history, architecture, and horticulture. Pick a garden of interest to explore or drop down into Palm Canyon. Spend the remainder of your time relaxing in front of the Botanical Building or around the Bea Evenson Fountain.

Half Day: Spend a little more time at the sights above, then select a museum to explore. Alternatively, catch a puppet show at the Marie Hitchcock Theater. Afterwards, you might have time for a quick ride on the carousel or a browse around the studios of Spanish Village Art Center. Cap things off with lunch in the Sculpture Court Café.

Full Day: Consider purchasing a one-day discount pass from the visitor center if you want to tackle several museums. Depending on when you visit, enjoy a free concert at the Spreckels Organ Pavilion, a cultural dance at the House of Pacific Relations International Cottages, or join a guided walking tour. Active types can hit one of the more intensive hiking trails, while others can rest their feet at an IMAX or 3-D movie in the Fleet Center or Natural History Museum, respectively. In the evening, dine at the beautiful Prado restaurant, or catch a show at the Old Globe Theatre.

WHAT'S FREE WHEN

Many freebies can be found in Balboa Park, both on a weekly basis and at special times of the year. Free **Ranger Tours** depart from the visitor center Tuesdays and Sundays at 1 pm, providing an overview of the history, architecture, and horticulture of the park. On Saturdays at 10 am, volunteers offer a rotating selection of thematic **Offshoot Tours,** also free of charge and departing from the visitor center. If you prefer to explore on your own, head to the visitor center to pick up a free garden tour map.

The free concerts at the **Spreckels Organ Pavilion** take place Sunday afternoons at 2 pm year-round and on Monday evenings in summer. Also at the Speckels Organ Pavilion, the **Twilight in the Park Summer Concert Series** offers various performances Tuesday, Wednesday, and Thursday from 6:15 to 7:15.

The **Timken Museum of Art** is always free, as is admission to the **House of Pacific Relations International Cottages,** although the latter are only open on Sundays. The **Centro Cultural de la Raza** and **Veterans Museum & Memorial Center** are free, but a donation is requested at each. You can explore the studios at the **Spanish Village Art Center** at no charge, although you just might be tempted to purchase a unique souvenir.

A fantastic deal for residents of San Diego County and active-duty military and their families is **Free Tuesdays in the Park,** a rotating schedule of free admission to most of Balboa Park's museums.

The **San Diego Zoo** is free for kids under 12 the whole month of October.

The **December Nights** festival on the first Friday and Saturday of that month includes free admission (and later hours) to most of the Balboa Park museums. The outdoor events during the festival make it something not to miss.

DISCOUNT: PASSPORT TO BALBOA

The visitor center offers a selection of Passport to Balboa discount passes that are worth considering if you plan on visiting several museums. The Passport ($45 adult, $24 children ages 3–12) offers one-time admission to 14 museums and attractions over the course of seven days. If you are also planning on visiting the zoo, the Zoo/Passport Combo might be a good choice ($75 adult/ $39 child). A new single-day pass includes entry to your choice of 5 out of the 14 options ($35 adult).

TIPS

- Hop aboard the free trams that run every 8–10 minutes, 8:30 am–6:00 pm daily, with extended summer hours.

- Wear comfortable shoes—you'll end up walking more than you might expect. Bring a sweater or light jacket for the evening drop in temperature.

- Don't be afraid to wander off the main drag. Discovering a hidden space of your own is one of the highlights of a trip to Balboa.

- Balboa Park is a good bet for the odd rainy day—the museums are nice and dry, and many of the park's buildings are connected by covered walkways.

- Make reservations for the Prado restaurant; it's popular with both visitors and locals alike.

- If you aren't receiving the discount, consider avoiding participating museums on Free Tuesdays, as they can become overcrowded.

- Don't overlook the 6th Avenue side of the park, between the Marston House and the Cabrillo Bridge. There are several pathways and open fields that make for a quiet escape.

PARKING

Parking within Balboa Park, including at the zoo, is free. From the Cabrillo Bridge, the first parking area you come to is off El Prado to the right. Don't despair if there are no spaces here; you'll see more lots as you continue along El Prado. Alternatively, you can park at Inspiration Point on the east side of the park, off Presidents Way. Free trams run from Inspiration Point to the visitor center and museums. Valet parking is available outside the House of Hospitality on weekends and on weekday evenings, except Monday.

EXPLORING BALBOA PARK

BALBOA PARK WALK

While Balboa Park as a whole is huge, many of its top attractions are located within reasonable walking distance. A straight shot across the **Cabrillo Bridge,** through the **Plaza de Panama** and on to the **Bea Evenson Fountain** will take you past several of the park's architectural gems, including the **California Building, House of Charm,** and **House of Hospitality.** Many of the parks museums are housed in the buildings lining the way. This route also encompasses the **Alcazar Garden** and **Botanical Building.** From the fountain, a quick jaunt across the pedestrian footbridge leads you into the **Desert Garden** and **the Inez Grant Parker Memorial Rose Garden.** Back at the fountain, your walking tour can continue by heading north towards the **San Diego Zoo.** This will take you past the **Spanish Village Art, Carousel,** and **Miniature Railroad** en route. Alternatively, double back to the Plaza de Panama and head south towards the **Spreckels Organ Pavilion.** Continuing on from here, a loop will take you past **Palm Canyon,** the **International Cottages,** the **Marie Hitchcock Puppet Theater,** several more museums, and the **Japanese Friendship Garden.**

CLOSE UP

20 Things We Love to Do in Balboa Park

1. Be awestruck with each stroll over Cabrillo Bridge

2. Visit the pandas at the San Diego Zoo

3. Enjoy a picnic on the lawns of the Botanical Building

4. Stop and smell the roses in one of the gorgeous gardens

5. Listen to a concert at the Spreckels Organ Pavilion

6. Get cultured under the stars at the Old Globe's Shakespeare Festival

7. Reach for the brass ring while riding the Carousel

8. Escape the city on a hiking trail

9. Browse the studios at Spanish Village Art Center

10. Enjoy the lights and decorations at December Nights

11. Feel the eerie stillness of the park when the fog rolls in

12. Catch a world-premiere musical, with preshow dining at the Prado

13. Go for a run, either solo or in one of the many races at the park

14. Observe a refined game of lawn bowls

15. Pick up a new sport at Morley Field

16. Find something new—a hidden courtyard, a remote trail—with each visit

17. Watch a movie under the stars at Screen on the Green

18. Play a round of golf, either Frisbee or the traditional variety

19. Eat new foods and watch cultural performances at the Pacific Relations Cottages

20. People-watch at the Bea Evenson Fountain

While the above routes provide a broad overview, there are several walking opportunities for those seeking more focused explorations of the park. Those wishing to experience the numerous gardens in depth will appreciate the excellent "Gardens of Balboa Park Self-Guided Walk," available free of charge at the visitor center. History and architecture buffs might consider buying a self-guided walking tour pamphlet from the visitor's center, or taking the briefer audio tour. Opportunities for hiking abound, from a brief journey through **Palm Canyon** to more strenuous hikes through **Florida Canyon** or on the **Old Bridle Trail**. Stop in the visitor center for maps and guidance before setting out.

TOP ATTRACTIONS

★ **Alcazar Garden.** The gardens surrounding the Alcazar Castle in Seville, Spain, inspired the landscaping here; you'll feel like royalty resting on the benches by the exquisitely tiled fountains. The flower beds are ever-changing horticultural exhibits featuring more than 7,000 annuals for a nearly perpetual bloom. Bright orange-and-yellow poppies appear in spring and deep rust, and crimson chrysanthemums arrive in fall. ⊠ *1439 El Prado, Balboa Park.*

Bea Evenson Fountain. A favorite of barefoot children, this fountain shoots cool jets of water upwards of 50 feet. Built in 1972 between the Fleet

The lily pond outside the Botanical Building is a beautiful spot to take a break.

Center and Natural History Museum, the fountain offers plenty of room to sit and watch the crowds go by. ⊠ *East end of El Prado, Balboa Park.*

Fodor's Choice ★ **Botanical Building.** The graceful redwood-lath structure, built for the 1915 Panama–California International Exposition, now houses more than 2,000 types of tropical and subtropical plants plus changing seasonal flower displays. Ceiling-high tree ferns shade fragile orchids and feathery bamboo. There are benches beside miniature waterfalls for resting in the shade. The rectangular pond outside, filled with lotuses and water lilies that bloom in spring and fall, is popular with photographers. ⊠ *1550 El Prado, Balboa Park* ☎ *619/239–0512* ⊠ *Free* ⊗ *Fri.–Wed. 10–4.*

★ **Cabrillo Bridge.** The park's official (and pedestrian-friendly) gateway soars 120 feet above the canyon floor. Crossing the 1,500-foot bridge into the park provides awe-inspiring views of the California Tower and El Prado beyond. ⊠ *On El Prado, at the 6th Ave. park entrance, Balboa Park.*

☾ ★ **Carousel.** Suspended an arm's length away on this antique merry-go-round is the brass ring that could earn you an extra free ride (it's one of the few carousels in the world that continue this bonus tradition). Hand-carved in 1910, the carousel features colorful murals, big-band music, and bobbing animals including zebras, giraffes, and dragons; real horsehair was used for the tails. ⊠ *1889 Zoo Pl., behind zoo parking lot, Balboa Park* ☎ *619/239–0512* ⊠ *$2* ⊗ *11-5; Mid-June–Labor Day, daily; rest of yr, weekends and school holidays.*

Fodor's Choice ★ **Globe Theatres.** Even if you're not attending a play, this complex, comprising the Cassius Carter Centre Stage, the Lowell Davies Festival Theatre, and the Old Globe Theatre, is a pleasant place to relax between museum visits. Theater classics such as *The Full Monty* and *Dirty*

Balboa's Best Bets

With so much on offer, Balboa Park truly has something for everyone. Here are some best bets based on area of interest.

ARTS AFICIONADOS
Old Globe Theatre

Museum of Photographic Arts

San Diego Art Institute

San Diego Museum of Art

SDAI: Museum of the Living Artist

Spanish Village Art Center

Spreckels Organ Pavilion

Timken Museum of Art

ARCHITECTURE BUFFS
Bea Evenson Fountain

Cabrillo Bridge

California Building and Tower

Casa de Balboa

House of Charm

House of Hospitality

CULTURAL EXPLORERS
Centro Cultural de la Raza

House of Pacific Relations

Mingei International Museum

HISTORY JUNKIES
Museum of San Diego History

San Diego Museum of Man

San Diego Natural History Museum

Veterans Museum

NATURE LOVERS
Alcazar Garden

Botanical Building

Inez Grant Parker Memorial Rose Garden

Japanese Friendship Garden

Palm Canyon

SCIENCE AND TECHNOLOGY GEEKS
Reuben H. Fleet Science Center

San Diego Air and Space Museum

San Diego Automotive Museum

KIDS OF ALL AGES
Carousel

Marie Hitchcock Puppet Theater

Miniature Railroad

San Diego Hall of Champions

San Diego Model Railroad Museum

San Diego Zoo

Rotten Scoundrels, both of which later performed on Broadway, premiered on these stages. The theaters, done in a California version of Tudor style, sit between the sculpture garden of the San Diego Museum of Art and the California Tower. A gift shop (hours vary, but open at least one hour prior to curtain and through intermission) sells posters, cards, and brightly colored puppets. ✉ *1363 Old Globe Way, Balboa Park* ☎ *619/234–5623* ⊕ *www.theoldglobe.org.*

House of Hospitality. At the Balboa Park visitor center in this building, you can pick up schedules and route maps for the free trams that operate around the park. Audio tours are also available ($5), as is the Passport to Balboa Park Combo Pass, which affords entry to 14 museums and the zoo for $75 adults ($39 children); for $45 ($24 children), a seven-day pass is available for those who prefer to visit the museums without zoo entry. There is also a single-day pass for $35 for admission to your choice of 5 out of the 14 museums.

In addition, you can pick up an event guide that details the current museum and theater offerings, as well as excellent free park tours that depart from here (or call for a schedule). Also note the beautiful

3

structure itself. A late 1990s rebuilding of the 1915 original, it has won awards for its painstaking attention to historical detail; 2,000 paint scrapes were taken, for example, to get the art deco colors exactly right. ⊠ *1549 El Prado, Balboa Park* ☎ *619/239–0512* ⊕ *www.balboapark. org* ☉ *Daily 9:30–4:30.*

House of Pacific Relations. This is not really a house but a cluster of red tile–roof stucco cottages representing some 30 foreign countries. The word "pacific" refers to the goal of maintaining peace. The cottages, decorated with crafts and pictures, are open Sunday afternoons, when you can chat with transplanted natives and sample different ethnic foods. From the first Sunday in March through the last Sunday in October, folk-song and dance performances are presented on the outdoor stage around 2 pm—check the schedule at the park visitor center. Across the road is the Spanish colonial–style **United Nations Building.** Inside, the United Nations Association's International Gift Shop, open daily, has reasonably priced crafts, cards, and books. ⊠ *2191 Pan American Pl., Balboa Park* ☎ *619/234–0739* ⊕ *www.sdhpr.org* ▨ *Free, donations accepted* ☉ *Sun. noon–4.*

Fodor'sChoice **Inez Grant Parker Memorial Rose Garden and Desert Garden.** These neigh-
★ boring gardens sit just across the Park Boulevard pedestrian bridge and offer gorgeous views over Florida Canyon. The formal rose garden contains 2,500 roses representing nearly 200 varieties, and blooms most months of the year. The adjacent Desert Garden provides striking contrast, with 2.5 acres of succulents and desert plants seeming to blend into the landscape of the canyon below. ⊠ *Near Park Blvd. pedestrian footbridge, Balboa Park.*

Japanese Friendship Garden. A koi pond with a waterfall, a 60-foot-long wisteria arbor, a tea pavilion, and a large activity center are highlights of the park's authentic Japanese garden, designed to inspire contemplation and evoke tranquility. You can wander the peaceful paths, meditate in the traditional stone and Zen garden, or, at times, learn such arts as origami and flower arranging at the activity center. The development of an additional 9 acres is underway and will include a traditional tea house and a cherry orchard. ⊠ *2215 Pan American Rd., Balboa Park* ☎ *619/232–2721* ⊕ *www.niwa.org* ▨ *$4* ☉ *Fall/winter/spring: Tues.– Sun. 10–4; summer: Mon.–Fri. 10–5, Sat.–Sun. 10–4.*

CLOSE UP

From Undeveloped Mesa to Urban Oasis

Looking at the intricate designs of Balboa Park today, it is hard to imagine its humble beginnings as empty scrubland on the outskirts of town.

1868: City leaders designate 1,400 acres of undeveloped land above Alonzo Horton's New Town (now San Diego's downtown) as a public park, known then as "City Park."

1892: Horticulturalist and entrepreneur Kate Sessions negotiates with the city to plant 100 trees within the park each year in return for the use of a 32-acre parcel of parkland to house her nursery business. In accordance with the deal, Sessions, the "Mother of Balboa Park," begins to transform the scrub-filled mesa into the landscaped oasis it is today.

1910: A local contest renames the park "Balboa Park" after Vasco Nuñez de Balboa, a European explorer who claims the first sighting of the Pacific Ocean.

1915–1916: Balboa Park hosts the Panama-California Exhibition, in honor of the Panama Canal's successful completion. Several buildings are constructed for the expo, including the Spreckels Organ Pavilion, and the Houses of Charm and Hospitality. The Cabrillo Bridge and El Prado walkway are laid out, and the park takes on much of its current character.

1935–1936: Balboa Park welcomes another major fair, the California Pacific International Exhibition, during the Great Depression. The House of Pacific Relations International Cottages as well as several buildings designed by lead architect Richard Requa are added to the park.

Mingei International Museum. All ages will enjoy the Mingei's colorful and creative exhibits of folk art, featuring toys, pottery, textiles, costumes, and curios from around the globe. Traveling and permanent exhibits in the high-ceilinged, light-filled museum include everything from antique American carousel horses to the latest in Japanese ceramics. The name "Mingei" comes from the Japanese words *min*, meaning "all people," and *gei*, meaning "art." Thus the museum's name describes what you'll find under its roof: "art of all people." The gift shop carries artwork from cultures around the world, from Zulu baskets to Turkish ceramics to Mexican objects, plus special limited tie-in items for major exhibitions. ✉ *House of Charm, 1439 El Prado, Balboa Park* ☎ *619/239–0003* ⊕ *www.mingei.org* ✆ *$7* ☺ *Tues.–Sun. 10–4.*

Palm Canyon. Heading down into this lush canyon near the House of Charm provides an instant escape into another landscape. More than 450 palms are planted in two acres, with a small hiking trail emerging by the Balboa Park Club. ✉ *South of the House of Charm, Balboa Park.*

☺
★ **San Diego Air and Space Museum.** By day, the streamlined edifice looks like any other structure in the park; at night, outlined in blue neon, the round building appears—appropriately enough—to be a landed UFO. Every available inch of space in the rotunda is filled with exhibits about aviation and aerospace pioneers, including examples of enemy planes from the world wars. All in all, there are 63 full-size aircraft on the floor and literally hanging from the rafters, and interactive

exhibits that kids love. In addition to exhibits from the dawn of flight to the jet age, the museum also displays a growing number of space-age exhibits, including the actual Apollo 9 command module. A collection of real and replicated aircraft fills the central courtyard, and a behind-the-scenes tour on Monday, Wednesday, and Friday allows you to watch volunteers restoring aircraft or creating replicas. ⌧ *2001 Pan American Plaza, Balboa Park* ☎ *619/234–8291* ⊕ *www.sandiegoairandspace.org* ⌧ *$16.50, restoration tour $5 extra* ۞ *Daily 10–4:30, until 5:30 Memorial Day–Labor Day.*

> **HISTORY REVEALED**
>
> While demurely posing as a butterfly garden today, the history behind the Zoro Garden is far racier. Tucked between the Casa de Balboa and the Fleet Center, this area showcased a nudist colony during the 1935–1936 Exposition.

★ **San Diego Museum of Art.** Known primarily for its Spanish Baroque and Renaissance paintings, including works by El Greco, Goya, Rubens, and van Ruisdael, San Diego's most comprehensive art museum also has strong holdings of South Asian art, Indian miniatures, and contemporary California paintings. An outdoor Sculpture Court and Garden exhibits both traditional and modern pieces. The IMAGE (Interactive Multimedia Art Gallery Explorer) system allows you to call up the highlights of the museum's collection on a computer screen and custom-design a tour, call up historical information on the works and artists, and print color reproductions. The museum's goal is to "connect people to art and art to people," so its exhibits tend to have broad appeal, and if traveling shows from other cities come to town, you can expect to see them here. Lectures, concerts, and film events are also on the roster. Free docent tours are offered throughout the day. **Sculpture Court Café by Giuseppe.** For a leisurely lunch, take respite in the Sculpture Court Café by Giuseppe, in the outdoor sanctuary of the Museum's Sculpture Court and Garden. The café serves a selection of artisan pizzas, grilled burgers, and steak, as well as gourmet sandwiches and salads. ☎ *619/702–6373* ۞ *Tues.– Sun. 11–3, until 4 Sundays in summer* ⌧ *1450 El Prado, Balboa Park* ☎ *619/232–7931* ⊕ *www.sdmart.org* ⌧ *$12* ۞ *Tues.–Sat. 10–5, Sun. noon–5; Memorial Day–Labor Day until 9 Thurs.*

☾ **San Diego Museum of Man.** If the facade of this building—the landmark California Building—looks familiar, it's because filmmaker Orson Welles used it and its dramatic tower as the principal features of the Xanadu estate in his 1941 classic, *Citizen Kane.* Inside, exhibits at this highly respected anthropological museum focus on Southwestern, Mexican, and South American cultures. Carved monuments from the Mayan city of Quirigua in Guatemala, cast from the originals in 1914, are particularly impressive. Exhibits might include examples of intricate beadwork from across the Americas, the history of Egyptian mummies, or the lifestyles of the Kumeyaay peoples who inhabited San Diego before Europeans arrived. Especially cool for kids is the hands-on Children's Discovery Center. ⌧ *California Bldg., 1350 El Prado, Balboa Park* ☎ *619/239–2001* ⊕ *www.museumofman.org* ⌧ *$10* ۞ *Daily 10–4:30.*

Continued on page 64

Polar bear, San Diego Zoo

LIONS AND TIGERS AND PANDAS:
The World-Famous San Diego Zoo

From cuddly pandas and diving polar bears to 6-ton elephants and swinging great apes, San Diego's most famous attraction has it all. Nearly 4,000 animals representing 800 species roam the 100-acre zoo in expertly crafted habitats that replicate the animals' natural environments. While the pandas get top billing, there are plenty of other cool creatures to see here, from teeny-tiny mantella frogs to two-story-tall giraffes. But it's not all just fun and games. Known for its exemplary conservation programs, the zoo educates visitors on how to go green and explains its efforts to protect endangered species.

SAN DIEGO ZOO TOP ATTRACTIONS

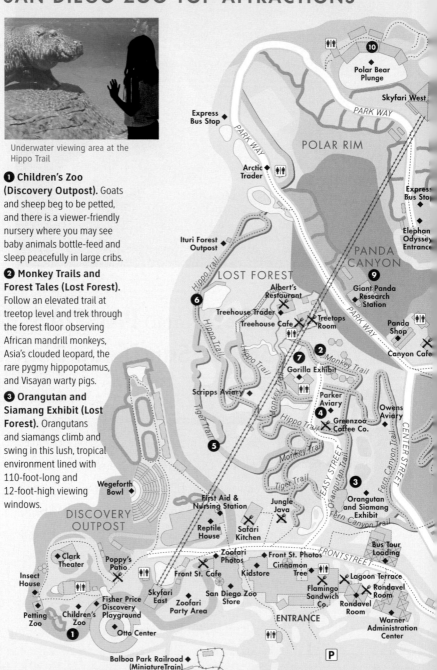

Underwater viewing area at the Hippo Trail

❶ Children's Zoo (Discovery Outpost). Goats and sheep beg to be petted, and there is a viewer-friendly nursery where you may see baby animals bottle-feed and sleep peacefully in large cribs.

❷ Monkey Trails and Forest Tales (Lost Forest). Follow an elevated trail at treetop level and trek through the forest floor observing African mandrill monkeys, Asia's clouded leopard, the rare pygmy hippopotamus, and Visayan warty pigs.

❸ Orangutan and Siamang Exhibit (Lost Forest). Orangutans and siamangs climb and swing in this lush, tropical environment lined with 110-foot-long and 12-foot-high viewing windows.

Polar Bear Plunge
10
Skyfari West
PARK WAY
Express Bus Stop
POLAR RIM
Arctic Trader
Express Bus Stop
Elephant Odyssey Entrance
Ituri Forest Outpost
PANDA CANYON
LOST FOREST
Giant Panda Research Station
Albert's Restaurant
Treehouse Trader
Treetops Room
Panda Shop
Treehouse Cafe
6
Canyon Cafe
2
Monkey Trail
7
Gorilla Exhibit
Scripps Aviary
Parker Aviary
Owens Aviary
4
Greenzoo Coffee Co.
Hippo Trail
5
CENTER STREET
Tiger Trail
Monkey Trail
Wegeforth Bowl
Tiger Trail
Jungle Java
Orangutan Trail
3
Orangutan and Siamang Exhibit
First Aid & Nursing Station
Fern Canyon Trail
DISCOVERY OUTPOST
Reptile House
Safari Kitchen
Bus Tour Loading
Clark Theater
Poppy's Patio
Zoofari Photos
Front St. Photos
FRONT STREET
Insect House
Front St. Cafe
Kidstore
Cinnamon Tree
Lagoon Terrace
Rondavel Room
Skyfari East
San Diego Zoo Store
Flamingo Sandwich Co.
Rondavel Room
Petting Zoo
Children's Zoo
Fisher Price Discovery Playground
Zoofari Party Area
ENTRANCE
Warner Administration Center
1
Otto Center
Balboa Park Railroad (MiniatureTrain)
P

④ Scripps, Parker, and Owens Aviaries (Lost Forest). Wandering paths climb through the enclosed aviaries where brightly colored tropical birds swoop between branches inches from your face.

⑤ Tiger Trail (Lost Forest). The mist-shrouded trails of this simulated rainforest wind down a canyon. Tigers, Malayan tapirs, and Argus pheasants wander among the exotic trees and plants.

⑥ Hippo Trail (Lost Forest). Glimpse huge but surprisingly graceful hippos frolicking in the water through an underwater viewing

window and buffalo cavorting with monkeys on dry land.

⑦ Gorilla Exhibit (Lost Forest). The gorillas live in one of the zoo's bioclimatic zone exhibits modeled on their native habitat with waterfalls, climbing areas, and an open meadow. The sounds of the tropical rain forest emerge from a 144-speaker sound system that plays CDs recorded in Africa.

⑧ Sun Bear Forest (Asian Passage). Playful beasts claw apart the trees and shrubs that serve as a natural playground for climbing, jumping, and general merrymaking.

⑨ Giant Panda Research Station (Panda Canyon). An elevated pathway provides visitors with great access

Lories at Owen's Aviary

to the zoo's most famous residents in their side-by-side viewing areas. The adjacent discovery center features lots of information about these endangered animals and the zoo's efforts to protect them.

⑩ Polar Bear Plunge (Polar Rim). Watch polar bears take a chilly dive from the underwater viewing room. There are also Siberian reindeer, white foxes, and other Arctic creatures here. Kids can learn about the Arctic and climate change through interactive exhibits.

⑪ Elephant Odyssey. Get a glimpse of the animals that roamed Southern California 12,000 years ago and meet their living counterparts. The 7.5-acre, multispecies habitat features elephants, California condors, jaguars, and more.

⑫ Koala Exhibit (Outback). The San Diego Zoo houses the largest number of koalas outside Australia. Walk through the exhibit for photo ops of these marsupials from Down-Under curled up on their perches or dining on eucalyptus branches.

MUST-SEE ANIMALS

❶ GORILLA

This troop of primates engages visitors with their human-like expressions and behavior. The youngsters are sure to delight, especially when hitching a ride on mom's back. Up-close encounters might involve the gorillas using the glass partition as a backrest while peeling cabbage. By dusk the gorillas head inside to their sleeping quarters, so don't save this for your last stop.

❷ ELEPHANT

Asian and African elephants coexist at the San Diego Zoo. The larger African elephant is distinguished by its big flapping ears—shaped like the continent of Africa—which it uses to keep cool. An elephant's trunk has over 40,000 muscles in it—that's more than humans have in their whole body.

❸ GIANT PANDA

The San Diego Zoo is well-known for its giant panda research and conservation efforts, and has had five successful panda births. You'll likely see parents Bai Yun ("White Cloud") and Gao-Gao ("Big-Big") with their youngest baby Yun Zi ("Son of Cloud").

❹ KOALA

While this collection of critters is one of the cutest in the zoo, don't expect a lot of activity from the koala habitat. These guys spend most of their day curled up asleep in the branches of the eucalyptus tree—they can sleep up to 20 hours a day. Although eucalyptus leaves are poisonous to most animals, bacteria in koalas' stomachs allow them to break down the toxins.

❺ POLAR BEAR

The trio of polar bears is one of the San Diego Zoo's star attractions, and their brand-new exhibit gets you up close and personal. Visitors sometimes worry about polar bears living in the warm San Diego climate, but there is no cause for concern. The San Diego-based bears eat a lean diet, thus reducing their layer of blubber and helping them keep cool.

DID YOU KNOW?

Bamboo is the panda's dietary staple—they can consume 84 pounds of it a day—and the zoo grows 69 species of bamboo to ensure they have plenty of variety.

PLANNING YOUR DAY AT THE ZOO

Left: Main entrance of the San Diego Zoo. Right: Sunbear

PLANNING YOUR TIME

Plan to devote at least a half-day to exploring the zoo, but with so much to see it is easy to stay a full day or more.

If you're on a tight schedule, opt for the guided **35 minute bus tour** that lets you zip through three-quarters of the exhibits. However, lines to board the busses can be long, and you won't get as close to the animals.

Another option is to take the **Skyfari Aerial Tram** to the far end of the park, choose a route, and meander back to the entrance. The Skyfari trip gives a good overview of the zoo's layout and a spectacular view.

The **Elephant Odyssey,** while accessible from two sides of the park, is best entered from just below the Polar Rim. The extremely popular **Panda exhibit** can develop long lines, so get there early.

The zoo has three **live shows:** *Sea Lions Rock!* and *Soar-A Symphony in Flight* feature trained animal performers, and the *Dr. Zoolittle Show* is a zany science demonstration.

BEFORE YOU GO

■ To avoid ticket lines, purchase and print tickets online using the zoo's Web site.

■ To avoid excessive backtracking or a potential meltdown, plan your route along the zoo map before setting out. Try not to get too frustrated if you lose your way, as there are exciting exhibits around every turn and many paths intersect at several points.

■ The zoo offers a variety of program extras, including behind-the-scenes tours, backstage pass animal encounters, and sleepover events. Call in advance for pricing and reservations.

AT THE ZOO

■ Don't forget to explore at least some of the exhibits on foot—a favorite is the lush Tiger Trail.

■ If you visit on the weekend, find out when the Giraffe Experience is taking place. You can purchase leaf–eater biscuits to hand feed the giraffes!

■ Splurge a little at the gift shop: your purchases help support zoo programs.

■ The zoo rents strollers, wheelchairs, and lockers; it also has a first-aid office, a lost and found, and an ATM.

Fern Canyon, San Diego Zoo

GETTING HERE AND AROUND

The zoo is easy to get to, whether by bus or car.

Bus Travel: Take Bus No. 7 and exit at Park Boulevard and Zoo Place.

Car Travel: From Downtown, take Route 163 north through Balboa Park. Exit at Zoo/Museums (Richmond Street) and follow signs.

Several options help you get around the massive park: express buses loop through the zoo and the Skyfari Aerial Tram will take you from one end to the other. The zoo's topography is fairly hilly, but moving sidewalks lead up the slopes between some exhibits.

QUICK BITES

There is a wide variety of food available for purchase at the zoo from food carts to ethnic restaurants such as the Pan-Asian **Canyon Cafe.**

One of the best restaurants is **Albert's** ($), near the Gorilla exhibit, which features grilled fish, homemade pizza, and fresh pasta along with a full bar.

SERVICE INFORMATION

✉ 2920 Zoo Dr., Balboa Park

☎ 619/234–3153; 888/697–2632 Giant panda hotline

⊕ www.sandiegozoo.org

💲 $40 adult, $30 children (3-11) includes Skyfari and bus tour; 2-Visit Pass ($76 adult, $56 children age 3-11); zoo parking free

🚌 AE, D, MC, V

🕙 June 24–Sept. 5, daily 9–9; Sept. 6–Oct. 2, daily 9–6; Oct. 3–Dec. 8, daily 9–5; Dec. 9–June 23, daily 9–6; Children's Zoo and Skyfari ride generally close 1 hr earlier.

SAN DIEGO ZOO SAFARI PARK

About 45 minutes north of the zoo in Escondido, the 1,800-acre San Diego Zoo Safari Park is an extensive wildlife sanctuary where animals roam free—and guests can get close in escorted caravans and on backcountry trails. This park and the zoo operate under the auspices of the San Diego Zoo's nonprofit organization; joint tickets are available. ⇨ *See Chapter 15: North County and Environs for more information.*

Stairs lead down to the lush Palm Canyon, which has more than 58 species of palms.

San Diego Model Railroad Museum. At 27,000 square feet, this is the largest indoor operating railroad museum in North America. The four main displays, built and maintained by local model railroad clubs, represent California railroads in "miniature," with the track laid on scale models of actual San Diego County terrain. When these impressive exhibits are in operation, you can hear the sounds of chugging engines, screeching brakes, and shrill whistles. A Toy Train Gallery contains an interactive Lionel exhibit that includes a camera car hooked up to a TV set showing an engineer's-eye view of the layout. Children under 15 get in free with an adult. ⊠ *Casa de Balboa, 1649 El Prado, Balboa Park* ☎ *619/696–0199* ⊕ *www.sdmrm.org* ☜ *$7* ☉ *Tues.–Fri. 11–4, weekends 11–5.*

San Diego Natural History Museum. There are 7.5 million fossils, dinosaur models, and even live reptiles and other specimens here. Favorite exhibits include the Foucault Pendulum, suspended on a 43-foot cable and designed to demonstrate the Earth's rotation, and *Ocean Oasis,* the world's first large-format film about Baja California and the Sea of Cortés. Regional environment exhibits are highlighted, and traveling exhibits also stop here. Included in admission are 3-D films shown at the museum's giant-screen theater. Call ahead for information on films, lectures, and free guided nature walks. ⊠ *1788 El Prado, Balboa Park* ☎ *619/232–3821* ⊕ *www.sdnhm.org* ☜ *$17* ☉ *Daily 10–5.*

San Diego Zoo.

Fodor'sChoice ⇨ *See the highlighted listing in this chapter.*
★

★ **Spanish Village Art Center.** More than 200 local artists, including glassblowers, enamel workers, woodcarvers, sculptors, painters, jewelers, and photographers rent space in these 41 red tile–roof studio-galleries that were set up for the 1935–36 exposition in the style of an old Spanish village, and they give demonstrations of their work on a rotating basis. Spanish Village is a great source for one-of-a-kind, truly memorable gifts. ⊠ *1770 Village Pl., Balboa Park* ☎ *619/233–9050* ⊕ *www. spanishvillageart.com* ⊠ *Free* ☉ *Daily 11–4.*

★ **Spreckels Organ Pavilion.** The 2,400-bench-seat pavilion, dedicated in 1915 by sugar magnates John D. and Adolph B. Spreckels, holds the 4,518-pipe Spreckels Organ, the largest outdoor pipe organ in the world. You can hear it at one of the year-round, free, 2 pm Sunday concerts, regularly performed by civic organist Carol Williams and guest artists. On Monday evenings from mid-June to August, internationally renowned organists play evening concerts. In winter the park's Christmas tree and life-size Nativity display turn the pavilion into a seasonal wonderland. ⊠ *2211 Pan American Rd., Balboa Park* ☎ *619/702–8138* ⊕ *www.sosorgan.com.*

WORTH NOTING

Casa de Balboa. This building on El Prado's southeast corner houses three museums: the Museum of Photographic Arts, the Museum of San Diego History, and the San Diego Model Railroad Museum. ⊠ *1649 El Prado, Balboa Park.*

Centro Cultural de la Raza. An old water tower was converted into this center for Mexican, indigenous, and Chicano arts and culture. Attractions include a gallery with rotating exhibits and a theater, as well as a collection of mural art, a fine example of which may be seen on the tower's exterior. ⊠ *2004 Park Blvd., Balboa Park* ☎ *619/235–6135* ⊕ *www. centroculturaldelaraza.org* ⊠ *Donation suggested* ☉ *Tues.–Sun. noon–4.*

House of Charm. This structure was rebuilt from the ground up in the mid-1990s to replicate the Spanish Mission style of the original expo building. Inside, you'll find the Mingei International Museum of Folk Art and the San Diego Art Institute. ⊠ *1439 El Prado, Balboa Park* ☉ *Mingei Museum, Tues.–Sun. 10–4; Art Institute, Tues.–Sat. 10–4, Sun. noon–4.*

Ⓒ ★ **Marie Hitchcock Puppet Theater.** One of the last of its kind, this puppet theater has been presenting shows for more than 60 years. Performances incorporate marionettes, hand puppets, rod puppets, shadow puppets, and ventriloquism, while the stories range from traditional fairy tales to folk legends and contemporary puppet plays. Pantomime, comedy, and music round out the program. Kids will be wide-eyed at the short, energy-filled productions. ⊠ *2130 Pan American Plaza, Balboa Park* ☎ *619/544–9203* ⊕ *www.balboaparkpuppets.com* ⊠ *$5* ☉ *Showtimes mid-June–Labor Day, Wed.–Sun. 11, 1, 2:30; Sept.–mid-June, Wed.–Fri. 10 and 11:30, weekends 11, 1, 2:30.*

Marston House. George W. Marston (1850–1946), a San Diego pioneer

SHOPPING SPREE

Balboa Park is an excellent place to shop for unique souvenirs and gifts. In addition to the wonderful artwork for sale in Spanish Village, several museums and the visitor center have excellent stores. Of particular note are the shops at the Reuben Fleet Science Center, the Mingei Museum, the United Nations Association and, of course, the zoo.

and philanthropist who financed the architectural landscaping of Balboa Park—among his myriad other San Diego civic projects—lived in this 16-room home at the northwest edge of the park. Designed in 1905 by San Diego architects Irving Gill and William Hebbard, it's a classic example of the American Arts and Crafts style, which emphasizes simplicity and functionality of form. On the 5-acre grounds is a lovely English Romantic garden, as interpreted in California. ✉ *3525 7th Ave., Balboa Park* ☎ *619/298–3142* ⊕ *www.marstonhouse.org* 🖼 *$8* ⊙ *Fri.–Sun. 10–4:30, guided tours every half hour.*

☾ **Miniature Railroad.** Adjacent to the zoo parking lot and across from the carousel, a pint-size 48-passenger train runs a ½-mi loop through four tree-filled acres of the park. The engine of this rare 1948 model train is one of only 50 left in the world. ✉ *2885 Zoo Pl., Balboa Park* ☎ *619/239–0512* 🖼 *$2* ⊙ *June–Aug., daily 11–6:30; Sept.–May, weekends and school holidays 11–4:30.*

☾ **Morley Field Sports Complex.** In addition to the 2-mi fitness course and baseball diamonds, the park's athletic center has a flying-disc golf course where players toss their Frisbees over canyons and treetops to reach the challenging "holes"—wire baskets hung from metal poles. Morley Field also has a public pool, a velodrome, an archery range, playgrounds, and boccie, badminton, and tennis courts. The website has a downloadable program guide with complete listings and times. The complex is at the northeast corner of Balboa Park, across Park Boulevard and Florida Canyon. ✉ *2221 Morley Field Dr.* ☎ *619/525–8262* ⊕ *www.sandiego. gov/park-and-recreation/centers/morley.html.*

Museum of Photographic Arts. World-renowned photographers such as Ansel Adams, Imogen Cunningham, Henri Cartier-Bresson, and Edward Weston are represented in the permanent collection, which includes everything from 19th-century daguerreotypes to contemporary photojournalism prints and Russian Constructivist images (many by Alexander Rodchenko). The 28,000-square-foot facility has a state-of-the-art theater for screening cinema classics, as well as a learning center. ✉ *Casa de Balboa, 1649 El Prado, Balboa Park* ☎ *619/238–7559* ⊕ *www.mopa.org* 🖼 *$6 museum* ⊙ *Tues.–Sun. 10–5; Memorial Day–Labor Day open until 9 Thurs.*

Museum of San Diego History. The San Diego Historical Society maintains its research library in the basement of the Casa de Balboa and organizes shows on the first floor. Permanent and rotating exhibits, which are often more lively than you might expect, survey local urban history after 1850, when California entered the Union. A 100-seat theater hosts public lectures, workshops, and educational programs, and a gift shop carries a good selection of books on local history as well as reproductions of old posters and other historical collectibles. ✉ *Casa de Balboa, 1649 El Prado, Balboa Park* ☎ *619/232–6203* ⊕ *www.sandiegohistory.org* 🖼 *$6* ⊙ *Tues.–Sun. 10–5.*

☾ **Reuben H. Fleet Science Center.** The Fleet Center's clever interactive exhibits
★ are artfully educational. You can reconfigure your face to have two left sides, or, in "Do, Undo" replay an instant video clip, and watch yourself moving in both forward and reverse. The IMAX Dome Theater, which screens exhilarating nature and science films, was the world's first, as is the Fleet's new "NanoSeam" (seamless) dome ceiling that doubles as

a planetarium. The Nierman Challenger Learning Center—a realistic mock mission-control and futuristic space station—is a big hit. ✉ *1875 El Prado, Balboa Park* ☎ *619/238–1233* ⊕ *www.rhfleet.org* ✉ *Gallery exhibits $10, gallery exhibits and 1 IMAX film $14.50, or 2 IMAX films $19.50* ◷ *Daily 10:00 am; closing hrs vary from 5 to 9, call ahead.*

San Diego Automotive Museum. Even if you don't know a choke from a chassis, you're bound to admire the sleek designs of the autos in this impressive museum. The core collection is composed of vintage motorcycles and cars, ranging from a 1905 Tourist to a 1970 AMX 3, as well as a series of rotating exhibits from collections around the world. Even non–car buffs will love the *Fabulous Car of Louis Mattar,* which was ingeniously kitted out to set the cross-country endurance record in 1952, when it drove nonstop 6,320 miles from San Diego to New York City and back. A video display shows some highlights, such as changing the tire while in motion, or pouring a glass of water from the onboard tap. There's an ongoing automobile restoration program, and an extensive automotive research library. ✉ *2080 Pan American Plaza, Balboa Park* ☎ *619/231–2886* ⊕ *www.sdautomuseum.org* ✉ *$8* ◷ *Daily 10–5, last admission at 4:30.*

⟳ **San Diego Hall of Champions.** In a 70,000-square-foot building, this museum celebrates local jock heroes—such as baseball great Ted Williams and basketball star Bill Walton—via a vast collection of memorabilia, uniforms, paintings, photographs, and computer and video displays. In keeping with the progressive nature of the San Diego sports community, there are also exhibits of such extreme sports as skateboarding, surfing, and street luge. ✉ *Federal Bldg., 2131 Pan American Plaza, Balboa Park* ☎ *619/234–2544* ⊕ *www.sdhoc.com* ✉ *$8* ◷ *Daily 10–4:30.*

SDAI: Museum of the Living Artist. Outside juries decide which works created by members of the Art Institute will be displayed in rotating shows, which change every four to six weeks. Painting, sculpture, mixed media, digital art, and photography are represented—everything except crafts, reserved for the excellent small gift shop. The David Fleet Young Artists Gallery shows art created by students at area schools. ✉ *House of Charm, 1439 El Prado, Balboa Park* ☎ *619/236–0011* ⊕ *www. sandiego-art.org* ✉ *$3* ◷ *Tues.–Sat. 10–4, Sun. noon–4.*

Timken Museum of Art. Somewhat out of place in the architectural scheme of the park, this modern structure is made of travertine imported from Italy. The small museum is a true jewelbox, housing works by major European and American artists as well as a superb collection of Russian icons. ✉ *1500 El Prado, Balboa Park* ☎ *619/239–5548* ⊕ *www. timkenmuseum.org* ✉ *Free* ◷ *Tues.–Sat. 10–4:30, Sun. 1:30–4:30.*

Veterans Museum and Memorial Center. Housed in what was the old Naval Hospital Chapel, this museum displays memorabilia and artifacts from different conflicts and branches of service. Several large murals detail well-known battles and moments in military history. The museum is located east of Park Boulevard, in an area known as Inspiration Point. ✉ *2115 Park Blvd., Balboa Park* ☎ *619/239–2300* ⊕ *www. veteranmuseum.org* ✉ *$5* ◷ *Tues.–Sun. 10–4.*

Old Town and Uptown

WORD OF MOUTH

"Old Town is the historical settlement of the early Spanish/Mexican settlers . . . very old buildings, like shops, a schoolhouse, blacksmith's shop, plus Mexican restaurants and a Mexican shopping bazaar . . . My kids always loved it, as well as the Presidio nearby. It is an old fort up on the hill above."

—lcuy

4

GETTING ORIENTED

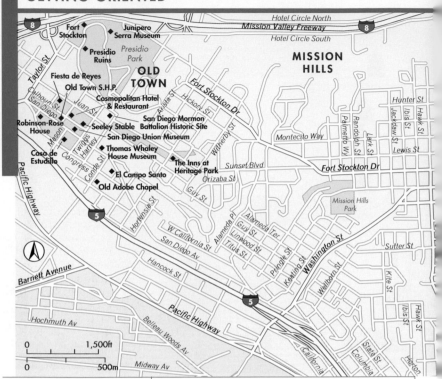

GETTING HERE

Old Town and Uptown are northwest and north of Balboa Park, respectively. Access to Old Town is easy thanks to the nearby Old Town Transit Center. Ten bus lines stop here, as do the San Diego Trolley and the Coaster commuter rail line. Two large parking lots linked to the Old Town Historic Park by an underground pedestrian walkway ease some of the parking congestion.

Uptown is best explored by car, although several bus routes do serve the area. Both metered street parking and pay-and-display lots are available.

TOP REASONS TO GO

Step back in time: Experience the early days of San Diego, from its beginnings as a remote military outpost and mission to the development of the first town plaza.

Architectural delights: Take an architectural journey through San Diego's history. Discover the pueblo- and clapboard-style structures of Old Town and the ornate Victorian gems in Heritage Park. Then head up the hill to view wonderfully preserved early-20th-century homes in Uptown.

Scare yourself silly: A nighttime visit to the Thomas Whaley House Museum, "the most haunted house in America," is sure to give you goose bumps.

Tortillas and margaritas: Enjoy the convivial atmosphere at one of the many Mexican eateries in Old Town.

Live like a local: Explore the vibrant shopping, dining, and nightlife of Uptown's unique neighborhoods.

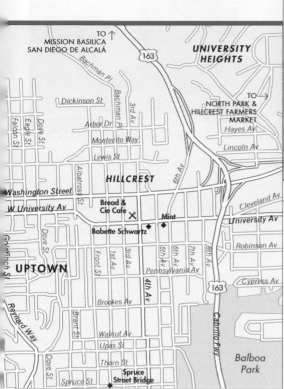

4

PLANNING YOUR TIME

It takes about two hours to walk through Old Town. Try to time your visit to coincide with the free daily tours given by costumed park staff. They depart at 11 and 2 from the Robinson-Rose House Visitor Center and take about one hour. If you go to Presidio Park, definitely consider driving up the steep hill from Old Town.

The highlight of an Uptown tour is exploring the heart of Hillcrest, located at the intersection of University and 5th avenues. Plan to drive or catch a bus between neighborhoods, then explore on foot.

FESTIVALS

The Uptown neighborhoods host a variety of events throughout the year like free summer concerts at Trolley Barn Park. Hillcrest hosts the annual LGBT Pride event every July. In late summer, Cityfest rocks the neighborhood with live music, food stalls, and beer gardens. Old Town celebrates Cinco de Mayo and the Old Town Art Festival held in October.

QUICK BITES

Fiesta de Reyes. If traveling back in time has left you tired and hungry, Old Town's Fiesta de Reyes has several options for a quick recharge. To the right when you enter from the plaza, **La Panaderia** serves a variety of empanadas as well as homemade *churros* (strips of fried dough) and hot chocolate. **Viva el Café,** toward the rear of the courtyard, features desserts and specialty coffee drinks. If you visit between Friday and Sunday, look for the simple booth marked **Street Tacos** for a quick meal to go. ⊠ *2754 Calhoun St., Old Town* ☎ *619/297–3100.*

Bread and Cie Café. Its delicious loaves are distributed around San Diego, but visitors to Hillcrest can go to the source at Bread and Cie Café. Pastries, soups, salads, sandwiches, and of course, plenty of bread are served in a bustling atmosphere. Enjoy a heavenly cappuccino alfresco, or sit inside to watch the commotion from the open kitchen. ⊠ *350 University Ave., Hillcrest* ☎ *619/683–9322.*

Sightseeing
★★★★☆
Nightlife
★★★★☆
Dining
★★★★★
Lodging
★★☆☆☆
Shopping
★★★★☆

San Diego's Spanish and Mexican roots are most evident in Old Town and the surrounding hillside of Presidio Park. Visitors can experience settlement life in San Diego from Spanish and Mexican rule to the early days of U.S. statehood. Nearby, the vibrant neighborhoods within Uptown showcase their unique blend of historical charm and modern urban community.

Updated by
Claire Deeks
van der Lee

As the first European settlement in Southern California, **Old Town** began to develop in the 1820s. However, its true beginnings took place on a nearby hillside in 1769 with the establishment of a Spanish military outpost and the first of California's missions, San Diego de Alcalá. In 1774 the hilltop was declared a presidio reál, a fortress built by the Spanish empire, and the mission was relocated along the San Diego River. Over time, settlers moved down from the presidio to establish Old Town. A central plaza was laid out, surrounded by adobe and, later, wooden, structures. San Diego became an incorporated U.S. city in 1850, with Old Town as its center. In the 1860s, however, the advent of Alonzo Horton's New Town to the southeast caused Old Town to wither. Efforts to preserve the area began early in the 20th century, and Old Town became a state historic park in 1968.

Today Old Town is a lively celebration of history and culture. The **Old Town San Diego State Historic Park** re-creates life during the early settlement, while San Diego Avenue buzzes with art galleries, gift shops, festive restaurants, and open-air stands selling inexpensive Mexican handicrafts.

Unconventional among San Diego's neighborhoods, **Uptown** encompasses the unique communities of Hillcrest, North Park, and University Heights, all pedestrian-friendly. In addition to its cultural diversity, Uptown is embraced for its urban boldness, retro style, upscale eateries, and artistic flair.

One of the city's most interesting neighborhoods, **Hillcrest** is San Diego's center for the gay community and artists of all types. Its streets are filled with cafés, thrift shops, boutiques, and a superb collection of restaurants.

North Park, named for its location north of Balboa Park, is centered at the intersection of University Avenue and 30th Street. It has a thriving business district and, despite renovations upgrading the neighborhood, care has been taken to maintain North Park's vintage atmosphere. **University Heights** features a compact, but attractive, center. A stroll along Park Boulevard reveals a range of coffee shops, bars, and ethnic eateries.

EXPLORING OLD TOWN

OLD TOWN TOUR

Because of the steep hills leading up to Heritage Park and Presidio Park, it's best to use a car to see all of Old Town's sights.

Visit the information center at Robinson-Rose House on Wallace Street, facing Old Town Plaza, to orient yourself to the various sights in **Old Town San Diego State Historic Park.** When you've had enough history, cross north on the west side of the plaza to **Fiesta de Reyes**, where you can shop or stop for a bite to eat. Walk down San Diego Avenue, which flanks the south side of Old Town's historic plaza, east to Harney Street and the **Thomas Whaley Museum.** It's best to hop in a car at this point for the next sights. Continue east 2½ blocks on San Diego Avenue beyond Arista Street to **El Campo Santo** cemetery. **Heritage Park** is perched on a hill above Juan Street, north of the museum and cemetery. Drive west on Juan Street and north on Taylor Street, which leads to Presidio Drive. This takes you up the hill on which **Presidio Park** sits.

TOP ATTRACTIONS

Fiesta de Reyes. North of San Diego's Old Town Plaza lies the area's unofficial center, built to represent a colonial Mexican square. This collection of shops and restaurants around a central courtyard in blossom with magenta bougainvillea, scarlet hibiscus, and other flowers in season reflect what it might have looked like in the early California days, from 1821 to 1872, complete with shops stocked with items reminiscent of that era. More than a dozen shops are open, and there are also three restaurants, including **Casa de Reyes,** serving Mexican food. If you are lucky, you might catch a mariachi band or folklorico dance performance on the plaza stage—check the Web site for times and upcoming special events. This area, formerly operated as Plaza del Pasado, and, before that, Bazaar del Mundo, was rechristened as Fiesta de Reyes in mid-2009. ⊠ *2754 Calhoun St., Old Town* ☎ *619/297–3100* ⊕ *www.fiestadereyes.com* ☉ *Shops 10–9 daily.*

Heritage Park. A number of San Diego's important Victorian buildings are the focus of this 7.8-acre park, up the Juan Street hill near Harney Street. The buildings, moved here and restored by Save Our Heritage Organization, include Southern California's first synagogue, a one-room Classical Revival structure built in 1889 for Congregation Beth Israel. The most interesting of the park's six former residences might be the Sherman Gilbert House, which has a widow's walk and intricate carving on its decorative trim. It was built for real-estate dealer John Sherman in 1887 at the then-exorbitant cost of $20,000—indicating just how profitable the booming housing market could be. All the houses, some of which may seem surprisingly colorful, do in fact accurately represent the bright

Fodor's Choice
★

4

CLOSE UP

California's Padre President

San Diego, the first European settlement in Southern California, was founded by Father Junípero Serra in July 1769. A member of the Franciscan order, Father Serra was part of a larger expedition chartered by King Charles III of Spain and headed by explorer Don Gaspar de Portola to travel north from Baja California and occupy the territory known then as Alta California.

When they arrived in San Diego, the Spaniards found about 20,000 Kumeyaay Indians living in a hundred or so villages along the coast and inland. The missionaries attempted to convert them to Christianity, and taught them agricultural and other skills so they could work what would become the missions' vast holdings.

Mission San Diego de Alcalá, established on a hillside above what is now Mission Valley, was the first of the 21 missions that the Franciscans ultimately built along the coast of California. After establishing the mission and presidio in San Diego, Serra and Portola moved on, founding the Mission San Carlos Borromeo and presidio at Monterey.

Father Serra, the padre president of California, established nine missions. Besides those at San Diego and Monterey, there were: San Antonio de Padua, 1771; San Gabriel, 1771; San Luis Obispo, 1772; Dolores, 1776; San Juan Capistrano, 1776; Santa Clara, 1777; and San Buenaventura, 1782. He personally oversaw the planning, construction, and staffing of each of these, and conferred the sacraments. His work took him from Carmel to locations up and down the length of California. It's estimated that during this period he walked more than 24,000 mi in California visiting missions.

The missions comprised millions of acres and were in fact small self-sufficient cities with the church as the centerpiece. In addition to converting the Indians to Christianity and teaching them European ways, the padres managed farming, education, and industries such as candle making and tanning. San Diego is the southernmost mission, while the mission at Sonoma, San Francisco Solano, the last to be founded, in 1823, is the northernmost; each was established a day's walk—about 30 mi—from the previous one and was linked to El Camino Highway. The missions were the earliest form of lodging in the Golden State, known far and wide for the hospitality they afforded visitors. You can trace the steps of Father Serra along El Camino Real by driving U.S. 101, the historic route that traverses coastal California from south to north.

—Bobbi Zane

tones of the era. Management of the park was recently transferred to a hospitality firm, and renovation of the buildings is underway. For visitors looking to stay overnight in a historic setting, four of the houses should be converted into "The Inns at Heritage Park" during the lifespan of this book. The park remains open during this process, with the synagogue and Senlis Cottage open to visitors daily from 9 to 5. The McConaughy House hosts the Old Town Gift Emporium, a gift shop specializing in Victorian porcelain dolls (Thursday–Tuesday 10–5). ⊠ *2455 Heritage Park Row, Old Town* ☎ *619/819–6009* ⊕ *www.heritageparksd.com.*

Old Town celebrates Mexican culture with live music and entertainment at the Cinco de Mayo festival.

⏱ **Old Town San Diego State Historic Park.** The six square blocks on the site
Fodor's Choice of San Diego's original pueblo are the heart of Old Town. Most of the
★ 20 historic buildings preserved or re-created by the park cluster around
Old Town Plaza, bounded by Wallace Street on the west, Calhoun Street
on the north, Mason Street on the east, and San Diego Avenue on the
south. The plaza is a pleasant place to rest, plan your tour of the park,
and watch passersby. San Diego Avenue is closed to vehicle traffic here.

Some of Old Town's buildings were destroyed in a fire in 1872, but
after the site became a state historic park in 1968, reconstruction and
restoration on the structures that remained began. Seven of the original
adobes are still intact. The tour pamphlet available at Robinson-Rose
House gives details about all the historic houses on the plaza and in
its vicinity; a few of the more interesting ones are noted below. Several
reconstructed buildings serve as restaurants or as shops purveying wares
reminiscent of those that might have been available in the original Old
Town; Racine & Laramie, a painstakingly reproduced version of San
Diego's first (1868) cigar store, is especially interesting. The noncom-
mercial houses are open daily 10 to 5 (until 4 in winter); none charges
admission, though donations are appreciated. Free tours depart daily
from the Robinson-Rose House at 11 and 2. ■**TIP➜** The covered wagon
in Old Town Plaza makes for a great photo opportunity.

Also worth exploring in the plaza area are the free **Dental Museum,
Mason Street School, Wells Fargo History Museum, First San Diego
Courthouse, Casa de Machado y Silvas Commercial Restaurant Museum,**
and the **Casa de Machado y Stewart.** Ask at the visitor center for locations.

Robinson-Rose House. The Robinson-Rose House, on Wallace Street facing Old Town Plaza, was the original commercial center of Old San Diego, housing railroad offices, law offices, and the first newspaper press. Built in 1853 but in ruins at the end of the 19th century, it has been reconstructed and now serves as the park's visitor center and administrative headquarters. It contains a model of Old Town as it looked in 1872, as well as various historic exhibits. Just behind the Robinson-Rose House is a replica of the Victorian-era Silvas-McCoy house, originally built in 1869. ⊠ *4002 Wallace St., Old Town* ☎ *619/220–5422.*

Cosmopolitan Hotel and Restaurant. On Mason Street, at the corner of Calhoun Street, is the Cosmopolitan Restaurant/Casa de Bandini, once one of the prettiest haciendas in San Diego. Built in 1829 by a Peruvian, Juan Bandini, the house served as Old Town's social center during Mexican rule. Albert Seeley, a stagecoach entrepreneur, purchased the home in 1869, built a second story, and turned it into the Cosmopolitan Hotel, a way station for travelers on the daylong trip south from Los Angeles. It later served as a store and a factory. It is set to reopen in the summer of 2010 as the restored Cosmopolitan Hotel and restaurant.

Seeley Stable. Next door to the Cosmopolitan building, this became San Diego's stagecoach stop in 1867 and was the transportation hub of Old Town until near the turn of the 19th century, when trains became the favored mode of travel. The stable houses a collection of horse-drawn vehicles, some so elaborate that you can see where the term "carriage trade" came from. Also inside are Western memorabilia, including an exhibit on the California vaquero, the original American cowboy, and a collection of Native American artifacts. ⊠ *2630 Calhoun St., Old Town.*

Casa de Estudillo. The Casa de Estudillo was built on Mason Street in 1827 by San Diego's first County Assessor, José Antonio Estudillo, in collaboration with his father, the commander of the San Diego Presidio, José María Estudillo. The largest and most elaborate of the original adobe homes, it was occupied by members of the Estudillo family until 1887. It was purchased and restored in 1910 by sugar magnate and developer John D. Spreckels, who advertised it in bold lettering on the side as "Ramona's Marriage Place." Spreckels's claim that the small chapel in the house was the site of the wedding in Helen Hunt Jackson's popular novel *Ramona* had no basis; that didn't stop people from coming to see it, however. ⊠ *4001 Mason St., Old Town.*

San Diego Union Museum. This New England–style, wood-frame house was prefabricated in the eastern United States and shipped around Cape Horn in 1851. The building has been restored to replicate the newspaper's offices of 1868, when the first edition of the *San Diego Union* was printed. ⊠ *2602 San Diego Ave., Old Town* ⊠ *4002 Wallace St., Old Town* ☎ *619/220–5422* ⊕ *www.parks.ca.gov.*

Presidio Park. The hillsides of the 40-acre green space overlooking Old Town from the north end of Taylor Street are popular with picnickers, and many couples have taken their wedding vows on the park's long stretches of lawn, some of the greenest in San Diego. You may encounter enthusiasts of the sport of grass-skiing, gliding over the grass and down the hills on their wheeled-model skis. ■ **TIP→** Grab a cardboard box to try grass-sledding the low-tech way. It's a nice walk from Old Town to the summit if you're in good shape and wearing the right shoes—it should take about half an hour. You can also drive to the top of the park via Presidio Drive, off Taylor Street.

If you do decide to walk, look in at the **Presidio Hills Golf Course** on Mason Street. It has an unusual clubhouse that incorporates the ruins of Casa de Carrillo, the town's oldest adobe, constructed in 1820. At the end of Mason Street, veer left on Jackson Street to reach the **presidio ruins,** where adobe walls and a bastion have been built above the foundations of the original fortress and chapel. Archaeology students from San Diego State University who excavated the area have marked off the early chapel outline, although they reburied the artifacts they uncovered in order to protect them. Also on-site are the 28-foot-high **Serra Cross,** built in 1913 out of brick tiles found in the ruins, and a bronze **statue of Father Serra.** Take Presidio Drive southeast and you'll come to the site of **Fort Stockton,** built to protect Old Town and abandoned by the United States in 1848. Plaques and statues also commemorate the Mormon Battalion, which enlisted here to fight in the battle against Mexico. ⊠ *1 block north of Old Town San Diego State Historic Park, Old Town.*

★ **Thomas Whaley House Museum.** Thomas Whaley was a New York entrepreneur who came to California during the gold rush. He wanted to provide his East Coast wife with all the comforts of home, so in 1857 he had Southern California's first two-story brick structure built, making it the oldest double-story brick building on the West Coast. The house, which served as the county courthouse and government seat during the 1870s, stands in strong contrast to the Spanish-style adobe residences that surround the nearby historic plaza and marks an early stage of San Diego's "Americanization." A garden out back includes many varieties of Old Garden roses from before 1867, when roses were first hybridized. The place is perhaps most famed, however, for the ghosts that are said to inhabit it. Starting at 7 pm, admission is by guided tour offered every half hour with the last tour departing at 9:30 pm. The nighttime tours are geared more toward the supernatural aspects of the house than is the daytime self-guided tour. ⊠ *2476 San Diego Ave., Old Town* ☎ *619/297–7511* ⊕ *www.whaleyhouse.org* ✉ *$6 before 5 pm, $10 after 5* ☉ *Sept.–May, Sun.–Tues. 10–5, Thurs.–Sun. 10–9:30; June–Aug., daily 10–9:30.*

AMERICA'S MOST HAUNTED

Built on a former gallows site in 1856, the Whaley House is one of 30 houses designated by the Department of Commerce to be haunted. Legend has it that the house is inhabited by seven spirits, making it the "most haunted house in America." Listen for the sound of heavy footsteps, said to belong to the ghost of Yankee Jim Robinson, a convict hanged on the site in 1852. Less ominous are sightings of the Whaley family's fox terrier scampering about the house.

4

WORTH NOTING

El Campo Santo. The old adobe-wall cemetery established in 1849 was, until 1880, the burial place for many members of Old Town's founding families—as well as for some gamblers and bandits who passed through town. Antonio Garra, a chief who led an uprising of the San Luis Rey Indians, was executed at El Campo Santo in front of the open grave he had been forced to dig for himself. These days the small cemetery is a peaceful stop for visitors to Old Town. Most of the markers give only approximations of where the people named on them are buried; some of the early settlers laid to rest at El Campo Santo actually reside under San Diego Avenue. ⊠ *North side of San Diego Ave. S, between Arista and Ampudia Sts., Old Town* ▭ *No credit cards.*

4

Junípero Serra Museum. The hill on which San Diego's original Spanish presidio (fortress) and California's first mission were perched is now the domain of a Spanish Mission–style museum established, along with Presidio Park, by department store magnate and philanthropist George Marston in 1929 to commemorate the history of the site from the time it was occupied by the Kumeyaay Indians through its Spanish, Mexican, and American periods. Artifacts include Kumeyaay baskets, Spanish riding gear, and a painting that Father Serra would have viewed in Mission San Diego de Alcalá. The education room has hands-on stations where kids can grind acorns in *metates* (stones used for grinding grain), dig for buried artifacts with archaeology tools, or dress up in period costumes—one represents San Diego founding father Alonzo Horton. Ascend the tower to compare the view you'd have gotten before 1929 with the one you have today. The museum, now operated by the San Diego Historical Society, is at the north end of Presidio Park, near Taylor Street. ⊠ *2727 Presidio Dr., Presidio Park* ☏ *619/297–3258* ⊕ *www. sandiegohistory.org* ⊒ *$6* ☉ *Weekends 10–5.*

OFF THE
BEATEN
PATH

Mission Basilica San Diego de Alcalá. It's hard to imagine how remote California's earliest mission once must have been; these days, it's accessible by major freeways (I–15 and I–8) and by the San Diego Trolley. Mission San Diego de Alcalá, the first of a chain of 21 missions stretching northward along the coast, was established by Father Junípero Serra on Presidio Hill in 1769 and moved to this location in 1774. There was no greater security from enemy attack here: Padre Luis Jayme, California's first Christian martyr, was clubbed to death by the Kumeyaay Indians he was trying to convert in 1775. The present church is the fifth built on the site; it was reconstructed in 1931 following the outline of the 1813 church. It measures 150 feet long but only 35 feet wide because, without easy means of joining beams, the mission buildings were only as wide as the trees that served as their ceiling supports were tall. Father Jayme is buried in the sanctuary; a small museum named for him documents mission history and exhibits tools and artifacts from the early days. From the peaceful palm-bedecked gardens out back you can gaze at the 46-foot-high *campanario* (bell tower), the mission's most distinctive feature; one of its five bells was cast in 1802. ⊠ *10818 San Diego Mission Rd., Mission Valley* ✧ *From I–8 east, exit and turn left on Mission Gorge Rd., turn left on Twain Rd. and the mission will be on the right* ☏ *619/281–8449* ⊕ *www.missionsandiego.com* ⊒ *$3 donation suggested* ☉ *Daily 9–4:45.*

San Diego Mormon Battalion Historic Site. Operated by the Church of Jesus Christ of Latter-day Saints, this site tells the story of the formation of the Mormon Battalion and their journey to San Diego. The battalion of just under 500 men left Council Bluffs, Iowa, on July 20, 1846, for a grueling six-month, roughly 2,000-mi infantry march during the Mexican-American war. Approximately 80 women and chil-

dren accompanied the group. Upon their arrival in San Diego, members of the Battalion were involved in the development of Old Town. Opened in early 2010 after a major remodel, the Mormon Battalion building features impressive set designs and multimedia exhibits. Guides in period costumes lead visitors through a series of rooms representing stages of the journey. Talking picture frames and other interactive features keep things interesting. At the end of the tour, visitors can learn more about members of the Battalion in the Research Room, or pan for gold out back. ⊠ *2510 Juan St., Old Town* ☎ *619/298–3317* ⊕ *www.lds.org/placestovisit* ⊠ *Free* ☉ *Daily 9–9.*

EN ROUTE The route from Old Town to Hillcrest passes through the historic neighborhood of **Mission Hills** with its delightful examples of early-20th-century architecture. From the top of Presidio Park, take Presidio Drive into the heart of this residential area. A left on Arista Street and a right on Fort Stockton Drive takes you past wonderfully preserved Spanish Revival, Craftsman, and Prairie-style homes, to name a few. Many local residents fine-tune their green thumbs at the **Mission Hills Nursery** (⊠ *1525 Ft. Stockton Dr.*), founded in 1910 by Kate Sessions, the "Mother of Balboa Park." Continuing on Fort Stockton Drive, a right on Goldfinch Street and a left on University Avenue will take you into the Hillcrest section of Uptown. For more information on this historic San Diego neighborhood, visit the Mission Hills Heritage Organization at ⊕ *www.missionhillsheritage.org.*

EXPLORING UPTOWN

TOP ATTRACTIONS

Fodor's Choice ★ **Hillcrest.** The large retro Hillcrest sign over the intersection of University and 5th avenues makes an excellent landmark at the epicenter of this vibrant section of Uptown. Strolling along University Avenue between 4th and 6th avenues from Washington Street to Robinson Avenue will reveal a mixture of retail shops and restaurants. National chains such as American Apparel and Pinkberry coexist alongside local boutiques, bookstores, and coffee shops. ⊠ *Centered around University Ave. and 5th Ave., Hillcrest.*

A few blocks east, another interesting stretch of stores and restaurants runs along University Avenue to Normal Street. If you are visiting Hillcrest on Sunday between 9 and 2 be sure to explore the Hillcrest Farmer's Market.

Gay-friendly Hillcrest is one of the hippest nabes in San Diego.

Babette Schwartz. Be sure to peek inside this quirky shop for an amusing assortment of gifts. ✉ *421 University Ave., Hillcrest.*

Mint. This shop offers a hip selection of men's and women's footwear. ✉ *525 University Ave., Hillcrest.*

Pomegranate Home. Pomegranate Home offers a great selection of home decor and accessories. ✉ *1037 University Ave., Hillcrest.*

Taste. Stop in for a delicious sampling of cheeses and other gourmet goods. ✉ *1243 University Ave., Hillcrest.*

☙ **Hillcrest Farmers' Market.** One of San Diego's best farmers' markets, this
★ weekly bazaar offers everything from vegan fruit pies and strawberry lemonade to homemade hummus and Turkish kabobs. A wide assortment of fresh produce and flowers are delivered straight from San Diego's local farms. Several vendors dish up food to enjoy on the spot, making this an excellent choice for a quick lunch. ✉ *3960 Normal St., between Blaine Ave. and Lincoln Ave., Hillcrest* ☎ *619/237–1632* ⊕ *www.sdfarmbureau.org* ☙ *Sun. 9–2 pm.*

QUICK BITES

Claire de Lune. With a focus on urban community, Claire de Lune, a living-room-style coffeehouse, will lure you in with its velvet couches, live jazz, wooden floors, and upstairs lounge. Their mouthwatering desserts include carrot cake, chocolate éclairs, and raspberry cheesecake. White dragon tea and tropical star are considered house-brewed favorites. ✉ *2906 University Ave., North Park* ☎ *619/688-9845.*

WORTH NOTING

Birch North Park Theatre. Built in 1928, this stunning period theater seats 730 and is owned by the Lyric Opera San Diego. Considered the jewel of North Park, the theater was reopened in October 2005 after extensive renovations. Known for its excellent acoustics, the theater features a wide selection of concerts and productions from opera to quartets. The original lobby now serves as the entrance to the West Coast Tavern restaurant and bar. ⊠ *2891 University Ave., North Park* ☎ *619/239–8836* ⊕ *www.birchnorthparktheatre.net.*

North Park. Named for its location north of Balboa Park, this evolving neighborhood is home to an exciting array of restaurants, bars, and shops. High-end condominiums and local merchants are often cleverly disguised behind historic signage from barbershops, bowling alleys, and theater marquees of a bygone era. The stretch of Ray Street near University Avenue is home to several small galleries that are fun to browse. ⊠ *Centered around University Ave. and 30th St., North Park.*

Urban Solace. Head here for upscale American comfort food and their Sunday bluegrass brunch. ⊠ *3823 30th St., North Park.*

Pigment. This shop has a charming selection of high-design housewares, gifts for baby, and incredible hanging glass succulent planters. ⊠ *3827 30th Ave., North Park.*

Off the Record. Across from the Birch North Park Theatre, peruse the vintage vinyl at Off the Record, a surviving member of a dying breed. ⊠ *2912 University Ave., North Park.*

Spruce Street Bridge. Constructed in 1912 by Edwin Capps, this 375-foot suspension bridge originally served as a passageway between isolated neighborhoods and trolley lines. Spanning across Kate Sessions Canyon (commonly referred to as Arroyo Canyon), today this wobbly bridge is considered one of San Diego's best-kept secrets, with its scenic and somewhat hair-raising stroll over treetops below. ⊠ *Spruce St. and 1st Ave., Hillcrest.*

☺ **University Heights.** Tucked between Hillcrest and North Park, this small but charming neighborhood is centered on Park Boulevard.

El Zarape. Join locals clamoring for fish tacos or lobster burritos at El Zarape. ⊠ *4642 Park Blvd., University Heights.*

Cream Coffee Bar. Coffee lovers can get their fix at Cream Coffee Bar. ⊠ *4496 Park Blvd., University Heights.*

Small Bar. Beer lovers will want to check out the selection at Small Bar. ⊠ *4628 Park Blvd., University Heights.*

Diversionary Theatre. This acclaimed theater specializes in productions with predominately gay and lesbian themes. ⊠ *4545 Park Blvd., University Heights.*

Trolley Barn Park. Kids will love the playgrounds here, just around the corner on Adams Ave. The park is also home to free family concerts in the summer. ⊠ *Adams Ave. between Georgia and Alabama sts., University Heights* ⊠ *Park Blvd. and Madison Ave., University Heights.*

Mission Bay, Beaches, and SeaWorld

WORD OF MOUTH

"To combat the crowds at SeaWorld, you could go when it first opens, getting a stamp on your exit, go back to your hotel in the afternoon for a nap, then return in the evening for shows and fireworks."

—itsv

GETTING ORIENTED

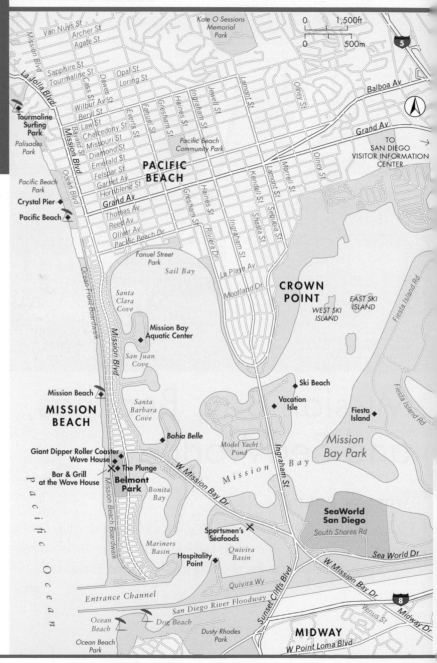

TOP REASONS TO GO

Sun and sand: With sand stretching as far as the eye can see, Mission and Pacific beaches represent the classic Southern California beach experience.

Bustling boardwalk: College kids partying at the bars, families grilling in front of their vacation homes, and kids playing in the sand—take in the scene with a stroll along the Mission Beach boardwalk.

Shamu mania: Even parents will find themselves falling in love with this charming killer whale at one of SeaWorld's spectacular shows.

Bayside delights: A quiet respite from the nearby beaches, Mission Bay is ringed with peaceful pathways, playgrounds, and parks.

Get out on the water: Catch a wave, paddle a kayak, or rev a Jet Ski at this irresistible water-sports playground.

QUICK BITES

Sportsmen's Sea Foods. This waterside eatery serves good fish-and-chips, seafood salads, and sandwiches to eat on the inelegant but scenic patio—by the marina, where sportfishing boats depart daily—or to take out to your chosen picnic spot. ✉ 1617 Quivira Rd., Mission Bay ☎ 619/224–3551.

The Bar and Grill at the Wave House. This spot is a great place to grab a drink or meal while taking in the view of surfers on the nearby wave machine. ✉ Mission Beach Boardwalk at Belmont Park, Mission Bay ☎ 858/228–9283.

There is no shortage of dining options inside **SeaWorld**. Roast beef sandwiches and the like are served at the **Deli**, while **Seaside Coffee and Bakery** offers a variety of fresh baked goods. Healthier fare is the order of the day at the huge **Shipwreck Reef Cafe**, where tropical birds, sea turtles, and other critters are on display near your table.

GETTING HERE

SeaWorld, Mission Bay, and Mission and Pacific beaches are all served by public bus routes 8 and 9. Many local hotels offer shuttle service to and from SeaWorld. There is a free parking lot at Belmont Park, although it can quickly fill during busy times.

PLANNING YOUR TIME

You may not find a visit to SeaWorld fulfilling unless you spend at least half a day; a full day is recommended. Belmont Park is open daily, but not all its rides are open year-round. The Mission Beach Boardwalk and the miles of trails around Mission Bay are great for a leisurely bike ride. On foggy days, particularly in late spring or early summer, the beaches can be overcast in the morning with the fog burning off as the day wears on.

5

SEAWORLD SAN DIEGO

SeaWorld is best known as the home of beloved killer whale Shamu. One of the world's largest marine-life amusement parks, SeaWorld is spread over 189 tropically landscaped bayfront acres—and it continues to expand.

(above) Acrobatic dolphins perform at SeaWorld's newest show, Blue Horizons. (lower right) Shamu steals the show at Believe. (upper right) You can purchase food to feed the flamingos at Flamingo Cove.

SeaWorld's highlights are its large-arena entertainments. With Shamu as the headliner, the park's signature show, **Believe,** brings down the house. **Blue Horizons,** new in 2010, brings dolphins, pilot whales, tropical birds, and aerialists together in a spectacular performance.

The majority of SeaWorld's exhibits are walk-through marine environments such as **Shark Encounter,** where you come face-to-face with several species of sharks while passing through a 57-foot clear acrylic tube. **Wild Arctic** starts out with a simulated helicopter ride to the North Pole and features beluga whales, walruses, and polar bears.

SeaWorld also wows the crowd with its adventure rides like **Journey to Atlantis,** with a heart-stopping 60-foot plunge, and **Shipwreck Rapids,** where you careen down a river in an inner tube encountering waterfalls.

DISCOUNTS AND DEALS

The San Diego 3-for-1 Ticket ($129 for adults, $99 for children ages 3 to 9) offers five consecutive days of unlimited admission to SeaWorld, the San Diego Zoo, and the San Diego Wild Animal Park. Look for SeaWorld specials at Mission Bay area hotels; some offer admission deals or free shuttle service to and from the park. Be sure to ask when you book.

SEAWORLD IN A DAY

The highlights of any visit to Sea World are the shows, so review the current performance schedule (available online or when you arrive at the park) and plan your visit accordingly. Shows are fairly short—about 20 minutes—so you can see several in a day.

SeaWorld is busiest in the middle of the day, so thrill seekers should tackle the adventure rides either at the beginning or end of your visit. Unless it is very hot, consider braving the soakers—**Journey to Atlantis, Shipwreck Rapids,** and sitting in the arenas' **Splash Zones**—in close secession, and then changing into dry clothes.

For an interactive experience, focus on the feeding stations and touch pools. The friendly bottlenose dolphins at **Rocky Point Preserve** just might let you pet them while the hands-on **California Tide Pool** features San Diego's indigenous marine life. At **Forbidden Reef** you can feed bat rays, while hungry sea lions await you at **Pacific Point.**

The standouts among the walk-through marine exhibits are the **Penguin** and **Shark Encounters,** as well as **Wild Arctic.** Those with little ones 42 inches and under should make time for the rides and play equipment at the **Sesame Street Bay of Play.**

It is easy for your SeaWorld visit to become a very full day. While saving either **Believe** or **Blue Horizons** for a finale can be great, if you get too tired you might end up missing a main attraction.

POPULAR ADD-ONS

The 30-minute **Dolphin Interaction Program** ($190) lets you feed, touch, and give behavior signals to bottlenose dolphins. A less expensive treat ($39 adults, $19 children) is the **Dine with Shamu** package, which includes a buffet lunch or dinner. The one-hour **Behind-the-Scenes Tour** ($13 adults, $11 children) takes you into backstage training areas.

TIPS

■ Pack a change of clothes for after the soaker rides and shows; you can rent a locker to stow belongings. Remember sunscreen and hats.

■ Get your hand stamped upon exiting the park to be able to return later the same day.

■ Don't miss the **Bayside Skyride** ($4) over Mission Bay for a great aerial view.

■ Arrive at shows at least 30 minutes early to get front-row seats and be prepared to get wet.

■ Steer kids towards the Trader's Cove gift shop, located near the Turtle Pool, where all items are priced $10 or less.

SERVICE INFORMATION

✉ 500 SeaWorld Dr., near west end of I–8, Mission Bay ☎ 800/257–4268 ⊕ www.seaworld.com 🎫 $69.99 adults, $61.99 kids; parking $12 cars, $8 motorcycles, $17 RVs and campers; pet boarding available for $10, bring bowls and food ▭ AE, D, MC, V ⊙ Daily 10–dusk; extended hrs in summer.

5

Sightseeing
★★★★☆

Nightlife
★★★☆☆

Dining
★★☆☆☆

Lodging
★★★☆☆

Shopping
★☆☆☆☆

Mission Bay and the surrounding beaches is the aquatic playground of San Diego. The choice of activities available is astonishing, and the perfect weather makes you want to get out there and have fun. If you're craving a little downtime after all that activity, there are plenty of peaceful spots to relax and simply soak up the sunshine.

Updated by
Claire Deeks
van der Lee

Mission Bay welcomes visitors with its protected waters and countless opportunities for fun. The 4,600-acre **Mission Bay Park** is the place for water sports like windsurfing, sailing, and water-skiing. With 19 mi of beaches and grassy areas, it's also a great place for a picnic. At the south end of the bay lies **SeaWorld**, one of San Diego's most popular attractions.

Heading west on Mission Bay Drive to the ocean, the Giant Dipper roller coaster rises into view welcoming visitors to the **Belmont Park** amusement park and to **Mission Beach.** Mission Boulevard runs north along a two block–wide strip embraced by the Pacific Ocean on the west and the bay on the east. Mission Beach is a famous and lively fun zone for families and young people both; if it isn't party time at the moment, it will be five minutes from now. The pathways in this area are lined with vacation homes, many for rent by the week or month. Those fortunate enough to live here year-round have the bay as their front yard, with wide sandy beaches, volleyball courts, and—less of an advantage—an endless stream of sightseers on the sidewalk.

North of Mission Beach is the college-packed party town of **Pacific Beach,** or "PB" as locals call it. The laid-back vibe of this surfer's mecca draws in free-spirited locals who roam the streets on skateboards and beach cruisers, in the local uniform of board shorts, bikinis, and baseball caps. Lining the main strip of Grand and Garnet avenues are tattoo parlors, smoke shops, vintage stores, and coffeehouses. The energy level peaks during happy hour, when PB's cluster of nightclubs, bars, and 150 restaurants open their doors to those ready to party.

EXPLORING MISSION BAY, BEACHES, AND SEAWORLD

PLANNING A DAY AT THE BEACHES AND BAY

A day spent at Mission Bay or the surrounding beaches can be as active or leisurely as you like.

If you want to play in the water, the bay is a great place to kayak, sail, or try some stand-up paddleboarding. If you're into surfing, be sure to check out the waves at **Crystal Pier** in Pacific Beach. A new kind of surfing experience is available at the **Wave House** at **Belmont Park**, where the Flow Rider lets you catch a continuous wave.

If you want to keep active on land, the Bayside Walk and Bike Path is a great place to jog or ride along the bay. Beach Cruiser bike rentals are widely available. For a more leisurely stroll and some people-watching, head to the **Mission Beach Boardwalk.** At the south end of Mission Beach try your hand at some typically Californian beach volleyball.

If you'd rather take it easy, just find a spot to lay out your towel anywhere along Mission or Pacific beach and soak up the sun. If you tire of the sand, enjoy a picnic at **Hospitality Point** or enjoy the view from one of the restaurants at Paradise Point Resort and Spa. As the day winds down, the happy-hour crowd is just heating up along Garnet Avenue in Pacific Beach. Alternatively, head to the Bahia Resort Hotel, where you can catch the *Bahia Belle* for a cruise around the bay.

If you are traveling with kids, a day at **SeaWorld** should be high on your list. There is plenty of family fun beyond SeaWorld, too. The protected beaches of the bay are popular spots for youngsters. The well-paved, peaceful Bayside Walk and Bike Path winds past picnic tables, grassy areas, and playgrounds, making it an ideal family spot. For a more lively contrast, cross the street to reach the Mission Beach Boardwalk, a classic boardwalk popular with young, hip surfers. At the south end lies **Belmont Park,** which includes an amusement park, the **Wave House,** and the **Giant Dipper** wooden roller coaster.

TOP ATTRACTIONS

Bahia Belle. At the dock of the Bahia Resort Hotel, on the eastern shores of West Mission Bay Drive, you can board this restored stern-wheeler for a sunset cruise of the bay and party until the wee hours. There's always music, mostly jazz, rock, and blues, and on Friday and Saturday nights the music is live. You can imbibe at the *Belle*'s full bar, which opens at 9:30 pm, but many revelers like to disembark at the Bahia's sister hotel, the Catamaran Resort, and have a few rounds before reboarding (the boat cruises between the two hotels, which co-own it, stopping to pick up passengers every half hour). Crusies after 9:30 pm are adults-only, but most cruises get a mixed crowd of families, couples, and singles. ⊠ *998 W. Mission Bay Dr., Mission Bay* ☎ *858/539–7779* ⌦ *$10 for unlimited cruising; cruisers must be at least 21 after 9:30 pm; free for guests of Bahia and Catamaran hotels* ⊙ *Sept.–Nov. and Feb.–May, Fri. and Sat. 6:30 pm–12:30 am, departures every hr on the ½ hr; June, Wed.–Sat. 6:30 pm–12:30 am; July–Labor Day, daily 6:30 pm–12:30 am; closed Dec. yearly and Jan. in odd-numbered years.*

★ **Belmont Park.** The once-abandoned amusement park between the bay and Mission Beach Boardwalk is now a shopping, dining, and recreation complex. Twinkling lights outline the **Giant Dipper,** an antique wooden roller coaster on which screaming thrill-seekers ride more than 2,600 feet of track and 13 hills (riders must be at least 4 feet,

> **MISSION BAY WARNING**
>
> Swimmers at Mission Bay should note signs warning about water pollution; on occasions when heavy rains or other events cause pollution, swimming is strongly discouraged.

2 inches tall). Created in 1925 and listed on the National Register of Historic Places, this is one of the few old-time roller coasters left in the United States. The **Plunge,** an indoor swimming pool, also opened in 1925, and was the largest—60 feet by 125 feet—saltwater pool in the world at the time (it's had freshwater since 1951). Johnny Weismuller and Esther Williams are among the stars who were captured on celluloid swimming here. Other Belmont Park attractions include a video arcade, a submarine ride, bumper cars, a tilt-a-whirl, and an antique carousel. Belmont Park also has the most consistent wave in the county at the **Wave House,** where the FlowRider provides surfers and bodyboarders a near-perfect simulated wave on which to practice their skills. The rock wall challenges both junior climbers and their elders. ⊠ *3146 Mission Blvd., Mission Bay* ☎ *858/488–1549, 858/228–9300 for pool* ⊕ *www. belmontpark.com* ✉ *$6 for roller coaster, other rides cost $2 to $5, or buy a full-day unlimited ride package $22.95 for 50" and over, $15.95 for under 50"; pool $7 for one-time entry* ⊙ *Park opens at 11 daily, ride operation varies seasonally; pool weekdays noon–4 pm, and 8–10 pm, weekends noon–8 pm.*

Crystal Pier. Stretching out into the ocean from the end of Garnet Avenue, Crystal Pier is Pacific Beach's landmark. A stroll to the end of the pier reveals fishermen hoping for a good catch, while surfers make catches of their own in the waves below. ⊠ *At the end of Garnet Ave., Pacific Beach.*

★ **Mission Bay Park.** Mission Bay Park is San Diego's monument to sports and fitness. This 4,600-acre aquatic park has 27 mi of shoreline including 19 mi of sandy beaches. Playgrounds and picnic areas abound on the beaches and low grassy hills. On weekday evenings, joggers, bikers, and skaters take over. In the daytime, swimmers, water-skiers, windsurfers, anglers, and boaters—some in single-person kayaks, others in crowded powerboats—vie for space in the water. ⊠ *2688 E. Mission Bay Dr., off I-5 at Exit 22 East Mission Bay Drive, Mission Bay* ☎ *858/581–7602 Park Ranger's Office* ⊕ *www.sandiego.gov* ✉ *Free.*

Mission Beach Boardwalk. The cement pathway lining the sand from the southern end of Mission Beach north to Pacific Beach is always bustling with activity. Cyclists ping the bells on their beach cruisers to pass walkers out for a stroll alongside the oceanfront homes. Vacationers kick back on their patios, while friends play volleyball in the sand. The activity picks up alongside Belmont Park and the Wavehouse, where people stop to check out the action on the FlowRider wave. ⊠ *Alongside the sand from Mission Beach Park to Pacific Beach, Mission Beach.*

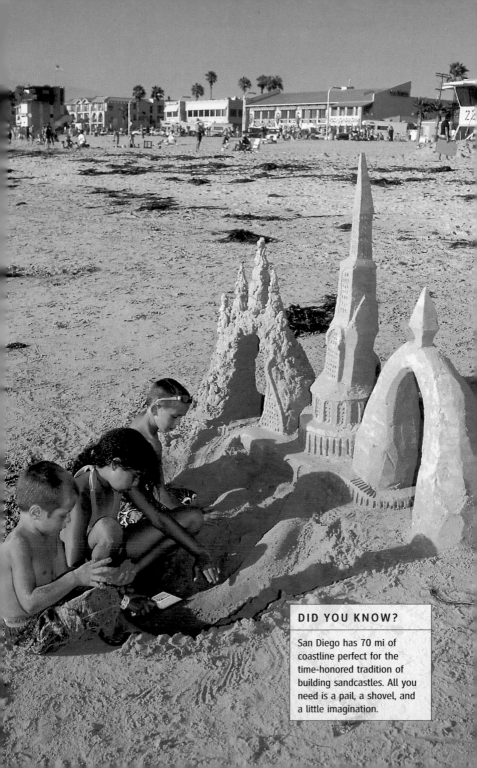

DID YOU KNOW?

San Diego has 70 mi of coastline perfect for the time-honored tradition of building sandcastles. All you need is a pail, a shovel, and a little imagination.

BEST BEACHES

The long expanse of sand running from Mission to Pacific beach is some of the most popular in San Diego with locals and visitors alike. There is an energetic atmosphere among the throngs of beachgoers—the boardwalks bustle with activity, and surf culture reigns supreme.

⇨ *For more information on Mission Bay's Beaches, see Chapter 12: Beaches.*

Mission Beach. The 2-mi stretch of sand that makes up Mission Beach extends north to Belmont Park and draws huge crowds on summer weekends. This is a great place for people-watching along the board-walk and on the volleyball courts at the southern tip.

Pacific Beach. PB picks up where Mission Beach leaves off and extends north to Crystal Pier. Parking is tough, but the scene on Ocean Front Walk and the party atmosphere may just be worth it.

Tourmaline Surfing Park. Technically part of Pacific Beach, a portion of this stretch of water is designated for surfing only.

SeaWorld San Diego.

Fodor's Choice ★ ⇨ *See the highlighted listing in this chapter.*

Vacation Isle. Ingraham Street bisects this island, providing two distinct experiences for visitors. The west side is taken up by the Paradise Point Resort & Spa, but you don't have to be a guest to enjoy the hotel's lushly landscaped grounds and bay-front restaurants. The water-ski clubs congregate at **Ski Beach** on the east side of the island, where there's a parking lot as well as picnic areas and restrooms. Ski Beach is the site of the annual Bayfair (formerly called the Thunderboat Regatta), held in September. At the model yacht pond on the south side of the island, children and young-at-heart adults take part year-round in motorized miniature boat races. ⊠ *Mission Bay.*

WORTH NOTING

Fiesta Island. The most undeveloped area of Mission Bay Park, this is popular with bird-watchers (there's a large protected nesting site for the California tern at the northern tip of the island) as well as with dog owners—it's the only place in the park where pets can run free. At Christmas the island provides an excellent vantage point for viewing the bay's Parade of Lights. In July the annual Over-the-Line Tournament, a competition involving a unique local version of softball, attracts thousands of players and oglers.

Hospitality Point. Enjoy lunch in this pretty, secluded spot, which has a view of sailboats and yachts entering the open sea. At the entrance to Hospitality Point, the City of San Diego Park and Recreation Department supplies area maps and other recreational information. ⊠ *2500 Quivira Ct., Mission Bay* ☎ *619/525–8213* ⊕ *www.sandiego.gov/park-and-recreation* ☾ *Weekdays 8–4:30.*

La Jolla

WORD OF MOUTH

"In La Jolla, you can combine the 'day at the beach' with shopping, walking and eating, plus . . . Torrey Pines State Park (just a little north)."

—sf7307

GETTING ORIENTED

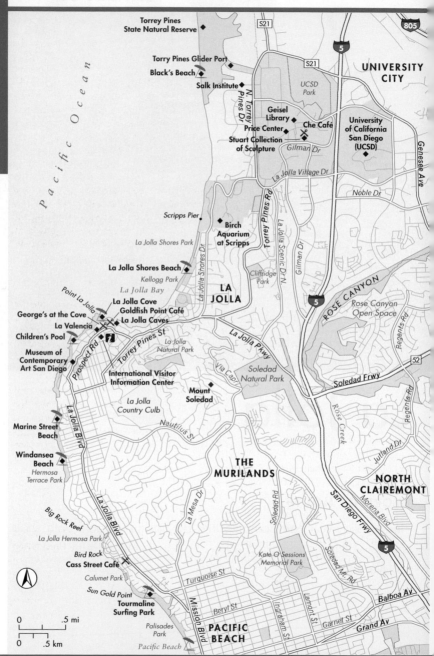

Torrey Pines
State Natural Reserve

Torry Pines Glider Port
Black's Beach
Salk Institute

N. Torrey Pines Dr

S21

S21

805

5

UNIVERSITY
CITY

UCSD
Park

Geisel
Library   Che Café
Price Center
Stuart Collection
of Sculpture   Gilman Dr

University
of California
San Diego
(UCSD)

Genesee Ave

La Jolla Village Dr

Noble Dr

Scripps Pier

Pacific Ocean

Birch
Aquarium
at Scripps

Torrey Pines Rd

La Jolla Scenic Dr N.

Gilman Dr

La Jolla Shores Park

La Jolla Shores Beach
Kellogg Park
La Jolla Bay

La Jolla Shores Dr

Cliffridge
Park

LA
JOLLA

5

ROSE CANYON

Rose Canyon
Open Space

Regents Rd

Point La Jolla

La Jolla Cove
George's at the Cove   Goldfish Point Café
La Valencia   La Jolla Caves
Children's Pool
Museum of
Contemporary
Art San Diego

Prospect Rd

Torrey Pines St

La Jolla
Natural Park

La Jolla Pkwy

Via Capri

Soledad
Natural Park

52

Regents Rd

Soledad Frwy

Rose Creek

International Visitor
Information Center

Mount
Soledad

La Jolla
Country Culb

Nautilus St

Marine Street
Beach

Windansea
Beach
Hermosa
Terrace Park

La Jolla Blvd

THE
MURILANDS

La Mesa Dr

Soledad Rd

San Diego Frwy

NORTH
CLAIREMONT

Morena Blvd

Jutland Dr

Big Rock Reef

La Jolla Hermosa Park

Bird Rock
Cass Street Café
Calumet Park

Sun Gold Point
Tourmaline
Surfing Park

Palisades
Park

Pacific Beach

Mission Blvd

Turquoise St

Beryl St

PACIFIC
BEACH

Kate O' Sessions
Memorial Park

Soledad Mt. Rd

Ingraham St

Lamont St

Garnet St

Grand Av

Balboa Av

5

0   .5 mi
0   .5 km

TOP REASONS TO GO

Promenade above the cove: The winding pathways above La Jolla Cove offer stunning views of the surf and sea lions below.

Shop till you drop: La Jolla's chic boutiques and galleries are San Diego's answer to Rodeo Drive. You may even spot a celebrity as you browse on Prospect Street and Girard Avenue.

Aquatic adventures: Hop in a kayak or strap on scuba gear to explore La Jolla's marine preserve.

Luxe living: Experience the good life at top-notch spas and restaurants. Or just gawk at multimillion-dollar mansions and their denizens running errands in Ferraris.

Torrey Pines State Beach and Reserve: Play the links, hike the trails, relax on the beach, or hang glide off the cliffs.

QUICK BITES

Cass Street Cafe. A breakfast of the excellent buttery croissants or brioches at the Cass Street Cafe is good preparation for time at Windansea Beach. ⊠ 5550 La Jolla Blvd., La Jolla ☎ 858/454–9094.

Goldfish Point Café. If you are looking for a casual breakfast or lunch overlooking La Jolla Cove, the Goldfish Point Café is sure to hit the spot without breaking the bank. ⊠ 1255 Coast Blvd., La Jolla ☎ 858/459–7407.

George's at the Cove. This restaurant complex may be one of the best-known spots in La Jolla for its incredible views of La Jolla Cove. While the main restaurant, George's California Modern, is an upscale affair, the Ocean Terrace on the top level is a great place for a casual meal. The cocktail list is inventive, and specialties like the Baja fish tacos or Neiman Ranch burger are delicious. Come for lunch or a sunset dinner. ⊠ 1250 Prospect St., La Jolla ☎ 858/454–4244.

GETTING HERE

If you enjoy meandering, the best way to approach La Jolla from the south is to drive on Mission Boulevard through Mission and Pacific beaches, past the crowds of in-line skaters, bicyclists, and sunbathers. The congestion eases up as the street becomes La Jolla Boulevard. Road signs along La Jolla Boulevard and Camino de la Costa direct drivers and bicyclists past homes designed by respected architects such as Irving Gill. As you approach the village, La Jolla Boulevard turns into Prospect Street.

PLANNING YOUR TIME

La Jolla's highlights can be seen in a few hours with a visit to La Jolla Village and the cove followed by a scenic drive along the coast and up through Torrey Pines.

The village and La Jolla Cove are easily explored on foot, but it's a steep walk between the two. Parking can be tough, so don't hold out for a better spot. Greater La Jolla is best explored by car or bus route 30.

VISITOR INFORMATION

International Visitor Information Center. La Jolla branch is a great resource for information and coupons. ⊠ 7966 Herschel Ave, Herschel at Prospect St., La Jolla ☎ 619/236–1212 ⊕ www.sandiego.org ⊙ Hrs. vary, generally 11–4.

6

Sightseeing
★★★★☆

Nightlife
★★☆☆☆

Dining
★★★★☆

Lodging
★★★☆☆

Shopping
★★★★☆

La Jollans have long considered their village to be the Monte Carlo of California, and with good cause. Its coastline curves into natural coves backed by verdant hillsides covered with homes worth millions. La Jolla is both a natural and cultural treasure trove. The upscale shops, galleries, and restaurants of La Jolla Village satisfy the glitterati, while secluded trails, scenic overlooks, and abundant marine life provide balance and refuge.

Updated by
Claire Deeks
van der Lee

Although **La Jolla** is a neighborhood of the city of San Diego, it has its own postal zone and a coveted sense of class; the ultrarich from around the globe own second homes here—the seaside zone between the neighborhood's bustling downtown and the cliffs above the Pacific has a distinctly European flavor—and old-money residents maintain friendships with the visiting film stars and royalty who frequent the area's exclusive luxury hotels and private clubs. Development and construction have radically altered the once serene and private character of the village, but it has gained a cosmopolitan air that makes it a popular vacation resort.

The Native Americans called the site La Hoya, meaning "the cave," referring to the grottoes that dot the shoreline. The Spaniards changed the name to La Jolla (same pronunciation as La Hoya), "the jewel," and its residents have cherished the name and its allusions ever since.

Prospect Street and Girard Avenue, the village's main drags, are lined with expensive shops and office buildings. Through the years the shopping and dining district has spread to Pearl and other side streets. La Jolla's nightlife sometimes seems a bit somnolent, although there are some lively bars that cater primarily to the younger crowd. Their elders dine at any of several fine restaurants and then may stop by the Whaling Bar at lovely old La Valencia hotel for a Whaler, a nightcap of sweet liqueurs, cream, and ice cream. It's a good drink, but watch out—it packs an unexpected punch.

EXPLORING LA JOLLA

LA JOLLA DRIVING TOUR

A drive through La Jolla reveals the breadth of its attractions, from quiet cliff-side overlooks to the bustling village galleries, all framed by the sparkling waters of the coves below. At the intersection of La Jolla Boulevard and Nautilus Street, turn toward the sea to reach **Windansea Beach**, one of the best surfing spots in town. **Mount Soledad**, about 1½ mi east on Nautilus Street, is La Jolla's highest spot. In the village itself you'll find the town's cultural center, the **Museum of Contemporary Art San Diego**, on the less trafficked southern end of Prospect. A bit farther north, at the intersection of Prospect Street and Girard Avenue, sits the pretty-in-pink hotel **La Valencia**, looking out onto the village's great natural attraction, **La Jolla Cove**, which can be accessed from Coast Boulevard, one block to the west. Past the far northern point of the cove, a trail leads down to **La Jolla Caves**.

> ### WORD OF MOUTH
>
> "If you drive up to La Jolla (and you should!), end your afternoon at George's at the Cove...Outdoor rooftop dining, great food at reasonable prices, and a view you won't forget. Sunset is spectacular!"
> —agsimpkins

The beaches along La Jolla Shores Drive north of the caves are some of the finest in the San Diego area, with long stretches allotted to surfers or swimmers. Nearby is the campus of the Scripps Institution of Oceanography. The institution's **Birch Aquarium at Scripps** is inland a bit, off Torrey Pines Road.

La Jolla Shores Drive eventually curves onto Torrey Pines Road, off which you'll soon glimpse the world-famous **Salk Institute**, designed by Louis I. Kahn. The road that leads to the institute ends at the cliffs used as the **Torrey Pines Glider Port**. The hard-to-reach stretch of sand at the foot of the cliffs is officially named Torrey Pines City Park Beach, but locals call it **Black's Beach** because the distinguished Black family, members of whom still reside in La Jolla, once owned a vast estate high above it. At the intersection of Torrey Pines Road and Genesee Avenue you'll come to the northern entrance of the huge campus of the **University of California at San Diego** and, a bit farther north, to the stretch of wilderness that marks the end of what most locals consider San Diego proper, **Torrey Pines State Natural Reserve**.

TOP ATTRACTIONS

Birch Aquarium at Scripps. The largest oceanographic exhibit in the United States, maintained by the Scripps Institution of Oceanography, sits at the end of a signposted drive leading off North Torrey Pines Road. More than 60 tanks are filled with colorful saltwater fish, and a 70,000-gallon tank simulates a La Jolla kelp forest. A special exhibit on sea horses features several examples of the species, plus mesmerizing sea dragons and a sea horse nursery. Besides the fish themselves, attractions include a gallery based on the institution's ocean-related research, and interactive educational exhibits on a variety of environmental issues. ⊠ *2300 Expedition Way, La Jolla* ☎ *858/534–3474* ⊕ *www.aquarium.ucsd.edu* ⊡ *$12, parking free for 3 hrs* ⊙ *Daily 9–5, last ticket sold at 4:30.*

6

BEST BEACHES

Framed in scenic coves and backed by dramatic cliffs, La Jolla's beaches are legendary. Challenging surf breaks, an underwater marine park, and expansive stretches of sand offer something for everyone. Look out over the sparkling waters to see seals frolicking in the surf, or lie back in the sand and watch hang gliders soar overhead.

⇨ *For more information on La Jolla's beaches, see Chapter 12: Beaches.*

Black's Beach. This secluded stretch of sand is considered one of the most beautiful beaches in San Diego. Black's Beach was clothing-optional for many years; although nudity is now prohibited by law, many people still shed their suits whenever the authorities are out of sight.

🌣 **Children's Pool.** This shallow bay was once a great place to bring the kids to swim. Nowadays, it's the best place on the coast to view harbor seals. Good thing kids enjoy that almost as much as playing in the waves.

🌣 **Fodor's** Choice ★ **La Jolla Cove.** Truly the jewel of La Jolla, "the Cove" is one of the prettiest spots on the West Coast.

🌣 **La Jolla Shores.** One of the most popular beaches in San Diego, La Jolla Shores features a wide sandy beach and calm waves perfect for swimming and beginner surf lessons.

Torrey Pines State Beach. This popular beach is located just below the Torrey Pines State Reserve. Bring your picnic here after an invigorating hike in the reserve.

Windansea Beach. Incredible views, secluded spots, and world-class waves make this a favorite beach for couples and surfers.

🌣 **La Jolla Caves.** It's a walk of 145 sometimes slippery steps down a tunnel to Sunny Jim, the largest of the caves in La Jolla Cove and the only one reachable by land. This is a one-of-a-kind local attraction, and worth the time if you have a day or two to really enjoy La Jolla. The man-made tunnel took two years to dig, beginning in 1902; later, a shop was built at its entrance. Today La Jolla Cave Store, a throwback to that early shop, is still the entrance to the cave, which was named Sunny Jim after a 1920s cartoon character. The shop sells jewelry and watercolors by local artists. ⊠ *1325 Coast Blvd. S, La Jolla* ☎ *858/459–0746* ⊕ *www. cavestore.com* 🖾 *$4* ⊙ *Daily 10–5.*

Fodor's Choice ★ **Museum of Contemporary Art San Diego (MCASD).**
⇨ *See the highlighted listing in this chapter.*

Fodor's Choice ★ **Torrey Pines State Natural Reserve.** *Pinus torreyana*, the rarest native pine tree in the United States, enjoys a 1,700-acre sanctuary at the northern edge of La Jolla. About 6,000 of these unusual trees, some as tall as 60 feet, grow on the cliffs here. The park is one of only two places in the world (the other is Santa Rosa Island, off Santa Barbara) where the Torrey pine grows naturally. The reserve has several hiking trails leading to the cliffs, 300 feet above the ocean; trail maps are available at the park station. Wildflowers grow profusely in spring, and the ocean panoramas are always spectacular. When in this upper part of the park,

DID YOU KNOW?

Goldfish Point in La Jolla is named after the garibaldi damselfish, which resemble goldfish, found in these waters. The garibaldi is California's official marine fish.

MUSEUM OF CONTEMPORARY ART SAN DIEGO

✉ *700 Prospect St., La Jolla* ☎ *858/454–3541* ⊕ *www. mcasd.org* 🖼 *$10, ages 25 and under are free, free·3rd Thurs. of the month 5–7* ⊙ *Thurs.–Tues. 11–5.*

TIPS

■ Be sure to also check out MCASD's downtown branch; admission is good for seven days and valid at both locations. See Chapter 2: Downtown for MCASD's downtown branch.

■ Get in free the third Thursday of every month from 5 to 7.

■ Informative and insightful exhibit tours are offered free of charge weekends at 2, and the third Thursday of the month at 6.

■ If you miss the weekly tours, free mobile phone and podcast audio tours are available for most exhibits. You can even borrow an iPod if you've left yours at home.

■ Head to the museum's X Store for unique cards and gifts.

■ The pleasant courtyard at the museum café is a great spot to relax and recharge.

Driving along Coast Boulevard, it is hard to miss the mass of watercraft jutting out from the rear of the Museum of Contemporary Art San Diego (MCASD) La Jolla location. *Pleasure Point* by Nancy Rubins is just one example of the mingling of art and locale at this spectacular oceanfront setting.

HIGHLIGHTS

The oldest section of La Jolla's branch of San Diego's contemporary art museum was originally a residence, designed by Irving Gill for philanthropist Ellen Browning Scripps in 1916. In the mid-1990s the compound was updated and expanded by architect Robert Venturi, who respected Gill's original geometric structure and clean Mission-style lines while adding his own distinctive touches. The result is a striking contemporary building that looks as though it's always been here.

The light-filled Axline Court serves as the museum's entrance and does triple duty as reception area, exhibition hall, and forum for special events, including the glittering Monte Carlo gala each September, attended by the town's most fashionable folk. Inside, the museum's artwork gets major competition from the setting: you can look out from the top of a grand stairway onto a landscaped garden that contains permanent and temporary sculpture exhibits, as well as rare 100-year-old California plant specimens and, beyond that, to the Pacific Ocean.

California artists figure prominently in the museum's permanent collection of post-1950s art, but the museum also includes examples of every major art movement through the present—works by Andy Warhol, Robert Rauschenberg, Frank Stella, Joseph Cornell, and Jenny Holzer, to name a few. Important pieces by artists from San Diego and Tijuana were acquired in the 1990s. The museum also gets major visiting shows.

respect the various restrictions. Not permitted: picnicking, smoking, leaving the trails, dogs, alcohol, or collecting plant specimens.

You can unwrap your sandwiches, however, at Torrey Pines State Beach, just below the reserve. When the tide is out, it's possible to walk south all the way past the lifeguard towers to Black's Beach over rocky promontories carved by the waves (avoid the bluffs, however; they're unstable). **Los Peñasquitos Lagoon** at the north end of the reserve is one of the many natural estuaries that flow inland between Del Mar and Oceanside. It's a good place to watch shorebirds. Volunteers lead guided nature walks at 10 and 2 on most weekends. ⊠ *N. Torrey Pines Rd. exit off I–5 onto Carmel Valley Rd. going west, then turn left (south) on Coast Hwy. 101, La Jolla* ☎ *858/755–2063* ⊕ *www. torreypine.org* ⊠ *Parking $10* ⊙ *Daily 8–dusk.*

> ## GOLDEN TRIANGLE
>
> High-tech research-and-development companies, attracted by the proximity of the University of California at San Diego, the Scripps Institution of Oceanography, and the Salk Institute, have developed huge state-of-the-art compounds east of I–5. The area along La Jolla Village Drive and Genesee Avenue has become a proving ground for futuristic buildings, including the striking Michael Graves–designed Aventine complex and the huge, white Mormon Temple, easily spotted while traveling up the freeway.

6

University of California at San Diego. The campus of one of the country's most prestigious research universities spreads over 1,200 acres of coastal canyons and eucalyptus groves, where students and faculty jog, bike, and rollerblade to class. If you're interested in contemporary art, check out the **Stuart Collection of Sculpture**—17 thought-provoking, site-specific works by artists such as Nam June Paik, William Wegman, Niki de St. Phalle, Jenny Holzer, and others arrayed around the campus. UCSD's **Price Center** has a well-stocked, two-level bookstore—the largest in San Diego—and a good coffeehouse, Espresso Roma. Look for the postmodern **Geisel Library**, named for longtime La Jolla residents Theodor "Dr. Seuss" Geisel and his wife, Audrey. For campus culture, political views, vegan dishes, and live music, head to the **Che Café** located in Building 161, painted in bright murals. Bring quarters for the parking meters, or cash or a credit card for the parking structures, since free parking is available only on weekends. ⊠ *Exit I–5 onto La Jolla Village Dr. going west; take Gilman Dr. off-ramp to right and continue on to information kiosk at campus entrance on Gilman Dr., La Jolla* ☎ *858/534–4414 campus tour information* ⊕ *www.ucsd.edu* ⊙ *90-min campus tours Sun. at 2 from South Gilman Information Pavilion; reserve before noon Thurs.*

WORTH NOTING

La Valencia. Mediterranean-style La Valencia, operating as a luxury hotel since 1926, has long been a gathering spot for Hollywood celebrities; in the 1940s Gregory Peck would invite friends to the hotel's Whaling Bar to try to persuade them to participate in one of his favorite projects, La Jolla Playhouse, now one of the city's leading cultural institutions. Today the hotel's grand lobby, with floor-to-ceiling windows overlooking

La Jolla Cove, is a popular wedding spot, and the **Whaling Bar** has the air of a private club for the town's mon-eyed families. ⊠ *1132 Prospect St., La Jolla* ☎ *858/454–0771, 800/451–0772* ⊕ *www.lavalencia.com.*

Mount Soledad. La Jolla's highest spot can be reached by taking Nautilus Street to La Jolla Scenic Drive South, and then turning left. Proceed a few blocks to the park, where parking is plentiful and the views are astound-ing, unless the day is hazy. The top of the mountain is an excellent van-tage point from which to get a sense of San Diego's geography: looking down from here you can see the coast from the county's northern border to the south far beyond downtown. ⊠ *6905 La Jolla Scenic Dr. S, La Jolla.*

Salk Institute. The world-famous biological-research facility founded by polio vaccine developer Jonas Salk sits on 27 clifftop acres. The twin structures that modernist architect Louis I. Kahn designed in the 1960s in consultation with Dr. Salk used poured concrete and other low-main-tenance materials to clever effect. The thrust of the laboratory–office complex is outward toward the Pacific Ocean, an orientation accentu-ated by a foot-wide "Stream of Life" that flows through the center of a travertine marble courtyard between the buildings. Architects-to-be and building buffs enjoy the free tours of the property; register online two days in advance. You can, however, stroll at will through the dra-matic courtyard—simultaneously monumental and eerie. ⊠ *10010 N. Torrey Pines Rd., La Jolla* ☎ *858/453–4100* ⊕ *www.salk.edu* ☎ *Free* ⊙ *Grounds weekdays 8:30–5; architectural tours weekdays at noon. Reservations required.*

★ **Torrey Pines Glider Port.** On days when the winds are just right, gliders line the cliffs, waiting for the perfect gust to carry them into the sky. Seasoned hang gliders and paragliders with a good command of the current can soar over the sea for hours, then ride the winds back to the cliffs. Less-experienced fliers sometimes land on the beach below, to the cheers and applause of the sunbathers who scoot out of the way. Tan-dem courses with certified instructors are also available for those who have ever wanted to try hang gliding, paragliding, or sailplane flying.

Cliff Hanger Cafe. If you want to take in the spectacular views and enjoy the action with your feet planted firmly on the ground, grab a deli sand-wich here. ☎ *858/452–9858* ⊠ *2800 Torrey Pines Scenic Dr., La Jolla* ☎ *858/452–9858* ⊕ *www.flytorrey.com* ⊙ *Daily 9–5.*

Point Loma and Coronado

WITH HARBOR AND SHELTER ISLANDS

WORD OF MOUTH

"[E]at at Point Loma Seafoods and then drive up to Cabrillo national monument and see the lighthouse . . . the views are incredible."
—ksucat

GETTING ORIENTED

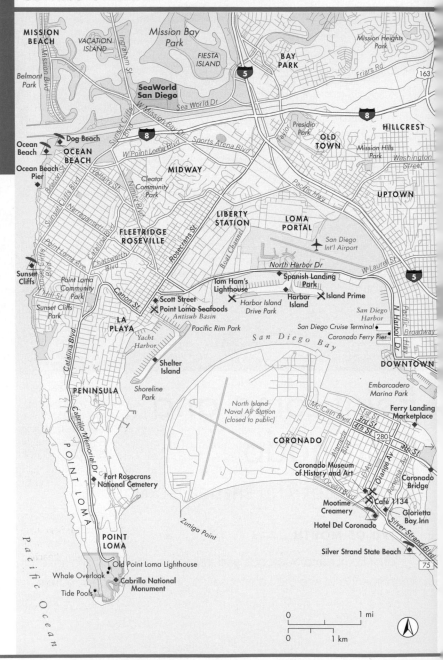

TOP REASONS TO GO

Point Loma's panoramic views: Take in the view from the mountains to the ocean at Cabrillo National Monument. Come evening, watch the sun go down at Sunset Cliffs.

The Hotel Del: As the grande dame of San Diego, the historic Hotel Del Coronado charms guests and visitors alike with her graceful architecture and oceanfront setting.

Boating paradise: San Diego's picturesque marinas are filled with sportfishing charters and ultraluxury yachts.

Sandy beaches: The long stretches of sand on Coronado are family-friendly, while Fido will love swimming at Ocean Beach's Dog Beach.

Military might: From the endless rows of white headstones at Fort Rosecrans National Cemetery to the roar of fighter jets over North Island Naval Air Station, San Diego's strong military ties are palpable.

QUICK BITES

Point Loma Seafoods. The freshest fish to be found along Point Loma's shores comes from this shop behind the Vagabond Inn. There's a fish market as well as an adjacent take-out counter selling prepared hot or cold foods. ⊠ *2805 Emerson St., Point Loma* ☎ *619/223–1109.*

Cafe 1134. You can get a good curried tuna sandwich on French bread to accompany your espresso at this hip mini-bistro. ⊠ *1134 Orange Ave., Coronado* ☎ *619/437–1134.*

Mootime Creamery. For a deliciously sweet pick-me-up, check out the rich ice cream, frozen yogurt, and sorbet made fresh daily on the premises. Dessert nachos made from waffle-cone chips are an unusual addition to an extensive sundae menu. Look for the statue of Elvis on the sidewalk in front. ⊠ *1025 Orange Ave., Coronado* ☎ *619/435–2422.*

GETTING HERE

Bus 84 serves Cabrillo National Monument on Point Loma, although a transfer is required from Bus 28, near Shelter Island. For Harbor Island, the hearty can walk from the Embarcadero or catch a bus to the airport and walk from there.

Coronado is accessible via the arching blue 2.2-mi-long San Diego–Coronado Bay Bridge, which offers breathtaking views of the harbor and downtown. Alternatively, pedestrians and bikes can reach Coronado via the popular ferry service. Bus 904 meets the ferry and travels as far as Silver Strand State Beach. Bus 901 runs daily between the Gaslamp Quarter and Coronado.

PLANNING YOUR TIME

If you're interested in seeing the tide pools at Cabrillo National Monument, call ahead or check the weather page of the *Union-Tribune* to find out when low tide will occur. Scott Street, with its Point Loma Seafoods, is a good place to find yourself at lunchtime, and Sunset Cliffs Park is where you want to be at sunset.

A leisurely stroll through Coronado takes at least an hour, more if you stop to shop or walk along the family-friendly beaches. Whenever you come, if you're not staying overnight, remember to get back to the dock in time to catch the final ferry out at 9:30 (10:30 on weekends).

7

CABRILLO NATIONAL MONUMENT

Cabrillo National Monument marks the site of the first European visit to San Diego, made by 16th-century explorer Juan Rodríguez Cabrillo. Cabrillo landed at this spot, which he called San Miguel, on September 15, 1542. Today the 160-acre preserve with its rugged cliffs and shores and outstanding overlooks is one of the most frequently visited of all the national monuments.

(above) Point Loma from the water, as Cabrillo would have seen it in 1542. (lower right) Old Point Loma Lighthouse stood watch for 36 years. (upper right) Cabrillo's statue adorns the visitor center.

Catching sight of a whale from the cliffs of Cabrillo National Monument can be a highlight of a wintertime visit to San Diego. More accessible sea creatures can be seen in the tide pools at the foot of the monument's western cliffs.

On land, trails lead down the hillside through sagebrush and cactus. Overlook points offer spectacular views from the desert mountains to downtown and beyond. The informative visitor center and the lighthouse give a historical perspective to this once-remote promontory.

SERVICE INFORMATION

The visitor center, located next to the statue of Cabrillo, presents films and lectures about Cabrillo's voyage, the sea-level tide pools, and migrating gray whales.

✉ *1800 Cabrillo Memorial Dr., Point Loma*
☎ *619/557-5450*
⊕ *www.nps.gov/cabr*
🎫 *$5 per car, $3 per person entering on foot or by bicycle* ☉ *Park daily 9–5.*

A HALF DAY AT CABRILLO NATIONAL MONUMENT

A **statue of Cabrillo** overlooks downtown from a windy promontory, where people gather to admire the stunning panorama over the bay, from the snowcapped San Bernardino Mountains, 130 mi north, to the hills surrounding Tijuana to the south. The stone figure standing on the bluff looks rugged and dashing, but he is a creation of an artist's imagination— no portraits of Cabrillo are known to exist.

The moderately steep **Bayside Trail,** 2½ mi round-trip, winds through coastal sage scrub, curving under the cliff-top lookouts and taking you ever closer to the bay-front scenery. You cannot reach the beach from this trail, and must stick to the path to protect the cliffs from erosion and yourself from thorny plants and snakes—including rattlers. You'll see prickly pear cactus and yucca, fragrant sage, and maybe a lizard, rabbit, or hummingbird. The climb back is long but gradual, leading up to the old lighthouse.

Old Point Loma Lighthouse's oil lamp was first lighted in 1855 and was visible from the sea for 25 mi. Unfortunately, it was too high above the cliffs to guide navigators trapped in Southern California's thick offshore fog. In 1891 a new lighthouse was built 400 feet below. The restored old lighthouse is open to visitors. An exhibit in the Assistant Keepers Quarters next door tells the story of the Old Lighthouse, the daily lives of the keepers, how lighthouses work, and the role they played in the development of early maritime commerce along the West Coast. On the edge of the hill near the old lighthouse sits a refurbished radio room containing displays of U.S. harbor defenses at Point Loma used during World War II.

■**TIP➔** Restrooms and water fountains are plentiful, but, except for vending machines at the visitor center, there's no food. Exploring the grounds consumes time and calories; pack a picnic and rest on a bench overlooking the sailboats.

WHALE-WATCHING

The western and southern cliffs of Cabrillo National Monument are prime whale-watching territory. A sheltered **viewing station** has wayside exhibits describing the great gray whales' yearly migration from Baja California to the Bering and Chukchi seas near Alaska. High-powered telescopes help you focus on the whales' water-spouts. Whales are visible on clear days from late December through early March, with the highest concentration in January and February. Note that when the whales return north in spring, they are too far out in the ocean to be seen from the monument.

TIDE POOLS

When the tide is low you can walk on the rocks around saltwater pools filled with starfish, crabs, anemones, octopuses, and hundreds of other sea creatures and plants. Tide pooling is best when the tide is at its lowest so call ahead or check tide charts online before your visit. Exercise caution on the slippery rocks.

7

Although Coronado is actually an isthmus, easily reached from the mainland if you head north from Imperial Beach, it has always seemed like an island and is often referred to as such. To the west, Point Loma protects the center of the city from the Pacific's tides and waves. Both Coronado and Point Loma share stately homes, sandy beaches, private marinas, and prominent military installations. Nestled between the two, recreational Harbor and Shelter islands owe their existence to dredging in the bay.

Updated by
Claire Deeks
van der Lee

In 1950 San Diego's port director decided to raise the shoal that lay off the eastern shore of Point Loma above sea level with the sand and mud dredged up during the course of deepening a ship channel in the 1930s and '40s. The resulting peninsula, **Shelter Island,** became home to several marinas and resorts, many with Polynesian details that still exist today, giving them a retro flair. Following the success of nearby Shelter Island, in 1961 the U.S. Navy used the residue from digging berths deep enough to accommodate aircraft carriers to build another recreational island, adjacent to the airport. The result, **Harbor Island,** is known for its views of the bay and the downtown skyline. It is a popular spot to watch the Parade of Lights each December, when local boat owners dress their craft in elaborate holiday light displays and embark on a festive procession around the bay. The hilly peninsula of **Point Loma** curves west and south into the Pacific and provides protection for San Diego Bay. Its maritime roots are evident, from its longtime ties to the U.S. Navy to its bustling sportfishing and sailing marinas. The funky community of **Ocean Beach** coexists alongside the stately homes of **Sunset Cliffs** and the honored graves at **Fort Rosecrans National Cemetery.** Its high elevations and sandy cliffs provide incredible views, and make Point Loma a visible local landmark.

As if freeze-framed in the 1950s, **Coronado's** quaint appeal is captured in its old-fashioned storefronts, well-manicured gardens, and charming

BEST BEACHES

On Point Loma's beaches surfers and even dogs join in on the fun. The wide beaches and gentle waves of nearby Coronado have been entertaining families for well over a century.

⇨ *For more information on the beaches of Point Loma and Coronado, see Chapter 12: Beaches.*

POINT LOMA
Ocean Beach and Dog Beach. Humans head to the southern Ocean Beach to swim and sunbathe and surfers congregate around the Ocean Beach Pier. The small beach to the north, known as Dog Beach, is one of the few beaches in the country where dogs can play leash-free.

Sunset Cliffs. Popular with surfers and sunbathers seeking privacy among the small coves, this makes for a better viewpoint than swimming beach.

CORONADO
♺ **Coronado Beach.** The north end of the beach, nearest the Naval Air Station, offers views of fighter jets landing and taking off as well as an off-leash dog area, while the south end has views of the Hotel Del Coronado. This is the widest expanse of beach in San Diego County and is great for families.

♺ **Silver Strand State Beach.** The stretch of sand that runs along Silver Strand Boulevard from the Hotel Del Coronado to Imperial Beach is a perfect family gathering spot, with restrooms and lifeguards. The shallow shoreline and minimal crowds also make it a popular spot for kite surfing.

7

Ferry Landing Marketplace. The streets of Coronado are wide, quiet, and friendly, and many of today's residents live in grand Victorian homes handed down for generations. Naval Air Station North Island was established in 1911 on Coronado's north end, across from Point Loma, and was the site of Charles Lindbergh's departure on the transcontinental flight that preceded his famous solo flight across the Atlantic. Coronado's long relationship with the U.S. Navy and its desirable real estate have made it an enclave for military personnel; it's said to have more retired admirals per capita than anywhere else in the United States.

EXPLORING POINT LOMA AND HARBOR AND SHELTER ISLANDS

POINT LOMA TO HARBOR ISLAND DRIVING TOUR

Take Catalina Boulevard all the way south to the tip of Point Loma to reach **Cabrillo National Monument**. North of the monument, as you head back into the neighborhoods of Point Loma, you'll see the white headstones of **Fort Rosecrans National Cemetery**. Continue north on Catalina Boulevard to Hill Street and turn left to reach the dramatic **Sunset Cliffs**, at the western side of Point Loma near Ocean Beach. Park to tour the dramatic cliff tops and the boiling seas below, but be cautious because the cliffs can be unstable. Signs generally warn you where not to go. Head north on Sunset Cliffs Boulevard until you reach Newport Avenue, where you will make a left to enter the heart of **Ocean Beach.** If you have your dog with you, head north to **Ocean Beach's Dog Beach** or check out surfers from the **Ocean Beach Pier** off Niagara Avenue. Just before the pier, turn left onto Newport Avenue, OB's main drag.

Return to Sunset Cliffs Boulevard and backtrack south to take a left on Point Loma Avenue. Turn left at Canon Street, which leads toward the peninsula's eastern (bay) side. Almost at the shore you'll see **Scott Street**, Point Loma's main commercial drag. Scott Street is bisected by Shelter Island Drive, which leads to **Shelter Island.** For another example of what can be done with tons of material dredged from a bay, go back up Shelter Island Drive, turn right on Rosecrans Street, another right on North Harbor Drive, and a final right onto **Harbor Island.**

TOP ATTRACTIONS

Cabrillo National Monument.

Fodor's Choice ⇨ *See the highlighted listing in this chapter.*
★

Fort Rosecrans National Cemetery. In 1934, 8 of the 1,000 acres set aside for a military reserve in 1852 were designated as a burial site. About 97,000 people are now interred here; it's impressive to see the rows upon rows of white headstones that overlook both sides of Point Loma just north of the Cabrillo National Monument. Some of those laid to rest at this place were killed in battles that predate California's statehood; the graves of the 17 soldiers and one civilian who died in the 1874 Battle of San Pasqual between troops from Mexico and the United States are marked by a large bronze plaque. Perhaps the most impressive structure in the cemetery is the 75-foot granite obelisk called the Bennington Monument, which commemorates the 66 crew members who died in a boiler explosion and fire onboard the USS *Bennington* in 1905. The cemetery, visited by many veterans, is still used for burials. ⊠ *Cabrillo Memorial Dr., Point Loma* ☎ *619/553–2084* ☉ *Weekdays 8–4:30, weekends 9–5.*

Harbor Island. Restaurants and high-rise hotels dot the inner shore of this 1½-mi-long man-made peninsula adjacent to the airport. The bay's shore is lined with pathways, gardens, and scenic picnic spots.

Tom Ham's Lighthouse. On the west point, Tom Ham's Lighthouse restaurant has a U.S. Coast Guard–approved beacon shining from its tower. ⊠ *2150 Harbor Island Dr., Harbor Island* ☎ *619/291–9110* ⊕ *www. tomhamslighthouse.com.*

Island Prime and C-level Lounge. On the east end point, you can enjoy a killer view of the downtown skyline. ⊠ *880 Harbor Island Dr., Harbor Island* ☎ *619/298–6802* ⊕ *www.cohnrestaurants.com* ⊠ *Harbor Island Dr., Harbor Island.*

Ocean Beach Pier. This T-shape pier is a popular fishing spot and home to the Ocean Beach Pier Café and a small tackle shop. Constructed in 1966, it is the longest concrete pier on the West Coast and a perfect place to take in views of the harbor, ocean, and Point Loma peninsula. Surfers flock to the waves that break just below. ⊠ *1950 Abbott St., Point Loma.*

Shelter Island. This reclaimed peninsula now supports towering palms, a cluster of resorts, restaurants, and side-by-side marinas. The center of San Diego's yacht-building industry, boats in every stage of construction are visible in Shelter Island's yacht yards. A long sidewalk runs past boat brokerages to the hotels and marinas that line the inner shore, facing

Point Loma. On the bay side, fishermen launch their boats and families relax at picnic tables along the grass, where there are fire rings and permanent barbeque grills. Within walking distance is the huge Friendship Bell, given to San Diegans by the people of Yokohama, Japan, in 1960 and the Tunaman's Memorial, a statue commemorating San Diego's once-flourishing fishing industry. ⊠ *Shelter Island Dr., Shelter Island.*

★ **Sunset Cliffs.** As the name suggests, the 60-foot-high bluffs on the western side of Point Loma south of Ocean Beach are a perfect place to watch the sun set over the sea. To view the tide pools along the shore, use the staircase off Sunset Cliffs Boulevard at the foot of Ladera Street.

The dramatic coastline here seems to have been carved out of ancient rock. The impact of the waves is very clear: each year more sections of the cliffs are posted with caution signs. Don't ignore these warnings—it's easy to lose your footing and slip in the crumbling sandstone, and the surf can be extremely rough. The small coves and beaches that dot the coastline are popular with surfers drawn to the pounding waves and neighborhood locals who name and claim their special spots. The homes along the boulevard—pink stucco mansions beside shingled Cape Cod–style cottages—are fine examples of Southern California luxury. ⊠ *Sunset Cliffs Blvd., Point Loma.*

BEACH-TOWN THROWBACK

At the northern end of Point Loma lies the chilled-out, hippyesque town of Ocean Beach, commonly referred to as "OB." The main thoroughfare of this funky neighborhood is dotted with dive bars, coffeehouses, surf shops, and 1960s diners. Bursting with character, OB is a magnet for everyone from surfers and musicians to children and artists. Newport Avenue, generally known for its boisterous bars, is also home to San Diego's largest antiques district. Fans of OB applaud its resistance to "selling out" to upscale development, whereas detractors lament its somewhat scruffy edges.

7

WORTH NOTING

Scott Street. Running along Point Loma's waterfront from Shelter Island to the old Naval Training Center on Harbor Drive, this thoroughfare is lined with deep-sea fishing charters and whale-watching boats. It's a good spot to watch fishermen (and women) haul marlin, tuna, and puny mackerel off their boats.

Spanish Landing Park. Across from the western end of Harbor Island, on the mainland's Spanish Landing Park, a bronze plaque marks the arrival in 1769 of a party from Spain that headed north from San Diego to conquer California. The group combined the crews of two ships, the *San Carlos* and the *San Antonio,* and a contingent that came overland from Baja California. As part of a beautification program, the city has begun installing whimsical, if sometimes monumental, artworks in this park, which is less visited than many city parks and therefore a quiet enclave in which to spend a peaceful hour or two. If you're the hardy type, you can walk from here to the Embarcadero, and then into the heart of downtown. ⊠ *Harbor Island.*

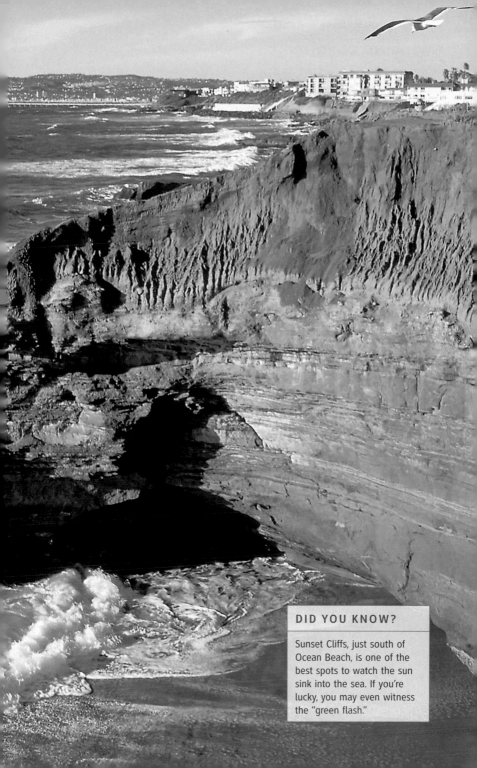

DID YOU KNOW?

Sunset Cliffs, just south of Ocean Beach, is one of the best spots to watch the sun sink into the sea. If you're lucky, you may even witness the "green flash."

EXPLORING CORONADO

CORONADO WALK

Coronado is easy to navigate without a car. When you leave the ferry, you can explore the shops at the **Ferry Landing Marketplace** and from there rent a bicycle or catch the shuttle bus that runs down **Orange Avenue**, Coronado's main street. Get off the bus at 10th Street and Orange to pick up a map at the Coronado Visitor Center, in the lobby of the **Coronado Museum of History and Art**, and then keep strolling along the boutique-filled promenade until you reach the **Hotel Del Coronado** at the end of Orange Avenue. Right across the street from the Hotel Del is the **Glorietta Bay Inn**, another of the island's outstanding early structures. If you've brought your swimsuit, you might continue on to **Silver Strand State Beach**—just past the Hotel Del, Orange Avenue turns into Silver Strand Boulevard, which soon resumes its original across-the-bridge role as Route 75.

TOP ATTRACTIONS

☺ **Ferry Landing Marketplace.** This collection of shops at Ferry Landing is
★ on a smaller scale than the Embarcadero's Seaport Village, but you do get a great view of the downtown San Diego skyline. Located along San Diego Bay, the little shops and restaurants resemble the gingerbread domes of the Hotel Del Coronado. If you want to rent a bike or in-line skates, stop in at **Bikes and Beyond** (✉ *1201 1st St., #122, Coronado* ☎ *619/435–7180*). ✉ *1201 1st St., at B Ave., Coronado* ☎ *619/435–8895*.

Fodor's Choice **Hotel Del Coronado.** One of San Diego's best-known sites, the hotel has
★ been a National Historic Landmark since 1977. It has a colorful history, integrally connected with that of Coronado itself. The Hotel Del, as natives call it, was the brainchild of financiers Elisha Spurr Babcock Jr. and H. L. Story, who saw the potential of Coronado's virgin beaches and its view of San Diego's emerging harbor. The hotel opened in 1888, just 11 months after construction began.

The Del's distinctive red-tile roofs and Victorian gingerbread architecture have served as a set for many movies, political meetings, and extravagant social happenings. It's speculated that the Duke of Windsor may have first met Wallis Simpson here. Eleven presidents have been guests of the Del, and the film *Some Like It Hot*—starring Marilyn Monroe, Jack Lemmon, and Tony Curtis—used the hotel as a backdrop.

Broad steps lead up to the main, balconied lobby, which is adorned with grand oak pillars and ceiling and opens out onto a central courtyard and gazebo. To the right is the cavernous **Crown Room**, whose arched ceiling of notched sugar pine was constructed without nails. A lavish Sunday brunch is served here from 9:30 to 1. During the holidays, the hotel hosts Skating by the Sea, an outdoor beachfront ice-skating rink open to the public.

Although the pool area is reserved for hotel guests, several surrounding dining patios make great places to sit back and imagine the scene during the 1920s, when the hotel rocked with good times. To the right, the Windsor Lawn provides a green oasis between the hotel and the beach. Behind the pool area, an attractive shopping arcade features a classic candy shop as well as several fine clothing and accessories stores. ■**TIP➔** Even if you don't happen to be saying at the Del, gazing out over the ocean while enjoying a drink at the Sun Deck Bar and Grill makes for a great escape. If it's chilly, the fire pits and sofa seating are very inviting.

The History Gallery displays photos from the Del's early days, and books elaborating on its history and that of Kate Morgan, the hotel's resident ghost, are sold along with logo apparel and gifts in the hotel's 15-plus shops. In early 2008 the Del unveiled $150 million in luxury enhancements, including 78 new cottages and villas, a signature restaurant, a wine room, and a spa. The resort recently published a new book titled *Building the Dream: The Design and Construction of the Hotel Del Coronado*. Tours of the Del are available Tuesday and Friday at 10:30, Saturday and Sunday at 2, and cost $15. Reservations are required through the **Coronado Visitor Center** (✉ *1100 Orange Ave., Coronado* ☎ *619/437–8788* ⊕ *www.coronadovisitorcenter.com*), which is open weekdays 9–5, weekends 10–5 year-round. ✉ *1500 Orange Ave., Coronado* ☎ *619/435–6611* ⊕ *www.hoteldel.com.*

Orange Avenue. Coronado's business district and its villagelike heart, this is surely one of the most charming spots in Southern California. Slow-paced and very "local" (the city fights against chain stores), it's a blast from the past, although entirely up to date in other respects. The military presence—Coronado is home to the U.S. Navy Sea, Air and Land (SEAL) forces—is reflected in shops selling military gear and places like McP's Irish Pub, the unofficial SEALs headquarters and a family-friendly stop for a good, all-American meal. Many clothing boutiques, home-furnishings stores, and upscale restaurants cater to visitors with deep pockets, but you can buy plumbing supplies, too, or get a genuine military haircut at Crown Barbers. **Bay Books.** Peruse a selection from the huge magazine collection while sipping a latte at the sidewalk café at San Diego's largest independent bookstore. ✉ *1029 Orange Ave., Coronado* ☎ *619/435–0070.*

WORTH NOTING

Coronado Museum of History and Art. The neoclassical First Bank of Commerce building, constructed in 1910, holds the headquarters and archives of the Coronado Historical Association, a museum, the Coronado Visitor Center, the Coronado Museum Store, and Tent City Restaurant. The collection celebrates Coronado's history with photographs and displays of its formative events and major sights. Two galleries have permanent displays, while a third hosts traveling exhibits. For information on the town's historic houses, pick up a copy of the inexpensive *Promenade Through the Past: A Brief History of Coronado and its Architectural Wonders* at the museum gift shop. The book traces a 60-minute walking tour of the architecturally and historically significant buildings that surround the area. The tour departs from the museum lobby on Wednesday at 10:30 am and costs $10 (reservations required). ✉ *1100 Orange Ave., Coronado* ☎ *619/435–7242* ⊕ *www.coronadohistory.org* ▨ *$4 suggested donation* ☉ *Weekdays 9–5, weekends 10–5.*

Glorietta Bay Inn. The former residence of John Spreckels, the original owner of North Island and the property on which the Hotel Del Coronado stands, is now a popular hotel. On Tuesday, Thursday, and Saturday mornings at 11 it's the departure point for a fun and informative 1½-hour walking tour of a few of the area's 86 officially designated historic homes. It includes—from the outside only—some spectacular mansions and the Meade House, where L. Frank Baum, author of *The Wizard of Oz*, wrote additional Oz stories. ⊠ *1630 Glorietta Blvd., Coronado* ☎ *619/435–3101, 619/435–5993 tour information* ⊠ *$14 for historical tour.*

**EN
ROUTE** **Chicano Park.** San Diego's Mexican-American community is centered in Barrio Logan, under the San Diego–Coronado Bay Bridge on the downtown side. Chicano Park, spread along National Avenue from Dewey to Crosby streets, is the barrio's recreational hub. It's worth taking a short detour to see the huge murals of Mexican history painted on the bridge supports at National Avenue and Dewey Street; they're among the best examples of folk art in the city. ⚠ With its somewhat isolated location under the bridge, visiting this site after dark is not recommended.

Where to Eat

WORD OF MOUTH

"If you go to the Prado (which I love), try their tres leches cake for dessert if you like that sort of thing. It is the best version I've ever had. I would try to do it for happy hour after the zoo."

—ncounty

Updated
by Maren
Dougherty

San Diego's proximity to Mexico makes it an attractive destination for anything wrapped in a tortilla. Go surfside to try the city's best fish tacos, or drive up to any local Mexican joint for a burrito stuffed with carne asada (thinly sliced marinated beef).

Among the more formal restaurants in town, there has been a movement toward using sustainable, locally sourced meat, seafood, and produce. While most of the top restaurants offer seasonal California fare, San Diego also boasts excellent ethnic cuisines available at all prices.

With the recent economic tough times, most restaurants—whether a neighborhood burger joint, gourmet pizzeria, or a high-end restaurant—are looking to offer diners more value for less money. This emphasis on affordability often is presented as early- or late-night dining specials, but also extends to the wine lists, where smart sommeliers are offering more wines from value regions like France's Loire and Languedoc, and countries like Chile and South Africa.

Downtown is packed with restaurants, but many can be touristy, so it's a good idea to be selective. The übertrendy Gaslamp Quarter delights visitors looking for innovative concepts with nightlife appeal. The gentrified Little Italy district has become a center for affordable Italian fare as well as surprises like English pubs and supper clubs with live music. Modern restaurants and cafés thrive in the East Village neighborhood, an area of luxury condos near PETCO Park.

The Uptown neighborhoods centered by Hillcrest—an urbane district with San Francisco flavor—is a mix of bars and independent restaurants. Mission Valley, the heart of the city's shopping district, abounds with big restaurants of varying quality. And scenic La Jolla offers some of the best fine dining in the city. Ethnic cuisine remains popular in the Gaslamp Quarter, Hillcrest, and Convoy Street, a hub for Chinese, Korean and Vietnamese fare. In Chula Vista you'll find authentic Mexican food, while Coronado—the peninsula city across San Diego Bay—has casual neighborhood eateries and extravagant hotel dining rooms with dramatic water views.

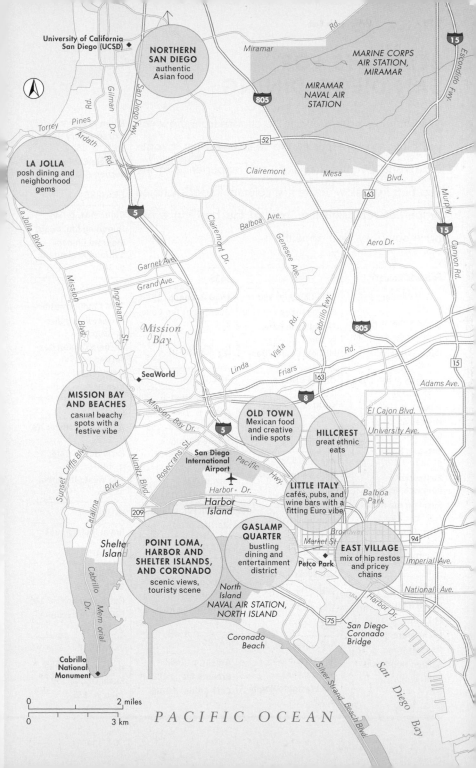

University of California
San Diego (UCSD) ◆

**NORTHERN
SAN DIEGO**
authentic
Asian food

Miramar

**MARINE CORPS
AIR STATION,
MIRAMAR**

**MIRAMAR
NAVAL AIR
STATION**

15

Escondido Fwy.

805

Torrey Pines
Ardath

Gilman Dr.

San Diego Fwy.

52

LA JOLLA
posh dining and
neighborhood
gems

Clairemont   *Mesa*   Blvd.

163

5

Balboa Ave.

Aero Dr.

15

Murphy Canyon Rd.

La Jolla Blvd.

Garnet Ave.

Grand Ave.

Clairemont Dr.

Genesee Ave.

805

Mission Blvd.

Ingraham St.

*Mission
Bay*

Linda   Vista   Rd.

Cabrillo Fwy.

Rd.

15

Adams Ave.

◆ SeaWorld

Friars

163

8

El Cajon Blvd.

University Ave.

**MISSION BAY
AND BEACHES**
casual beachy
spots with a
festive vibe

Mission Bay Dr.

OLD TOWN
Mexican food
and creative
indie spots

HILLCREST
great ethnic
eats

Sunset Cliffs Blvd.

Nimitz Blvd.

Rosecrans St.

5

San Diego
International
Airport

Pacific   Hwy.

LITTLE ITALY
cafés, pubs, and
wine bars with a
fitting Euro vibe

*Balboa
Park*

Catalina   Blvd.

209

Harbor · Dr.

*Harbor
Island*

**GASLAMP
QUARTER**
bustling
dining and
entertainment
district

Broadway

94

Market St.

*Shelter
Island*

**POINT LOMA,
HARBOR AND
SHELTER ISLANDS,
AND CORONADO**
scenic views,
touristy scene

EAST VILLAGE
mix of hip restos
and pricey
chains

Imperial Ave.

Petco Park ◆

National Ave.

Cabrillo Dr.

Memorial

*North
Island*
**NAVAL AIR STATION,
NORTH ISLAND**

75

Harbor Dr.

**Cabrillo
National
Monument** ◆

*Coronado
Beach*

**San Diego-
Coronado
Bridge**

*San Diego
Bay*

Silver Strand Beach Blvd.

0 ⟶ 2 miles
0 ⟶ 3 km

PACIFIC   OCEAN

BEST BETS FOR SAN DIEGO DINING

With hundreds of restaurants to choose from, how will you decide where to eat? We've selected our favorite restaurants by price, cuisine, and experience in the Best Bets list below. In the first column, Fodor's Choice properties represent the "best of the best" in every price category. Bon appétit!

Fodor'sChoice★

A. R. Valentien, $$$, p. 150

Bread & Cie, ¢, p. 142

Café Chloe, $, p. 130

Cucina Urbana, $, p. 140

George's at the Cove, $$$$, p. 152

Jsix, $$, p. 132

Mistral, $$, p. 157

Nine-Ten, $$$, p. 154

Ortega's Bistro, $, p. 143

Restaurante Romesco, $$, p. 162

Sushi on the Rock, $ p. 155

Taka, $$, p. 135

By Price

¢

Bread & Cie, p. 142

El Zarape, p. 147

Lucha Libre, p. 147

Phuong Trang, p. 161

Saffron Noodles & Saté, p. 143

$

Café Chloe, p. 130

Cucina Urbana, p. 140

Farm House Café, p. 148

Michele Coulon Dessertier, p. 154

Ortega's Bistro, p. 143

Sushi on the Rock, p. 155

$$

Ave 5, p. 138

Barbarella, p. 150

Jsix, p. 132

Mistral, p. 157

Quarter Kitchen, p. 134

Restaurante Romesco, p. 162

Searsucker, p. 135

Sushi Ota, p. 150

Taka, p. 135

$$$

A. R. Valentien, p. 150

Nine-Ten, p. 154

Nobu, p. 133

The Westgate Room, p. 136

$$$$

1500 Ocean, p. 157

George's at the Cove, p. 152

By Cuisine

AMERICAN

A.R. Valentien, p. 150

Ave 5, p. 138

Bankers Hill, p. 138

Jimmy's Famous American Tavern, p. 159

Jsix, p. 132

Nine-Ten, p. 154

Searsucker, p. 135

Starlite, p. 147

ASIAN

Harney Sushi, p. 147

Saffron Noodles & Saté, p. 143

Sushi on the Rock, p. 155

CAFÉS

Azucar, p. 158

Bread & Cie, p. 142

Café Chloe, p. 130

Karen Krasne's Extraordinary Desserts, p. 136

Michele Coulon Dessertier, p. 154

CHINESE

China Max, p. 160

Dumpling Inn, p. 161

Emerald Chinese Seafood Restaurant, p. 161

DESSERTS

Café Chloe, p. 130

Extraordinary Desserts, p. 136

Michele Coulon Dessertier, p. 154

Nine-Ten, p. 154

Viva Pops, p. 145

FRENCH

Bertrand at Mister A's, p. 138

Farm House Café, p. 148

The Westgate Room, p. 136

INDIAN

Royal India, p. 134

ITALIAN

Barbarella, p. 150

BiCE, p. 131

Cucina Urbana, p. 140

Pizzeria Arrivederci, p. 143

JAPANESE

Hane Sushi, p. 140

Sushi Ota, p. 150

Taka, p. 135

LATIN/MEXICAN

El Zarape, p. 147

Isabel's Cantina,
p. 149

Lucha Libre, p. 147

Ortega's Bistro,
p. 143

MEDITERRANEAN

Mama's Bakery &
Lebanese Deli, p. 146

Mistral, p. 157

Restaurante
Romesco, p. 162

PIZZA

Barbarella, p. 150

Cucina Urbana, p. 140

Pizzeria Arrivederci,
p. 143

Pizzicato Pizza, p. 140

SEAFOOD

Blue Water Seafood
Market & Grill, p. 146

El Pescador, p. 152

Fish Market, p. 131

Oceanaire Seafood
Room, p. 133

STEAKHOUSES

Lou & Mickey's, p. 133

Morton's, p. 133

Puerto La Boca,
p. 137

VEGETARIAN

Kous Kous Moroccan
Bistro, p. 142

Saffron Noodles &
Saté, p. 143

Starlite, p. 147

Tender Greens, p. 159

By Experience

BRUNCH

Barbarella, p. 150

Bread & Cie, p. 142

Café Chloe, p. 130

Nine-Ten, p. 154

BUSINESS MEALS

Ave 5, p. 138

George's at the Cove,
p. 152

Oceanaire Seafood
Room, p. 133

Taka, p. 135

Zodiac, p. 145

COCKTAILS

Cucina Urbana, p. 140

Jsix, p. 132

Oceanaire, p. 133

Starlite, p. 147

DINING WITH KIDS

Corvette Diner Bar &
Grill, p. 158

Hodad's, p. 159

Ortega's Bistro,
p. 143

Pizzeria Arrivederci,
p. 143

Rimel's Rotisserie,
p. 154

Tartine, p. 158

Tender Greens, p. 159

GOOD FOR GROUPS

Emerald Chinese
Seafood Restaurant,
p. 161

Oceanaire Seafood
Room, p. 133

Red Pearl Kitchen,
p. 134

Royal India, p. 134

URBN Coal Fired
Pizza, p. 146

HOTEL DINING

A.R. Valentien, p. 150

Jsix, p. 132

Mistral, p. 157

Nine-Ten, p. 154

The Westgate Room,
p. 136

OUTDOOR DINING

1500 Ocean, p. 157

A.R. Valentien, p. 150

Barbarella, p. 150

Café Chloe, p. 130

Osteria Romantica,
p. 154

PRE-THEATER

Ave 5, p. 138

Bankers Hill, p. 138

Café Chloe, p. 130

Farm House Café,
p. 148

ROMANTIC

Bertrand at Mister A's,
p. 138

Chez Loma, p. 157

George's at the Cove,
p. 152

Mistral, p. 157

Whisk'n'ladle, p. 156

SINGLES SCENE

George's at the Cove,
p. 152

JRDN at Tower 23,
p. 149

Oceanaire Seafood
Room, p. 133

Red Pearl Kitchen,
p. 134

TRENDY

Jsix, p. 132

Neighborhood, p. 130

Nobu, p. 133

Prepkitchen, p. 154

Quarter Kitchen,
p. 134

Searsucker, p. 135

Stingaree, p. 135

WATER VIEWS

Fish Market, p. 131

George's at the Cove,
p. 152

JRDN, p. 149

Marine Room, p. 153

Mistral, p. 157

WINE LISTS

1500 Ocean, p. 157

A.R. Valentien, p. 150

George's at the Cove,
p. 152

Mistral, p. 157

Vela, p. 135

8

BANKER'S HILL

Once just a place to find a title insurance broker's office or to visit your attorney or banker, the central Banker's Hill is the next up-and-coming dining neighborhood in San Diego.

(above) For an upscale happy hour, stop into Ave 5. (lower right) Bertrand at Mister A's is a local favorite with updated takes on French classics. (upper right) Olives at Cucina Urbana.

A mix of well-landscaped older homes with pedigrees from prominent architects, high-rise condos, and businesses, Banker's Hill offers gorgeous views ranging from Balboa Park's greenery in the east to the San Diego Bay in the west. The recent influx of new condo dwellers has attracted the attention of several independent restaurateurs who are among the best in the city. San Diegans have long visited the area for classics like the circa-1970s Mister A's and Extraordinary Desserts. Now the neighborhood boasts standouts for French, Asian, and Italian food mixed in with divey bars, old Chinese food haunts, and delis.

Banker's Hill draws an eclectic mix of foreign travelers to a mostly hip and affluent mix of young professionals and foodies who live nearby.

HAPPY HOUR

Beyond drink specials, some spots in Banker's Hill offer great deals for afternoon cocktails coupled with a late lunch or early dinner. One of the best is at **Ave 5** (✉ *2760 Fifth Ave.* ☎ *619/542-0394* ✛ *2:D6*) when drinks are $3–$7 during its daily 5–8 pm happy hour. **Pizzicato Pizza** (✉ *2420 Fifth Ave.* ☎ *619/232-9000* ✛ *2:D6*), a gourmet pie shop, serves a slice and a glass of wine or beer for $7.

WHAT'S HOT IN BANKER'S HILL?

If you're craving upscale Mexican food in hip surroundings, the energetic new **Barrio Star** (✉ 2706 5th Ave. ☎ 619/501–7827 ✛ 2:D6) from chef Isabel Cruz should satisfy with pulled pork tacos, chicken tamales, a Mexican Caesar salad, and flourless spiced chocolate cake. Don't miss the Latin-inflected cocktails like the blackberry martini spiked with jalapeño.

Bankers Hill (✉ 2202 4th Ave. ☎ 619/231–0222 ✛ 1:D1) is a popular pick for dinner or drinks. The upscale bar and grill, by renowned chef Carl Schroeder, offers high-quality, gently priced dishes like deviled farmer's market eggs, Cabernet-braised short ribs, and buttermilk fried chicken. The space is warm and woodsy with a living garden wall.

Vegetarians, raw foodists, and people who like an especially fresh and green meal should visit **Evolution Fast Food** (✉ 2949 Fifth Ave. ☎ 619/550–1818 ✛ 2:D6) for tempting items like Mexican-spiced veggie burgers with house-made guacamole, wrap sandwiches, faux chicken tenders, sweet potato fries, and the well-stocked salad bar. There's even a parking lot and a drive-through window open until 8 pm.

After years of working for San Diego's reigning sushi chef Yukito Ota, student Roger Nakamura, with the help of his master, opened his own place. The result is **Hane Sushi** (✉ 2760 5th Ave. ☎ 619/260–1411 ✛ 2:D6), where the delectable presentations range from simple Japanese classics like tuna sashimi to Nakamura's more modern and playful creations including the Caterpillar and salmon-crunch rolls.

Don't be put off by the retro sign in front of **Marketplace Deli** (✉ 2601 Fifth Ave. ☎ 619/239–8361 ✛ 2:E6). Inside it's a surprisingly modern and well-stocked grocery, wine shop, and liquor store. It's a lunchtime favorite for people from area offices and Balboa Park because of the amazingly varied and affordable sandwiches and salads made daily. Local favorites include the California sandwich with turkey, avocado, bacon, and sprouts; the Albacore Melt; and the Greek salad.

UP FOR A DRINK?

Besides the creative Italian-style fare, **Cucina Urbana**'s (✉ 505 Laurel St. ☎ 619/239–2222 ✛ 2:D6) clever cocktails are introducing a whole new crowd to Italian *amaros* (spice-infused spirits) and liqueurs. The Averna Manhattan features the dark Sicilian amaro, while orange-rhubarb Aperol stars in a twist on the Negroni. Pleasantly bitter Campari becomes downright appealing in the Pompelmo, blended with muddled grapefruit, vodka, and sparkling wine.

If you're in the mood for a down-and-dirty drink with locals, then head over to **Nunu's** (✉ 3537 5th Ave. ☎ 619/295–2878 ✛ 2:E5). The cocktails come fast and they're strong—the hardest part is snagging a booth from one of the groups that look like they're permanent residents. And while it's not going to appear on any list of haute cuisine, Nunu's does a very tasty burger and excellent hot fries.

8

LA JOLLA

Offering panoramic water views, romantic terraces, and pedestrian-friendly streets, La Jolla is a favorite among tourists and well-heeled San Diegans.

(above) George's at the Cove's California Modern dining room serves award-winning cuisine. (lower right) Arrive before dusk to snag a table at George's Ocean Terrace. (upper right) Sweets at Michele Coulon Dessertier.

With the affluent local community and abundance of celebrity visitors, the overall quality of restaurants in this seaside resort community is pretty high. La Jolla offers everything from historic diners and breakfast spots to Moroccan restaurants with mid-meal dance performances, modern California-style sushi bars, and high-end hotel dining rooms with water views. To work up an appetite, stroll the streets and meander through art galleries, walk along La Jolla Cove, or take a hike down the bluff to the beach. Because it's a popular destination, reservations are a good idea, especially on weekends. Parking can be a challenge too, but there are a few parking garages along Prospect Avenue. The "view" restaurants are tempting, but be wary of committing to a full meal at ones that aren't mentioned here or elsewhere in the chapter.

SUSHI SAMBA

La Jolla has a trio of restaurants serving sushi and world-class local sea urchin. For a traditional setting, head to **Toshi San** (⊠ 7614 Fay Ave. ☎ 858/456–4545 ✛ 3:A2). **Zenbu** (⊠ 7660 Fay Ave. ☎ 858/454–4540 ✛ 3:A2) delivers high-end dishes like prime beef cooked on a hot stone and buttery tuna belly. **Sushi on the Rock** (⊠ 1025 Prospect St. ☎ 858/459–3208 ✛ 3:A2) is a winner for rolls and happy hour.

ROOMS WITH A VIEW

It's a "sad but truism" that many restaurants with great views serve food that isn't so hot. Many less-than-dedicated operators figure that the gorgeous vista will help make up for any deficiencies in the flavor department. Here are some exceptions to that rule:

George's Ocean Terrace (✉ *1250 Prospect St.* ☎ *858/454–4244* ✛ *3:A2*) is one of the busiest spots in the village and for good reason: the casual bistro above George's California Modern has an expansive view of the ocean, where you can glimpse boats and sometimes whales. Order a bowl of their signature black bean, broccoli, and chicken soup; Asian-style chicken wings; or grilled swordfish with red-pepper sauce.

For a more upscale experience, head downstairs to **George's California Modern**, which offers excellent high-end fare. Chef Trey Foshee's menu offers seasonal dishes like local-catch grilled octopus salad with tzatziki sauce; and scallop, lemon, and tarragon ravioli. ✛ *3:A2*

Tucked into a hillside above the cove, **Brockton Villa** (✉ *1235 Coast Blvd.* ☎ *858/454–7393* ✛ *3:B2*) serves three meals a day, but they excel at brunch and lunch when ocean views are best. Snag a seat by the fireplace and order the soufflélike Coast Toast or a layered bagel-and-smoked-salmon sandwich.

Cody's La Jolla (✉ *8030 Girard Ave.* ☎ *858/459–0040* ✛ *3:A2*) serves up a slice of ocean view along with American fare like voluminous omelets and grilled chicken sandwiches with Gruyère and crisp pancetta.

At **Goldfish Point Cafe** (✉ *1255 Coast Blvd.* ☎ *858/459–7407* ✛ *3:B2*) the menu is very light, limited to coffee, teas, pastries, and a few sandwiches. But it's easily the most affordable romantic spot in La Jolla. They also welcome dogs with free treats and a bowl of water.

JUST DESSERTS

Michele Coulon Dessertier (✉ *7556 Fay Ave.* ☎ *858/456–5098* ⊕ *www.dessertier.com* ✛ *3:B2*) is a warm place for desserts like an organic berry tart, carrot cake, or a piece of Torte Lion filled with caramel, Belgian chocolate, and nuts.
Lean & Green (✉ *7825 Fay Ave.* ☎ *858/459–5326* ✛ *3:A2*) serves up organic smoothies with acai berries and blueberries, and guiltless orange juice-and-vanilla shakes.
Or sit at the bar at **Nine-Ten** (✉ *910 Prospect St.* ☎ *858/964–5400* ⊕ *www.nine-ten.com* ✛ *3:A2*) and experience one of Jack Fisher's delightful seasonal desserts like a local fig napoleon or lemon verbena panna cotta.

8

NORTH PARK

You won't find million-dollar views or nightclubs with bottle service, but North Park offers some of the best and most eclectic food in San Diego. This central neighborhood has become a hub of art and culinary innovation, featuring many independently owned restaurants, bars, art galleries, and boutiques. Comprising mostly young hipsters and middle-aged professionals, the community has a fun and low-key vibe; you're bound to stumble upon live music, trivia night, karaoke, or an open-mic night.

It's hard to think of a style of food not found here. Starting at the intersection of University Avenue and 30th Street, it's possible to walk in any direction and find inexpensive spots serving Peruvian, vegetarian, Mexican, Southern, and Asian cuisines, as well as dessert cafes, wine bars, gastropubs, and gourmet coffee and tea houses.

If you're in town on the 30th of the month, head to North Park for the monthly 30th on 30th night, when area eateries have food and drink specials, such as $2 wines and $3 appetizers.

(above) Crazee Burger is known for its unusual sandwiches. (lower right) Non-meat eaters can also find a respectable Caprese salad at Crazee Burger. (upper right) A slice from Lefty's.

GOOD BURGER

North Park has no shortage of burger joints. If you like your burgers chargrilled and maybe topped with pastrami, head to **Western Steakburger** (✉ *2730 University Ave.* ☎ *619/296–7058* ✛ *2:G4*). **Crazee Burger** (✉ *4201 30th St.* ☎ *619/282–6044* ✛ *3:G3*), features about 30 burgers, including ostrich, alligator with curry fruit tapenade, or a kangaroo version with horseradish sauce.

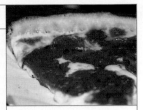

TOWER OF PIZZA

It could take a week to experience all the pizzas in North Park. **Sicilian Thing Pizza** (✉ *4046 30th St.* ☎ *619/282–3000* ✛ *2:G4*) cuts pizza in squares, but the real draw is the zesty sauce and the airy Sicilian-style crust. A highlight is the Barack-oli Ricotta pie, named for our U.S. commander-in-chief.

Lefty's Chicago Pizzeria (✉ *3448 30th St.* ☎ *619/295–1720* ✛ *2:G5*) specializes in thick-crust pizzas famous in Chicago; the simplest ones are the best.

If New York– and Italian-style pizzas could procreate, the result would be the pies at **Pizzeria Luigi** (✉ *2121 El Cajon Blvd.* ☎ *619/294–9417* ✛ *2:F3*) with their impossibly thin crusts topped with pepperoni or meatballs and ricotta.

Chic decor with white marble and twinkling lights accompanies the pies at **Alexander's** (✉ *3391 30th St.* ☎ *619/281–2539* ✛ *2:H5*). Try the gourmet-style affairs like the White Room with white garlic, ricotta, mozzarella, and pesto-dressed chicken.

ON TAP

The eclectic international mix at the **Ritual Tavern** (✉ *4095 30th St.* ☎ *619/283–1618* ✛ *2:G4*), a cottage-y bar with a pleasant patio includes Zatec Bright Lager from the Czech Republic, Ace Hard Apple Cider from Sonoma, and the intense Young's Double Chocolate Stout from England. The menu includes beer-centric dishes like beer-battered fried vegetables, mussels steamed with the draft beer of your choice, and ice-cream floats with chocolate stout.

With a staff of beer lovers, you're sure to find something appealing at **Toronado** (✉ *4026 30th St.* ☎ *619/282–0456* ✛ *2:G4*), a pub that's often packed thanks to a beer list that's arguably the best in town. They feature many local brews, including Trigger Hoppy, a Belgian IPA style; California Honey, a creamy ale; and Sticky Stout, an homage to the Russian Imperial style.

NATURAL FLAVOR

North Park is endowed with restaurants that focus on fresh, locally sourced, and sustainably grown cuisine. As the name suggests, **Rancho's Mexican & Vegetarian Cuisine** (✉ *3910 30th St.* ☎ *619/574–1288* ✛ *2:G4*) serves up healthy, Mexican-accented fare ranging from vegan chili dogs and tofu enchiladas to lobster torta sandwiches to eat in or take out. **The Linkery** (✉ *3794 30th St.* ☎ *619/255–8778* ✛ *2:G4*) put itself on the national foodie map for using local and artisanal ingredients like sustainably raised meats from local farmers. Try their house-made sausages. **Sea Rocket** (✉ *3382 30th St.* ☎ *619/255–7049* ✛ *2:G4*) is an earnest, slow food–minded spot that uses fresh local seafood in its wholesome dishes, like grilled sardines and fish tacos.

8

SAN DIEGO DINING PLANNER

EATING OUT STRATEGY

It's not too long after arriving in a new city that you start wondering, where should we eat? With hundreds of San Diego restaurants and cafés competing for your attention, it may seem like a daunting question. But fortunately, our expert writers and editors have done most of the legwork. The selections here represent the best this city has to offer—from hot dogs to haute cuisine. *Search "Best Bets" for top recommendations by price, cuisine, and experience.* Sample local flavor in the neighborhood features. Or find a review quickly in the alphabetical listings. Bon appétit!

DINING HOURS

Unless otherwise noted, the restaurants listed in this guide are open daily for lunch and dinner. Lunch is typically served 11:30 pm to 2:30 pm, and dinner service in most restaurants begins at 5:30 pm and ends at 10 pm, though a number of establishments serve until 11 pm or later on Friday and Saturday nights.

RESERVATIONS

We mention reservations in reviews only when they're essential or not accepted. But reservations are usually a good idea—a venue may be booked solid or rented out for a special event, so it's best to call ahead. Especially for fine-dining restaurants, reserve as far ahead as you can, and reconfirm when you arrive in town.

WHAT TO WEAR

San Diego restaurants have given up trying to require dressy attire. It's a casual city for men and women alike, with designer jeans and a trendy top as the typical going-out uniform. A few dress-up places remain. Otherwise, a "come-as-you-are" attitude generally prevails.

CHILDREN

San Diego welcomes all kinds of diners, including children, though some of the more formal establishments and expense-account steak houses probably are inappropriate venues for kids. Children's menus can be found here and there, but staff at most establishments will cheerfully offer a few suggestions for the younger set if asked. The restaurants we recommend for families with children are marked with a ۞ symbol.

TIPPING AND TAXES

In most restaurants, tip the waiter 16% to 20%. (To figure out a 20% tip quickly, just move the decimal point one place to the left on your total and double that amount.) Note that checks for parties of six or more may already include the tip. At the bar, tip at least $1 per drink; for coat check, tip $1 per item. Never tip the maître d' unless you're out to impress your guests or expect to pay another visit soon. Also, be prepared for a city tax of 8.75% to appear on your bill.

PARKING

With the boom of new apartments and condominiums in Little Italy, parking near many of its restaurants has become a problem. Try to find valet parking or a spot in a surface lot. Downtown, there's Parkade, a controlled-price public parking garage at the corner of 6th Avenue and K Street, which usually has ample parking even in the evening. There's also a local San Diego Trolley stop that's less than two blocks from Little Italy's India Street restaurant row. If you use the trolley to get to downtown and Gaslamp Quarter restaurants, you can avoid parking fees that may exceed $20 and valets who expect tips.

SMOKING

Smoking is banned in restaurants, but some permit it on their terraces.

PRICES

Meal prices in San Diego have caught up with those of other major metropolitan areas, despite the fact that the city's serious dining scene is still developing. Especially in districts like La Jolla, the Gaslamp Quarter, and Coronado, high rents and popularity with tourists lead to more expensive entrées. But with the economic downturn, many restaurants around town are offering extra value with fixed-price menus and early-dining specials.

Some restaurants listed are marked with a price range ($$–$$$, for example). This indicates one of two things: either the average cost straddles two categories or, if you order strategically, you can get out for less than what most diners spend.

WHAT IT COSTS					
	¢	$	$$	$$$	$$$$
Restaurants	under $10	$10–$18	$19–$27	$28–$35	over $35

Prices are per person for a main course or equivalent combination of smaller plates (e.g., tapas, sushi), excluding 8.75% sales tax.

ORIENTATION

Throughout the chapter, you'll see mapping symbols and coordinates (✢ 3:F2) after property names or reviews. *To locate the property on a map, turn to the San Diego Dining and Lodging Atlas at the end of this chapter.* The first number after the ✢ symbol indicates the map number. Following that is the property's coordinate on the map grid.

RESTAURANT REVIEWS

Listed alphabetically within neighborhoods. Use the coordinate (✢ 1: B2) at the end of each listing to locate a site on the San Diego Dining and Lodging Atlas following this chapter.

DOWNTOWN

The East Village is one of the hippest areas of downtown with its urbane mix of independent restaurants serving everything from French bistro fare and burgers to Thai food and artisan-baked bread. It is located just east of the Gaslamp Quarter, which is known as much for the nightlife as the eateries. Many restaurants in the Gaslamp Quarter are pricey chains and tourist-driven concepts along 4th, 5th, and 6th avenues. They range from casual spots for burgers, sushi, and tacos to stylish restaurants serving fresh seafood, Italian cuisine, and aged steaks. Heading north from downtown, Little Italy offers a mix of mostly Italian spots and markets.

EAST VILLAGE

¢

CAFÉ

×**Bread on Market.** The baguettes at this artisanal bakery near the PETCO Park baseball stadium are every bit as good as the ones you'd buy in Paris. Focaccia and other superior loaves are the building blocks for solid sandwiches, which range from the turkey special with honey mustard and cranberry sauce to a vegan sandwich with locally grown avocado. The menu extends to a daily soup, a fruit-garnished cheese plate, and an appetizing Mediterranean salad. If you have a sweet tooth, try the peanut butter and chocolate-chip cookies, coconut macaroons, and biscotti with hazelnut and chocolate. ✉ *730 Market St., East Village* ☎ *619/795–2730* ⊕ *www.breadonmarket. com* ⊗ *No dinner* ✛ *1:E4.*

$

FRENCH

Fodor'sChoice

★

×**Café Chloe.** The intersection of 9th and G is now the meeting point for San Diego's café society, thanks to the superchic and friendly Café Chloe. Surrounded by luxury high-rises, hotels, and boutiques, this pretty, Parisian spot is frequented by the area's residents for breakfast, lunch, dinner, and weekend brunch. Start the day with whole-wheat pancakes and sour-cherry sauce; lunch on smoked trout and apple salad or a casserole of macaroni, pancetta, and Gorgonzola; or enjoy duck confit or steak frites for dinner. Enjoy wines by the glass, imported teas, and coffee with desserts like seasonal fruit tarts or chocolate pot de crème. It's a lovely place to spend the afternoon. ✉ *721 9th Ave., East Village* ☎ *619/232–3242* ✛ *1:E4.*

¢

AMERICAN

×**Neighborhood.** There's no ketchup in the house—the young owners (inspired by the famous Father's Office in Los Angeles) don't want anything to mar the flavor of their perfectly seasoned burgers topped with pickled daikon or spicy Cajun sauce and served on artisanal buns. One local favorite is the 777 Burger with tomato confit and béarnaise. They also serve smoked, porter-braised beef ribs, chorizo corn dogs, and fennel frites with white balsamic vinegar. Wash it down with one of the many international artisan beers such as Delirium Tremens on tap and Pliny the Elder by Russian River Brewing Co., Belgian triple ale aged in Jim Beam casks, or wines by the glass. ✉ *777 G St., East Village* ☎ *619/446–0002* ⊕ *www.neighborhoodsd.com* ⌲ *Reservations not accepted* ✛ *1:E4.*

EMBARCADERO

$$
SEAFOOD
✕ Fish Market. Fresh mesquite-grilled, steamed, and skewered fish and shellfish are the specialty at this informal restaurant. There's also an excellent shellfish bar that serves crab cocktails and steamed clams. The Monday through Thursday happy hour brings specials on snacks like oysters and smoked-trout quesadillas, as well as drink deals. The view is stunning: enormous plate-glass windows look directly out onto the harbor. A more formal restaurant upstairs, Top of the Market, is expensive but worth the splurge and is the place to find such rarities as Pacific swordfish with pumpkin risotto and ricotta salata. ⊠ *750 N. Harbor Dr., Embarcadero* ☎ *619/232–3474 Fish Market, 619/234–4867 Top of the Market* ⊕ *www.thefishmarket.com* ✛ *1:A4.*

$$
ECLECTIC
✕ Roy's Restaurant. The old San Diego Yacht Club restaurant has been transformed into a modern and inviting space that overlooks the marina, showcasing chef Roy Yamaguchi's version of Hawaiian cuisine that's fused with French techniques and flourishes. Inventive sushi such as a delicious surf-and-turf roll draped in Kobe beef give way to delicate lobster potstickers and Szechuan baby back ribs. Entrées run from the original macadamia-crusted mahimahi in lobster-studded beurre blanc sauce to a pork porterhouse. Desserts, like a hot chocolate soufflé, are served with island-style warmth. ⊠ *333 W. Harbor Dr., Embarcadero* ☎ *619/239–7697* ⊕ *www.roysrestaurant.com* ✛ *1:C5.*

GASLAMP QUARTER

$$$
ITALIAN
✕ BiCE. After two years of anticipation, BiCE Ristorante brings its refined, big-city style of Italian cuisine to San Diego with a gleaming new space in the Gaslamp Quarter. This sleek, dinner-only restaurant led by Italian-born chef Mario Cassineri offers a cheese-and-salumi bar, dishes like gnocchi with asiago cheese, veal with saffron risotto, and fresh sea bass. Waiters deliver professional service and informed opinions on the extensive Italian wine list, while the bar features local artisanal and imported beers and appropriate cocktails like the Il Rutino, with Aperol and prosecco. ⊠ *425 Island Ave., Gaslamp Quarter* ☎ *619/239–2423* ⊕ *www.bicesandiego.com* ☽ *No lunch* ✛ *1:D5.*

$$$
SEAFOOD
✕ Blue Point Coastal Cuisine. If there's a convention in town, Blue Point gets jammed with diverse diners who share a taste for sophisticated seafood. The menu swims with classics like crab three ways, seared ahi tuna in ginger port butter with an ahi spring roll, and mussels in tomato-saffron broth. The small but serious oyster bar, which serves both raw and imaginatively prepared shellfish, offers a warm-up for a menu of more seafood, plus chicken and steaks. The wine list is impressive, and the service is efficient and friendly. The airy dining room has gleaming woodwork and walls of windows looking onto 5th Avenue and Market Street, a prime corner for people-watching. ⊠ *565 5th Ave., Gaslamp Quarter* ☎ *619/233–6623* ☽ *No lunch* ✛ *1:E4.*

$$$
MEXICAN
✕ Candelas. The scents and flavors of imaginative Mexican cuisine with a European flair permeate this handsome, romantic restaurant and nightspot in the shadow of San Diego's tallest residential towers. Candles glow everywhere around the small, comfortable dining room. There isn't a burrito or taco in sight. Fine openers such as black bean soup and watercress salad with bacon and pistachios give way to main courses like local

8

DINING WITH KIDS

The most popular "kid magnet" in town is **Corvette Diner Bar & Grill in Point Loma's Liberty Station** (✉ 2965 Historic Decatur Rd., Point Loma ☎ 619/542–1476 ⊕ www.crg.com ✛ 4:C1), which hosts many kiddie birthday parties thanks to a 1950s menu and decor, and singing servers. Children are well received at **Tender Greens** in Liberty Station (✉ 2400 Historic Decatur Rd., Point Loma ☎ 619/226–6245 ⊕ www.tendergreensfood.com ✛ 4:C1) and big crowd-pleasing places like **P.F. Chang's** (✉ 7707 Friar's Rd., Mission Valley ☎ 619/260–8484 ⊕ www.pfchangs.com ✛ 2:C2) and the **Cheesecake Factory** in Mission Valley (✉ 7067 Friar's Rd., Mission Valley ☎ 619/683–2800 ⊕ www.thecheesecakefactory.com ✛ 2:C2).

Kearny Mesa's Convoy Street has Chinese restaurants that specialize at lunchtime in dim sum (myriad small dishes). Youngsters who have never tried them may be delighted by egg rolls, fried pork dumplings, and fried shrimp rolls. California-style Mexican cuisine that's usually a hit with kids is not hard to find, especially in the bustling Old Town area, where **Old Town Mexican Café** (✉ 2489 San Diego Ave., Old Town ☎ 619/297–4330 ⊕ www.oldtownmexcafe.com ✛ 2:A4) offers high chairs and crayons to kids. Fish tacos are a standard here, but if you're not sure what your kids will like, try a cheese quesadilla (melted cheese in a flour tortilla), chips, or rolled tacos with guacamole. Always sample the salsa before offering it to your little ones, as it's often spicy.

lobster stuffed with mushrooms, jalapeño peppers, and aged tequila; or tequila-flamed jumbo prawns over creamy, seasoned goat cheese. The adjacent bar pours many elegant tequilas and has become a popular, often jam-packed nightspot. They also serve a Mexican-style breakfast on weekends. ✉ 416 3rd Ave., Gaslamp Quarter ☎ 619/702–4455 ✛ 1:D5.

$ **✕ The Field.** A family-run pub decorated with artifacts from an Irish
IRISH farm, the Field has character to spare. Both on the outdoor terrace and indoors, diners enjoy solid meals of Irish stew, corned beef and cabbage, Gaelic steak with an Irish whisky–peppercorn sauce or, best of all, a *boxty*, a lacy but substantial potato pancake served crisp and hot with such fillings as sage-accented chicken or Irish bacon and cheese. As the evening wears on, the crowd grows younger, livelier, louder, and sometimes rowdier. A traditional Irish breakfast is served on weekends, and there's dancing and music on Sunday. ✉ 544 5th Ave., Gaslamp Quarter ☎ 619/232–9840 ⊕ www.thefield.com ✛ 1:D5.

$$ **✕ Jsix.** Creative and carefully prepared seafood reigns on this menu that
AMERICAN reflects the diverse flavors found along the West Coast from Mexico
Fodor's Choice to Washington. Chef Christian Graves favors fresh, light fare, using
★ sustainably raised seafood such as the tarragon and dijon mussels and seared albacore with avocado puree. Non-seafood options include vegetarian butternut squash ravioli, chicken and dumplings, and pork chop with apple-brandy butter sauce. The cheeses, salami, and house-made pickles are excellent. Desserts are made with equal care, and the bar boasts cocktails made with seasonal fruit. The eclectic decor includes blown-glass pendant lights, a series of culinary paintings by a local art-

ist, and a dramatically backlighted bar. ⊠ *616 J St., Gaslamp Quarter* ☎ *619/531–8744* ⊕ *www.jsixrestaurant.com* ✛ *1:E5.*

$$ ✕ **Lou & Mickey's.** Just across the street from the San Diego Convention
STEAK Center, this handsome, 1940s-style establishment lures with thick steaks and lamp chops, meaty seafood cuts like the unusual T-bone of Alaskan halibut, richly sauced pastas, and chicken dishes of surprising flavor and sophistication. For a special splurge, start with a shellfish platter of oysters, clams, shrimp, mussels, and lobster, then move on to the $50-per-serving Alaskan king crab legs. If you're on a budget, visit at lunch for the tasty meatloaf po' boy sandwich, or the monumental cheeseburger served with a good pound of hot fries. Either way, plan on finishing with an impressive wedge of key lime pie. ⊠ *224 5th Ave., Gaslamp Quarter* ☎ *619/237–4900* ⊕ *www.louandmickeys.com* ✛ *1:D5.*

$$$$ ✕ **Morton's, The Steakhouse.** Housed in the soaring Harbor Club towers
STEAK near both the San Diego Convention Center and the Gaslamp Quarter, Morton's teems with conventioneers out for a night on the town. The newly expanded Bar 12-21 offers an extensive list of original cocktails and tasty appetizers such as filet mignon sliders. For the main event, servers present the menu by wheeling up a cart laden with crimson prime steaks, behemoth lamb chops, and huge Maine lobsters that may wave their claws in alarm when they hear the prices quoted (based on the market, but always astronomical). Expect a treat, since this restaurant knows how to put on a superb spread that takes the concept of indulgence to new heights. ⊠ *Harbor Club, 285 J St., Gaslamp Quarter* ☎ *619/696–3369* ⊕ *www.mortons.com* ☾ *No lunch* ✛ *1:D5.*

$$$ ✕ **Nobu.** This outpost of Nobu Matsuhisa's restaurant empire in the
JAPANESE Hard Rock Hotel is known for inventive and fresh sushi and hot dishes created with a modern Japanese-Peruvian flair. The sexy if rather noisy room with scorched ash wood treatments and jade-green walls makes a cool space to enjoy Nobu classics like white fish *tiradito* with yuzu citrus, lobster in wasabi sauce, or succulent black cod with miso glaze. If you're feeling slightly adventurous, let the sushi chef's whims guide you through a delicious *omakase* tasting menu—just be sure to tell them what you'd like to spend. More than a few diners have ended up with a surprise bill in the hundreds. ⊠ *Hard Rock Hotel, 207 5th Ave., Gaslamp Quarter* ☎ *619/814–4124* ⊕ *www.noburestaurants.com* ☾ *No lunch* ✛ *1:E5.*

¢ ✕ **O'Brothers Burgers.** A pair of San Diego brothers created this spot in
AMERICAN Horton Plaza mall where everything is organic from the grass-fed-beef burgers to the onion rings to the brown paper napkins. The modern red and brown decor features counters inlaid with recycled glass, reclaimed wood, and contemporary pendant lights. The Western Burger with barbecue sauce, bacon, and onion rings is a favorite; vegetarians will like the portobello mushroom burgers, the side salad that comes with the burgers, and the house-made brownies. ⊠ *188 Horton Plaza, Gaslamp Quarter* ☎ *619/615–0909* ⊕ *www.obrothersburgers.com* ⊘ *Reservations not accepted* ✛ *1:D4.*

$$$ ✕ **Oceanaire Seafood Room.** Engineered to recall an ocean liner from the
SEAFOOD 1940s, Oceanaire is a bit put-on but admirable for the long bar serving classic cocktails, oysters, and sashimi, and a carefully prepared menu of up to 25 daily "fresh catches," with many specialties ranging

8

from convincing Maryland crab cakes and oysters Rockefeller to richly stuffed California sole, a luxurious one-pound pork chop, and irresistible hash brown potatoes. Executive chef Sean Langlais creates a daily menu that may include the deliciously hot, spice-fired "angry" pink snapper. Service is a casual thing in San Diego, which makes the professional staff here all the more notable. ⊠ *400 J St., Gaslamp Quarter* ☎ *619/858–2277* ⊕ *www.theoceanaire.com* ☽ *No lunch* ✛ *1:D5.*

$$ ✕ **Quarter Kitchen at the Andaz Hotel.** This spacious modern restaurant in
AMERICAN the $100 million Andaz Hotel (formerly the Ivy Hotel) is a must-see. The seasonal dinner menu by chef de cuisine Michael Liotta ranges from steaks and wonderful wine-braised short ribs to seafood standouts like the crispy salmon with sweet and sour beets. Come for the scene, the impressive wine list, and tasty desserts—a favorite is the orange tart with chocolate ganache. Valet parking is $20–$30 but complimentary for diners Sunday–Thursday. ⊠ *600 F St., Gaslamp Quarter* ☎ *619/814–2000* ⊕ *www.quarterkitchen.com* ✛ *1:E4.*

$$ ✕ **RA Sushi Bar Restaurant.** Servers in semisensational T-shirts challenge a
JAPANESE young clientele to strive for sexy "attitude" in this small, intimate space carved out of a former department store. Two ultrahip bars—one for cocktails, one for sushi, both for being seen mostly—fuel the popularity, bolstered by a dining-room menu from which you can make a meal out of the many appetizers, such as sesame chicken wings, assorted sashimi, and scallops in spicy "dynamite" sauce. Otherwise, choose sushi combination plates, chicken or pork katsu, apple teriyaki salmon, and hearty noodle dishes. With snacks and drinks for $2–$7, the weekday happy hour is one of the best in downtown. ⊠ *474 Broadway, Gaslamp Quarter* ☎ *619/321–0021* ⊕ *www.rasushi.com* ✛ *1:D3.*

$ ✕ **Red Pearl Kitchen.** Vivid red Venetian plaster walls, a loungey vibe, and
ASIAN a widely varied menu of pan-Asian fare make Red Pearl Kitchen unique among San Diego's Asian restaurants. Diners embark on a culinary journey with dishes like pineapple and Kobe beef satay, honey-chili-glazed chicken wings, spicy meatballs, and steamed pork buns, all of which are designed for sharing. Pair them with sake and wine, or creative cocktails. It's a great place to bring a group. On weekends the bar and lounge are dominated by exuberant twentysomethings—and the service can become harried and nonchalant. ⊠ *440 J St., Suite 108, Gaslamp Quarter* ☎ *619/231–1100* ⊕ *www.redpearlkitchen.com* ✛ *1:D5.*

$$ ✕ **Royal India.** Experience cuisine once reserved for royalty as brothers
INDIAN Sam and Jag Kambo lovingly re-create their mother's north Indian recipes. Everything from the mint chutney to the smoky tomato sauce that graces the chicken *tikka masala* is made from scratch. Dining here is first-rate, whether it's the daily lunch buffet or the sumptuous dinners that include sizzling chili-lemon chicken kebabs, indulgent lamb korma, and garlic naan bread. Elegant but comfortable decor is highlighted by a carved antique maple bar, stunning chandeliers, and golden arches from a palace in Jodhpur. Don't miss the imported Indian beers, mango martinis, or desserts, including mango mousse and rice pudding redolent of warm spices. ⊠ *329 Market St., Gaslamp Quarter* ☎ *619/269–9999* ⊕ *www.royalindia.com* ✛ *1:D4.*

$$ ✕ **Searsucker.** The much-hyped first restaurant of *Top Chef* finalist Brian
AMERICAN Malarkey opened in summer 2010 in the middle of the Gaslamp Quarter.
Since then it has maintained its buzz, attracting patrons with its fun urban
decor and experimental dishes like swordfish with drunken cherries and
beef cheeks over goat cheese dumplings. The flavor combinations are
mostly successful, particularly when paired with comfort-food sides like
bacon grits and grilled asparagus. Chef Malarkey adds to the lively vibe
when he makes his rounds to chat with diners. ⊠ *611 5th Ave., Gaslamp
Quarter* ☎ *619/233–7327* ⊕ *www.searsucker.com* ✛ *1:E4.*

$$ ✕ **Stingaree.** You wouldn't expect to find fine cuisine at a hip, three-level
AMERICAN nightclub, but then you discover Stingaree. Chef Antonio Friscia wows
with dishes like crab risotto with sweet summer corn; smoked duck with a
whiskey cherry sauce; and smoked jidori chicken. Dress to impress at Stingaree, which is done in ultramod tones of chocolate, turquoise, and orange.
Though bottle service reigns here, the spectacular wine list ranges from
reasonable labels from California and France to once-in-a-lifetime bottles
such as Domaine de la Romanée Conti. A generous happy hour offers 50%
off beef sliders or lamb meatballs from 5 to 7 pm Wednesday to Friday.
On weekends the dining room rocks; buying dinner allows you to skip the
long line and $20 club admission; be prepared for crowds and bouncers
with attitude. ⊠ *454 6th Ave., Gaslamp Quarter* ☎ *619/544–9500* ⊕ *www.
stingsandiego.com* ☽ *Closed Sun. and Mon. No lunch* ✛ *1:E5.*

$$ ✕ **Taka.** Even though it's on a prominent corner, Taka modestly lets its
JAPANESE pristine fish imported from around the world and its creative presen-
Fodor's Choice tations attract a crowd each night. Start with one of the sushi chef's
★ appetizers such as monkfish liver with ponzu; slices of tender hamachi
sashimi; or a special box-press sushi with shrimp, tuna, and crab topped
with pickled seaweed and caviar. Hot dishes include crispy soft-shell
crab and an East-meets-West-style New York steak. This restaurant is
a favorite with Japanese visitors. ⊠ *555 5th Ave., Gaslamp Quarter*
☎ *619/338–0555* ⊕ *www.takasushi.com* ☽ *No lunch* ✛ *1:E5.*

¢ ✕ **The Tin Fish.** On the rare rainy day, the staff takes it easy at this eatery
SEAFOOD less than 100 yards from the PETCO Park baseball stadium (half of
its 100-odd seats are outdoors). Musicians entertain some evenings,
making this a lively spot for dinners of grilled and fried fish, as well as
seafood burritos and tacos. The quality here routinely surpasses that
at grander establishments. Service hours vary with the day of the week
and whether it's baseball season or not, but generally Tin Fish is open
from 11 am to 10 pm Sunday through Thursday and until midnight on
weekends. ⊠ *170 6th Ave., Gaslamp Quarter* ☎ *619/238–8100* ⊕ *www.
thetinfish.net* ⌃ *Reservations not accepted* ✛ *1:E6.*

$$ ✕ **Vela.** With a name that means "sail" in Latin, Vela in the new Bay-
AMERICAN front Hilton hotel, concentrates on cuisine and wines from coastal
areas around the globe. Chef Adam Bussell creates dishes including
roasted fennel and parsnip soup, 72-hour braised short rib, and seasonal preparations of New Zealand king salmon and local white sea
bass. The restaurant, which overlooks the bay, has rather avant-garde
staff uniforms and decor set off by striking light fixtures with an ocean
motif. ⊠ *1 Park Blvd., Gaslamp Quarter* ☎ *619/321–4284* ⊕ *www.
hiltonsandiegobayfront.com* ⌃ *Reservations essential* ✛ *1:E6.*

8

$$$ ✕**The Westgate Room.** Normandy-born chef Fabrice Hardel oversees the
FRENCH preparation of three meals a day and writes seasonal menus with high-
end fare mixing French and Asian flavors such as grilled salmon with
spring onions and shitake mushrooms, but usually offers classics like
Dover sole meunière and New York steak with potato foam. The $42
Sunday brunch in the opulent Le Fontainebleau Room—with made-to-
order crepes, omelets, and seafood dishes—is one of the best in town.
⊠ *Westgate Hotel, 1055 2nd Ave., Gaslamp Quarter* ☎ *619/557–3655*
⊕ *www.westgatehotel.com* ✛ *1:D3.*

LITTLE ITALY

$$ ✕**Anthology.** Executive chef Todd Allison seeks to create fare that's as
AMERICAN finely tuned as the music. Contemporary jazz, rock, and blues music is
played live here by artists including Diane Schuur, the Gin Blossoms,
and Joe Sample. The modern three-level dining room features a contemporary top-floor patio and wonderful acoustics. Stick to simple choices
such as the scallops, roasted chicken, Caesar salad, and sticky toffee
pudding. Check the schedule in advance; the venue is closed on most
Sundays and Mondays. ⊠ *1337 India St., Little Italy* ☎ *619/595–0300*
⊕ *www.anthologysd.com* ☾ *Usually closed Sun. and Mon.* ✛ *1:C3.*

$ ✕**Buon Appetito.** This charmer serves old-world-style cooking in a casual
ITALIAN but somewhat sophisticated environment. Choose a table on the breezy
sidewalk or in a room jammed with art and fellow diners. Baked eggplant *all'amalfitana*, in a mozzarella-topped tomato sauce, is a dream
of a dish (in San Diego, tomato sauce doesn't get better than this). Consider also sea bass in mushroom sauce, hearty seafood cioppino, and
expert osso buco paired with affordable and varied wines. The young
Italian waiters' good humor makes the experience fun. ⊠ *1609 India
St., Little Italy* ☎ *619/238–9880* ✛ *1:C2.*

$$ ✕**Indigo Grill.** Chef-partner Deborah Scott uses inspirations from Mexico
SOUTHWESTERN to Alaska to infuse her contemporary Southwestern cuisine. Indigo Grill
has an interior with natural wood and stone accents, and a broad terrace
whose cool breezes do nothing to moderate the chilies that heat such offer-
ings like a stacked beet salad, pecan-crusted trout, and salmon roasted
on a wooden plank. Creative desserts like the coconut crème brûlée is so
generous in size that it can satisfy two with ease. Increasing competition
in the neighborhood hasn't come near to cooling this hot spot's popular-
ity. ⊠ *1536 India St., Little Italy* ☎ *619/234–6802* ☾ *No lunch.* ✛ *1:C2.*

$ ✕**Karen Krasne's Extraordinary Desserts.** The sleek, newer branch of the
CAFÉ original Karen Krasne's pastry shop near Balboa Park is a few blocks
east of India Street, which is Little Italy's main drag. It's worth a trip
for Paris-perfect cakes, tarts, and pots-de-crème. A converted commer-
cial space that has won architectural awards, this café offers a serene
atmosphere in which to enjoy Krasne's unusual and delicious break-
fasts, lunches, and light dinners. The shop also offers artisanal cheeses,
private-blend teas, and made-on-premises chocolates and ice creams.
The panini sandwiches are creative and filling. ⊠ *1430 Union St., Little
Italy* ☎ *619/294–7001* ⊕ *www.extraordinarydesserts.com* ✛ *1:C2.*

$$ ✕**Po Pazzo.** An eye-catching creation from leading Little Italy restaura-
ITALIAN teurs Joe and Lisa Busalacchi, Po Pazzo earns its name, which means
"a little crazy," by mixing a lively bar with a restaurant serving modern

Italian fare. A steak house with an accent, this stylish eatery offers attractive salads and thick cuts of prime beef, as well as a top-notch presentation of veal chops Sinatra style with mushrooms, tomatoes, and onions; and Sicilian rib-eye steak that defines richness. ⊠ *1917 India St., Little Italy* ☎ *619/238–1917* ✛ *1:C2.*

$ ✗ **Princess Pub & Grille.** Packed to the rafters during any televised Brit-
BRITISH   ish football (soccer) championship, this cheerful neighborhood place is the unofficial headquarters of transplanted Brits, Australians, and New Zealanders. The selection of imported beers and ales, most of them from the United Kingdom, is quite impressive, and the menu complements them well with Anglophile favorites like sausage rolls, fish-and-chips, and spicy chicken curry. The roasted lamb sandwiches also have a loyal following. Breakfast brings eggs with bangers (sausages) and baked beans. The patrons seem equally fond of conversation and darts. ⊠ *1665 India St., Little Italy* ☎ *619/702–3021* ⊕ *www. princesspubandgrille.com* ✛ *1:C2.*

$$ ✗ **Puerto La Boca.** Named for a waterfront neighborhood in Buenos Aires
ARGENTINE   that was home to generations of newly arrived Italian immigrants, this handsome restaurant is at the gateway to an area filling up with trendy boutiques, including a Harley-Davidson showroom. Like the cooking in Buenos Aires, the menu marries the traditional Argentine love of beef—and lots of it—with traditional Italian recipes and techniques, and the results are entirely satisfying. A long list of sizable steaks is crowned by the *parrillada*, a feast of beef cuts, sausage, sweetbreads, and chicken served on a tabletop grill. The sliced tomatoes in a creamy Roquefort sauce open the meal perfectly, and if you don't want beef, try the unusual "Bombonera" pizza with prosciutto, heart of palm, and olives, which shares its name with the B.A. soccer stadium where the Boca Juniors play. ⊠ *2060 India St., Little Italy* ☎ *619/234–4900* ⊕ *www.puertolaboca.com* ✛ *1:C2.*

$$ ✗ **Trattoria Fantastica.** Sicilian flavors abound on the menu, which is high-
ITALIAN   lighted by such offerings as a salmon salad at lunch, osso buco, and the pasta *palermitana*—rigatoni with spicy sausage, olives, capers, and marinara sauce. Many pastas come with cargoes of fresh seafood, and the pizzas baked in the stone oven are robust and beautifully seasoned. Call ahead if you want to score a table in the shady courtyard, and keep this in mind as a snack break for beautiful pastries, remarkable gelato, and freshly brewed Italian coffees. ⊠ *1735 India St., Little Italy* ☎ *619/234–1735* ⊕ *www.trattoriafantastica.com* ✛ *1:C2.*

¢   ✗ **The Waterfront.** Not a destination for children, this historic bar and
AMERICAN   eatery, which opened in the 1930s and claims to be San Diego's oldest watering hole, is an attraction for anyone in search of a local, working-class atmosphere. The bar has supported the elbows of tuna fishermen and aviation workers in earlier eras and now attracts lawyers, construction workers, and other souls hungry for bar food such as a $7.50 bowl of chili, excellent burgers, fish-and-chips, and other great-tasting grub, including fish tacos. The Waterfront serves from early morning until 2 am. ⊠ *2044 Kettner Blvd., Little Italy* ☎ *619/232–9656* ⊕ *www. waterfrontbarandgrill.com* ✛ *1:B1.*

8

AROUND BALBOA PARK

BALBOA PARK

$$$ ✕ **The Prado.** This beautiful restaurant in the historic House of Hospital-
ECLECTIC   ity on Balboa Park's museum row brings an inventive, contemporary
menu to an area where picnic lunches or hot dogs from a nearby cart
are the only other options. The striking Spanish–Moorish interior has
painted ceilings and elaborate glass sculptures, and the bar is a fashion-
able pre- and post-theater destination for light nibbles with Latin, Ital-
ian, and Asian flavors and creative drinks. In the dining room, servers
offer dishes that range from lunchtime grilled mahimahi tacos and a
fancy pressed salad of baby arugula, strawberries, dried figs, and asiago
cheese to saffron-scented lobster paella and roasted sea bass. ⊠ *1549
El Prado, Balboa Park* ☎ *619/557–9441* ✛ *2:F6.*

BANKER'S HILL

$$ ✕ **Ave 5.** American cuisine gets a French twist at this inviting spot serv-
AMERICAN   ing fine seasonal cuisine and cocktails. The trio of Nicolas Carbonne
and brothers Brian and Colin MacLaggan have created a clean-feeling,
brick-walled space with an art gallery feel. Start with filet mignon car-
paccio with capers, aged Parmesan, and white truffle oil, or pickled
beet salad with apples, Stilton, and pancetta. Excellent mains include
pepper-crusted albacore tuna and saffron mussel sauce, and duck
confit with potato croquettes. Weekend brunch and desserts shine as
well; the fromage blanc cheesecake is not to be missed. ⊠ *2760 5th
Ave., Banker's Hill* ☎ *619/542–0394* ⊕ *www.avenue5restaurant.com*
☉ *Closed Mon.* ✛ *2:D6.*

$ ✕ **Bankers Hill.** Chef Carl Schroeder of Market Restaurant + Bar brought
AMERICAN   his creative way with seasonal and local fare to this more affordable
eatery in early 2010. The updated take on a bar and grill features open
beam ceilings, a zinc bar, a cozy patio, and a living wall of succulents.
Expect upscale comfort dishes like house-made potato chips and dip,
crispy BBQ pork tacos, and steak frites paired with eclectic wines and
cocktails. ⊠ *2202 4th Ave., Banker's Hill* ☎ *619/231–0222* ⊕ *www.
bankershillsd.com* ✛ *1:D1.*

$ ✕ **Barrio Star.** The latest effort by chef Isabel Cruz of Isabel's Cantina
MEXICAN   and up-and-coming chef Todd Camburn puts a fresh, distinctive, and
rather refined spin on classic Mexican fare. In this airy space done in
bright colors, feast on grilled sweet corn slathered in spicy lime butter,
a Caesar salad with cilantro and toasted pumpkin seeds, slow-roasted
pork carnitas tacos with house-made tortillas, flourless Mexican chocolate cake, and Latin-inspired cocktails. ⊠ *2706 5th Ave., Banker's Hill*
☎ *619/501–7827* ⊕ *www.barriostar.com* ✛ *2:D6.*

$$$ ✕ **Bertrand at Mister A's.** Restaurateur Bertrand Hug's sumptuous 12th-
FRENCH   floor dining room offers serene decor, contemporary paintings, and
a view that stretches to Mexico, making it perfect for a sunset cock-
tail. Chef Stephane Voitzwinkler creates luxurious seasonal dishes such
as lobster strudel, black truffle macaroni and cheese, and Wagyu rib-
eye steak with béarnaise sauce. The dessert list encompasses a galaxy
of sweets. Service, led by the charming Hug, is expert and attentive.
⊠ *2550 5th Ave., 12th Floor, Banker's Hill* ☎ *619/239–1377* ⊕ *www.*

SUGAR RUSH

In the Gaslamp Quarter, stop for a sweet treat at Ghiradelli Ice Cream and Chocolate Shop at 643 5th Ave., between G St. and Market St.

bertrandatmisteras.com ⚖ *Reservations essential* ☾ *No lunch weekends* ⊹ *2:D6.*

$
ITALIAN
Fodor'sChoice
★

✕**Cucina Urbana.** Proprietor Tracy Borkum transformed the former Laurel into a casual and stylish Cal-Italian spot that's quickly become one of the most popular tables in town. Weathered wood treatments, boho floral tablecloths covered in butcher paper, and creamy vinyl barrel chairs wrapped in burlap signal the sea change. Nothing on the dinner menu is more than $20, and diners can pop into the retail wine room, select a bottle, and drink it with dinner for just a $7 corkage fee. The ricotta gnocchi bathed in brown butter and fried sage are the best yet; fried squash blossoms sing; and polenta boards mixed tableside are creative and satisfying. The best entrées include a pork milanese with artichoke salad, and short-rib pappardelle. Sit at the cozy bar and watch the chefs turn out bubbly, thin-crust pizzas topped with wild mushroom and taleggio cheese or pancetta fried egg and potatoes, or find a spot at the main bar for a clever cocktail crafted from seasonal fruit and Italian liqueurs. ✉ *505 Laurel St., Banker's Hill* ☎ *619/239–2222* ⊕ *www. sdurbankitchen.com* ⚖ *Reservations essential* ⊹ *2:D6.*

$$
JAPANESE

✕**Hane Sushi.** An airy and open room with a fresh Japanese aesthetic is the setting for pristine and contemporary sushi by Roger Nakamura. The chef spent years learning his craft from Yukito Ota of Sushi Ota fame. Sushi purists will be happy with the toro, fresh local uni, golden eye snapper, and other delicacies imported from Japan. Modernists will like the creative rolls. ✉ *2760 5th Ave., Banker's Hill* ☎ *619/260–1411* ☾ *Closed Mon.* ⊹ *2:D6.*

¢
ITALIAN

✕**Pizzicato Pizza.** Everything from the dough for the gourmet pizzas to the salads is made fresh daily at Pizzicato, a concept that originated in Portland. Lunchtime brings panini stuffed with Tuscan meatballs, as well as grilled vegetable salads and lunch specials for under $8. Popular pizzas include the four-cheese with sausage and mushrooms; a Thai-style pizza with shrimp, peanut sauce, and roasted sweet peppers; and the molto carne with prosciutto, pepperoni, and Italian sausage. ✉ *2420 5th Ave., Banker's Hill* ☎ *619/232–9000* ⊕ *www. pizzicatopizza.com* ⊹ *2:D6.*

OLD TOWN AND UPTOWN

Hillcrest and the nearby Uptown district, formed by the neighborhoods of University Heights and North Park, are a mecca for affordable and diverse ethnic dining and entertainment. Most of these spots are independently owned by restaurateurs who are there to make sure their customers are happy. It's an easy walking neighborhood that's open to everyone but is considered the center of San Diego's gay community.

The historic adobe buildings clustered in the center of Old Town is where California first started; it's the first permanent encampment of Spanish settlers. Obviously, it's Mexican food that reigns here, though many of the restaurants that were once independently owned have become very commercial. Still, Old Town offers a few choices for affordable and authentic cuisine.

CLOSE UP

Where to Refuel Around Town

San Diego has a few homegrown chains as well as many stand-alone eateries that will amiably fill you up without demanding too much cash in return.

Burger Lounge (⊕ *www. burgerlounge.com*) specializes in juicy burgers made from grass-fed Tallgrass Beef—besides skipping grain, the cows were also raised without growth hormones or antibiotics. The four locations in Kensington (✉ *4116 Adams Ave.* ☎ *619/584–2929*), Coronado (✉ *922 Orange Ave.* ☎ *619/435–6835*), La Jolla (✉ *1101 Wall St.* ☎ *858/456–0196*), and Little Italy (✉ *1608 India St.* ☎ *619/237–7878*) share a retro-mod orange and white decor and hearty side dishes like onion rings and house-made French fries, sodas, and malts.

A vast and varied homegrown chain specializing in seafood is the **Brigantine** (multiple locations, see ⊕ *www. thebrigantine.com*), which offers a cozy atmosphere and a menu that ranges from fish tacos to fresh oysters, grilled swordfish with avocado butter, and wok-charred ahi tuna in every corner of San Diego County. The happy hours at any of the Brigantine (aka "The Brig" to locals) restaurants are popular for the beer-battered fish tacos for a song.

The Mission, a local minichain open only for breakfast and lunch, has three locations: Mission Beach (✉ *3795 Mission Blvd.* ☎ *858/488–9060*), North Park (✉ *2801 University Ave.* ☎ *619/220–8992*), and the East Village (✉ *1250 J St.* ☎ *619/232–7662*). They all fulfill their mission as a breakfast-and-lunch destination (there's no service after 3 pm) with a menu that runs

the gamut from banana-blackberry pancakes to a Zen breakfast complete with tofu and brown rice, to creative black-bean burritos and a smoked turkey sandwich. Or if you're in the mood for excellent Mexican-style comfort fare, head to **Achiote** (⊕ *www.achioterestaurants. com*) in San Ysidro (✉ *4419 Camino de la Plaza* ☎ *619/690–1494*) and Otay Mesa (✉ *2110 Birch Rd.* ☎ *619/482–0307*)—the omelet with chipotle cream sauce is muy rico. Sushi lovers should head to **Harney Sushi** in Old Town (✉ *3964 Harney St.* ☎ *619/295–3272*) and Oceanside (✉ *301 Mission Ave.* ☎ *760/967–1820* ⊕ *www.harneysushi.com*) for California-style sushi and superfresh fish with a rocking atmosphere that includes DJ booths and a sexy modern Asian design.

If there's something for everyone at the Mission, the statement is equally true of San Diego's enormously popular **Sammy's Wood-fired Pizza** (multiple locations; see ⊕ *www.sammyspizza.com*) chain. With convenient outlets in La Jolla, Mission Valley, and the Gaslamp Quarter, Sammy's makes friends with oversize salads, a vast selection of pizzas, entrées, and pastas, and the fun "messy sundae," which lives up to its name.

Besides chains, keep these streets or neighborhoods in mind for refueling: funky Ocean Beach, famed for its easygoing breakfast places; Little Italy (India Street), with endless Italian options; and Hillcrest in the vicinity of the 5th Avenue–University Avenue intersection, a buffet of international cuisines. If you want Asian, Convoy Street is the place to go.

8

To the east of Balboa Park is the shopper's paradise of Mission Valley, where big-box restaurants cater to refueling shoppers on their way to or from one of the area's massive malls—Fashion Valley and Mission Valley Center—which are just blocks apart. Mission Valley also includes the Hotel Circle area of San Diego, which includes plenty of tourist and business hotels, and a large golf course that can be seen from Interstate 8, the east-west freeway that feeds into Mission Valley. The area isn't known for groundbreaking cuisine, but it has lots of satisfying casual and fast-casual spots.

HILLCREST

$
INDIAN

✗**Bombay Exotic Cuisine of India.** Notable for its elegant dining room with a waterfall, Bombay employs a chef whose generous hand with raw and cooked vegetables gives each course a colorful freshness reminiscent of California cuisine, though the flavors definitely hail from India. Try the tandoori lettuce-wrap appetizer and any of the stuffed *kulchas* (a stuffed flatbread). The unusually large selection of curries may be ordered with meat, chicken, fish, or tofu. The curious should try the *dizzy noo shak*, a sweet and spicy banana curry. Try the family-style tasting menu, which includes appetizer, tasting portions of four entrées, naan, and mango mousse dessert for $29 per person. ✉ *Hillcrest Center, 3960 5th Ave., Suite 100, Hillcrest* ☎ *619/297–7777* ⊕ *www.bombayrestaurant.com* ✛ *2:D4.*

¢
CAFÉ
Fodor'sChoice
★

✗**Bread & Cie.** There's a brisk East Coast air to this artsy urban bakery and café known for being one of San Diego's first and best artisanal bread bakers. Owner Charles Kaufman is a former New Yorker and filmmaker, who gave Bread & Cie a sense of theater by putting bread ovens imported from France on center stage. The mix served from daybreak to sunset includes warm focaccia covered in cheese and vegetables, crusty loaves of black olive bread, gourmet granola with Mediterranean yogurt, bear claws, and first-rate cinnamon rolls. Lunch on house-made quiche; panini filled with pastrami, turkey, and pesto; or Brie and honey, washed down with tea, coffee, upscale soft drinks, beer, or wine. ✉ *350 University Ave., Hillcrest* ☎ *619/683–9322* ✛ *2:D4.*

$
AMERICAN

✗**Hash House A Go Go.** Expect to wait an hour or more for weekend breakfast at this splashy Hillcrest eatery, whose walls display photos of farm machinery and other icons of Middle America but whose menu takes a Southern-accented look at national favorites. The nearly grotesquely supersize portions are the main draw here; at breakfast, huge platters carpeted with fluffy pancakes sail out of the kitchen, while at noon customers favor the overflowing chicken pot pies crowned with flaky pastry. The parade of old-fashioned good eats continues at dinner with hearty meat and seafood dishes, including the grand sage-flavored fried chicken, bacon-studded waffles, and meatloaf stuffed with roasted red pepper, spinach, and mozzarella with a side of mashed potatoes. ✉ *3628 5th Ave., Hillcrest* ☎ *619/298–4646* ⊕ *www.hashhouseagogo.com* ✛ *2:C2.*

$
MOROCCAN

✗**Kous Kous Moroccan Bistro.** Settle into the low-cushioned seating and let the sensual atmosphere of the room draped in imported fabrics with Moroccan lanterns transport you to somewhere far away for the evening. Moroccan-style couscous makes a tasty bed for a variety of dishes by chef Moumen Nouri including tagines with chicken, merguez sausage, or vegetables, grilled skewers loaded with meat and salads like *khizzou* of roasted carrots with ginger. The food is flavorful without being spicy; the strawberries with orange flower water are a delicious way to end the meal. ⊠ *3940 4th Ave., Hillcrest* ☎ *619/295–5560* ⊕ *www.kouskousrestaurant.com* ☉ *No lunch.* ✛ *2:D4.*

$ ✕ **Ortega's Bistro.** Californians have long flocked to Puerto Nuevo, the
MEXICAN "lobster village" south of San Diego in Baja California. When a member
☾ of the family that operates several Puerto Nuevo restaurants opened
Fodor'sChoice Ortega's, it became an instant sensation, since it brought no-nonsense,
★ authentic Mexican fare straight to the heart of Hillcrest. The specialty of choice is a whole lobster prepared Baja-style and served with superb beans, rice, and made-to-order tortillas, but there are other fine options, including melt-in-the-mouth carnitas (slow-cooked pork), made-at-the-table guacamole, and grilled tacos filled with *huitlacoche* corn mushrooms and Mexican herbs. The pomegranate margaritas are a must, as is the special red salsa if you like authentic spice. ⊠ *141 University Ave., Hillcrest* ☎ *619/692–4200* ⊕ *www.ortegasbistro.com* ✛ *2:D4.*

$ ✕ **Pizzeria Arrivederci.** The superhot oven in this restaurant run by a
ITALIAN native of Sorrento adds an authentic toasty flavor to pizzas topped
☾ with forest mushrooms and smoky *scamorza* cheese, or perhaps *alla messicana,* a Mexican-style pie whose topping includes pork sausage, cilantro, and crushed red peppers. The list of imaginative pizzas is long (yes, you can get a pepperoni pizza, too), but there are also expertly made pastas such as penne in creamy vodka sauce with smoked salmon, and penne in pungent puttanesca sauce. Start with a well-priced glass or bottle of wine and a plate of roasted peppers with anchovies or the shrimp and white-bean salad with arugula. The young waiters from Italy treat guests well. ⊠ *3789 4th Ave., Hillcrest* ☎ *619/542–0293* ⊕ *www.arrivederciristorante.com* ✛ *2:D4.*

¢ ✕ **Saffron Noodles and Saté.** Comfortable outdoor tables on a narrow
THAI sidewalk and inexpensive prices make this and the neighboring Saffron Thai Grilled Chicken takeout worth a short detour from Old Town. The simple menu has spicy and mild noodle soups; stir-fried noodles with chicken, beef, pork, or shrimp; and a couple of uncommon Vietnamese and Thai-Indian noodle dishes bathed with aromatic sauces. Go next door for the namesake grilled half chicken served with jasmine rice, tart-sweet cucumber salad, and savory house-made peanut sauce. The room has a minimalist look but is sunny and comfortable. ⊠ *3737 India St., Hillcrest* ☎ *619/574–7737* ⊕ *www.saffronsandiego.com* ✛ *2:B5.*

$$ ✕ **Sambuca Italian Bistro.** This cozy, candlelit restaurant, with reason-
ITALIAN able prices and a well-prepared menu, differs more than a bit from the competition. Dishes marked "signature" are particularly noteworthy, like the Sambuca shrimp appetizer with a lime-garlic sauce. Creamy cheese sauce makes the four-cheese penne pasta with lobster an extravagant treat, while there's delicious subtlety to the roasted chicken with brandied Gorgonzola sauce. There are daily specials on weekdays. ⊠ *3888 4th Ave., Hillcrest* ☎ *619/298–8700* ⊕ *www. sambucabistro.com* ✛ *2:D4.*

8

Pepper-crusted tuna is a popular dish at Ave 5 in Banker's Hill.

MISSION VALLEY

$ ✕ **King's Fish House.** This warehouse-size restaurant is wildly popular
SEAFOOD with shoppers at Mission Valley's many malls, owing to extremely
friendly and efficient service, tanks filled with lively lobsters, and a
daily-changing menu with a fine selection of freshly shucked oysters.
Specialties include New Orleans–style barbecued shrimp and a full-size
New England clambake complete with red potatoes and sweet corn
on the cob. Seasonal fish and shellfish are char-grilled, deep-fried, sautéed, steamed, and skewered, and the menu obliges meat eaters with
a convincing cheeseburger, roasted chicken, and grilled sirloin. When
jammed, the scene recalls a train station—and sounds like one, too.
✉ *825 Camino de la Reina N, Mission Valley* ☎ *619/574–1230* ⊕ *www.
kingsfishhouse.com* ✥ *2:E2.*

¢ ✕ **Mr. Peabody's Burgers & Ale.** Burgers and beer are an unbeatable com-
AMERICAN bination anywhere, but especially within a stone's throw of the pricey
Fashion Valley mall. Friendly and informal, this bustling eatery is fine
for kids during lunch, but perhaps not after that. The attractions range
from the domestic, microbrew, and imported beers and juicy half-pound
burgers to a variety of tacos, like the ones with seasoned ground turkey
and a satisfying, gently priced rib-eye steak. Order a basket of excellent
fries or onion rings for the table, but not both, because the portions
are beyond huge. ✉ *6110 Friars Rd., Mission Valley* ☎ *619/542–1786*
⊕ *www.mrpeabodys.net* ✍ *Reservations not accepted* ✥ *2:B2.*

$ ✕ **Ricky's Restaurant.** Chain feeders haven't driven out all of San Diego's
AMERICAN old-line family restaurants, and this unpretentious place on the quiet
☾ fringe of Mission Valley remains dear to the city's heart after 44 years.
A traditional three-meals-daily restaurant, Ricky's serves big portions

of unassuming, well-prepared, all-American cooking, like steak with all the trimmings for $16, but is famed for its breakfasts, when savory corned-beef hash and fluffy strawberry Dutch baby and oven-baked omelets are the rule. The spectacular apple pancake, a souf-flélike creation that takes 20 minutes to bake, arrives burning hot and is irresistible to the last molecule of molten cinnamon sugar. Ricky's popularity never wanes. ⊠ *2181 Hotel Circle S, Mission Valley* ☎ *619/291–4498* ✛ *2:B3.*

$ ✕**The Zodiac.** Men like to lunch at
AMERICAN this elegant room in the luxurious Neiman Marcus department store as much as the ladies, who enjoy cool chardonnay and the restaurant's complimentary chicken consommé and hot popovers with strawberry butter. Salads abound, but there's serious competition from the dressy lobster club sandwich, sea scallops, and Gorgonzola-crusted filet mignon. The desserts are as self-indulgent as some of the well-heeled patrons, and this is by far the best place to dine in Fashion Valley, which is universally regarded as San Diego's leading shopping center. ⊠ *Neiman Marcus, Fashion Valley, 7027 Friars Rd., Mission Valley* ☎ *619/542–4450* ⊗ *Closed Sun. No dinner* ✛ *2:C2.*

> ## SAN DIEGO'S BOUNTY
>
> Sunny San Diego is one of the premier agricultural areas in the country. Visit a farmers' market and have a taste: spring is the season for cherimoyas and strawberries, summer brings peaches and boysenberries, autumn is the time for apples and pears, and winter is abundant with tangerines and grapefruit. There's a different market every day of the week; check the list of farmers' markets around the county at ⊕ *www.sdfarmbureau.org.*

NORMAL HEIGHTS

¢ ✕**Blind Lady Ale House.** The stars here are the artisanal and craft beers on
AMERICAN tap; chef Aaron LaMonica creates a beer-friendly menu of seasonal and casual fare including pizzas, burgers, and salads. The room is warm and informal with lots of natural wood treatments and natural light flooding in the large front windows. Service is casual, too: diners order at the counter and then find a seat. ⊠ *3416 Adams Ave., Normal Heights* ☎ *619/255–2491* ⊕ *www.blindladyalehouse.com* ⚑ *Reservations not accepted* ⊗ *Closed Mon. No lunch on weekdays.* ✛ *2:H2.*

¢ ✕**Viva Pops.** Frozen treats are elevated to an art form at this funky and
ECLECTIC colorful shop in the Adams Avenue corridor where owner Lisa Altmann creates popsicles from organic seasonal fruits. The nectarine-basil and strawberry pops shine in summer; cool weather brings flavors like pomegranate, pineapple chili, blood orange, and creamy passion fruit, while Mexican chocolate and lavender-lemonade are available year-round. Be sure to bring cash, as they don't accept credit cards. ⊠ *3330 Adams Ave., Normal Heights* ☎ *619/795–1080* ⊕ *www.ilovevivapops.com* ⊟ *No credit cards* ⊗ *Closed Mon.* ✛ *2:H2.*

NORTH PARK

$$ ✕**The Linkery.** The menu at this earthy farm-to-table-style restau-
AMERICAN rant reads like a Who's Who of seasonal produce and the area's top organic farms. House-made sausages such as chicken-mushroom and

8

kaisekreiner (spicy Vienna-style pork sausage with cheese) and smoky poblano pork lend the casual restaurant its name, but there's lots of vegetarian fare, too, including a vegan roast with eggplant and squash, and lasagna stuffed with garden vegetables. Entrées include black cod with house-pickled ginger and haricots verts, and a ranch-style ham-and-egg sandwich. They also house-cure country ham, Italian coppa, and lardo, and they fire up the grill for Sunday cookouts. The well-chosen wine and beer list

> ### OLD VINES
>
> Napa and Sonoma counties in Northern California might get all the publicity when it comes to wine, but California viticulture got its start in San Diego—Old Town to be exact. There are no vines there anymore, but the San Diego Wine & Culinary Center (⊠ *200 Harbor Dr.* ☎ *619/231–6400*) pours wines from all of the best vintners in the region.

includes cask-conditioned ales and even mead. ⊠ *3794 30th St., North Park* ☎ *619/255–8778* ⊕ *www.thelinkery.com* ✛ *2:G4.*

¢ | MIDDLE EASTERN
✕ **Mama's Bakery & Lebanese Deli.** This little house converted into a restaurant serves some of the best authentic Lebanese fare in San Diego County. The key is the *saji*, a superheated oven that's used to cook a flatbread by the same name. The warm herb bread might be wrapped around garlicky marinated chicken, hummus, and vegetables, or made into the Manakeesh Ultimate, a combination of yogurt cheese, herbs, tomatoes, olives, and fresh mint. Try the hearty seasoned ground beef *kafta* plate that includes house-made hummus, basmati rice, green salad, and pita bread. For dessert, don't resist the buttery baklava filled with cashews or pistachio nuts. ⊠ *4237 Alabama St., North Park* ☎ *619/688–0717* ✛ *2:F3.*

¢ | PIZZA
✕ **URBN Coal Fired Pizza.** A few blocks east of 30th Street (North Park's restaurant row), a 5,000-square-foot warehouse is home to this chic and casual pizza spot. Hip young locals chow down on coal-fired New Haven–style pies, fresh salads, and cheese boards. Try the carbalicious mashed potato pizza pie topped with pancetta, fresh mozzarella, and Parmesan. Linger with a local brew or a craft cocktail off the extensive drink list. ⊠ *3085 University Ave., North Park* ☎ *619/255–7300* ✛ *2:H5.*

OLD TOWN

$ | SEAFOOD
✕ **Blue Water Seafood Market & Grill.** Take one bite of the fresh, perfectly grilled fish at this seafood spot and you'll forget about the no-frills decor. Placing an order at the counter is a three-step process. First, choose the type of fish (mahimahi, swordfish, and seared ahi are popular). Next, tell them how to season it (lemon butter, garlic butter, teriyaki, or chipotle). Finally, decide whether you'd like it served as a sandwich, over salad, or on a plate with rice. Be sure to confirm prices prior to ordering, as they fluctuate according to market availability. ⊠ *3367 India St., Old Town* ☎ *619/497–0914* ⊕ *www.bluewater. sandiegan.com* ✛ *2:B5.*

$$$ | MEXICAN
✕ **El Agave.** A Mexico City native brings authentic regional Mexican fare to an otherwise touristy area. Be sure to try quesadillas filled with mushrooms and manchego cheese; grilled shrimp bathed in

bright, smoky guajillo chili sauce; and chicken in a slow-simmered mole sauce. Try one of the more than 2,000 tequilas, which make El Agave the largest "tequileria" in the United States. The collection includes artisanal tequilas dating to the 1930s and some infused with jalapeño chilies. ⊠ *2304 San Diego Ave., Old Town* ☎ *619/220–0692* ⊕ *www.elagave.com* ⟡ *2:A4.*

$$ ✗ **Harney Sushi.** People in the know come here for super-fresh California-
JAPANESE style sushi and modern Asian cuisine served up in a sexy atmosphere with a live DJ spinning popular music and R&B favorites. The restaurant is decorated in high-end modern Asian art and moody lighting; there's also a heated outdoor patio. Inventive sushi rolls include the Rolls Royce with lobster tempura and the Afterburner with yellowtail and spicy crab in ponzu sauce. Chef Anthony Sinsay adds a molecular flair to dishes like the cold-smoked hamachi, miso-glazed pork belly with ginger "air," and the liquid-center chocolate gyoza with apricot foam. ⊠ *3964 Harney St., Old Town* ☎ *619/295–3272* ⊕ *www. harneysushi.com* ☽ *No lunch on weekends.* ⟡ *2:A4.*

¢ ✗ **Lucha Libre.** On any given weekday at lunch, you're sure to see a line of
MEXICAN locals from nearby offices waiting for their favorite Lucha Libre picks. The lines don't lie the food here is worth the wait. Named for a form of Mexican wrestling that often involves brightly colored masks, the restaurant's hot-pink walls and shiny booths create a fun and family-friendly atmosphere. There is an array of gourmet tacos and burritos on the menu; the Surfin' California burrito packed with grilled steak, shrimp, french fries, avocado, and chipotle sauce is a favorite. There are also many meatless options. ⊠ *1810 W. Washington St., Old Town* ☎ *619/296–8226* ⊕ *www.tacosmackdown.com* ⟡ *2:B5.*

$ ✗ **Starlite.** Starlite attracts a diverse and discerning crowd to a some-
AMERICAN what quiet stretch of India Street with its solid seasonal fare and understated midcentury vibe that's won design awards. Chef Marguerite Grifka covers the gamut of tony comfort food from Belgian-style fries and marinated olives to organic macaroni and cheese, juicy roasted chicken, and a fish of the day paired with mushrooms and bitter greens. Cocktails are just as creative and seasonal as the cuisine; in hot weather the Starlite Mule in a copper cup is the perfect way to cool off. ⊠ *3175 India St., Old Town* ☎ *619/358–9766* ⊕ *www. starlitesandiego.com* ⟡ *2:C6.*

UNIVERSITY HEIGHTS

¢ ✗ **El Zarape.** There's a humble air to this cozy Mexican taquería, but
MEXICAN one bite of the signature scallop tacos and you'll realize something special is happening in the kitchen. Inside the satiny corn tortilla, seared bay scallops mingle with tangy white sauce and shredded cheese. Or perhaps you'll prefer sweet pieces of lobster meat in oversize quesadillas; burritos filled with chiles rellenos; or the original beef, ham, and pineapple Aloha burrito. No matter, nearly everything is fantastic at this busy under-the-radar eatery that's part of a developing independent restaurant row in University Heights. Mexican beverages, including the sweet-tart hibiscus-flower drink *jamaica* and the cinnamon rice drink *horchata*, and house-made flan and rice pudding round out the menu. ⊠ *4642 Park Blvd., University Heights* ☎ *619/692–1652* ⟡ *2:F3.*

8

$ ✕ **Farm House Cafe.** Chef Olivier Biouteau and his wife, Rochelle, are
FRENCH living their dream of owning a French country restaurant. Escargot
risotto; salmon with roasted fingerling potatoes, chorizo, and flageo-
let beans; flat-iron steak frites; and even a perfect burger paired with
affordable wines are among the delights that await. It's a cozy room,
so call ahead; regulars like to fill the seats at the bar. Be sure to save
room for house-made desserts such as the apple tartelette with honey ice
cream, a changing pot de crème with Scottish shortbread, or Olivier's
chocolate truffles. ✉ *2121 Adams Ave., University Heights* ☎ *619/269–
9662* ⊕ *www.farmhousecafesd.com* ✛ *2:F3.*

MISSION BAY, BEACHES, AND SEAWORLD

This sprawling area, which includes Pacific Beach, is all about great
views of the water, sandy beaches, and relaxation. Most of the restaurants here are casual spots that diners can visit in T-shirts and board
shorts or little sundresses and flip-flops. Food available here is similarly
laid-back. Burgers and tacos are easy to find, but so are sushi, Mexican,
and Thai food. Many of the restaurants here are bars at heart that serve
food and quickly transform around 9 pm, but several venues including
JRDN, Isabel's Cantina, and Gringo's serve food that's notable.

MISSION BAY

$$ ✕ **Red Marlin.** A multimillion-dollar renovation of the Hyatt Regency
SEAFOOD Mission Bay has turned a historic restaurant—with soaring ceilings
and 120-degree views of Mission Bay—into a bright and modern space
specializing in seafood. Start with a pot of clams steamed with bacon
and garlic, a blue crab cake with preserved lemon and a salad, then
move on to seared sea scallops with pumpkin risotto or a grilled filet
mignon. The Taste of Red Marlin three-course menu is $35 ($50 with
wine pairings) and changes weekly. ✉ *1441 Quivira Rd., Mission Bay*
☎ *619/221–4868* ✛ *3:C6.*

PACIFIC BEACH

$ ✕ **Andrés Restaurant.** For more than two decades, Andrés was San
CARIBBEAN Diego's sole outpost for solid, savory Cuban and Puerto Rican cui-
sine. In a nondescript building in the Morena Boulevard home-fur-
nishings district near Pacific Beach, Andrés is not much to look at, but
the enclosed-patio dining room is comfortable, and servers smile as
they place heaped-high plates of breaded steak, roast pork, and grilled
marinated fish in front of impressed diners. For Cuban home cook-
ing at its best, order the *picadillo*, a ground-beef hash with bold and
piquant flavors and avoid the often-overcooked pollo asado. Like all
entrées, they're accompanied by oceans of delicious black beans and
mountains of rice. Nothing ever changes here, which is how the regulars
like it. ✉ *1235 Morena Blvd., Pacific Beach* ☎ *619/275–4114* ⊕ *www.
andresrestaurantsd.com* ✛ *3:E6.*

$$ ✕ **Caffe Bella Italia.** Contemporary northern Italian cooking as prepared
ITALIAN in Italy is the rule at this simple dinner-only restaurant near one of the
main intersections in Pacific Beach. The menu presents Neapolitan-style
macaroni with sausage and artichoke hearts in spicy tomato sauce, pizzas baked in a wood-fired oven, linguine with clams, mussels, white fish,

and salmon, plus formal entrées like chicken breast sautéed with Marsala wine and mushrooms, and slices of rare filet mignon tossed with herbs and topped with arugula and Parmesan shavings. Impressive daily specials include beet-stuffed ravioli in creamy saffron sauce. ⊠ *1525 Garnet Ave., Pacific Beach* ☎ *858/273–1224* ⊕ *www.caffebellaitalia. com* ◑ *No lunch* ✠ *3:C4.*

$$ ✗ **Gringo's Cantina.** About a stone's throw from the ocean in the heart of
MEXICAN lively Pacific Beach, this sizable restaurant often seems to be having a party. A good variety of margaritas and fine tequilas helps fuel the atmosphere, but so does a menu cleverly divided between Mexican casual fare like quesadillas, enchiladas, burritos, and fajitas, and authentic regional specialties from the Mexican heartland. The latter includes dishes like *chile Colorado* (beef stew with New Mexico chilies) and *cochinita pibil* (roasted pork spiced with pickled onions). The dressed-up *queso fundido*, which is melted Oaxacan cheese with crumbled chorizo sausage, makes a great shared starter. ⊠ *4474 Mission Blvd., Pacific Beach* ☎ *858/490–2877* ⊕ *www.gringoscantina.com* ✠ *3:B5.*

$ ✗ **Isabel's Cantina.** A funky mix of Asian and Latin fare mingles on the
ECLECTIC inventive menu at this popular beachy restaurant created by chef and cookbook author Isabel Cruz. A huge teak Buddha reposes coolly in one corner, playing yin to the yang of spicy Latin-inspired fare. The day starts early with coconut French toast, soy-chorizo scramble with black beans, and healthy egg-white dishes. Lunch and dinner dishes include crispy wontons with ahi tuna, steak and chicken lettuce wraps, fragrant Buddha bowls of soba noodles and vegetables in coconut and lemongrass broth, spicy roasted dragon chicken, and grilled salmon with house-made salsas. Save room for the house-made desserts including sautéed bananas and decadent flourless chocolate cake. Chef's table dinners offer a chance to learn about Cruz's approach to cuisine while having a unique dining experience in the kitchen. ⊠ *966 Felspar St., Pacific Beach* ☎ *858/272–8400* ⊕ *www.isabelscantina.com* ✠ *3:C5.*

$$ ✗ **JRDN.** With some 300 seats, this ocean-facing restaurant, pro-
AMERICAN nounced Jordan, in the beach-chic boutique-style Tower23 Hotel might seem overwhelming, but the seating is divided between a long, narrow outdoor terrace and a series of relatively intimate indoor rooms. Chef David Warner presents modern steakhouse fare including chops and steaks with sauces of the diner's choosing, lightened with lots of seasonal produce and a raw bar menu. Weekend brunch and lunch have a similar appeal, with dishes like blue-crab eggs Benedict with citrus hollandaise, eggplant panino, or a salad of smoked tri-tip over spinach and fingerling potatoes. On Friday and Saturday the bar is the place to see and be seen in Pacific Beach for under-30 types, and it's jammed after 9 pm. Just note that the hotel serves breakfast only to guests during the week. ⊠ *723 Felspar St., Pacific Beach* ☎ *858/270–5736* ✠ *3:B5.*

$ ✗ **Lanna.** This small, attractive Thai restaurant loads its tables with
THAI lush fresh flowers. On the eastern edge of Pacific Beach, Lanna serves a number of house specialties that are not found elsewhere, such as "talay Thai," a batter-fried fish fillet topped with a green-apple salad, onions, and cashews; spice-braised duck in a deep, dark, wonderfully

8

fragrant red curry sauce; and "Spicilicious Seafood," a mix of shrimp, squid, mussels, and scallops stir-fried in a chili-garlic sauce. The kitchen demonstrates considerable talent, and servers are prompt and gracious. ✉ *4501 Mission Bay Dr., Pacific Beach* ☎ *858/274–8424* ⊕ *www. lannathaicuisine.com* ✛ *3:D4.*

$$ **✕ Sushi Ota.** Wedged into a minimall between a convenience store and
JAPANESE a looming medical building, Sushi Ota initially seems less than auspicious. Still, San Diego–bound Japanese businesspeople frequently call for reservations before boarding their trans-Pacific flights. Look closely at the expressions on customers' faces as they stream in and out of the doors, and you can see the eager anticipation and satisfied glows that are products of San Diego's best sushi. Besides the usual California roll and tuna and shrimp sushi, sample the specialties that change daily such as sea urchin or surf clam sushi, and the soft-shell crab roll or the *omakase* tasting menu. Sushi Ota offers the cooked as well as the raw. There's additional parking behind the mall. It's hard not to notice that Japanese speakers get the best spots, and servers can be abrupt. ✉ *4529 Mission Bay Dr., Pacific Beach* ☎ *858/270–5670* ⊕ *www.sushiotamenu. info* ⚑ *Reservations essential* ☽ *No lunch Sat.–Mon.* ✛ *3:D4.*

LA JOLLA

Some of the area's top gems in the culinary sense are found in La Jolla. The best create fine Californian, Italian, Asian, and French cuisine that showcases San Diego's abundant local produce and seafood. The enclave is also packed with fun spots that attract lots of tourists year-round but there are many neighborhood favorites on the side streets that offer good food and inviting decor. The ocean-view restaurants along Prospect Street are very popular, so it's important to plan ahead if you want to secure a table.

$$$ **✕ A. R. Valentien.** Known for his insistence on in-season, fresh-today
AMERICAN produce and seafood, chef Jeff Jackson writes menus daily for this cozy
Fodor's Choice room in the luxurious, Craftsman-style Lodge at Torrey Pines. His take
★ on food combinations is simultaneously simple and inventive, like appetizers of smoked trout with potatoes and turnips, and porcini mushroom and chestnut soup with bacon and apple. A three-course tasting menu explores the day's market through the eyes of a talented chef. At lunch on the outdoor terrace, consider the off-menu "Drugstore" hamburger, a minispectacle on a great big bun. ✉ *11480 N. Torrey Pines Rd., La Jolla* ☎ *858/777–6635* ⊕ *www.lodgeattorreypines.com* ✛ *3:B1.*

$$ **✕ Barbarella.** With the sunny patio brightened by year-round blooms
ITALIAN and the menu of casual Cal-Italian fare, it's not hard to see why Barbarella attracts many visitors to La Jolla Shores area. For locals, the other part of the charm is owner Barbara Beltaire, who works the room joking with regulars and even swiping a french fry or two. The warm, woodsy room is accented with original work by local artists and a mosaic-tile pizza oven decorated by Niki de Saint Phalle. The seasonal menu ranges from crispy wild-mushroom pizzas, mussels, and zucchini fritti in a silver cup to oversize burgers topped with marinated red onions and blue cheese, and a whole stone-roasted fish

Talking Tacos

Even though terms like taco, burrito, enchilada, and tostada are as common as macaroni and cheese to San Diegans, don't count on any residents to agree on where to find the best ones. That's because tacos are as individual as spaghetti sauce and come in endless variations from small, authentic Mexico City-style tacos to Cal-Mex versions in crunchy shells topped with cheddar cheese.

The most traditional style of taco features a small soft corn tortilla pressed from corn masa dough and filled with shredded beef, carne asada (roasted beef), braised tongue in green sauce, spicy marinated pork, or deep-fried fish or seafood. Tortillas made from white flour are out there, too, but they're not nearly as tasty.

Garnishes usually include a drizzle of salsa and a squeeze of tart Mexican lime (a small citrus similar to the Key lime that's juicier than the large lime commonly found in the United States), along with chopped cilantro and onion. Whole radishes topped with lime juice and a sprinkle of salt are served on the side.

Mama Testa's (✉ *1417 University Ave., Suite A, Hillcrest* ☎ *619/298–8226* ⊕ *www.mamatesta.com* ✛ *2:E4*) shows the diversity of regional Mexican tacos with ones that are fried, steamed, and grilled. The salsa bar, which offers at least eight different selections including a spicy peanut salsa, is unparalleled. The restaurant's name (a suggestive double entendre in Spanish) and the colorful decor inspired by Mexican *lucha libre* wrestling and *loteria* are all part of the fun.

If you can't make it across the border, check out **Tacos El Gordo**, a well-known Tijuana taco franchise that has branches in Chula Vista (✉ *689 H St.* ☎ *619/691–8848*), Imperial Beach (✉ *3265 Palm Ave.* ☎ *619/424–7427*), and National City (✉ *1940 Highland Ave.* ☎ *619/474–5033*). Carne asada and seasoned pork adobada tacos on small freshly made tortillas are popular, but El Gordo also offers more exotic fillings like *sesos* (brain) or *tripa* (intestines). Look for their distinctive red-and-white sign, since there are imitators.

Most casual San Diego restaurants offer some version of the fish taco, either with batter-fried white fish or grilled fish topped with a mayonnaise-based tangy white sauce, shredded cabbage, lime, and salsa. A combination plate almost always includes seasoned rice and beans, either soupy or refried beans that are smooth and creamy thanks to the addition of lots of fat. Both syles of beans are crowned with melted shredded cheese and usually support a small raft of shredded lettuce dabbed with a bit of sour cream. Any empty spaces (you shouldn't see more of the plate than the rim) will be hidden by the preferred combination of tacos, enchiladas, chiles rellenos, and burritos.

What are those? Enchiladas can be filled with cheese, chicken, or beef and topped with savory, mostly mild red or green chili sauce. Chiles rellenos are mild, deep-fried peppers stuffed with cheese and then baked in tomato and chili sauce. Burritos are flour tortillas filled with beans, rice, and shredded meat.

8

of the day. Barbarella is packed on weekends, so reservations are a must. ☒ *2171 Ave. de la Playa, La Jolla* ☎ *858/454–7373* ⊕ *www. barbarellarestaurant.com* ✛ *3:B2.*

$ ✗**Barolo.** This cozy, candlelit restaurant in the Golden Triangle's Renais-
ITALIAN sance Towne Center boasts specialties like veal scallops with pesto, and goat-cheese-and-pear-stuffed ravioli. The mixed-greens salad with shrimp and avocado nicely kicks off a meal that may go on simply to a mushroom and ham pizza, homemade gnocchi, chicken Marsala, or grilled salmon. Ask for a banquette table and enjoy the suave, eager-to-please service. ☒ *8935 Towne Center Dr., La Jolla* ☎ *858/622–1202* ⊕ *www.barolos.com* ☽ *No lunch weekends* ✛ *3:E1.*

$$$ ✗**Cafe Japengo.** Framed by marbled walls and accented with bamboo
ASIAN trees and unusual black-iron sculptures, this Pacific Rim restaurant serves Asian-inspired cuisine with many North and South American touches. The seared ahi napoleon and the char siu duck salad are guaranteed to wake up your taste buds. There's also a selection of grilled, wood-roasted, and wok-fried entrées; try the braised short ribs with risotto or the sake-marinated prawns. The sushi is always fresh, and many regard it as the liveliest sushi bar in town. Service can be slow, but the pace in the bar, crowded with young locals on the make, is fast and energetic. If you savor quiet, avoid weekend evenings. ☒ *Aventine Center, 8960 University Center La., La Jolla* ☎ *858/450–3355* ⊕ *www. cafejapengo.com* ☽ *No lunch weekends* ✛ *3:D1.*

$ ✗**El Pescador.** This low-key fish market and café in the heart of La
SEAFOOD Jolla village is popular with locals for its simply prepared fresh fish. Try a fillet—maybe halibut, mahimahi, salmon, or tuna—lightly grilled and piled on a soft torta roll with shredded lettuce, tomato, and onions. Other choices include ceviche, sashimi plates, Dungeness crab salad, sautéed mussels with sourdough bread, and excellent fish tacos. Seats are few, and tables often end up being shared, but the food is worth the wait. ☒ *627 Pearl St., La Jolla* ☎ *858/456–2526* ⊕ *www. elpescadorfishmarket.com* ✛ *3:A2.*

$ ✗**Elijah's.** This large, somewhat sterile-looking, brightly lighted deli-
AMERICAN catessen serving New York–style Jewish, Russian, and even some Mexican fare such as breakfast burritos is in the La Jolla village area near I–5. Prominent are towering sandwiches, blintzes, smoked fish plates, and specialties like "mish-mosh" soup, which combines noodles, matzo balls, and shredded crepes in a big bowl of steaming chicken broth. Count on hearty breakfasts, reliable chopped liver, and dinners like chicken-in-the-pot and savory beef brisket. The restaurant makes impressive Reuben sandwiches, a combination of corned beef or pastrami, sauerkraut, Swiss cheese, and Thousand Island dressing on rye bread. Service is quick and friendly. One of San Diego's best art-movie theaters is 50 feet away. ☒ *8861 Villa La Jolla Dr., La Jolla* ☎ *858/455–1462* ⊕ *www.elijahsrestaurant.com* ✛ *3:D1.*

$$$$ ✗**George's at the Cove.** An extensive makeover brought an updated look
AMERICAN to this eternally popular restaurant overlooking La Jolla Cove. Hol-
Fodor'sChoice lywood types and other visiting celebrities can be spotted in George's
★ California Modern, the sleek main dining room with its wall of windows. Simpler, more casual preparations of fresh seafood, beef, and

JRDN (pronounced Jordan) in the Tower23 Hotel is a great spot for a sunset dinner.

lamb reign on the new menu that chef Trey Foshee enlivened with seasonal produce from local specialty growers. Give special consideration to succulent roasted chicken with escarole, local swordfish with prosciutto-wrapped gnocchi, and cider-glazed Niman Ranch pork chops. For more informal dining and a sweeping view of the coast, try the rooftop Ocean Terrace. ✉ *1250 Prospect St., La Jolla* ☎ *858/454-4244* ⊕ *www.georgesatthecove.com* ⌘ *Reservations essential* ✛ *3:A2.*

¢

AMERICAN

✗ **JK Burgers & Hot Dogs.** Fans of good messy burgers and hot dogs head here when they get a craving for this filling and affordable fare. Ownership change brings a new decor featuring paintings and photos by San Diego artists and photographers. But the new owners are still serving Chicago-style Vienna-brand beef hot dogs dressed in mustard, onion, relish, chopped tomatoes, tiny hot peppers, celery salt, and dill pickles—but never ketchup. New menu additions include salads, fish-and-chips, and turkey burgers along with juicy Italian beef sandwiches, chili cheeseburgers, and barbecued ribs. ✉ *8935 Towne Center Dr., La Jolla* ☎ *858/622-0222* ✛ *3:E1.*

$$$$

FRENCH

✗ **Marine Room.** Gaze at the ocean from this venerable La Jolla Shores mainstay and, if it's during an especially high tide, feel the waves race across the sand and beat against the glass. Long-running chef Bernard Guillas takes a bold approach to combining ingredients. Creative seasonal menus score with "trilogy" plates that combine three meats, sometimes including game, in distinct preparations. Exotic ingredients show up in a variety of dishes, including Bengali cashew-spiced prawns, sesame-peppered ahi tuna, and a rack of lamb with violet mustard. ✉ *2000 Spindrift Dr., La Jolla* ☎ *866/644-2351* ⊕ *www.marineroom.com* ✛ *3:B2.*

$ ✕ **Michele Coulon Dessertier.** A "dessertier" confects desserts, a job that
CAFÉ Michele Coulon does exceedingly well with organic produce and
☺ imported chocolate in the back of a small, charming shop in the heart
of La Jolla. Moist chocolate-chip scones, the colorful raspberry pin-
wheel *bombe* (a molded dessert of cake, jam, almond macaroons, and
ice-cream filling), the berry-frangipane tart, and a decadent chocolate
mousse cake are a few treats. This is not just a place for dessert, however. Lunch is served weekdays (the store is open 9 to 4), and the simple
menu includes quiche Lorraine (baked fresh daily) and salads. ✉ *7556
Fay Ave., La Jolla* ☏ *858/456–5098* ⊕ *www.dessertier.com* ☽ *Closed
Sun. No dinner* ✛ *3:B2.*

$$$ ✕ **Nine-Ten.** Many years ago, the elegant Grande Colonial Hotel in the
AMERICAN heart of La Jolla "village" housed a drugstore owned by actor Gregory
Fodor's Choice Peck's father. In the sleekly contemporary dining room that now occu-
★ pies the space, acclaimed chef Jason Knibb serves satisfying seasonal
fare at breakfast, lunch, and dinner. At night the perfectly executed
menu may include tantalizing appetizers like Jamaican jerk pork belly or
lamb sugo. The kitchen's creative flair comes through with dishes such
as duck breast with pickled Swiss chard and ginger, and short ribs with
smoked shiitake mushroom puree. Delicious desserts include spiced
crumb cake with butternut ice cream and caramelized bacon. ✉ *910
Prospect St., La Jolla* ☏ *858/964–5400* ⊕ *www.nine-ten.com* ✛ *3:A2.*

$ ✕ **Osteria Romantica.** The name means "Romantic Inn," and with a
ITALIAN sunny location a few blocks from the beach in La Jolla Shores, the
look suggests a trattoria in Positano. The kitchen's wonderfully light
hand shows up in the tomato sauce that finishes the scampi and other
dishes, and in the pleasing Romantica salad garnished with figs and wal-
nuts. Savory pasta choices include lobster-filled *mezzelune* (half moons)
in saffron sauce, and wonderfully rich spaghetti *alla carbonara.* The
breaded veal cutlets crowned with chopped arugula and tomatoes is a
worthy main course. The warm, informal service suits the neighbor-
hood. ✉ *2151 Ave. de la Playa, La Jolla* ☏ *858/551–1221* ⊕ *www.
osteriaromantica.com* ✛ *3:B2.*

$ ✕ **Prepkitchen.** For a less expensive option in La Jolla, head to this gem,
AMERICAN known to fans as "PK." The low-key sister restaurant to Whisk'n'ladle
(also in La Jolla) offers a seasonal menu of soups, sandwiches, and
entrees. Standouts include the butternut squash ravioli, fusili Bolognese,
and a flavorful meatloaf melt served with house-made potato chips. If
you'd rather picnic than dine in, family meals meant to feed four to five
people are available for takeout. ✉ *7556 Fay Ave., La Jolla* ☏ *858/875–
7737* ⊕ *www.prepkitchen.com* ⚄ *Reservations not accepted* ✛ *3:B2.*

$ ✕ **Rimel's Rotisserie.** An affordable option in often-pricey La Jolla, this
AMERICAN comfy spot sometimes serves seafood caught that morning by fishermen
☺ who work for the owner. Other than market-priced "fresh catches" and
the $25 grass-fed filet mignon from the owner's Home Grown meat
shop, most items come in under $12, such as grilled mahimahi tacos
(served with rice, beans, and a powerful green chili-garlic salsa), grain-
fed chicken grilled on a mesquite-fire rotisserie, and "steaming rice
bowls" that actually are plates spread with jasmine rice, wok-cooked
vegetables, and grilled seafood with a variety of vegetables. This is one

of La Jolla's better choices for families. ✉ *1030 Torrey Pines Rd., La Jolla* ☎ *858/454–6045* ⊕ *www.rimelsrestaurants.com* ✛ *3:A2.*

$$
ASIAN

✕ **Roppongi Restaurant and Sushi Bar.** Roppongi was a hit from the moment it opened with chef Stephen Window's Asian-accented global menu. The contemporary dining room, done in wood tones and accented with a tropical fish tank, Buddhas, and other Asian statuary, has a row of comfortable booths along one wall. It can get noisy when crowded; tables near the bar are generally quieter. Order the imaginative Euro-Asian tapas as appetizers, or combine them for a full meal. Equally delicious are the crispy tofu, pan-seared scallops on potato pancakes, and the Mongolian duck quesadilla. Good entrées include Roppongi crab stack, Thai steak salad, grilled flat-iron steak with shishito peppers, and macadamia-crusted mahimahi with mango chutney. The creative sushi bar rocks. ✉ *875 Prospect St., La Jolla* ☎ *858/551–5252* ⊕ *www.roppongiusa.com* ✛ *3:A2.*

$
JAPANESE
Fodor's Choice
★

✕ **Sushi on the Rock.** This popular California-style sushi spot now operates just from its newest location, which boasts a patio with an ocean view. The restaurant opens at 11:30 am daily, though it gets busy around 5 with people wanting to nail a seat for the daily happy hour from 5 to 6:30 pm. There's something fun about Sushi on the Rock, from the young friendly sushi chefs to the comically named specialties, like the Slippery When Wet roll featuring tempura shrimp, eel, crab, and cucumber. Loads of original rolls include the Barrio Roll stuffed with fried white fish and spicy tomato salsa, the Ashley Roll that pairs seared tuna with soft-shell crab and tangy whole-grain mustard sauce, and the Bruce Lee with spicy crab, tuna, and avocado. Also try the Japanese-inspired dishes like pot stickers, Asian-style Caesar salad, and lobster mac and cheese. ✉ *1025 Prospect St., La Jolla* ☎ *858/459–3208* ⊕ *www.sushiontherock.com* ⌦ *Reservations not accepted* ✛ *3:A2.*

8

$$$
FRENCH

✕ **Tapenade.** Named after the Provençal black olive-and-anchovy paste, Tapenade specializes in the fresh cuisine of the south of France. The sunny cuisine matches the unpretentious, light, and airy room, lined with 1960s French movie posters, in which it is served. Fresh ingredients, a delicate touch with sauces, and an emphasis on seafood characterize the menu, which changes frequently. If you're lucky, it may include wild boar stewed in red wine, lobster with white corn sauce flavored with Tahitian vanilla, pan-gilded sea scallops, and desserts like chocolate fondant and profiteroles. The two-course "Riviera Menu" served at lunch for $21.95 is a fabulous steal. ✉ *7612 Fay Ave., La Jolla* ☎ *858/551–7500* ⊕ *www.tapenaderestaurant.com* ⊗ *No lunch weekends* ✛ *3:A2.*

$$$
SEAFOOD

✕ **Truluck's.** This Southern-style seafood restaurant with reasonably priced fish, steaks, and international wines boldly takes over a space that has been several restaurants in succession. This one stakes a claim with live piano music nightly and a menu of Alaskan king crab legs and Jonah crab. Monday they offer all-you-can-eat stone crab and side dishes for $49.95. The menu shows its Southern flair with sides like cheese grits and fried green tomatoes. The Chocolate Sack is a bed made of chocolate and stuffed with enough delicious pound cake, fresh berries, and warm chocolate to satisfy a crowd. ✉ *8990 University Center La.,*

La Jolla ☎ *858/453–2583* ⊕ *www.trulucks.com* ✛ *3:D1.*

$$
SEAFOOD
✕ **Whisk'n'ladle.** Whisk'n'ladle has earned national acclaim with its combination of casual comfort and a menu of ever-changing local fare. Appetizers include dishes like warm spinach salad with grilled butternut squash and seared scallops with caramelized endive. Larger plates feature black ink risotto and wild steelhead trout with Moroccan spices. By all means request a patio table when reserving at this hip, popular eatery that doubles as a fashion show of some of La Jolla's ladies who lunch. And the bar is worth a visit, too, with its original menu of cocktails like the tamarind margarita, passion-fruit vanilla mimosa, and pomegranate mojito. ✉ *1044 Wall St., La Jolla* ☎ *858/551–7575* ⊕ *www.whisknladle.com* ✛ *3:A2.*

WHEN THE GRUNIONS RUN

A generations-old San Diego tradition is heading to the beach during certain high tides—preferably when the moon is full—to hunt grunion. These small, barely edible fish come ashore during mating periods and "run" on the beach, causing great excitement among spectators. As the fish flop across the sand in search of adventure (as it were), bold individuals chase them down and scoop up a few with their hands—catching them by any other means is illegal. Beach-area businesses and eateries often know the date of the next run.

$$
ASIAN
✕ **Zenbu.** There's a cool California vibe to this cozy, moodily lighted sushi-and-seafood restaurant that serves some of the freshest fish in town and attracts a Who's Who of La Jolla. Restaurateur Matt Rimel runs a commercial fishing company and uses his connections to bring varied seafood from all over the world that excels, whether raw or cooked. Seasonal specialties include buttery *otoro* tuna belly and local sea urchin fresh from its spiny shell. Sushi, which can be pricey, ranges from simple nigiri to beautiful sashimi plates and original rolls like Salmon Spider, which combines soft-shell crab with fresh salmon. Cooked dishes run from noodle bowls and grass-fed Montana prime sirloin seared at the table on a hot stone, to whole fried rockfish or spicy "dynamite" lobster. ✉ *7660 Fay Ave., La Jolla* ☎ *858/454–4540* ⊕ *www.rimelsrestaurants.com* ☽ *No lunch* ✛ *3:A2.*

POINT LOMA, HARBOR AND SHELTER ISLANDS, AND CORONADO

Point Loma has a storied history as the center of the tuna-fishing industry and is developing into an area of charming neighborhood restaurants. In recent years, a couple of places have opened that specialize in simple, high-quality fare showcasing local ingredients. But most restaurants in Point Loma and on Harbor and Shelter islands are casual neighborhood spots or eateries with great views that cater to tourists and sailing enthusiasts.

Coronado is a picturesque community filled with neat wood-frame homes, the historic turrets of the Hotel Del Coronado, and one of the most beautiful beaches in the area. Though there are exceptions, many restaurants here rely on a steady stream of tourist traffic, so often the cuisine is adequate and somewhat expensive but not stellar.

CORONADO

$$$$ ✕ **1500 Ocean.** The fine-dining restaurant at Hotel Del Coronado offers
AMERICAN a memorable evening that showcases the best organic and naturally raised ingredients the region has to offer. Chef Brian Sinnott, who honed his technique in San Francisco, presents sublimely subtle dishes such as chilled king crab with compressed Asian pear salad; wild prawns with kale, smoked bacon, and shelled beans; and Kurobuta pork tenderloin with creamy polenta. The interior, at once inviting and elegant, evokes a posh cabana, while the terrace offers ocean views. An excellent international wine list and equally clever desserts and artisanal cheeses complete the experience. ⊠ *Hotel Del Coronado, 1500 Orange Ave., Coronado* ☎ 619/522–8490 ⊗ *No lunch* ✢ *4:G6.*

$$$ ✕ **Chez Loma.** A favorite with guests at nearby Hotel Del Coronado, this
FRENCH restaurant is tucked away on a side street. Chez Loma is located in a former private home with plenty of windows, attractive lighting, and an upstairs Victorian parlor where coffee and dessert are served. The more elaborate dishes among the carefully prepared French bistro menu are *boeuf bourguignon,* rack of lamb with balsamic marinade, and roasted salmon in a horseradish crust. The solid selection of desserts includes classics like chocolate soufflé and crème caramel. A specially priced early dinner menu, and two choices of fixed-price menus for $40 or $45 offer more value than the à la carte selections. ⊠ *1132 Loma Ave., Coronado* ☎ 619/435–0661 ⊕ *www.chezloma.com* ⊗ *Closed Mon. No lunch* ✢ *4:G6.*

$ ✕ **Coronado Brewing Company.** The carefully crafted beers, such as the
AMERICAN Islander Pale Ale (IPA) and Mermaid's Red Ale, are good by themselves, but they also make a tasty accompaniment to bratwurst and
Ⓒ beer-battered onion rings, served in huge portions. There's indoor seating, a pair of sidewalk terraces, and, best of all, a walled garden that provides a quiet haven from the bustle of Orange Avenue. Simple choices are the wisest, from the Philadelphia-style steak sandwich to wood-fired pizzas to baby back ribs basted with spicy, ginger-flavored barbecue sauce. It may be a brewery, but it's still popular with families. ⊠ *170 Orange Ave., Coronado* ☎ 619/437–4452 ⊕ *www. coronadobrewingcompany.com* ✢ *4:H4.*

$$ ✕ **Mistral.** Evocatively named after the warm wind that blows across
INTERNATIONAL southern France and Italy, the dinner-only fine-dining restaurant at
Fodor'sChoice Loews Coronado Bay Resort features polished southern French and
★ northern Italian cuisine built around naturally raised meats and organic local produce. The menu of fifth-generation French chef Patrick Ponsaty includes an arugula salad with figs and lavender honey, grilled prime beef tenderloin, and salmon with lobster emulsion. A well-edited wine list and house-made desserts like profiteroles with Valrhona chocolate sauce and vanilla ice cream complete the experience. The soft new decor plays up the sweeping views of the bay visible from every table. ⊠ *Loews Coronado Bay Resort, 4000 Coronado Bay Rd., Coronado* ☎ 619/424–4000 ⊗ *Closed Sun. and Mon. No lunch* ✢ *4:H6.*

8

$$$ ✕ **Sheerwater.** This casual but pricey all-day dining room is the primary
AMERICAN restaurant at Hotel Del Coronado. A spacious, breeze-swept terrace
enjoys extraordinary ocean views, while the indoor room can be on
the noisy side, especially when families are present. The menu offers
a local take on all-American fare, with dishes such as lobster bisque
with avocado-mango salsa, and splits the entrée list between meats like
filet mignon with *beurre blanc* or truffled béarnaise sauce, and seafood
offerings such as grilled salmon and mahimahi. ⊠ *Hotel Del Coronado,
1500 Orange Ave., Coronado* ☎ *619/435–6611* ✛ *4:G6.*

$ ✕ **Tartine.** There's always a dish of water for canine pals on the terrace
FRENCH of this French-inspired café a block from San Diego Bay. Popular sand-
↻ wiches include ham-and-Brie slathered with grain mustard, or Gorgon-
zola cheese, walnuts, mache, and sliced pears. Clever salads and soups
round out the daytime menu. Dinner brings a bruschetta of the day,
capellini with pomodoro sauce, bistro salad, and specials like chicken
under a brick with butternut squash risotto. The stars of the menu are
the house-made desserts such as lemon tart, blueberry streusel coffee
cake, and double-chocolate bread pudding. Continental breakfast com-
mences at 6 am when quiche and just-baked pastries silently command,
"Eat me!" This may be Coronado's best bet for casual but stylish fare.
⊠ *1106 1st St., Coronado* ☎ *619/435–4323* ⊕ *www.tartinecoronado.
com* ✛ *4:H4.*

HARBOR ISLAND

$$$$ ✕ **Island Prime and C Level Lounge.** This sizable eatery on the shore of
AMERICAN Harbor Island is two restaurants in one: the extravagant, dinner-only
Island Prime, and the much less formal (but not inexpensive) lunch-and-
dinner C Level Lounge, which has a choice terrace. Both venues tempt
with unrivaled views of downtown San Diego's ever-taller skyline. At
Island Prime, the menu of steaks and seafood lists most choices sim-
ply as "market price" (and when the bill arrives, it suggests that chef
Deborah Scott shops at a pretty extravagant market). Besides prime
steaks, pork chops, and lamb rack, the entrées include composed dishes
like the plank-roasted salmon with cucumber salsa. Lunch is the best
time at C Level Lounge, which serves hearty pastas and sandwiches.
Reservations are strongly suggested for Island Prime; C Level doesn't
take them. ⊠ *880 Harbor Island Dr., Harbor Island* ☎ *619/298–6802*
⊙ *No lunch at Island Prime* ✛ *4:F1.*

POINT LOMA

¢ ✕ **Azucar.** For a taste of Cuba in San Diego, head to this bakery. Ideal
CUBAN for a quick meal before shopping or hitting the beach, the friendly café
offers morning specialties such as raspberry scones with passion fruit
icing, ham quiche, and *café con leche* (sweet Cuban espresso with hot
milk). For lunch, try the slow-roasted pork sandwich with plantain
chips. ⊠ *4820 Newport Ave., Ocean Beach* ☎ *619/523–2020* ⊕ *www.
iloveazucar.com* ⊙ *No dinner.* ✛ *4:B1.*

$ ✕ **Corvette Diner Bar & Grill.** A San Diego County favorite for children's
AMERICAN parties and other family occasions, Corvette Diner rolled into a new
↻ location in 2009, but still showcases a real Corvette (changed yearly)
in a kitschy, 1950s-style dining room dominated by vintage movie

posters and singing servers. The new digs also feature a train-style dining car with old movies playing in the "windows." The menu has what you'd expect—macaroni and cheddar, plump burgers, piled-high deli sandwiches, spaghetti and meatballs, greasy chili-cheese fries, and thick milk shakes. The daily "Dine and Play Package" includes game cards. ⊠ *2965 Historic Decatur Rd., Point Loma* ☎ *619/542–1476* ✛ *4:C1.*

¢ ✕**Hodad's.** No, it's not a flashback.
AMERICAN The 1960s live on at this fabulously
☺ funky burger joint. Walls are covered with license plates, and the amiable servers with tattoos. Still, this is very much a family place, and Hodad's clientele often includes toddlers and octogenarians. Huge burgers are the thing, loaded with onions, pickles, tomatoes, lettuce, and condiments, and so gloriously messy that you might wear a swimsuit so you can stroll to the beach for a bath afterward. The minihamburger is good, the double bacon cheeseburger is breathtaking (and artery-clogging), as are the onion rings and seasoned potato wedges. ⊠ *5010 Newport Ave., Point Loma* ☎ *619/224–4623* ✛ *1:B1.*

$ ✕**Jimmy's Famous American Tavern.** A standout in the wave of recent gas-
AMERICAN tropubs, Jimmy's interior is industrial meets Americana. Head through the garage-style doors for a patio seat with a water view or gather at a cozy booth. The menu features elevated takes on backyard BBQ that include The Jimmy, a 10-ounce burger topped with pimento cheese, applewood smoked bacon, and jalapeño jelly. The buttermilk fried chicken breast is also worth a try. Check out the warm cinnamon donut holes at Sunday brunch. ⊠ *4990 N. Harbor Dr., Point Loma* ☎ *619/226–2103* ⊕ *www.j-fat.com* ✛ *4:B2.*

$ ✕**Sessions Public.** From the short rib sliders, duck confit Thai summer
AMERICAN rolls, and Serrano ham on the menu to the stuffed ducks adorning the walls, it's clear this is no vegetarian joint. Opened by Point Loma native Abel Kaase, the casual restaurant features farm-to-table fare and local craft beers. Highlights include the mussels, the certified Angus beef natural burger topped with gouda and arugula, and duck-fat fries served with garlic aioli. ■TIP➔ For post-dinner drinks, pop over to the adjacent Catalina Lounge, a favorite local dive bar with cheap drinks and friendly bartenders. ⊠ *4204 Voltaire St., Point Loma* ☎ *619/756–7715* ⊕ *www.sessionspublic.com* ☉ No lunch. ✛ *4:B1.*

$ ✕**Tender Greens.** "Farm-fresh ingredients served up with little fuss" is
AMERICAN the ethos behind this cafeteria-style spot in Liberty Station. Expect big
☺ salads like seared tuna Niçoise; Fra' Mani salami with shaved fennel, pecorino, and arugula; or chipotle chicken salad. Naturally raised beef and chicken are roasted and then tucked into sandwiches or served as a dinner plate with vegetables. House-made desserts round out the

A FISH TALE

From the 1930s to the early '70s, San Diego was the capitol of the American tuna-fishing industry. Visit Point Loma to see the remnants of the fishing industry or stop by Whole Foods for a sample of this favorite fish canned by American Tuna, a company formed by six local fishing families who only use poles—not nets—to catch premium albacore tuna in a sustainable way.

8

menu. ⊠ *2400 Historic Decatur Rd., Point Loma* ☎ *619/226–6254* ⊕ *tendergreensfood.com* ✛ *4:C1.*

$ ✗ **The Venetian.** The spacious back room of this neighborhood restau-
ITALIAN rant is actually a sheltered garden that you can enjoy in any weather. The menu takes a personal view of southern Italian cuisine, with house specialties like shrimp puttanesca, and bow-tie pasta tossed with pro-sciutto, peas, and mushrooms in a rose-tinted cream sauce. The well-priced selection of veal, chicken, and seafood dishes is excellent, but many regulars settle for the lavishly garnished antipasto salad and one of the tender-crusted pizzas. ⊠ *3663 Voltaire St., Point Loma* ☎ *619/223–8197* ⊕ *www.venetian1965.com* ✛ *4:B1.*

NORTHERN SAN DIEGO

Although mostly an industrial and residential area that doesn't attract many tourists, Kearny Mesa and Clairemont offer a diversity of small independent and ethnic restaurants. Convoy Street—the commercial heart of the busy Kearny Mesa area—is the unofficial Asian Restaurant Row of San Diego, and presents a comprehensive selection of Chinese, Korean, and Vietnamese restaurants, a number of which qualify as "Best in Class." Good food can be found very affordably here—just don't be put off by the simple interiors and the service, which some-times can seem somewhat abrupt or offhand due to cultural and lan-guage differences.

CLAIREMONT

$$ ✗ **Buga Korean B.B.Q. Restaurant.** The cook-it-yourself fun of Korean
KOREAN barbecue and Japanese-style shabu-shabu focuses attention on your table's built-in cooking unit, not on the modest surroundings. Sus-pended exhaust-fan hoods create something of a draft when the res-taurant is full of guests barbecuing sharply marinated cuts of meat and seafood. Shabu-shabu, a multicourse meal of paper-thin meats, vegetables, and noodles, is cooked in iron pots of boiling liquid that provide a final course of tasty broth. Order a combination barbecue dinner and expect a near avalanche of food. Pleasant servers explain how everything works. The restaurant is a few blocks west of the Convoy Street corridor. ⊠ *5580 Clairemont Mesa Blvd., Clairemont* ☎ *858/560–1010* ✛ *3:F2.*

KEARNY MESA

$ ✗ **China Max.** This good-looking Convoy Street eatery has won hundreds
CHINESE of loyal fans, not only because of the quality, variety, and authenticity of the cooking, but because a value-priced, late-supper menu is offered nightly from 9 to 11. Dishes not to be missed from the House Special menu include the lettuce "taco" stuffed with stir-fried shrimp, country-style *mei fun* noodles, dumplings filled with shrimp paste and Chinese chives, and pan-fried lamb chops in black-pepper sauce. Tanks teem with seafood, all market priced. The dim sum dumplings and pastries served at lunch may be San Diego's best. ⊠ *4698 Convoy St., Kearny Mesa* ☎ *858/650–3333* ⊕ *www.chinamaxsandiego.com* ✛ *3:G3.*

¢ ╳ **Dumpling Inn.** Modest, family-style, and delicious, this is in some
CHINESE ways the most likable of Convoy Street's Asian restaurants. The tiny
☺ establishment loads its tables with bottles of aromatic and spicy condiments for the boiled, steamed, and fried dumplings that are the
house specialty. These delicately flavored, hefty mouthfuls preface a
meal that may continue simply, with honey-glazed shrimp, or elaborately, with mini braised pork shank. Ask about daily specials, such
as shredded pork in plum sauce served on a sea of crispy noodles.
You may bring your own wine or beer; the house serves only tea and
soft drinks. ✉ *4619 Convoy St., #F, Kearny Mesa* ☎ *858/268–9638*
☾ *Closed Mon.* ✛ *3:G3.*

$$ ╳ **Emerald Chinese Seafood Restaurant.** Emerald is sought out by those
CHINESE who prefer elaborate, carefully prepared, and sometimes costly seafood
dishes. Even when the restaurant is full to capacity with 300 diners,
the noise level is moderate and conversation flows easily between bites
of the best Chinese cuisine in the area. Market-priced—and that can
be high—lobsters, clams, and fish reside in tanks until the moment of
cooking. Simple preparations flavored with scallions, black beans, and
ginger are among the most worthy. Other recommended dishes include
beef with Singapore-style satay sauce, honey-walnut shrimp, baked
chicken in five spices, Peking duck served in two savory courses, and,
at lunch, the dim sum. ✉ *3709 Convoy St., Kearny Mesa* ☎ *858/565–
6888* ✛ *3:H4.*

$$ ╳ **Jasmine.** This cavernous, Hong Kong–style establishment seats no
CHINESE fewer than 400 people; even so, there are frequently lines outside at
lunchtime on weekends, when groups arrive to enjoy fragrant soups,
steaming noodles, and dim sum from carts that constantly circle the
room. At dinner it's a hard choice between the seafood from the wall-
mounted tanks and "Peking duck two ways"—the crisp skin sand-
wiched in tasty buns as a first course, the meat deliciously stir-fried for
a savory follow-up. A supplementary menu of "special-priced dishes"
offers bargains like half of a roasted chicken for $7.50. At times servers
can be somewhat abrupt. ✉ *4609 Convoy St., Kearny Mesa* ☎ *858/268–
0888* ✛ *3:G3.*

$$ ╳ **Pampas Argentine Grill.** Meats, mostly cut in hefty portions, grilled
ARGENTINE and served with zesty chimichurri sauce are the main thrust of the
menu at this comfy steakhouse a few blocks east of the Convoy Street
restaurant row. Choices include rib eye, filet mignon, and strip steaks,
along with marinated boneless chicken, lamb, and the seafood of
the day. Reasonably priced and served for two or more, the "Parril-
lada Pampas" is a grilled-at-the-table feast of beef, spicy sausage, and
sweetbreads. The spacious restaurant is gently lighted and decorated
with paintings that strive for the romance of the tango. There's live
music on weekends—and a tango the last Friday of the month. ✉ *8690
Aero Dr., Kearny Mesa* ☎ *858/278–5971* ☾ *No dinner Mon. No lunch
weekends* ✛ *3:H4.*

¢ ╳ **Phuong Trang.** One of the most popular Vietnamese restaurants in San
VIETNAMESE Diego, Phuong Trang cooks up hundreds of appetizers, soups, noodle
dishes, and main courses, which can make choosing a meal a bewil-
dering process. Waiters tend to steer you to tasty offerings like fried

egg rolls, char-grilled shrimp paste wrapped around sugarcane, beef in grape leaves, and fresh spring rolls filled with pork and shrimp. Broken rice and a grilled pork chop make a satisfying meal. The large, relatively spare dining room gets packed, especially on weekends, but service is speedy, if sometimes curt. ⊠ *4170 Convoy St., Kearny Mesa* ☎ *858/565–6750* ✛ *3:G3.*

OFF THE BEATEN PATH

CHULA VISTA

$$ ✕**Restaurante Romesco.** Mediterranean bistro meets Baja California
MEDITERRANEAN   ingredients in this restaurant by Javier Plascencia and family, Tijuana's
Fodor'sChoice   renowned restaurateurs. The varied menu starts with salmon carpaccio
★   or tapas like the spicy shrimp dish *cazuelita de gambas* and ahi tuna tostadas. Daily happy hours from 3:30 to 6:30 and 9 to 10:30 bring half-price tapas and drinks. Exquisitely flavored entrées include lobster ravioli in brandy cream sauce and mesquite-grilled duck breast, while desserts run to crepes in tangy *cajeta,* goat milk caramel. Romesco offers a full bar and the rare chance to taste some of the fine wines made in Baja California Norte, Mexico's premier wine country. Service can be leisurely; request the check when you're close to finishing your meal. ⊠ *4346 Bonita Rd., Chula Vista* ☎ *619/475–8627* ⊕ *www. romescobajamed.com* ◷ *Closed Mondays* ✛ *4:H6.*

Where to Eat and Stay in San Diego

KEY
□ *Hotels*
■ *Restaurants*
■ *Restaurant in Hotel*
✥ *following dining and lodging reviews indicates a map-grid coordinate*

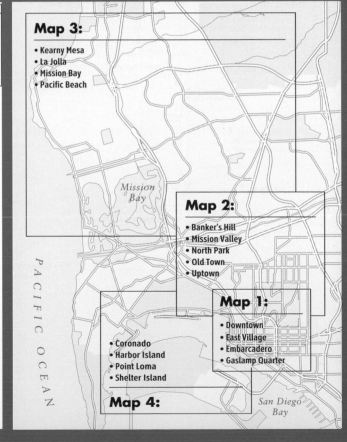

Map 3:
• Kearny Mesa
• La Jolla
• Mission Bay
• Pacific Beach
Mission Bay
Map 2:
• Banker's Hill
• Mission Valley
• North Park
• Old Town
• Uptown
PACIFIC OCEAN
Map 1:
• Downtown
• East Village
• Embarcadero
• Gaslamp Quarter
• Coronado
• Harbor Island
• Point Loma
• Shelter Island
Map 4:
San Diego Bay

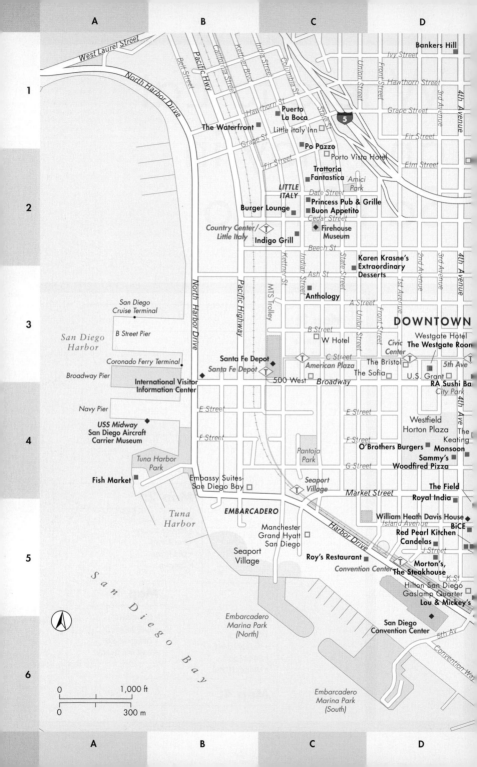

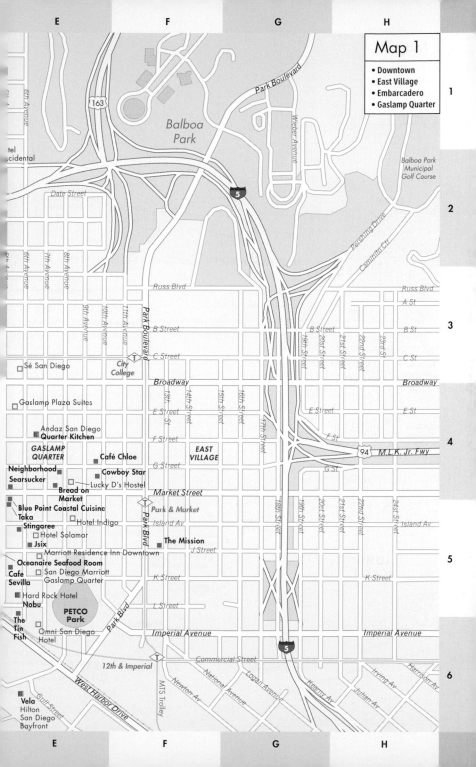

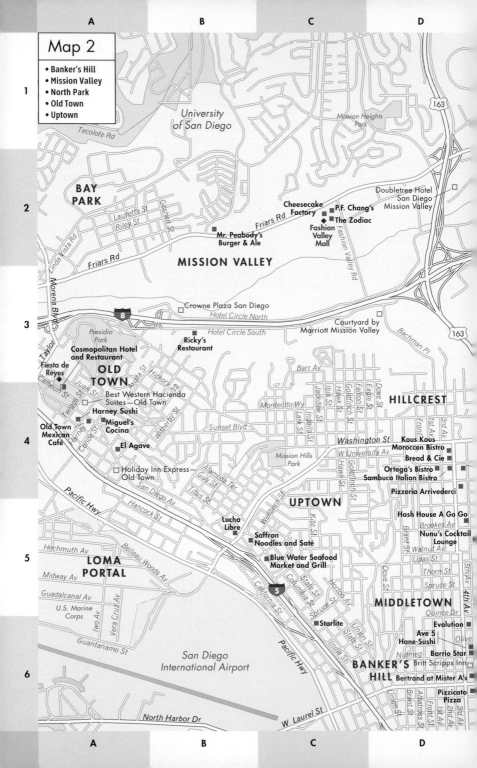

Map 2

- Banker's Hill
- Mission Valley
- North Park
- Old Town
- Uptown

A **B** **C** **D**

1

163

University of San Diego

Tecolote Rd

Mission Heights Park

2

BAY PARK

Lauretta St
Riley St

Goshen St

Friars Rd

Cheesecake Factory
P.F. Chang's
The Zodiac
Fashion Valley Mall

Doubletree Hotel San Diego Mission Valley

Mr. Peabody's Burger & Ale

Friars Rd

Morena Blvd

Friars Rd

MISSION VALLEY

Fashion Valley Rd

3

8

Crowne Plaza San Diego
Hotel Circle North
Hotel Circle South

Courtyard by Marriott Mission Valley

Bachman Pl

163

Presidio Park

Ricky's Restaurant

Cosmopolitan Hotel and Restaurant

Fiesta de Reyes

Taylor St

OLD TOWN

Juan St

Hickory St

Barr Av

HILLCREST

Eagle St
Dove St
Falton St
Ibis St
Jackdaw St
Goldfinch St
Hawk St

3rd Av
1st Av
Front St

Best Western Hacienda Suites—Old Town

Harney Sushi
Miguel's Cocina

Conde St
Harney St
Twiggs St
Arista St
Witherby St

Montecito Wy

Sunset Blvd

Lark St
Ingalls St

Washington St
W University Av

Kous Kous
Moroccon Bistro
Bread & Cie
Ortega's Bistro
Sambuca Italian Bistro
Pizzeria Arrivederci

4

Old Town Mexican Café

El Agave

Holiday Inn Express—Old Town

Calhoun St

San Diego Av

Alameda Ter
Guy St
Titus St

Mission Hills Park

Wellborn St
Kite St
Goldfinch St
Hawk St

UPTOWN

Hash House A Go Go

Brookes Av
Nunu's Cocktail Lounge
Walnut Av
Upas St
Thorn St
Spruce St

Front St
Brant St
Dove St

5

Pacific Hwy

Hancock St

Belleau Woods Av

Hochmuth Av

LOMA PORTAL

Midway Dr

Guadalcanal Av

U.S. Marine Corps

Guantanamo St

Iwo Av
Vera Cruz Av

Lucha Libre

Saffron Noodles and Saté

Blue Water Seafood Market and Grill

California St

5

Columbia St
State St
Spruce St
Union St
India St
Horton Av

Kite St

MIDDLETOWN

Quince Dr

Evolution

5th Av
4th Av

Ave 5
Hane-Sushi

Olive

6

San Diego International Airport

Pacific Hwy

North Harbor Dr

W Laurel St

Starlite

Nutmeg St
Barrio Star
Britt Scripps Inn

BANKER'S HILL

Bertrand at Mister A's

Pizzicato Pizza

Union St
Brant St
Albatross St
Front St
1st Av
2nd Av

A **B** **C** **D**

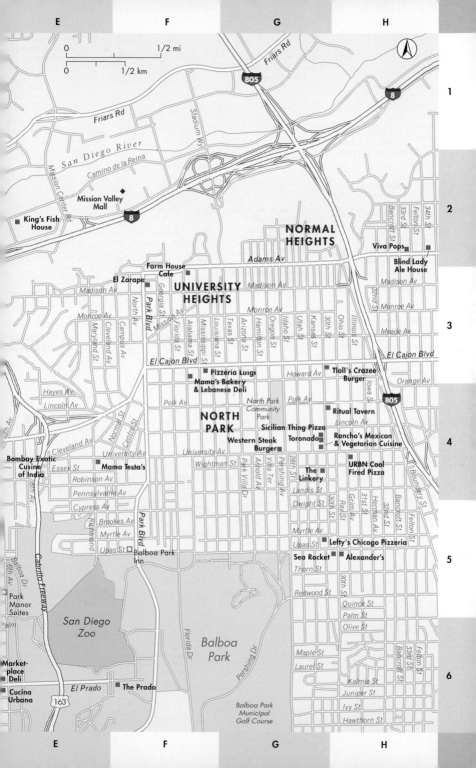

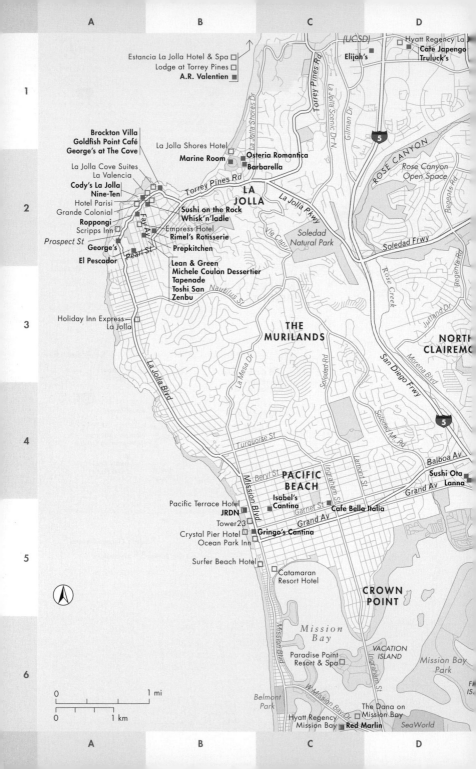

A **B** **C** **D**

1

Estancia La Jolla Hotel & Spa □
Lodge at Torrey Pines □
A.R. Valentien

(UCSD)
Elijah's
Hyatt Regency La □
Cafe Japengo
Truluck's

ROSE CANYON

Rose Canyon
Open Space

2

Brockton Villa
Goldfish Point Café
George's at The Cove

La Jolla Shores Hotel □
Marine Room □

Osteria Romantica
Barbarella

LA
JOLLA

La Jolla Cove Suites
La Valencia
Cody's La Jolla
Nine-Ten
Hotel Parisi
Grande Colonial
Roppongi
Scripps Inn □
Prospect St
George's
El Pescador

Sushi on the Rock
Whisk'n'ladle

Empress Hotel
Rimel's Rotisserie

Prepkitchen

Lean & Green
Michele Coulon Dessertier
Tapenade
Toshi San
Zenbu

La Jolla Pkwy

Via Capri

Soledad
Natural Park

Soledad Frwy

3

Holiday Inn Express
La Jolla □

THE
MURILANDS

Soledad Rd

San Diego Frwy

NORTH
CLAIREMO

Jutland Dr

Morena Blvd

4

Turquoise St

La Jolla Blvd

Beryl St

PACIFIC
BEACH

Ingraham St

Lamont St

Balboa Av

Sushi Ota
Lanna

Grand Av

5

Pacific Terrace Hotel
JRDN ■
Tower23 □
Crystal Pier Hotel □
Ocean Park Inn

Surfer Beach Hotel □

Mission Blvd

Isabel's
Cantina

Garnet St

Gringo's Cantina

Grand Av

Cafe Bella Italia

Catamaran
Resort Hotel □

CROWN
POINT

6

0   1 mi
0   1 km

Mission
Bay

Paradise Point
Resort & Spa □

Mission Blvd

VACATION
ISLAND

Ingraham St

Mission Bay
Park

Belmont
Park

Hyatt Regency
Mission Bay

W. Mission Bay Dr

The Dana on
Mission Bay □
Red Marlin

SeaWorld

A **B** **C** **D**

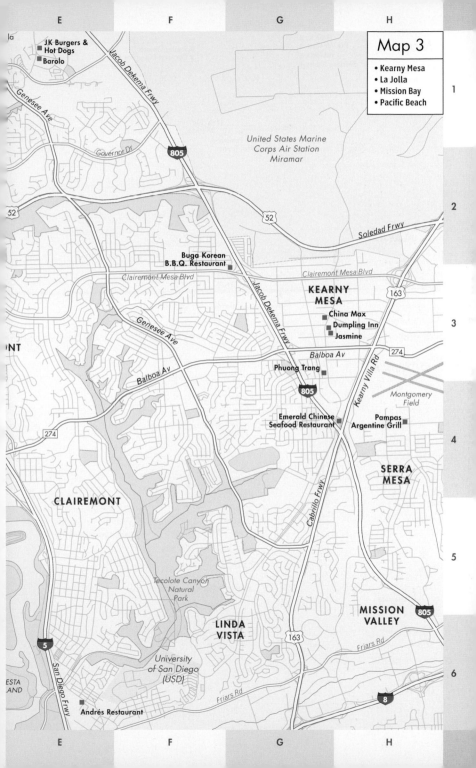

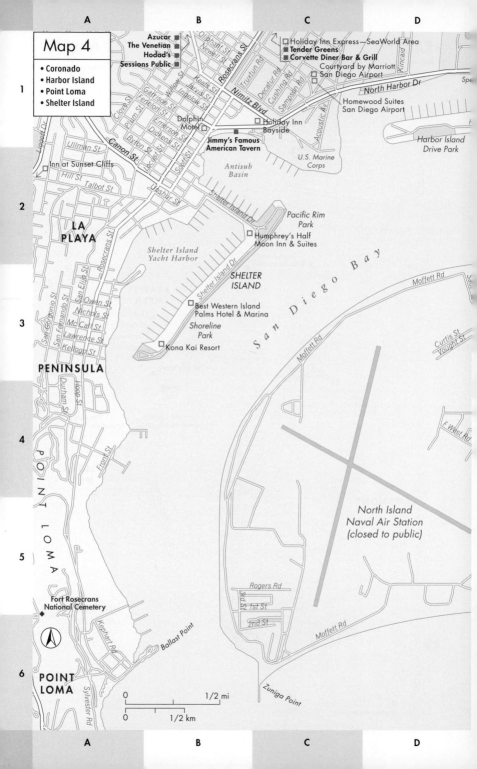

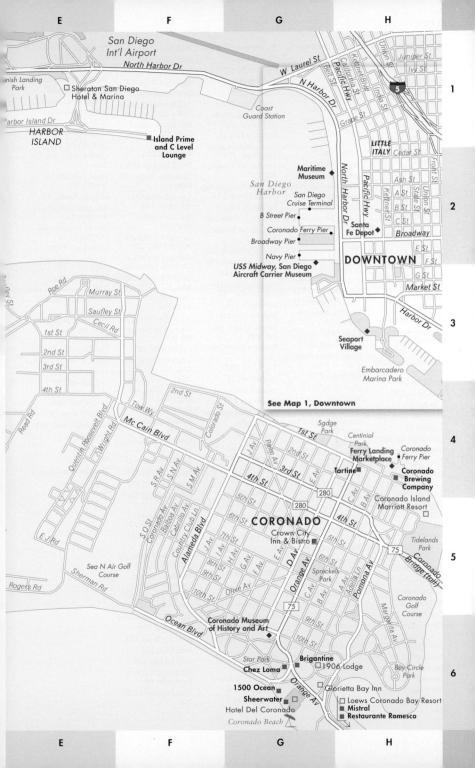

E   **F**   **G**   **H**

San Diego
Int'l Airport

North Harbor Dr

W Laurel St

...nish Landing
Park

Sheraton San Diego
Hotel & Marina

...Harbor Island Dr

**HARBOR
ISLAND**

Island Prime
and C Level
Lounge

Coast
Guard Station

N Harbor Dr

Pacific Hwy

Belt St

Kettner Blvd

California St

India St

Union St

Juniper St

Ivy St

5

1

Grape St

**LITTLE
ITALY** Cedar St

Front St

Ash St

A St

State St

B St

Union St

C St

Maritime
Museum

*San Diego
Harbor*

North Harbor Dr

Pacific Hwy

*San Diego
Cruise Terminal*

B Street Pier

Coronado Ferry Pier

Broadway Pier

Navy Pier

USS Midway, San Diego
Aircraft Carrier Museum

Santa
Fe Depot

Kettner St

Broadway

E St

DOWNTOWN

F St

G St

Market St

Harbor Dr

2

3

Roe Rd

Murray St

Saufley St

Cecil Rd

...fley St

1st St

2nd St

3rd St

4th St

2nd St

Colorado St

Tow Wy

2nd St

1st St

Sgdge
Park

Centinial
Park

Seaport
Village

*Embarcadero
Marina Park*

See Map 1, Downtown

4

Ferry Landing
Marketplace

Coronado
Ferry Pier

Read Rd

Quentin Roosevelt Blvd

Wright Rd

Mc Cain Blvd

J Av

Palm Av

3rd St

E Av

Tartine

**Coronado
Brewing
Company**

Coronado Island
Marriott Resort

Tidelands
Park

5

S R Av

S N Av

S M Av

4th St

CORONADO

4th St

Sea N Air Golf
Course

S O St

Coronado Av

Balboa Av

Cabrillo Av

Country Club Ln

Alameda Blvd

5th St

6th St

J Av

7th St

H Av

8th St

G Av

9th St

F Av

Olive Av

10th St

D Av

Crown City
Inn & Bistro

Spreckels
Park

Orange Av

C Av

B Av

A Av

Adella Ln

Pomona Av

6th St

5th St

9th St

Coronado
Golf
Course

Margarita Av

75

Coronado
Bridge (toll)

E J Rd

Rogers Rd

Sherman Rd

Ocean Blvd

Coronado Museum
of History and Art

10th St

75

Star Park

Chez Loma

Brigantine

1906 Lodge

Bay Circle
Park

6

1500 Ocean

Sheerwater

Hotel Del Coronado

Coronado Beach

Orange Av

Glorietta Bay Inn

Loews Coronado Bay Resort

Mistral

Restaurante Romesco

E   **F**   **G**   **H**

Where to Stay

WORD OF MOUTH

"We had a blast staying at Hotel Indigo. The view and the bar on the 9th floor is fabulous. Petco Park is smack in view."

—SOCALOC

Updated
by Maren
Dougherty

In San Diego, you could plan a luxurious vacation, staying at a hotel with 350-thread-count sheets, wall-mounted flat screens, and panoramic Pacific views. But with some flexibility—maybe opting for a partial-view room with standard TVs—it's possible to experience the city's beauty at half the price.

Any local will tell you two things about San Diego: No. 1, the weather really is perfect; and No. 2, the area's neighborhoods and beach communities offer great diversity, from lively urban vacations to laid-back beachfront escapes. In action-packed downtown, luxury hotels battle it out by offering the nicest perks, including outdoor infinity pools, in-room iPod docks, chauffeured rides in SUVs, and passes to the hotels' hip weekend parties. There are also hostels and some budget-friendly options toward the Little Italy part of town.

You'll need a car if you stay outside downtown, but the coastal communities are rich with lodging options. Across the bridge, Coronado's hotels and resorts offer access to a stretch of glistening white sand that's often recognized as one of the best beaches in the country. La Jolla offers many romantic, upscale ocean-view hotels and some of the area's best restaurants and specialty shopping. But it's easy to find a water view in any price range: surfers make themselves at home at the casual inns and budget stays of Pacific Beach. And if you're planning to fish, check out hotels located near the marinas in Shelter Island, Point Loma, or Coronado.

For families, Uptown, Mission Valley, and Old Town are close to Sea-World and the San Diego Zoo, offering good-value accommodations with extras like sleeper sofas and video games. Mission Valley is ideal for business travelers; there are plenty of well-known chain hotels with conference space, modern business centers, and kitchenettes for extended stays.

When your work (or sightseeing) is done, join the trendsetters flocking to downtown's Gaslamp Quarter for its hip restaurants and rooftop hotel bars that rival L.A.'s stylish scenes.

WHERE SHOULD I STAY?

	NEIGHBORHOOD VIBE	PROS	CONS
Downtown	Downtown's hub is the Gaslamp Quarter, an action-packed area with many hotels, boutiques, restaurants, and clubs. Little Italy and Embarcadero areas are quieter.	Close to food and night-life options for every age and taste. Quick walk or trolley ride to convention center. Won't need a car to get to many attractions.	Streets can be congested and noisy at night, particularly in the Gaslamp District and East Village. Overnight parking is expensive.
Uptown and Old Town	Quieter area north of downtown with more budget-friendly hotels. Old Town has a busy stretch of Mexican restaurants and historic sites.	Central location that's close to Balboa Park and major freeways. Good for business travelers. More inexpensive dining options.	Limited nightlife options. Feels more removed from San Diego's beachy feel. Mission Valley area lacks character; it's filled with malls and car lots.
Mission Bay, Beaches, and SeaWorld	Relaxed and casual beachside area with many resorts, golf courses, and parks. Largest man-made aquatic park in the country.	Right on the water. Can splurge on Jet Skis and other water sports or stick to BBQs and public playgrounds. Close to SeaWorld.	Resorts are spaced far apart, and area is somewhat removed from central San Diego. Watch for high resort fees and other not-so-obvious charges.
La Jolla	The "jewel" of San Diego, an affluent coastal area with a small-town atmosphere. Has a range of luxury hotels and a few value choices.	Gorgeous views. Close or right on the beach. Some of the best seafood restaurants and high-end shopping in the state. Safe area for walking.	Often congested, and parking can be nearly impossible in summer. Very expensive area. Has few hotels that cater to children.
Point Loma and Coronado with Harbor and Shelter Islands	Areas by the bay have historic and resort hotels, beaches, and tourist-oriented restaurants. Coronado and Point Loma are more residential, home to many military families.	Great views of the city, bay, and beaches. Near the airport. Convenient for boaters. Hotels tend to be family-friendly, with large rooms and pools.	Isolated from the rest of the city; you'll spend significant time commuting to other parts of San Diego, such as La Jolla and Balboa Park.

9

BEST BETS FOR SAN DIEGO LODGING

Fodor's offers a selective listing of quality lodging experiences. Here we've compiled our top recommendations. The very best properties—in other words, those that provide a particularly remarkable experience in their price range—are designated in the listings with a Fodor's Choice logo.

Fodor's Choice ★

1906 Lodge, $$, p. 193
Britt Scripps Inn, $$, p. 185
Catamaran Resort Hotel, $$$, p. 186
Courtyard by Marriott Mission Valley, $, p. 185
Grande Colonial, $$$, p. 189
Hard Rock Hotel, $$$, p. 180
Homewood Suites San Diego Airport, $$, p. 196
Hotel Del Coronado, $$$, p. 193
Hotel Solamar, $$, p. 180
Lodge at Torrey Pines, $$$$, p. 190
The Sofia Hotel, $$, p. 183
Westgate Hotel, $$, p. 184

By Price

¢

500 West, p. 179
Lucky D's Hostel, p. 182

$

Best Western Plus Hacienda Hotel–Old Town, p. 185
Courtyard by Marriott-Mission Valley, p. 185
Crown City Inn & Bistro, p. 193
The Cosmopolitan Hotel, p. 186
Park Manor Suites, p. 185

$$

Britt Scripps Inn, p. 185
The Dana on Mission Bay, p. 186
Grande Colonial, p. 189
Homewood Suites San Diego Airport, p. 196
Hotel Indigo, p. 180
Hotel Solamar, p. 180
The Sofia Hotel, p. 183

$$$

Catamaran Resort Hotel, p. 186

Hard Rock Hotel, p. 180
Hotel Del Coronado, p. 193
Pacific Terrace Hotel, p. 188
Paradise Point Resort & Spa, p. 188
Westgate Hotel, p. 184

$$$$

La Valencia, p. 190
Lodge at Torrey Pines, p. 190

By Experience

BEST BEACH

Catamaran Resort Hotel, p. 186
Hotel Del Coronado, p. 193
La Jolla Shores Hotel, p. 190
Paradise Point Resort & Spa, p. 188
Tower23, p. 189

BEST POOL

Andaz San Diego, p. 179

Hotel Solamar, p. 180
Hyatt Regency Mission Bay Spa & Marina, p. 188
La Valencia, p. 190
Loews Coronado Bay Resort, p. 195

BEST FOR ROMANCE

1906 Lodge, p. 193
Hotel Del Coronado, p. 193
Hotel Parisi, p. 189
Hotel Solamar, p. 180
The Lodge at Torrey Pines, p. 190

BEST SPA

Estancia La Jolla Hotel & Spa, p. 189
Loews Coronado Bay Resort, p. 195
Sè San Diego, p. 183

BEST VIEWS

Crystal Pier Hotel, p. 186
Hilton San Diego Bayfront, p. 188
Hyatt Regency Mission Bay Spa & Marina, p. 188
Inn at Sunset Cliffs, p. 196
Sheraton San Diego Hotel & Marina, p. 195

MOST TRENDY

Andaz San Diego, p. 179
The Keating Hotel, p. 180
Sè San Diego, p. 183
Tower23, p. 189

SAN DIEGO LODGING PLANNER

LODGING STRATEGY

Where should I stay? With hundreds of San Diego hotels in dozens of neighborhoods, it may seem like a daunting question. But fret not—our expert writers and editors have done most of the legwork. The selections here represent the best this sunny paradise has to offer—from the best budget motels to the sleekest boutique hotels. Scan "Best Bets" on the following pages for our top recommendations by price and experience. Or find a review quickly in the listings—search by neighborhood, then alphabetically. Happy hunting!

PARKING

Given the distances between attractions and limited public transportation routes, a car is almost a necessity for visitors to San Diego. That being said, a vehicle can significantly add to your expenses if you stay in the ritzier areas. Overnight parking in Coronado, La Jolla, and downtown's Gaslamp Quarter can be as high as $35 per night; in Uptown and Mission Bay it usually runs $10 to $15.

NEED A RESERVATION?

Book well in advance, especially if you plan to visit in summer, which is the busy season for most hotels. In spring and fall, conventions and sports events can fill every downtown hotel room. When you make reservations, ask about specials. Hotel packages are your best bet; deals range from arts and culture escapes to relaxing spa weekends. Check hotel Web sites for Internet specials and try to call a hotel directly; sometimes your effort will result in a lower rate. Several properties in the Hotel Circle area of Mission Valley offer reduced rates and even free tickets to the San Diego Zoo and other attractions. Many hotels also promote discounted weekend packages to fill rooms after convention and business customers leave town. Since the weather is great year-round, don't expect substantial discounts in winter. You can save on hotels and attractions by visiting the San Diego Convention and Visitors Bureau Web site (⊕ *www.sandiego.org*) for a free Vacation Planning Kit with a Travel Value Coupon booklet.

STAYING WITH KIDS

San Diego is a great year-round family destination. The area is full of hotels suited to a family's budget and/or recreational needs, and many allow kids under 18 to stay free with their parents. You'll find the most choices and diversity in and around Mission Bay, which is close to Sea-World, beaches, parks, and Old Town. Many Mission Bay hotels offer SeaWorld packages or discounts. Another central choice is Mission Valley, which has malls, movie theaters, and hotels that have become accustomed to kids running through the halls. Some resorts offer full- or half-day programs for kids that include swimming, arts and crafts, and trips to the Birch Aquarium. These programs are usually available only in summer and some holiday weekends. Look for "children's programs" within the italicized service information below each lodging review if these services are important to you. Properties that are especially kid-friendly are marked with ♔ throughout the chapter.

SERVICES

You can assume that all rooms have private baths, phones, and TVs, and are nonsmoking unless otherwise noted. Downtown hotels once catered primarily to business travelers, though the new boutique hotels are attracting hip leisure travelers to the area, while those at Mission Bay, in coastal locations such as Carlsbad and Encinitas, and at inland resort areas offer golf and other sports facilities, spa services, children's activities, and more.

If a particular amenity is important to you, ask for it; many hotels will provide extras upon request. Also double-check your bill at checkout. These days, hotels are fond of tacked-on charges such as a "minibar restocking fee" or cleaning charges for smokers. If a charge seems unreasonable, ask to remedy it at checkout. If you're traveling with pets, note that pet policies do change and some hotels require substantial cleaning fees of $50 to $100. A cautionary note to smokers: some hotels are entirely smoke-free, meaning even smoking outdoors is frowned upon or prohibited.

PRICES

The lodgings we list run from bare-bones basic to lavishly upscale. Note that even in the most expensive areas, you can find affordable rooms. High season is summer, and rates are lowest in fall. If an ocean view is important, request it when booking, but be aware that it will cost significantly more than a non-ocean-view room.

We always list a property's facilities, but we don't specify whether you'll be charged extra to use them; when pricing accommodations, always ask what's included. Our price categories are based on a hotel's standard double room (or suites, in all-suites properties) in non-holiday high season.

WHAT IT COSTS				
¢	$	$$	$$$	$$$$
Hotels　　under $100	$100–$199	$200–$299	$300–$400	over $400

Prices are for a standard double room in high (summer) season, excluding 10.5% tax.

USING THE MAPS

Throughout the chapter, you'll see mapping symbols and coordinates (⊹ 2:F3) after property names or reviews. *To locate the property on a map, turn to the San Diego Dining and Lodging Atlas located before this chapter.* The first number after the ⊹ symbol indicates the map number. Following that is the property's coordinate on the map grid. Hotel reviews have been abbreviated in this book. For expanded reviews please visit Fodors.com.

HOTEL REVIEWS

Listed alphabetically within neighborhoods. Use the coordinates (⊕ 2:F3) after property names or reviews to locate the property on the San Diego Dining and Lodging Atlas. The first number after the ⊕ symbol indicates the map number. Following that is the property's coordinate on the map grid.

DOWNTOWN

Lively, continuously revitalizing downtown is San Diego's hotel hub, with everything from budget chains to boutique and business hotels. Here's a part of Southern California where you won't need a car; you can walk or take the trolley to Seaport Village, the Embarcadero, the convention center, galleries and coffeehouses, and the Horton Plaza shopping center. Smack in the middle of downtown is the Gaslamp Quarter where you'll find nightlife options for every night of the week, ranging from 1920s-style jazz lounges to posh multilevel clubs.

¢ ⚏ **500 West.** An $8 million renovation in 2004 transformed San Diego's historic 1924 Armed Services YMCA Building into this hip, urban boutique hotel. **Pros:** near shops and restaurants; modern room decor; kitchen. **Cons:** small rooms; few double rooms; no air-conditioning. ⊠ *500 W. Broadway, Downtown* ☎ *619/234–5252, 866/500–7533* ⊕ *www.500westhotel.com* ↩ *259 rooms* ⌂ *In-room: no a/c, Wi-Fi. In-hotel: gym, laundry facilities* ⊕ *1:C4.*

$$$ ⚏ **Andaz San Diego.** This storied property opened as the Maryland Hotel in 1914, and later became a boardinghouse. **Pros:** central location; great scene; luxurious rooms. **Cons:** spotty service; pretentious attitude. ⊠ *600 F St., Downtown* ☎ *619/849–1234* ⊕ *www.andaz.com* ↩ *159 rooms, 17 suites* ⌂ *In-room: a/c, safe, Internet, Wi-Fi. In-hotel: restaurant, bar, pool, business center, parking, some pets allowed* ⊕ *1:E4.*

$ ⚏ **The Bristol.** Pop art by Peter Max and Andy Warhol on the walls marks the style of this splashy boutique hotel. **Pros:** modern rooms; centrally located; good value. **Cons:** noisy, somewhat seedy area. ⊠ *1055 1st Ave., Downtown* ☎ *619/232–6141, 888/745–4393* ⊕ *www. thebristolsandiego.com* ↩ *102 rooms* ⌂ *In-room: a/c, Wi-Fi. In-hotel: restaurant, bar, gym, parking* ⊕ *1:D3.*

$$ ⚏ **Embassy Suites–San Diego Bay.** The front door of each spacious, contemporary suite opens out onto a 12-story atrium, and rooms facing the harbor have spectacular views. **Pros:** new bathrooms; upgraded gym; good location. **Cons:** busy location; wildly varying room rates. ⊠ *601 Pacific Hwy., Embarcadero* ☎ *619/239–2400, 800/362–2779* ⊕ *www.sandiegobay.embassysuites.com* ↩ *337 suites* ⌂ *In-room: a/c, Wi-Fi. In-hotel: restaurant, bar, pool, gym, laundry facilities, parking* ⎮◎⎮ *Breakfast* ⊕ *1:B4.*

$ ⚏ **Gaslamp Plaza Suites.** On the National Register of Historic Places, this 10-story structure a block from Horton Plaza was built in 1913 as one of San Diego's first "skyscrapers." **Pros:** historic building; good location; well priced. **Cons:** books up early; smallish rooms. ⊠ *520 E St., Gaslamp Quarter* ☎ *619/232–9500, 800/874–8770* ⊕ *www.*

9

gaslampplaza.com ↝ *12 rooms, 52 suites* ⌂ *In-room: a/c, Wi-Fi. In-hotel: bar, parking* ⦿*Breakfast* ✛ *1:E4.*

$$$
Fodor'sChoice
★

⬚ **Hard Rock Hotel.** Self-billed as a hip playground for rock stars and people who just want to party like them, the Hard Rock Hotel is conveniently located near PETCO Park overlooking glimmering San Diego Bay. **Pros:** central location; great scene; luxurious rooms. **Cons:** pricey drinks; some attitude. ✉ *207 5th Ave., Gaslamp Quarter* ☎ *619/702–3000, 866/751–7625* ⊕ *www.hardrockhotelsd.com* ↝ *244 rooms, 176 suites* ⌂ *In-room: a/c, safe, Internet, Wi-Fi. In-hotel: restaurant, bar, pool, gym, spa, business center, parking* ✛ *2:E5.*

$$

⬚ **Hilton San Diego Bayfront.** This modern 30-story hotel overlooking San Diego Bay isn't a typical Hilton. **Pros:** close to the convention center; new rooms. **Cons:** awkward layout; pricey drinks. ✉ *1 Park Blvd., Downtown* ☎ *619/564–3333* ⊕ *www.hiltonsdbayfront.com* ↝ *1,160 rooms, 30 suites* ⌂ *In-room: a/c, safe, Wi-Fi. In-hotel: restaurant, bar, pool, gym, spa, parking, some pets allowed* ✛ *1:E6.*

$$

⬚ **Hilton San Diego Gaslamp Quarter.** Step into the modern and sophisticated lobby with its cozy lounge spaces and wood accents, and you'll know this isn't your run-of-the-mill chain hotel. **Pros:** nice decor; upscale lofts; near restaurants and shops. **Cons:** noisy area; somewhat gritty area. ✉ *401 K St., Gaslamp Quarter* ☎ *619/231–4040, 800/445–8667* ⊕ *www.hiltongaslamp.com* ↝ *240 rooms, 13 suites, 30 lofts* ⌂ *In-room: a/c, Internet. In-hotel: restaurant, bar, pool, gym, parking, some pets allowed* ✛ *1:D5.*

$$

⬚ **Hotel Indigo.** Smart spaces and great service for the business traveler is the ethos behind this chain of modern hotels. **Pros:** close to restaurants and bars; new rooms. **Cons:** somewhat noisy neighborhood. ✉ *509 9th Ave., East Village* ☎ *619/727–4000* ⊕ *www.hotelindigo.com/sandiego* ↝ *210 rooms, 5 suites* ⌂ *In-room: a/c, Wi-Fi. In-hotel: restaurant, bar, parking, some pets allowed* ✛ *1:E5.*

$$
Fodor'sChoice
★

⬚ **Hotel Solamar.** For its first entry onto San Diego's hotel scene, the Kimpton boutique hotel chain renovated an old warehouse, hitting the right notes with striking, high style. **Pros:** great restaurant; attentive service; upscale rooms. **Cons:** busy valet parking; bars are crowded on weekends. ✉ *435 6th Ave., Gaslamp Quarter* ☎ *619/531–8740, 877/230–0300* ⊕ *www.hotelsolamar.com* ↝ *217 rooms, 16 suites* ⌂ *In-room: a/c, safe, Wi-Fi. In-hotel: restaurant, bar, pool, gym, parking, some pets allowed* ✛ *1:E5.*

$$

⬚ **The Keating Hotel.** The Keating's 120-year-old historic exterior looks nothing like its new sexy interior, remade into a hotel in 2006. **Pros:** great location; boutique hotel; many amenities. **Cons:** industrial-feeling rooms; small lobby. ✉ *432 F St., Downtown* ☎ *619/814–5700, 877/753–2846* ⊕ *www.thekeating.com* ↝ *26 rooms, 9 suites* ⌂ *In-room: a/c, Wi-Fi. In-hotel: restaurant, bar, parking, some pets allowed* ✛ *1:D4.*

$

⬚ **Little Italy Inn.** This old-world-style bed-and-breakfast, in a renovated 1910 property, has 22 unique, well-appointed rooms. **Pros:** good location; historic property; free HBO. **Cons:** some shared baths; no parking; loud traffic area. ✉ *505 W. Grape St., Little Italy* ☎ *619/230–1600, 800/518–9930* ⊕ *www.littleitalyhotel.com* ↝ *21 rooms, 2 suites* ⌂ *In-room: a/c, safe, Wi-Fi* ⦿*Breakfast* ✛ *1:C1.*

Hard Rock Hotel

The Sofia Hotel

Versailles Room, Westgate Hotel

Family-Friendly Hotels

Got kids in tow? San Diego is designed for family fun; the year-round sunny, warm weather ensures lots of play days. The focus is on outdoor activities, such as surfing or swimming, but be sure to spend a day at Balboa Park's gardens, museums, and IMAX theater. Many hotels let kids under 18 stay free—just ask. And check into kids' activity programs, family-size suites, in-room Nintendo, or kitchenettes. Shop around for hotel packages, which often include tickets to local attractions.

Some of the high-end properties have special programs for kids; most occur in summer, some year-round. The famous **Hotel Del Coronado** has tons of activities, from surfing lessons and kayak tours to foosball and karaoke in "VIBZ," a year-round hangout for teens ages 13–17. The **Loews Coronado Bay Resort** has welcome gifts for children, a kids-only pool, a game library, and special menus. Some recreational fun is offered seasonally, such as sunset sails and gondola rides. And kids can bring their pets.

Across the bay, resorts on family-friendly Mission Bay cater to young ones. The **Catamaran Resort Hotel** holds science camps for kids ages 5–12. Offered daily in summer, the workshops focus on a range of topics, including the diversity of sea life and the physics of beach cruisers. At the **Lodge at Torrey Pines'** library, kids over age 12 can play pool or watch movies borrowed from the concierge; it's open from 8 am until 11 pm.

Smaller hotels in Mission Valley and La Jolla may not have organized programs but several offer extra amenities for kids and teens; the Courtyard by Marriott Mission Valley has a Nintendo Wii system in the lobby and board games that kids can borrow from the front desk.

¢ ☷ **Lucky D's Hostel.** A quick walk from PETCO Park and most of the major downtown bars and clubs, this no-frills hostel is a good pick for travelers who are content with shared bathrooms and sounds of drunk people stumbling home at 2 am. **Pros:** solo travelers can easily find friends here; central location; free dinner on some nights. **Cons:** can get very hot in summer; noisy; no on-site parking. ⊠ *615 8th Ave., East Village* ☎ *619/595–0000* ⊕ *www.luckydshostel.com* ⇄ *35 dorms, 5 private rooms* ⌂ *In-room: no a/c, safe, no TV, Wi-Fi. In-hotel: bar, laundry facilities, business center, some age restrictions* ⊹ *1:E4.*

$$ ☷ **Manchester Grand Hyatt San Diego.** Built primarily for business travelers,
☾ this hotel between Seaport Village and the convention center is the largest in San Diego, and its 33- and 40-story towers make it the West Coast's tallest waterfront hotel. **Pros:** great views; conference facilities; good location. **Cons:** very busy; some rooms dated. ⊠ *1 Market Pl., Embarcadero* ☎ *619/232–1234, 800/233–1234* ⊕ *www.manchestergrand.hyatt.com* ⇄ *1,530 rooms, 95 suites* ⌂ *In-room: a/c, safe, Internet, Wi-Fi. In-hotel: restaurant, bar, pool, tennis court, gym, spa, parking* ⊹ *1:C5.*

$$ ☷ **Marriott Residence Inn Downtown.** A home away from home for urbanites, the all-suites hotel opened in November 2009. **Pros:** spacious rooms; central location; pet-friendly. **Cons:** no room service; pricey

valet-only parking will add up quickly during an extended stay. ✉ *356 6th Ave., Gaslamp Quarter* ☎ *619/487–1200* ⊕ *www.marriott.com/ sanrg* ⇄ *240 suites* ৬ *In-room: a/c, safe, kitchen, Internet, Wi-Fi. In-hotel: bar, pool, gym, laundry facilities, business center, parking, some pets allowed* ❏ *Breakfast* ✛ *1:E5.*

$$ ▦ **Omni San Diego Hotel.** Welcoming business travelers who also want to catch the Cubs vs. Padres game, this modern masterpiece occupies the first 21 floors of a 32-story high-rise overlooking PETCO Park baseball stadium. **Pros:** great views; good location; modern setting. **Cons:** busy; crowded during baseball season. ✉ *675 L St., Gaslamp Quarter* ☎ *619/231–6664, 800/843–6664* ⊕ *www.omnihotels.com* ⇄ *478 rooms, 33 suites* ৬ *In-room: a/c, safe, Internet, Wi-Fi. In-hotel: restaurant, bar, pool, gym, parking, some pets allowed* ✛ *1:E6.*

$ ▦ **Porto Vista Hotel & Suites.** A \$15 million renovation turned this former budget motel into a contemporary hotel-motel with two additional buildings, a stylish restaurant and lounge, a business center, and a fitness center. **Pros:** new decor in common areas, some guest rooms, and the fitness center; free shuttle. **Cons:** small rooms, some still in need of updating. ✉ *1835 Columbia St., Little Italy* ☎ *619/544–0164, 800/800–8000* ⊕ *www.portovistasandiego.com* ⇄ *189 rooms, 22 suites* ৬ *In-room: a/c, Wi-Fi. In-hotel: restaurant, bar, laundry facilities, parking, some pets allowed* ✛ *1:C2.*

$$ ▦ **San Diego Marriott Gaslamp Quarter.** This 22-story hotel is in the midst of all the Gaslamp's restaurants and boutiques, a short walk to the trolley station, convention center, and PETCO Park. **Pros:** good views; modern decor; central location. **Cons:** rooftop bar can get rowdy; no pool. ✉ *660 K St., Gaslamp Quarter* ☎ *619/696–0234* ⊕ *www. marriott.com* ⇄ *291 rooms, 15 suites* ৬ *In-room: a/c, safe, Internet, Wi-Fi. In-hotel: restaurant, bar, gym, parking* ✛ *1:E5.*

$$ ▦ **Sè San Diego.** This Dodd Mitchell–designed hotel sets a new standard for luxury digs in San Diego. **Pros:** new rooms; centrally located; luxury amenities. **Cons:** expensive parking; sliding glass doors in bathrooms provide limited privacy. ✉ *1047 5th Ave., Downtown* ☎ *619/515–3000* ⊕ *www.sesandiego.com* ⇄ *181 rooms, 37 suites, 20 condos, 3 penthouses* ৬ *In-room: a/c, safe, Wi-Fi. In-hotel: restaurant, bar, pool, gym, spa, parking, some pets allowed* ✛ *1:E3.*

$$ ▦ **The Sofia Hotel.** A major remodeling in 2006 transformed the former Pickwick into a practical and stylish downtown destination. **Pros:** upscale room amenities; historic building; near shops and restaurants. **Cons:** next to bus station; busy area. ✉ *150 W. Broadway, Downtown* ☎ *800/826–0009* ⊕ *www.thesofiahotel.com* ⇄ *212 rooms, 4 suites* ৬ *In-room: a/c, safe, Internet, Wi-Fi. In-hotel: restaurant, bar, gym, business center, parking, some pets allowed* ✛ *1:D3.*

Fodor's Choice
★

$$ ▦ **U.S. Grant.** Stepping into the regal U.S. Grant not only puts you in the lap of luxury but also back into San Diego history; the 100-year-old building is on the National Register of Historic Sites. **Pros:** modern rooms; great location; near shopping and restaurants. **Cons:** small elevators; the hotel's many special events can make for a hectic atmosphere. ✉ *326 Broadway, Downtown* ☎ *619/232–3121, 800/237–5029* ⊕ *www.*

9

W Hotel

luxurycollection.com/usgrant ⇌ *270 rooms, 47 suites* ⌂ *In-room: a/c, safe, Internet, Wi-Fi. In-hotel: restaurant, bar, gym, parking* ✛ *1:D3.*

$$ 🖳 **W Hotel.** Come here for the trendy decor, fruity drinks, and upscale rooms. **Pros:** large lobby that's fun for people-watching; modern rooms; nice spa. **Cons:** expensive parking; not centrally located. ✉ *421 W. B St., Downtown* ☎ *619/398–3100, 877/822–0000* ⊕ *www.whotels.com/sandiego* ⇌ *258 rooms, 20 suites* ⌂ *In-room: a/c, safe, Internet, Wi-Fi. In-hotel: restaurant, bar, pool, gym, spa, parking, some pets allowed* ✛ *1:C3.*

$$ 🖳 **Westgate Hotel.** A modern high-rise near Horton Plaza hides what

Fodor's Choice must be the most opulent old-world-style hotel in San Diego. **Pros:**

★ elegant rooms; grand lobby, near shopping. **Cons:** formal atmosphere; somewhat gritty neighborhood. ✉ *1055 2nd Ave., Gaslamp Quarter* ☎ *619/238–1818, 800/221–3802* ⊕ *www.westgatehotel.com* ⇌ *223 rooms, 10 suites* ⌂ *In-room: a/c, Internet, Wi-Fi. In-hotel: restaurant, bar, gym, spa, parking* ✛ *1:D3.*

UPTOWN AND OLD TOWN

San Diego's Uptown area is close to the San Diego Zoo and Balboa Park, and includes the neighborhoods of Hillcrest, Mission Hills, Banker's Hill, North Park, and University Heights. There are few hotels, but the area offers pedestrian-friendly shopping and hip dive bars.

Dense with Mexican eateries, Old Town is the place to be for quick and easy access to house-made tortillas. The neighborhood is also home to historic adobe shops and museums. East of Old Town is Mission Valley, a suburban maze of freeways, shopping centers, and Hotel Circle, where many spacious and inexpensive lodging options are located.

MISSION VALLEY

$ ▦ **Courtyard by Marriott-Mission Valley.** Located in hotel-dense Mission

Fodor'sChoice Valley, this family-friendly hotel transformed from a Holiday Inn into a

★ Courtyard by Marriott in 2008. **Pros:** easy freeway access to area attrac-

☾ tions; good value; nice perks for families and business travelers. **Cons:** few stores and restaurants in walking distance; halls can be noisy with groups and kids. ✉ *595 Hotel Circle S, Mission Valley* ☎ *619/291–5720* ⊕ *www.courtyardsd.com* ⋑ *309 rooms, 8 suites* ⟁ *In-room: a/c, Internet, Wi-Fi. In-hotel: restaurant, pool, gym, laundry facilities, business center, parking* ⊹ *2:D3.*

$$ ▦ **Doubletree Hotel San Diego Mission Valley.** Near the Fashion Valley shopping mall and adjacent to the Hazard Center—which has a seven-screen movie theater, four major restaurants, a food pavilion, and more than 20 shops—the Doubletree is also convenient to Route 163 and I–8. **Pros:** centrally located; large rooms. **Cons:** dated bathrooms; few amenities. ✉ *7450 Hazard Center Dr.* ☎ *619/297–5466, 800/222–8733* ⊕ *www.doubletree.com* ⋑ *294 rooms, 6 suites* ⟁ *In-room: a/c, Internet, Wi-Fi. In-hotel: restaurant, bar, pool, tennis court, gym, laundry facilities, parking* ⊹ *2:D2.*

UPTOWN

¢ ▦ **Balboa Park Inn.** This budget guesthouse occupies four Spanish colonial–style 1915 residences connected by courtyards. **Pros:** good value; convenient location; continental breakfast. **Cons:** no parking; no on-site services; busy area. ✉ *3402 Park Blvd., North Park* ☎ *619/298–0823, 800/938–8181* ⊕ *www.balboaparkinn.com* ⋑ *26 suites* ⟁ *In-room: a/c, kitchen, Wi-Fi* ⦿ *Breakfast* ⊹ *2:F5.*

$$ ▦ **Britt Scripps Inn.** A block west of Balboa Park, in prominent Banker's

Fodor'sChoice Hill, this inn occupies the former mansion of the Scripps newspaper

★ family. **Pros:** intimate; historic building; upscale amenities. **Cons:** not near any nightlife. ✉ *406 Maple St., North Park* ☎ *888/881–1991* ⊕ *www.brittscripps.com* ⋑ *9 rooms* ⟁ *In-room: a/c, safe, Wi-Fi. In-hotel: parking* ⦿ *Breakfast* ⊹ *2:D6.*

$ ▦ **Park Manor Suites.** One of few lodgings within walking distance of Balboa Park, antique furniture, ornate mirrors, and the original 1926 ceiling grace the lobby of this seven-story historic hotel. **Pros:** spacious rooms; evening entertainment. **Cons:** no a/c; some rooms need renovation. ✉ *525 Spruce St., Banker's Hill* ☎ *619/291–0999* ⊕ *www. parkmanorsuites.com* ⋑ *4 rooms, 71 suites* ⟁ *In-room: no a/c, safe, kitchen, Wi-Fi. In-hotel: restaurant, bar, laundry facilities, business center, parking* ⦿ *Breakfast* ⊹ *2:E6.*

OLD TOWN

$ ▦ **Best Western Hacienda Hotel–Old Town.** Perched on a hill in the heart

☾ of Old Town, this hotel is known for its expansive courtyards, outdoor fountains, and a maze of stairs that connect eight buildings of guest rooms. **Pros:** airport shuttle; well-maintained outdoor areas. **Cons:** some rooms need renovating; complicated property layout. ✉ *4041 Harney St., Old Town* ☎ *619/298–4707* ⊕ *www.haciendahotel-oldtown.com* ⋑ *178 rooms, 21 suites* ⟁ *In-room: a/c, safe, Internet. In-hotel: restaurant, bar, pool, gym, laundry facilities, business center, parking* ⊹ *2:A4.*

9

$ 📺 **The Cosmopolitan Hotel.** With antique furniture, pull-chain toilets, and a veranda overlooking the Old Town State Historic Park, the Cosmo offers guests a taste of Victorian-era living. **Pros:** historic charm; huge suites; romantic. **Cons:** no TVs; public or street parking only. ✉ *2660 Calhoun St., Old Town* ☎ *619/297–1874* ⊕ *www. oldtowncosmopolitan.com* 🛏 *6 rooms, 4 suites* ⚭ *In-room: a/c, Wi-Fi. In-hotel: restaurant, bar, some pets allowed* ⏧ *Breakfast* ⚓ *2:A4.*

$ 📺 **Crowne Plaza San Diego.** After an $8 million renovation in mid-2007, the former Red Lion Hanalei Hotel is now a member of the InterContinental chain. **Pros:** near shopping; close to airport; updated rooms. **Cons:** near freeway; dated public areas; spotty service. ✉ *2270 Hotel Circle North, Mission Valley* ☎ *619/297–1101* ⊕ *www.ichotelsgroup. com* 🛏 *403 rooms, 14 suites* ⚭ *In-room: a/c, safe, Internet. In-hotel: restaurant, bar, pool, gym, spa, laundry facilities, parking, some pets allowed* ⚓ *2:B3.*

$ 📺 **Holiday Inn Express–Old Town.** Already an excellent value for Old Town, this cheerful property throws in such perks as a free breakfast buffet. **Pros:** good location; hot continental breakfast. **Cons:** smallish rooms; few nightlife options. ✉ *3900 Old Town Ave., Old Town* ☎ *619/299–7400, 800/465–4329* ⊕ *www.hioldtownhotel.com* 🛏 *125 rooms, 2 suites* ⚭ *In-room: a/c, Internet, Wi-Fi. In-hotel: pool, laundry facilities, parking* ⏧ *Breakfast* ⚓ *2:A4.*

MISSION BAY, BEACHES, AND SEAWORLD

Mission Bay Park, with its beaches, bike trails, boat-launching ramps, golf course, and grassy parks—not to mention SeaWorld—is a haven of hotels and resorts. Smaller hotels, motels, and hostels can be found nearby in Mission Beach and Pacific Beach. These coastal communities are popular among local twentysomethings for the many inexpensive dining and nightlife possibilities. The streets are also filled with surf shops and boutiques for picking up flip-flops, sundresses, and other beachy souvenirs. You can't go wrong with any of these beachfront areas, as long as the frenzied crowds at play don't bother you.

$$$ 📺 **Catamaran Resort Hotel.** Exotic macaws perch in the lush lobby of this
☾ appealing hotel on Mission Bay. **Pros:** recently upgraded rooms; spa;
Fodor's Choice free cruises. **Cons:** not centrally located. ✉ *3999 Mission Blvd., Mission
★ Beach* ☎ *858/488–1081, 800/422–8386* ⊕ *www.catamaranresort.com* 🛏 *311 rooms, 50 suites* ⚭ *In-room: a/c, safe, kitchen, Internet, Wi-Fi. In-hotel: restaurant, bar, pool, gym, spa, beach, parking* ⚓ *3:C5.*

$$$ 📺 **Crystal Pier Hotel.** Crystal Pier, a Pacific Beach landmark, had its grand opening in 1927; 10 years later, the first of the cottages was built. **Pros:** ocean view; historic hotel; on beach. **Cons:** few amenities; no air-conditioning in most; reservations fill up fast. ✉ *4500 Ocean Blvd., Pacific Beach* ☎ *858/483–6983, 800/748–5894* ⊕ *www. crystalpier.com* 🛏 *23 cottages, 6 suites* ⚭ *In-room: a/c, kitchen. In-hotel: beach, parking* ⚓ *3:B5.*

$$ 📺 **The Dana on Mission Bay.** There's a modern chic feel to the earth-tone lobby of this beach hotel, making it feel you've arrived somewhere much more expensive. **Pros:** water views; two pools. **Cons:** slightly confusing layout; not centrally located. ✉ *1710 W. Mission Bay Dr., Mission*

Courtyard by Marriott Mission Valley

Catamaran Resort Hotel

Britt Scripps Inn

Bay ☎ *619/222–6440, 800/445–3339* ⊕ *www.thedana.com* ➹ *259 rooms, 12 suites* ⚙ *In-room: a/c, Wi-Fi. In-hotel: restaurant, bar, pool, parking* ✛ *3:C6.*

WORD OF MOUTH

"One of the great things to enjoy about San Diego is its ocean and bay views. Shelter Island, Harbor Island, and Mission Bay fit the bill. They would be central so you can get to sites quickly and they provide a location where you can get the kids outside for those few minutes when they need to use up some energy—or an interesting (and maybe even romantic) stroll for adults."

—travelbuggie

$$$ ▦ **Hyatt Regency Mission Bay Spa &**
ⓒ **Marina.** This modern and stunning property has many desirable amenities, including balconies with excellent views of the garden, bay, ocean, or swimming pool courtyard (pools have 120-foot waterslides, plus a smaller slide on the kiddie pool). **Pros:** modern decor; eco-spa; water views. **Cons:** slightly hard to navigate surrounding roads; thin walls; not centrally located. ⊠ *1441 Quivira Rd., Mission Bay* ☎ *619/224–1234, 800/233–1234* ⊕ *www.hyatt.com* ➹ *354 rooms, 76 suites* ⚙ *In-room: a/c, Internet, Wi-Fi. In-hotel: restaurant, bar, pool, gym, spa, children's programs, business center, parking* ✛ *3:C6.*

$$ ▦ **Ocean Park Inn.** A 2009 renovation of this beachfront hotel outfitted guest rooms with new white comforters and flat-screen TVs. **Pros:** close to the beach, shops and restaurants; large rooms; enclosed outdoor pool is protected from the wind. **Cons:** bar noise carries to some rooms on the east side; common areas feel dated. ⊠ *710 Grand Ave., Pacific Beach* ☎ *858/483–5858* ⊕ *www.oceanparkinn.com* ➹ *73 rooms* ⚙ *In-room: a/c, safe, kitchen, Wi-Fi. In-hotel: pool, gym, beach, laundry facilities, parking* ⦾| *Breakfast* ✛ *3:B5.*

$$$ ▦ **Pacific Terrace Hotel.** Travelers love this terrific beachfront hotel and the ocean views from most rooms; it's a perfect place for watching sunsets over the Pacific. **Pros:** beach views; large rooms; friendly service. **Cons:** busy area; lots of traffic. ⊠ *610 Diamond St., Pacific Beach* ☎ *858/581–3500, 800/344–3370* ⊕ *www.pacificterrace.com* ➹ *61 rooms, 12 suites* ⚙ *In-room: a/c, safe, Wi-Fi. In-hotel: pool, gym, laundry facilities, parking* ⦾| *Breakfast* ✛ *3:B5.*

$$$ ▦ **Paradise Point Resort & Spa.** The beautiful landscape of this 44-acre
ⓒ resort on Vacation Isle has been the setting for a number of movies. **Pros:** water views; pools; good service. **Cons:** not centrally located; summer minimum stays; motel-thin walls. ⊠ *1404 Vacation Rd., Mission Bay* ☎ *858/274–4630, 800/344–2626* ⊕ *www.paradisepoint.com* ➹ *462 cottages* ⚙ *In-room: a/c, safe, Internet. In-hotel: restaurant, bar, pool, tennis court, gym, spa, beach, parking* ✛ *3:C6.*

$$ ▦ **Surfer Beach Hotel.** Choose this place for its great location—right on bustling Pacific Beach. **Pros:** beach location; ocean-view rooms; pool. **Cons:** busy area; dated rooms. ⊠ *711 Pacific Beach Dr., Pacific Beach* ☎ *858/483–7070, 866/251–2764* ⊕ *www.surferbeachhotel.com* ➹ *53 rooms, 16 suites* ⚙ *In-room: no a/c, Wi-Fi. In-hotel: restaurant, bar, pool, beach, laundry facilities, parking, some pets allowed* ✛ *3:B5.*

$$$ 🏨 **Tower23.** A neomodern masterpiece with a beachy vibe, this boutique hotel is a San Diego rarity, the first beachfront hotel to be built in the last decade. **Pros:** beach views; good location; hip decor. **Cons:** spotty service; busy area. ✉ *723 Felspar St., Pacific Beach* ☎ *866/869–3723, 858/270–2323* ⊕ *www.t23hotel.com* ➷ *38 rooms, 6 suites* ⚷ *In-room: a/c, safe, Wi-Fi. In-hotel: restaurant, bar, beach, business center, parking, some pets allowed* ✢ *3:B5.*

LA JOLLA

Multimillion-dollar homes line the beaches and hillsides of beautiful and prestigious La Jolla, a community about 20 minutes north of downtown. La Jolla Shores is a mile-long sandy beach that gets crowded in summer with kayakers, sunbathers, and students in scuba-diving classes. The village—the heart of La Jolla—is chockablock with expensive boutiques, art galleries, restaurants, and a grassy beachfront park that's popular for picnics and weddings. It may have an upscale European air, but don't despair if you're not driving up in an Aston Martin: this vacation spot has sufficient lodging choices for every budget.

$$ 🏨 **Empress Hotel.** Less glitzy than most neighboring lodging options in La Jolla, the five-story hotel attracts many business travelers and couples looking for a basic but comfortable place to stay. **Pros:** well-trained staff; near shops and restaurants; quiet street. **Cons:** not exciting for kids; some travelers report that noise carries between the thin walls. ✉ *7766 Fay Ave., La Jolla* ☎ *858/454–3001, 888/369–9900* ⊕ *www.empress-hotel.com* ➷ *69 rooms, 4 suites* ⚷ *In-room: a/c, safe, Wi-Fi. In-hotel: restaurant, gym, business center, parking* ⅇ|*Breakfast* ✢ *3:A2.*

$$ 🏨 **Estancia La Jolla Hotel & Spa.** La Jolla's newest resort was once the site of a famous equestrian ranch, Blackhorse Farms, where Thoroughbreds were trained. **Pros:** upscale rooms; nice spa; landscaped grounds. **Cons:** spotty service; not centrally located. ✉ *9700 N. Torrey Pines Rd., La Jolla* ☎ *858/550–1000, 877/437–8262* ⊕ *www.estancialajolla.com* ➷ *200 rooms, 10 suites* ⚷ *In-room: a/c, safe, Wi-Fi. In-hotel: restaurant, bar, pool, gym, spa, parking* ⅇ|*Breakfast* ✢ *3:B1.*

$$ 🏨 **Grande Colonial.** This white wedding cake–style hotel has ocean views and is in the heart of La Jolla village. **Pros:** near shopping; near beach; superb restaurant. **Cons:** somewhat busy street. ✉ *910 Prospect St., La Jolla* ☎ *858/454–2181, 800/826–1278* ⊕ *www.thegrandecolonial.com* ➷ *52 rooms, 41 suites* ⚷ *In-room: a/c, safe, kitchen, Wi-Fi. In-hotel: restaurant, bar, pool, parking* ✢ *3:A2.*

Fodor'sChoice
★

$$ 🏨 **Hotel Parisi.** A Zen-like peace welcomes you in the lobby, which has a skylighted fountain and is filled with Asian art. **Pros:** upscale amenities; modern decor; centrally located. **Cons:** one-room "suites"; staff can be aloof. ✉ *1111 Prospect St., La Jolla* ☎ *858/454–1511* ⊕ *www.hotelparisi.com* ➷ *29 suites* ⚷ *In-room: a/c, safe, Wi-Fi. In-hotel: parking* ⅇ|*Breakfast* ✢ *3:B2.*

$$ 🏨 **Hyatt Regency La Jolla.** This Hyatt is in the Golden Triangle area, about 10 minutes from the beach and the village of La Jolla. **Pros:** many restaurants; modern rooms; upscale amenities. **Cons:** busy hotel;

9

not centrally located. ⊠ *Aventine Center, 3777 La Jolla Village Dr., La Jolla* ☎ *858/552–1234, 800/233–1234* ⊕ *www.lajolla.hyatt.com* ⤴ *399 rooms, 20 suites* ♿ *In-room: a/c, safe, Internet, Wi-Fi. In-hotel: restaurant, bar, pool, tennis court, gym, parking* ⊹ *3:D1.*

$$ ▦ **La Jolla Cove Suites.** It may lack the charm of some properties in this exclusive area, but this motel with studios and suites (some with spacious oceanfront balconies) gives its guests the same first-class views of La Jolla Cove at lower rates. **Pros:** good value; ocean views; some large rooms. **Cons:** dated rooms; busy street. ⊠ *1155 Coast Blvd., La Jolla* ☎ *858/459–2621, 888/525–6552* ⊕ *www.lajollacove.com* ⤴ *25 rooms, 90 suites* ♿ *In-room: a/c, safe, kitchen, Wi-Fi. In-hotel: pool, parking, some pets allowed* ⏹*Breakfast* ⊹ *3:B2.*

$$$ ▦ **La Jolla Shores Hotel.** One of the few San Diego hotels actually on the
ⓒ beach, La Jolla Shores is located at La Jolla Beach and Tennis Club. **Pros:** on beach; great views; quiet area. **Cons:** not centrally located; unrenovated rooms are dated. ⊠ *8110 Camino del Oro, La Jolla* ☎ *619/567–4601, 877/346–6714* ⊕ *www.ljshoreshotel.com* ⤴ *127 rooms, 1 suite* ♿ *In-room: a/c, kitchen, Internet. In-hotel: restaurant, bar, pool, tennis court, gym, beach, laundry facilities, parking* ⊹ *3:B2.*

$$$$ ▦ **La Valencia.** This pink Spanish-Mediterranean confection drew Hollywood film stars in the 1930s and '40s with its setting and views of La Jolla Cove. **Pros:** upscale rooms; views; near beach. **Cons:** expensive; lots of traffic outside. ⊠ *1132 Prospect St., La Jolla* ☎ *858/454–0771, 800/451–0772* ⊕ *www.lavalencia.com* ⤴ *82 rooms, 16 villas, 15 suites* ♿ *In-room: a/c, safe, Wi-Fi. In-hotel: restaurant, bar, pool, gym, parking* ⊹ *3:B2.*

$$$$ ▦ **Lodge at Torrey Pines.** This beautiful Craftsman-style lodge sits on a
Fodor's Choice bluff between La Jolla and Del Mar and commands a coastal view. **Pros:**
★ upscale rooms; good service; near golf. **Cons:** not centrally located; expensive. ⊠ *11480 N. Torrey Pines Rd., La Jolla* ☎ *858/453–4420, 800/995–4507* ⊕ *www.lodgetorreypines.com* ⤴ *164 rooms, 6 suites* ♿ *In-room: a/c, safe, kitchen, Internet, Wi-Fi. In-hotel: restaurant, bar, golf course, pool, gym, spa, parking* ⊹ *3:B1.*

$$ ▦ **Scripps Inn.** You'd be wise to make reservations well in advance for this small, quiet inn tucked away on Coast Boulevard; its popularity with repeat visitors ensures that it's booked year-round. **Pros:** beach access; intimate feel; inexpensive parking. **Cons:** spotty service; motel layout; busy area. ⊠ *555 S. Coast Blvd., La Jolla* ☎ *858/454–3391* ⊕ *www.scrippsinn.com* ⤴ *7 rooms, 7 suites* ♿ *In-room: a/c, safe, kitchen, Wi-Fi. In-hotel: parking* ⏹*Breakfast* ⊹ *3:A2.*

Lodge at Torrey Pines

Grande Colonial

LODGING ALTERNATIVES

APARTMENT RENTALS

Travelers planning on more than a weekend with Shamu can find a variety of apartment and hotel options suitable for extended stays. Some of these properties also work well for larger families and groups looking for shared accommodations with full kitchens and eating areas.

If you're sticking to hotels, many properties with suites offer special weekly and monthly rates, especially during the off-season. Downtown's new **Marriott Residence Inn** has studios and one-bedroom suites with full-size refrigerators and two-burner stoves. **Homewood Suites San Diego Airport** offers a similar setup; the hotel also has two-bedroom suites and offers complimentary grocery shopping service and light dinner receptions on weeknights. Less expensive options include **Hotel Occidental**, a no-frills spot near Balboa Park, and downtown's **500 West**, both of which promote excellent deals for weekly stays. Long-term guests at 500 West have access to a shared kitchen, laundry facilities, and social hostel-like common areas. Lastly, another option downtown is **Lucky D's Hostel**, perfect for international students and young travelers looking for an inexpensive place to stay for a week or two.

Oakwood Apartments rents comfortable furnished apartments in several popular neighborhoods with maid service and linens; there's a one-week to 30-day minimum stay depending on locations. Parking can be difficult in some of these areas, so be sure to ask about private parking and any associated fees.

Many travelers recommend the online **Vacation Rentals by Owner** (VRBO) directory for condos and beach houses that owners rent directly to individuals. There are some risks involved, but VRBO offers money-back guarantees, which prevents much of the online fraud that plagues other sites like Craigslist.

Oakwood Apartments (☎ 800/888–0808 ⊕ www.oakwood. com). **Penny Realty** (☎ 800/748–6704 ⊕ www.missionbeach.com). **San Diego Sunset Vacation Rentals** (☎ 858/488–5204 ⊕ www. sandiegosunsetvacationrentals. com). **San Diego Vacation Rentals** (☎ 800/222–8281 ⊕ www. sdvr.com), **Vacation Rentals by Owner**(⊕ www.vrbo.com).

BED-AND-BREAKFASTS

San Diego is known more for its resorts and chain properties, but the city has several bed-and-breakfasts, most of which are in private homes and are well maintained and accommodating. Travelers hoping to stay in the Uptown neighborhoods near Balboa Park may find that bed-and-breakfasts are their best bet because there are few recommendable hotels but many activities and restaurants within walking distance. The San Diego Bed & Breakfast Guild lists a number of high-quality member inns. The Bed & Breakfast Directory for San Diego, maintained by a guild member, covers San Diego County.

Bed & Breakfast Directory for San Diego (☎ 800/619–7666 ⊕ www.bandbguildsandiego.org). **California Association of Bed and Breakfast Inns** (☎ 800/373–9251 ⊕ www.cabbi.com).

POINT LOMA AND CORONADO WITH HARBOR AND SHELTER ISLANDS

Coronado feels like something out of an earlier, more gracious era, making it a great getaway. The clean white beaches are some of the best in the state, and they're rarely crowded. But if you plan to see many of San Diego's attractions, you'll spend significant time commuting across the bridge or riding the ferry.

Harbor Island and Shelter Island, two man-made peninsulas between downtown and Point Loma, have grassy parks, tree-lined paths, and views of the downtown skyline. Closer to downtown, Harbor Island is less than five minutes from the airport. Shelter Island is next to Point Loma, a hilly community that's home to Cabrillo National Monument and a naval base.

CORONADO

$$ **1906 Lodge.** Smaller but no less luxurious than the sprawling beach resorts of Coronado, this lodge welcomes couples for romantic retreats two blocks from the ocean. **Pros:** welcoming staff; historic property; free underground parking. **Cons:** too quiet for families; no pool. ⊠ *1060 Adella Ave., Coronado* ☎ *619/437–1900, 866/435–1906* ⊕ *www.1906lodge.com* ☞ *6 rooms, 11 suites* ⚭ *In-room: a/c, safe, Wi-Fi. In-hotel: parking* ❘⚬❘ *Breakfast* ✛ *4:G6.*

Fodor's Choice ★

$$$ **Coronado Island Marriott Resort.** Near San Diego Bay, this snazzy hotel has rooms with great downtown skyline views. **Pros:** spectacular views; on-site spa; close to water taxis. **Cons:** not in downtown Coronado; difficult to find. ⊠ *2000 2nd St., Coronado* ☎ *619/435–3000, 800/543–4300* ⊕ *www.marriotthotels.com/sanci* ☞ *273 rooms, 27 suites* ⚭ *In-room: a/c, Wi-Fi. In-hotel: restaurant, bar, pool, tennis court, gym, spa, water sports, parking* ✛ *4:H5.*

$ **Crown City Inn & Bistro.** On Coronado's main drag, the Crown City Inn is close to shops, restaurants, and the beach. **Pros:** affordable; on-site restaurant; complimentary bikes. **Cons:** few amenities; somewhat dated rooms; a hike from downtown. ⊠ *520 Orange Ave., Coronado* ☎ *619/435–3116* ⊕ *www.crowncityinn.com* ☞ *35 rooms* ⚭ *In-room: a/c, Wi-Fi. In-hotel: restaurant, pool, laundry facilities, parking, some pets allowed* ✛ *4:G5.*

$$$ **Glorietta Bay Inn.** The main building on this property is an Edwardian-style mansion built in 1908 for sugar baron John D. **Pros:** great views; friendly staff; close to beach. **Cons:** mansion rooms are small; lots of traffic nearby. ⊠ *1630 Glorietta Blvd., Coronado* ☎ *619/435–3101, 800/283–9383* ⊕ *www.gloriettabayinn.com* ☞ *100 rooms* ⚭ *In-room: a/c, kitchen, Wi-Fi. In-hotel: pool, parking* ✛ *4:G6.*

$$$ **Hotel Del Coronado.** The Victorian-styled "Hotel Del," situated along 28 oceanfront acres, is as much of a draw today as it was when it opened in 1888. **Pros:** romantic; on the beach; hotel spa. **Cons:** some rooms are small; expensive dining; public areas are very busy. ⊠ *1500 Orange Ave., Coronado* ☎ *800/468–3533, 619/435–6611* ⊕ *www. hoteldel.com* ☞ *757 rooms, 65 suites, 43 villas, 35 cottages* ⚭ *In-room: a/c, safe, Wi-Fi. In-hotel: restaurant, bar, pool, gym, spa, beach, water sports, children's programs, business center, parking* ✛ *4:G6.*

Fodor's Choice ★

9

Hotel Del Coronado

1906 Lodge

$$$ ⊞ **Loews Coronado Bay Resort.** You can park your boat at the 80-slip
☾ marina of this romantic retreat, set on a secluded 15-acre peninsula
on the Silver Strand. **Pros:** great restaurants; lots of activities; lobby
worth lingering in. **Cons:** far from anything; somewhat confusing layout.
✉ *4000 Coronado Bay Rd., Coronado* ☎ *619/424–4000, 800/815–6397*
⊕ *www.loewshotels.com* ⤴ *402 rooms, 37 suites* ☾ *In-room: a/c, safe,
Wi-Fi. In-hotel: restaurant, bar, pool, tennis court, gym, spa, beach,
water sports, children's programs, parking, some pets allowed* ✛ *4:H6.*

HARBOR ISLAND

$$ ⊞ **Sheraton San Diego Hotel & Marina.** Of this property's two high-rises,
the smaller, more intimate Bay Tower has larger rooms, with sepa-
rate areas suitable for business entertaining; the more recently renovated Marina Tower has better sports facilities. **Pros:** water views; near
marina and airport; free airport shuttle. **Cons:** not centrally located.
✉ *1380 Harbor Island Dr., Harbor Island* ☎ *619/291–2900, 888/625–
5144* ⊕ *www.sheraton.com* ⤴ *1,001 rooms, 52 suites* ☾ *In-room: a/c,
safe, Internet. In-hotel: restaurant, bar, pool, tennis court, gym, spa,
parking* ✛ *4:E7.*

SHELTER ISLAND

$$ ⊞ **Best Western Island Palms Hotel & Marina.** This waterfront inn, with
an airy lobby brightened by skylights, a waterfall, and a Thai theme
expressed in gilt carvings and golden statues, is a good choice if you
have a boat to dock: the adjacent marina has guest slips. **Pros:** near
water; great room views; free tennis; free parking. **Cons:** not centrally
located; somewhat confusing area; average-size rooms; can be noisy.
✉ *2051 Shelter Island Dr., Shelter Island* ☎ *619/222–0561, 800/345–
9995* ⊕ *www.islandpalms.com* ⤴ *222 rooms, 60 suites* ☾ *In-room: a/c,
safe, kitchen, Wi-Fi. In-hotel: restaurant, bar, pool, tennis court, gym,
parking* ✛ *4:B3.*

$$ ⊞ **Humphrey's Half Moon Inn & Suites.** This sprawling South Seas–style
resort has grassy open areas with palms and tiki torches. **Pros:** water
views; near marina; nightlife on property. **Cons:** vast property; not
centrally located. ✉ *2303 Shelter Island Dr., Shelter Island* ☎ *619/224–
3411, 800/542–7400* ⊕ *www.halfmooninn.com* ⤴ *128 rooms, 54
suites* ☾ *In-room: a/c, safe, kitchen, Wi-Fi. In-hotel: restaurant, bar,
pool, gym, laundry facilities, business center, parking* ✛ *4:B2.*

$$ ⊞ **Kona Kai Resort.** This 11-acre property blends Spanish and Mediter-
ranean styles. **Pros:** quiet area; near marina; water views. **Cons:** not
centrally located; small rooms. ✉ *1551 Shelter Island Dr., Shelter Island*
☎ *619/221–8000, 800/566–2524* ⊕ *www.resortkonakai.com* ⤴ *124
rooms, 5 suites* ☾ *In-room: a/c, Wi-Fi. In-hotel: restaurant, bar, pool,
gym, spa, beach, parking* ✛ *4:B3.*

POINT LOMA

$$ ⊞ **Courtyard by Marriott San Diego Airport.** Located close to the new restaurants and shops of Liberty Station, this cheery, family-friendly hotel
offers travelers a break from the extra fees usually found at downtown and coastal hotels. **Pros:** modern rooms; near airport; friendly
service. **Cons:** unimpressive views. ✉ *2592 Laning Rd., Point Loma*
☎ *619/221–1900, 888/236–2427* ⊕ *www.marriott.com* ⤴ *200 rooms*

9

    ᴥ *In-room: a/c, Internet, Wi-Fi. In-hotel: restaurant, pool, gym, laundry facilities, business center, parking* ✛ *4:C1.*

¢ ⌨ **Dolphin Motel.** With rooms that cost less than a steak dinner for two, this family-run motel across from Fisherman's Landing is a great pick for solo travelers and couples on a budget. **Pros:** free parking, friendly staff. **Cons:** small rooms, thin walls, few amenities. ⊠ *2912 Garrison St., Point Loma* ☎ *619/758–1404, 866/353–7897* ⊕ *www.dolphinmotel.com/motel.html* ⟳ *31 rooms* ᴥ *In-room: a/c, Internet, Wi-Fi. In-hotel: parking* ⍥⊙⍥ *Breakfast* ✛ *4:B2.*

$ ⌨ **Holiday Inn Bayside.** If SeaWorld and the zoo aren't enough to sap kids
ᶜ⅃ of their energy, the outdoor activities here should do the trick. **Pros:** free parking; close to airport. **Cons:** dated lobby and common areas; not centrally located. ⊠ *4875 N. Harbor Dr., Point Loma* ☎ *619/224–3621, 800/662–8899* ⊕ *www.holinnbayside.com* ⟳ *227 rooms, 10 suites* ᴥ *In-room: a/c, Wi-Fi. In-hotel: restaurant, bar, pool, gym, laundry facilities, parking* ✛ *4:C1.*

$ ⌨ **Holiday Inn Express–SeaWorld Area.** In Point Loma near the West Mission Bay exit off I–8, this is a surprisingly cute and quiet lodging option despite proximity to bustling traffic. **Pros:** near SeaWorld; free breakfast; good service. **Cons:** not a scenic area; somewhat hard to find. ⊠ *3950 Jupiter St., Point Loma* ☎ *619/226–8000, 800/320–0208* ⊕ *www.seaworldhi.com* ⟳ *69 rooms, 2 suites* ᴥ *In-room: a/c, Wi-Fi. In-hotel: pool, laundry facilities, parking* ⍥⊙⍥ *Breakfast* ✛ *4:C1.*

$$ ⌨ **Homewood Suites San Diego Airport.** Families and business travelers
ᶜ⅃ on long trips will benefit from the space and amenities at this all-suites
Fodor's Choice hotel. **Pros:** warm staff; free parking; close to paths for joggers and
★ bikers. **Cons:** often crowded dining room. ⊠ *2576 Laning Rd., Point Loma* ☎ *619/222–0500* ⊕ *www.homewoodsuites.com* ⟳ *150 suites* ᴥ *In-room: a/c, safe, kitchen, Internet, Wi-Fi. In-hotel: pool, gym, laundry facilities, business center, parking* ⍥⊙⍥ *Breakfast* ✛ *4:C1.*

$ ⌨ **Inn at Sunset Cliffs.** Here you really do hear the sound of waves crashing against the shore. **Pros:** romantic; breathtaking views; friendly staff. **Cons:** exterior is slightly run-down; no elevator. ⊠ *1370 Sunset Cliffs Blvd., Point Loma* ☎ *619/222–7901, 866/786–2543* ⊕ *www.innatsunsetcliffs.com* ⟳ *24 rooms* ᴥ *In-room: a/c, kitchen, Wi-Fi. In-hotel: pool, beach, business center, parking* ✛ *4:A2.*

Nightlife

WORD OF MOUTH

"Although you are not planning on 'Girls Gone Wild' nightlife, you and some 20-something friends would be bored in La Jolla. Mission Beach or Pacific Beach for sure I would suggest. Stay close to Garnet Ave., or Grand Ave. or Mission Bay Dr. Go to La Jolla for the day, eat dinner there, shop, etc. but IMHO, don't stay there."
—lollylo25

Updated by
AnnaMaria
Stephens

A couple of decades ago, San Diego scraped by on its superb daytime offerings. When the city's smattering of neighborhood dives and dance clubs got stale, locals fled town for late-night benders in L.A. or Las Vegas. Those sleepy-after-dark days are over; San Diego now sizzles when the sun goes down.

The most obvious destination for visitors is the Gaslamp Quarter, a 16-block former red-light district gone glam. The downtown debauchery is slightly more modest these days—or at least legal, anyway. Between the Gaslamp and neighboring East Village, there's truly something for everyone, from secretive speakeasies to big, bangin' dance clubs and chic rooftop lounges to grimy dives. If you're staying in the Gaslamp, it's the perfect place to party. Some of the boutique hotels even have their own happening scenes. If you're driving from elsewhere, prepare to pay. Your best options: parking lots (prices start at $20) or valet (at some restaurants and clubs). If you don't mind a long trek—in other words, leave the stilettos at home—you can usually score spots 10 or more blocks from the action. Meters are free after 6 pm.

The epicenter of gay culture is Hillcrest, where you'll find bars and clubs catering primarily to the LGBT crowd—though everyone is welcome. East of Hillcrest is North Park, where hip twenty- and thirtysomethings hang out at edgy scenester hotspots (though locals complain that upscale new arrivals on the nightlife scene are ruining the underground vibe). Nearby South Park and University Heights also have a few cool offerings. A cab from downtown to any of these 'hoods costs about $15.

Pacific Beach tends to draw college kids who don't know when to say when, while Ocean and Mission Beaches pull laid-back surfers and their cohort. La Jolla, for the most part, is a snooze if you're in the mood to booze late at night.

Californians love their independent cafés and coffeehouses. San Diego's got plenty, especially in the Hillcrest and North Park neighborhoods in Uptown. Many offer tasty fare (from light pastries to full meals) alongside every possible caffeinated concoction. Some offer terrific live

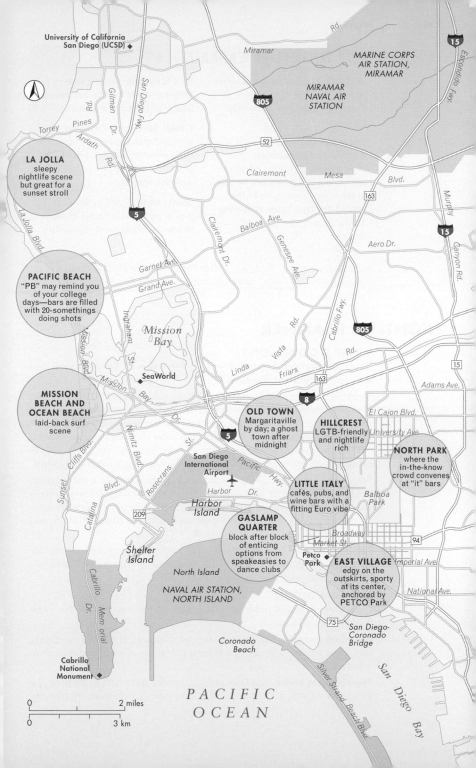

University of California
San Diego (UCSD) ◆

Miramar

MARINE CORPS
AIR STATION,
MIRAMAR

MIRAMAR
NAVAL AIR
STATION

Clairemont   Mesa   Blvd.

LA JOLLA
sleepy
nightlife scene
but great for a
sunset stroll

Balboa Ave.

Garnet Ave.

Grand Ave.

PACIFIC BEACH
"PB" may remind you
of your college
days—bars are filled
with 20-somethings
doing shots

Mission
Bay

SeaWorld ◆

Linda   Vista   Rd.

Friars

**MISSION
BEACH AND
OCEAN BEACH**
laid-back surf
scene

OLD TOWN
Margaritaville
by day; a ghost
town after
midnight

HILLCREST
LGTB-friendly
and nightlife
rich

El Cajon Blvd.

University Ave.

NORTH PARK
where the
in-the-know
crowd convenes
at "it" bars

San Diego
International
Airport

Harbor

LITTLE ITALY
cafés, pubs, and
wine bars with a
fitting Euro vibe

Balboa
Park

Harbor
Island

**GASLAMP
QUARTER**
block after block
of enticing
options from
speakeasies to
dance clubs

Broadway

Market St.

Petco
Park ◆

EAST VILLAGE
edgy on the
outskirts, sporty
at its center,
anchored by
PETCO Park

Imperial Ave.

National Ave.

Shelter
Island

North Island

NAVAL AIR STATION,
NORTH ISLAND

San Diego-
Coronado
Bridge

Cabrillo
National
Monument ◆

Coronado
Beach

San
Diego
Bay

PACIFIC
OCEAN

0 ———— 2 miles
0 ———— 3 km

TOP NIGHTLIFE EXPERIENCES

Real relaxation: Bask in the warm weather, drink in hand, on one of the city's many open-air, rooftop bars.

Pedal power: Dance the night away in the Gaslamp Quarter and then make a pedicab bicyclist do all the work to get you home. Just be sure to ask about prices upfront—the unregulated fares range from $5 to $15 for a short ride, depending on the driver.

Be a scenester: Order a shot of Jaeger and a PBR while watching a future "It" band at the Casbah.

C'mon, get happy: Pretend you're a local and grab the happy-hour drink deals with the working stiffs—it's a great excuse to tie one on while the sun's still shining.

Sports night: Swing by Bar Basic for a giant pizza and a pitcher of beer before the big game at PETCO Park.

entertainment, too. And, if a coffee buzz isn't the kind you're looking for, a handful also serve wine and beer. Hookah (also known as *shisha*) lounges are another popular bar alternative.

NIGHTLIFE PLANNER

WHAT'S GOING ON?

Don't just wander the streets looking for action. A little research will lead you in the right direction.

Scour the entertainment section of the city's daily paper, *The San Diego Union-Tribune* (⊕ *www.SignOnSanDiego.com*), for event listings and editorial suggestions. Of San Diego's two alternative-weeklies, the *Reader* (⊕ *www.sandiegoreader.com*) offers the most thorough online listings, covering everything from tiny shows to huge festivals. *San Diego CityBeat* (⊕ *sdcitybeat.com*) clues locals in to the edgiest underground events.

San Diego Magazine (⊕ *www.sandiegomagazine.com*) is a mainstream read for all walks of life; *Riviera* (⊕ *sandiego.modernluxury.com*) is younger, more upscale, and au courant. Both glossy monthlies have calendar sections and tips on topics such as haute nightlife attire and the hottest DJs.

Head to *Happy Hour Magazine* (⊕ *happyhourmagonline.com*) for happy-hour reviews and how-to tips, and ⊕ *DiscoverSD.com* for insider-y club write-ups.

THE LOWDOWN

All glammed up and ready for a big night on the town? Here are a few things to keep in mind:

Don't drink and drive. San Diego's laws are stringent. If you plan to drink, stay local or save a wad of cash for a cab ride—it's way cheaper than a lawyer.

Step outside to smoke. San Diegans who smoke have had to do it on the street since 1998, although you'll occasionally catch smokers covertly lighting up in crowded venues. You can usually smoke on open-air patios or just outside the front door, but look for posted rules to be sure.

Know the code. California casual doesn't cut it at a few of the Gaslamp's swankier spots. Dress codes vary, but the more common no-no's are sneakers, shorts, and baseball caps.

Last call for alcohol. The last chance for nightcaps is theoretically 2 am, but most bars stop serving around 1:30. Listen for the bartender's announcement.

NIGHTLIFE BY NEIGHBORHOOD

DOWNTOWN

BARS

Altitude Sky Lounge. This lounge, at the San Diego Marriott Gaslamp Quarter, occupies the hotel's 22nd-story rooftop. Location is everything—the views here (of the downtown skyline and PETCO Park) will give you a natural high. ⊠ *660 K St., Gaslamp Quarter* ☎ *619/696–0234.*

Bar Basic. This spot is always bustling, in part because it's right across from PETCO Park and a popular place to visit before seeing the Padres. True to its name, the Basic is reliable for the simple pleasures it dishes up: cold drinks and hot pizza. The garage-style doors at this former warehouse roll up and keep the industrial-chic space ventilated during the balmy summer. ⊠ *410 10th Ave., East Village* ☎ *619/531–8869.*

El Dorado. El Dorado means "The Gold," and that's exactly what this hip hangout has brought to a dodgy strip of downtown. The Wild West–theme cocktail lounge comes with creative drinks, cute bartenders, and in-demand local (and sometimes national) DJs, plus a pool table and a well-stocked jukebox. Save your own gold with a $5 happy hour that runs from 7 till 9 pm. ⊠ *1030 Broadway, Downtown* ☎ *619/237–0550.*

Hard Rock Hotel. Hard Rock Hotel draws A-list wannabes (and a few real celebs) to its two bars, the loungey 207 off the lobby and the rooftop bar, Float. Also a big ticket is Woodstock, the hotel's 9,000-square-foot outdoor event space. If you can't be a rock star, you might as well party like one. (Just be prepared to spend like one, too.) ⊠ *207 5th Ave., Gaslamp Quarter* ☎ *619/702–3000.*

Dick's Last Resort. The surly waitstaff and abrasive service at this dive bar are part of the gimmick, though might horrify Emily Post adherents. Despite (or probably because of) the rudeness, fun-loving party people pile into this barnlike restaurant and bar. Dick's has live music nightly, a solid beer list, and buckets of greasy grub. True to its name, this is a suitable "last resort" after a long night of drinking. ⊠ *345 4th Ave., Gaslamp Quarter* ☎ *619/231–9100.*

★ **East Village Tavern & Bowl.** This laid-back hot spot has 12 lanes for bowling, which means no more hauls to the suburbs for a night of tenpin bliss. Reservations are definitely recommended. Renting lanes is pricey during prime times, but if you consider that some nearby clubs charge a Jackson just for admission, East Village Tavern seems suddenly

10

Altitude Sky Lounge, atop the Marriott Gaslamp Quarter, keeps things hot with fire pits on chilly nights.

reasonable. From the expansive bar area you can watch sports on 33 flat screens, and the satellite radio plays an assortment of alt- and classic rock. ⊠ *930 Market St., East Village* ☎ *619/677–2695.*

Fodor's Choice **Ivy Rooftop and Ivy Nightclub.** These two bars offer a chiller version of ★ nightlife for Andaz San Diego visitors and hotel guests. Sink into a deep leather couch in the posh lobby Ivy Nightclub and Wine Bar or head to the spacious Ivy Rooftop, where you can swill cocktails poolside while gazing at gorgeous people or views of the city—both are abundant. ⊠ *600 F St., Gaslamp Quarter* ☎ *619/814–1000.*

Karl Strauss Brewing Company. San Diego's first microbrewery now has two locations, the original one in downtown and a newer outpost in La Jolla. This locale draws an after-work downtown crowd and later fills with beer connoisseurs from all walks of life. Beer-to-go by the gallon or half gallon is a very popular choice. The German-inspired pub food here is above average. ⊠ *1157 Columbia St., Downtown* ☎ *619/234–2739.*

The Local. Flip-flops are totally acceptable at this kick-back beach bar to the middle of the city, where tasty bar grub goes down well with the regional beers on tap. It's a favorite happy-hour haunt for downtown professionals and dwellers. ⊠ *1065 4th Ave., Downtown* ☎ *619/231–4447.*

LOUNGEsix. This trendy poolside bar on the fourth floor of the swank Hotel Solamar is a sexy spot for people-watching while sipping sangria or mango piña coladas, or noshing on snacks from the "slow food" menu. On cool evenings you can warm up by the roaring fire pit. ⊠ *435 6th Ave., Gaslamp Quarter* ☎ *619/531–8744.*

CLOSE UP

Cocktails with a View

Combine sun and socializing at these rocking outdoor bars.

ROOFTOP BARS
Altitude Skybar (Gaslamp Quarter)

Beach at the W Hotel (Downtown)

'Canes Bar and Grill (Mission Beach)

Ivy Rooftop at the Andaz San Diego (Gaslamp Quarter)

Firehouse PB (Pacific Beach)

Float at the Hard Rock Hotel (Gaslamp Quarter)

LOUNGEsix (Gaslamp Quarter)

Siren (Gaslamp Quarter)

Stingaree (Gaslamp Quarter)

Top of the Park (Hillcrest)

OUTDOOR PATIOS
Barefoot Bar and Grill (Mission Bay)

Brockton Villa (La Jolla)

Dick's Last Resort (Gaslamp Quarter)

ENO at the Hotel Del (Coronado)

Humphrey's by the Bay (Shelter Island)

JRDN (Pacific Beach)

Lei Lounge (University Heights)

Moondoggies (Pacific Beach)

Pacific Beach Bar & Grill (Pacific Beach)

Pannikin (La Jolla)

The Pearl Hotel (Point Loma)

Shakespeare Pub & Grille (Mission Hills)

Starlite (Mission Hills)

Urban Mo's (Hillcrest)

The Vine (Ocean Beach)

The Wine Cabana (Old Town)

Onyx Room/Thin. Although Onyx and Thin are separate clubs, they share the same owners and building, allowing for many options as you move back and forth between the two, sampling each bar's distinctive look and feel. Downstairs, Onyx feels like two bars in one. In front there's a mood-lighted cocktail lounge, and in the next room acid-jazz bands and DJs keep the crowds dancing on the tiny dance floor. Thin, upstairs, has a stainless-steel–heavy interior that could be the inside of a UFO. Thin is more conducive to the conversation-minded, although a DJ spins down-tempo acid jazz and funk tunes on weekends. The cover charges allow entrance to both clubs. ⊠ *852 5th Ave., Gaslamp Quarter* ☎ *619/235–6699.*

Patrick's II. Patrons enjoy live jazz, blues, and rock in this intimate Irish-themed setting, although actual Irish music is—ironically—somewhat rare. ⊠ *428 F St., Gaslamp Quarter* ☎ *619/233–3077.*

Prohibition. Prohibition is an underground jazz lounge with a slinky speakeasy style. Red lighting, dark wood, and leather tufted couches provide a cozy 1920s/'30s-inspired backdrop to the live jazz on weekends. ⊠ *548 5th Ave., Gaslamp Quarter* ☎ *619/663–5485.*

Side Bar. Shuttered for more than a year, Side Bar has reopened with new owners and a "more is more" decor. Painted birdcages hang from the loft ceiling, and the DJ spins from inside a giant cage, which also provides sturdy scaffolding for female go-go dancers on weekends.

10

The black-clad chandeliers and mismatched velvet couches (including one that once belonged to Paris Hilton) get an additional visual pop from the nudie paintings lining the walls. Fancy martinis are a must, and if you get hungry after last call, step next door to get some NYC-style pizza at Ciro's, open till 3 am. ⊠ *536 Market St., Gaslamp Quarter* ☎ *619/696–0946.*

Siren. On the fourth floor of the posh Sé Hotel, Sirens brings you gorgeous views and people—for a price. Like other Gaslamp locales, the drinks here don't come cheap, but such is life on a chaise lounge in a private cabana (those are extra, naturally). Note that the music shuts down after midnight. ⊠ *1047 5th Ave., Gaslamp Quarter* ☎ *619/515–3000.*

Tivoli. Established in 1885, this is the oldest bar in the Gaslamp. Rumor has it that Wyatt Earp himself threw back a whiskey or two in its early days. Perhaps old age accounts for its grungy veneer, but that doesn't stop locals from hitting this Western-loving dive for $9 pitchers of PBR and hot dogs. The jukebox and pool table keep the unruly in check. Is that a spittoon in the corner? ⊠ *505 6th Ave., Gaslamp Quarter* ☎ *619/232–6754.*

Top of the Hyatt. This lounge at the Manchester Grand Hyatt crowns the tallest waterfront building in California, affording great views of San Diego Bay, including Coronado to the west, the San Diego–Coronado Bridge and Mexico to the south, and Point Loma and La Jolla to the north. It's pricey and pretentious (don't you dare wear flip-flops), but this champagne-centric bar is putting the red light back in the Gaslamp (literally—the lighting is red). ⊠ *1 Market Pl., Downtown* ☎ *619/232–1234.*

★ **W Hotel.** The W Hotel has two bars, and even after several years on the scene and recent financial troubles, the boutique hotel continues to lure the young barhopping set. The ground-level Living Room encourages lounging with plush chairs and couches. Have a late-night nosh at the clearly named The Restaurant at the W and head for the beach—or, more accurately, Beach, the W's open-air rooftop with private cabanas, fire pits, and tons of heated sand covering the floor. On weekends, get here before 9 to avoid a line at the door. ⊠ *421 W. B St., Downtown* ☎ *619/398–3100.*

Fodor's Choice ★ **The Waterfront.** It isn't actually *on* the waterfront, but this was once the gathering spot for the Italian fishermen who used to live in the area. Now a local landmark, San Diego's oldest bar actually had an apartment building constructed around it rather than be torn down. It's also famous for its burgers, and it's still the hangout of some working-class heroes, even if most of the collars are now white. There's live jazz and blues many evenings. ✉ *2044 Kettner Blvd., Little Italy* ☎ *619/232–9656.*

Whiskey Girl. The happy-hour sports crowd loves Whiskey Girl for its 23 flat-screen and four projection-screen TVs. Tuesday through Thursday, bands play rockabilly and Top 40 music; DJs play nightly. This place has long been a major stop on the bachelorette party circuit. ✉ *600 5th Ave., Gaslamp Quarter* ☎ *619/236–1616.*

Yard House. It's a chain, yes, but you can't really go wrong with more than 100 beers on tap—which the restaurant/bar bills as the world's largest selection of draft beer. With a backdrop of classic rock and an unbeatable downtown location, Yard House goes the distance. ✉ *1023 4th Ave., Downtown* ☎ *619/233–9273.*

WINE BARS

The Cask Room. Learn the ins and outs of wine tasting or just savor a fine glass of white or red in a low-key but sophisticated environment. The staff is friendly and accommodating—don't be afraid to ask for samples before ordering. You might even end up chatting with the friendly owners. ✉ *550 Park Blvd., Downtown* ☎ *619/822–1606.*

The Grape. Swing by this pleasant place before or after dinner. The narrow wine bar could do without the cheesy wine-theme decor, but the mile-long wine list and lively ambience make up for it. Skip the unremarkable nibbles. ✉ *823 5th Ave., Downtown* ☎ *619/238–8010.*

Fodor's Choice ★ **Vin de Syrah.** This "spirit and wine cellar" sends you down a rabbit hole, or at least underground to a whimsical spot straight out of Alice in Wonderland, behind a hidden door (look for a handle in the grass wall). Inside you'll find visual delights (old grapevines suspended from the ceiling, vintage jars with flittering "fireflies," cozy chairs nestled around a faux fireplace and pastoral vista) that rival the culinary ones. The wine list is approachable and the charcuterie boards are exquisitely curated. ✉ *901 5th Ave., Downtown* ☎ *619/234–4166.*

COFFEEHOUSES

Extraordinary Desserts. Not just a delicious visual treat, with its lacy, laser-cut metal façade and elegant teak patio, Extraordinary Desserts also satisfies every sort of culinary craving, from savory to sweet and everything in between. The wine, beer, and bubbly list is très chic, too. ✉ *1430 Union St., Little Italy* ☎ *619/294–7001.*

Fumari Hookah Lounge. This relaxed café is a dark and cozy spot for smoking from a water pipe. The richly flavored tobaccos are worth the exorbitant price tag (around $20 for a bowl, except during the nightly happy hour from 7–8 pm), and the chill ambience makes it easy to hang out and hookah the evening away. ✉ *330 G St., Downtown* ☎ *619/238–4949.*

10

Upstart Crow. In downtown's charming Seaport Village, Upstart Crow is a bookstore and coffeehouse in one. The secluded upstairs space is ideal for chatting or flipping through the book you just bought. Irreverent gifts are sold, too. ⊠ *835 W. Harbor Dr., Downtown* ☎ *619/232–4855.*

DANCE CLUBS

★ **Ivy Nightclub.** A cavernous downstairs space with a decidedly naughty feel, this big-money, multilevel dance club in the Andaz San Diego hotel is one of the few places in town where you can bump and grind with sports stars and visiting celebs. ⊠ *600 F St., Gaslamp Quarter* ☎ *619/814–1000.*

On Broadway. This huge club in a former bank building used to be the hottest destination in town, but looks more and more like a dinosaur as the Gaslamp evolves around it. Still, on Friday and Saturday nights—the only nights it's open—scantily clad twentysomethings wait in a line that sometimes reaches around the block. Cover charges are steep and ordering drinks is a hassle, but the cool decor—marble floors, Greek columns, and original vault doors mixed with modern design elements—make it worth a visit, as do the computerized light shows, Leviathan sound system, and skilled DJs. ⊠ *615 Broadway, Gaslamp Quarter* ☎ *619/231–0011.*

★ **Stingaree.** In the posh Gaslamp Quarter, Stingaree occupies an old warehouse in the former red-light district. The owners spent approximately a gazillion dollars creating this smashing three-story space with translucent "floating" staircases and floor-to-ceiling water walls. There's a high-end restaurant and a dance club inside (the music tends to be of the Top 40 variety). Dress nicely—the air of exclusivity at this hangout is palpable, and to further prove the point, drinks are steep. ⊠ *454 6th Ave., at Island St., Gaslamp Quarter* ☎ *619/544–9500.*

Voyeur. This tiny club will leave you gasping for air—and loving it. It may be small and stifling, but Voyeur compensates for its size with creepy-cool decor (a mashup of skull/guns/Gothic weird stuff), a can't-hide bathroom in line with the club's name, a mesmerizing LED wall, gorgeous go-go girls, and cutting-edge electronic acts like MSTRKRFT and Bloody Beetroots. ⊠ *755 5th Ave., Gaslamp Quarter* ☎ *619/756–7678.*

OFF THE BEATEN PATH

Kava Lounge. This free-spirited underground dance club is a favorite of the nightlife-lovin' counterculture. The crowd is always eclectic and open-minded. DJs spin everything from downtempo to breakbeat, and organic cocktails keep sweaty bodies cool when the dance floor heats up. ⊠ *2812 Kettner Blvd., Middletown* ☎ *619/543–0933.*

JAZZ CLUBS

Fodor'sChoice

★ **Anthology.** The Rat Pack would be proud of the fine-tuned acoustics in this classy joint. The sleek, three-story club primarily books jazz acts, although it has also hosted Ozomatli as well as Herb Alpert. ⊠ *1337 India St., Little Italy* ☎ *619/595–0300.*

Croce's. Restaurateur Ingrid Croce (widow of singer-songwriter Jim Croce) books superb acoustic-jazz musicians, among others, in this intimate dinner joint and jazz cave. Son A. J. Croce frequently performs here. ⊠ *802 5th Ave., Gaslamp Quarter* ☎ *619/233–4355.*

For a bit of history, check out the Waterfront in Little Italy, San Diego's oldest bar.

Dizzy's. This is one of the few venues in town that's totally devoted to music and the arts. At the popular all-ages joint you can count on the best in jazz, visual and performance-art shows, and the occasional spoken-word event. Most shows are held at the San Diego Wine and Culinary Center, but check Dizzy's website for updated event information. ⊠ *San Diego Wine & Culinary Center, Harbor Towers, 200 Harbor Dr., Downtown* ☏ *858/270–7467* ⊕ *www.dizzysjazz.com.*

NIGHT BAY CRUISES

Hornblower Cruises. Take a dinner-dance cruise aboard the *Lord Hornblower*—the trip comes with fabulous views of the San Diego skyline. ⊠ *1066 N. Harbor Dr., Downtown* ☏ *800/668–4322.*

★ **Flagship Cruises and Events.** Flagship Cruises welcomes guests aboard with a glass of champagne as a prelude to nightly dinner-dance cruises. ⊠ *1050 N. Harbor Dr., Downtown* ☏ *619/234–4111, 800/442–7847.*

PIANO BARS

The Shout! House. Dueling pianos and rock-and-roll sing-alongs make for a festive, even boisterous, evening here. The Shout! House is open Tuesday through Sunday; make reservations or come early to get a good seat. ⊠ *655 4th Ave., Gaslamp Quarter* ☏ *619/231–6700.*

Fodor's Choice ★ **Westgate Hotel Plaza Bar.** The old-money surroundings, including leather-upholstered seats, marble tabletops, and a grand piano, make this bar one of the most elegant settings in San Diego. ⊠ *1055 2nd Ave., Gaslamp Quarter* ☏ *619/238–1818.*

ROCK, POP, HIP-HOP, FOLK, AND BLUES CLUBS

4th & B. Occupying a former bank, this club is open only when a concert is booked. All styles of music and occasional comedy acts take the stage. ⊠ *345 B St., Downtown* ☎ *619/231–4343.*

★ **House of Blues.** This branch of the renowned chain of clubs is a cavernous space decorated floor to ceiling with colorful folk art from HOB's huge collection. There's something going on here just about every night of the week, and Sunday's gospel brunch is one of the most praiseworthy events in town. Can we get a hallelujah? ⊠ *1055 5th Ave., Downtown* ☎ *619/299–2583.*

OFF THE BEATEN PATH

Casbah. Near the airport, the Casbah is a small club with a national reputation for showcasing up-and-coming acts. Nirvana, Smashing Pumpkins, and the White Stripes all played the Casbah on their way to stardom. For more than two decades, it's been the unofficial headquarters of the city's indie music scene. You can hear every type of band here—except those that sound like Top 40. ⊠ *2501 Kettner Blvd., Middletown* ☎ *619/232–4355.*

Over the Border. Cover bands usually play here on the weekends, but some of the top Latin rock bands make this unassuming cinder-block club a destination for fans of *rock en español* from both sides of the border. ⊠ *3008 Main St., Chula Vista, California* ☎ *619/427–5889.*

HEY, BIG SPENDER

You can dress to impress and bat your eyelashes, but unless you're a supermodel or a pro athlete, just about the only way to bypass a long queue or nab that corner booth at the most exclusive of San Diego's clubs and lounges is to arrange for bottle service. Just be forewarned: a lowly bottle of Jack Daniels will run you about $250.

OLD TOWN

BARS

El Agave Tequileria. Named for the agave cactus, whose sap is distilled into tequila, this restaurant's bar stocks hundreds of top-shelf brands that are as sip-worthy as the finest cognac. ⊠ *2304 San Diego Ave., Old Town* ☎ *619/220–0692.*

O'Hungry's. This landmark saloon is famous for its yard-long beers and live music. The seafaring decorative scheme inside is quite a contrast to the Mexican-theme Old Town San Diego State Historic Park just outside the doors. Be sure to drink up quickly—O'Hungry's closes weekdays at 9 and weekends at 11. ⊠ *2547 San Diego Ave., Old Town* ☎ *619/298–0133.*

WINE BARS

The Wine Cabana. This small bar opens to a spacious outdoor patio that has semiprivate cabanas where groups can hang out. You can bring your pooch anytime, or join other dog owners for Dog Day Afternoon, usually the second Sunday of the month. A nice and affordable selection of wines and a variety of flights and tastings has garnered the Wine Cabana a regular clientele. ⊠ *2539 Congress St., Old Town* ☎ *619/574–9463.*

CLOSE UP

San Diego On Tap

The secret is out: San Diego is the nation's best beer town, and not just according to *Men's Journal*, which hailed it as #1 in 2009, or *Food and Wine*, which raved about the city's remarkably innovative way with brews. In addition to more than 30 local breweries, San Diego has a stretch of beer-nerd heaven nicknamed the Belgian Corridor (30th Street in North/South Park), and restaurants that cater to hopheads with special pairing dinners. In addition, fall brings **San Diego's Beer Week** (⊕ *www.sdbw.org*), a supersize celebration that lasts 10 days.

You can find all styles of beer in San Diego, from the meek to the mighty, but many local brewers contend that our specialty is the big, bold Double IPA (also called an Imperial IPA). It's an India Pale Ale with attitude—and way too many hops for the weak at heart. Nearly every local brewery has its own version.

Here's a shortlist guide to the local scene:

Bars with the best microbrew selection: Blind Lady Ale House, Hamilton's Tavern, Live Wire, O'Brien's, Toronado

Best fests: One location and a seemingly endless supply of beer? Sounds like hops heaven. Try the Belgian Beer Fest (March), the San Diego Festival of Beers (September), and the Strong Ale Fest (December). Check ⊕ *www.sandiegobrewersguild.org* for more listings.

How to sample it all: Sign up for Brewery Tours of San Diego (⊕ *www.brewerytoursofsandiego.com*) to sample the best craft beers without a second thought about directions or designated drivers.

UPTOWN

BARS

Aero Club. Named for its proximity to the airport, this watering hole draws in twenty- and thirtysomethings with its pool tables, dominoes, and 20 beers on tap (including a few local brews). Drinks are cheap, which makes it a popular place to fuel up before heading downtown. Don't miss the cool fighting warplanes mural. ⊠ *3365 India St., Mission Hills* ☎ *619/297–7211.*

★ **Bar Pink.** Cheap drinks, live music, and a hip crowd explain the line that's usually waiting outside this bar co-owned by Rocket From the Crypt frontman John "Speedo" Reis. ⊠ *3829 30th St., North Park* ☎ *619/564–7194.*

Blind Lady Ale House. The Blind Lady pairs two of the best things on the planet: pizza and beer. Good luck getting a table at this popular hangout, which is decorated in resourced materials, from old wooden floors used as wall paneling to the giant '60s-era Hamm's billboard. The pizzas are Old World and organic, and the beer selection—while succinct—is out of this world. ⊠ *3416 Adams Ave., University Heights* ☎ *619/255–2491.*

10

San Diego's Best Breweries

Get your drink on at one of San Diego's top breweries. They're outside of the city center, but well worth the trek for beer aficionados.

AleSmith Brewing Co. This artisanal microbrewery offers small tours and tastings at its out-of-the-way locale in the Miramar area. Just how artisanal is it? The "Kopi Luwak" special edition of AleSmith's popular Speedway Stout is brewed with Civet coffee from Indonesia, made from rare and expensive coffee berries that have been eaten—and passed, undigested—by the Asian Palm Civet. If you can't pay a visit to the brewery, you can pick up AleSmith beers at area BevMo! stores. ✉ 9368 Cabot Dr., Scripps Ranch ☎ 858/549–9888.

Alpine Brewing Co. Well worth the mountain drive, this family-owned operation may be itty-bitty, but it's also a big champ: in 2006 it took the title of the fifth-best brewery in the nation from Beer Advocate. Brewmaster Pat McIlhenney, a former fire captain, has won national and international kudos for his hopped-up creations. Try four tasters for $1.50, or fill a growler, which holds a half gallon, for future imbibing. If they're on

tap, don't pass up Duet, Pure Hoppiness, or Exponential Hoppiness. Alpine recently opened a pub a few doors down where you can enjoy tasting flights of their various beers. ✉ 2351 Alpine Blvd., Alpine ☎ 619/445–2337.

Ballast Point Brewing Co. This isn't the best location for a casual visit, but if you're in the Miramar/Scripps Ranch area, swing by for a tasting. Otherwise, be on the lookout for their offerings at local brewpub: Sculpin and Dorado are especially awesome. ✉ 10051 Old Grove Rd., Suite B, Scripps Ranch ☎ 858/695–2739.

Stone Brewing Co. The Big Daddy of San Diego craft brewing, Stone Brewing Co. was founded by a couple of basement beer tinkerers in 1996; the company now exports its aggressively hoppy beers—instantly identifiable by their leering gargoyle labels—to bars and stores across the nation. Stone's impressive HQ is off the beaten path, but totally worth a visit for its free tours (with free tasters at the end!), vast on-tap selection (not just Stone beers), and hard-to-beat bistro eats. ✉ 1999 Citracado Pkwy., Escondido, California ☎ 760/471–4999.

★ **Hamilton's Tavern.** More commonly called Hammy's, this bar has one of the best beer lists in town. On the ceiling, lights strung between old beer taps twinkle as bright as the eyes of the suds-lovers who flock here. In between pours, grab something from Hammy's kitchen—the grilled-cheese menu offers some of the tastiest around. Hamilton's marks the start of 30th Street's unofficial "Belgian Corridor." ✉ 1521 30th St., South Park ☎ 619/238–5460.

Live Wire. This hip hole-in-the-wall, lures the pierced and tattooed kids in their twenties. A wide-ranging (and very loud) jukebox and TVs screening movies or music videos are the main entertainment in this fun dive, unless you count people-watching. And the cocktails as well as the excellent beers come in pint glasses, so pace yourself; the police lie in wait on nearby side streets. ✉ 2103 El Cajon Blvd., North Park ☎ 619/291–7450.

A night out at Bar Pink may leave you seeing pink elephants, the bar's mascots.

Nunu's. It might be the most popular mainstream bar in très gay Hillcrest, but don't expect a glitzy facade. This retro-cool hangout with intentionally dated decor sits within the tatty walls of a white-brick box that probably hasn't had a face-lift since the LBJ administration. ✉ *3537 5th Ave., Hillcrest* ☎ *619/295–2878.*

OFF THE BEATEN PATH

O'Brien's. Billed as "the Hoppiest Place on Earth," O'Brien's makes up for its tacky interior (pleather executive chairs?) with a world-class beer list. Owner Tom Nickel, one of San Diego's most notable beer connoisseurs, helps organize festivals and beer trips to Belgium when he's not perfecting his pub's offerings. Hidden among the Asian-oriented strip malls of Kearny Mesa, about 15 minutes north of downtown, O'Brien's is a must-visit for hardcore beer lovers. ✉ *4646 Convoy St., Kearny Mesa* ☎ *858/715–1745.*

10

Shakespeare Pub & Grille. This Mission Hills hangout captures all the warmth and camaraderie of a traditional pub in England—except here you can enjoy consistently sunny and warm weather on the sprawling patio. The bar hands pour from a long list of imported ales and stouts, and it's the place to watch soccer matches. ✉ *3701 India St., Mission Hills* ☎ *619/299–0230.*

Fodor's Choice **Starlite.** Bar-goers are dazzled by Starlite's award-winning interior
★ design, which includes rock walls, luxe leather booths, and a massive mirror-mounted chandelier. A hexagonal wood-plank entryway leads to a sunken white bar, where sexy tattooed guys and girls mix creative cocktails like the Starlite Mule, which is served in a copper mug. An iPod plays eclectic playlists that range from old-timey jazz and blues to obscure vintage rock. During warmer months, procuring a spot on

the outside wood-decked patio is an art form. ⌧ *3175 India St., Mission Hills* ☎ *619/358–9766.*

Toronado. Named in honor of the San Francisco beer bar by the same name, the Toronado is an essential stop along the Belgian Corridor and one of San Diego's favorite gathering spots. The beer list—both on tap and by the bottle—is hard to beat. It can get noisy, but after a drink or two you'll barely notice. The grub is good, too. ⌧ *4026 30th St., North Park* ☎ *619/282–0456.*

> ### NECTAR OF THE HIPSTER?
>
> The Starlite Mule—a potent signature concoction of organic vodka, ginger beer, bitters, and fresh lime juice—is just one of the reasons people pack it in at this hard-to-find hotspot (look for the sign).

True North. Many long-established locals hate this sports bar, eyeing its beefy bouncers and backwards baseball cap–wearing "bros" as a pox on their neighborhood's hip vibe. True North may be more Pacific Beach than North Park, but it also has a sun-soaked patio and the tastiest tater-tots in town. ⌧ *3815 30th St., North Park* ☎ *619/291–3815.*

U-31. U-31 ratchets up this neighborhood's nightlife potential with a spacious layout and stylish, custom-designed interior. Located at University and 31st, the aptly named U-31 is loungey except when DJs or live bands bring patrons to the dance floor. ⌧ *3112 University Ave., North Park* ☎ *619/584–4188.*

WINE BARS

★ **Wine Steals.** This room crackles with excitement on busy nights—you can actually hear the din of conversation from half a block away. A wide assortment of reasonably priced wines draws patrons in, and the freshly baked pizza keeps them in top form for imbibing. Check out their other locations in the East Village and Point Loma. ⌧ *1243 University Ave., Hillcrest* ☎ *619/295–1188.*

COFFEEHOUSES

Café Bassam. This Uptown café offers a Parisian-inspired coffee-sipping experience, complete with quirky decor. There's also a selection of wine and about 150 teas. It's open until midnight most nights. ⌧ *3088 5th Ave., Hillcrest* ☎ *619/557–0173.*

Claire de Lune. On a corner in artsy North Park, this café is revered for its redesign of the historic Odd Fellows building. High ceilings and huge arched windows give this wooden-floor hangout a funky charm. There are sofas and armchairs for lounging as well as tables for studying. Local musicians and poets take the stage on various nights. ⌧ *2906 University Ave., North Park* ☎ *619/688–9845.*

Fodor's Choice **Extraordinary Desserts.** This café lives up to its name, which explains ★ why there's often a line here, even though it has ample seating. Paris-trained Karen Krasne turns out award-winning cakes, tortes, and pastries of exceptional beauty (many are decorated with fresh flowers). The Japanese-theme patio invites you to linger over yet another coffee drink. There is a second location in Little Italy. ⌧ *2929 5th Ave., Hillcrest* ☎ *619/294–2132.*

Gelato Vero Caffe. A youthful crowd gathers here for authentic Italian ice cream and a second-floor view of the downtown skyline. The place is usually occupied by regulars who stay for hours at a time. ⊠ *3753 India St., Mission Hills* ☎ *619/295–9269.*

Urban Grind. This coffeeshop is popular with San Diego's gay community. It's a great place to meet locals, read a book, work on your laptop (there's free Wi-Fi), or simply people-watch.

It's open until later during the week (9 or 10 pm) than on weekends (6 or 7 pm), so call ahead for hours. ⊠ *3797 Park Blvd., Hillcrest* ☎ *619/299–4763.*

COMEDY AND CABARET

Lips. Patrons enjoy their dinner while drag queens entertain (a $3 to $5 per-person cover charge will be added to your check). The place is always a hit for birthdays and bachelorette parties, but fair warning to the conservative—the scene can get raunchy. The motto, "where the men are men and so are the girls," says it all. ⊠ *3036 El Cajon Blvd., North Park* ☎ *619/295–7900.*

National Comedy Theatre. Comedy fans stop by for competitive improv comedy contests on Friday and Saturday nights. ⊠ *3717 India St., Mission Hills* ☎ *619/295–4999.*

DANCE CLUBS

Bar Dynamite. Affectionately known to regulars as Bar D, in its heyday this was the hottest underground dance club around. It's still a pretty good bet for booty-shaking classic hip-hop, as well as mashups, reggae, and funk. The cover rarely tops $5. ⊠ *1808 W. Washington St., Mission Hills* ☎ *619/295–8743.*

★ **In Cahoots.** With a great sound system, large dance floor, and DJ, Cahoots is the destination of choice for cowgirls, cowboys, and city slickers alike. Free dance lessons are given every day, when seasoned two-steppers strut their stuff. A nightly happy hour is one of this bar's many lures. Tuesday is country karaoke night. ⊠ *5373 Mission Center Rd., Mission Valley* ☎ *619/291–1184* ⊘ *Closed Mon.*

Whistle Stop Bar. This is the place to get your groove on to indie, electro, and hip-hop, plus live bands on Friday. It's a tiny-but-banging locals' favorite just a few minutes from downtown, and though it gets hot and crowded, the dance floor is always happening on Saturday. Plus, the cover's usually five bucks. ⊠ *2236 Fern St., South Park* ☎ *619/284–6784.*

GAY NIGHTLIFE

Fodor'sChoice ★ **Baja Betty's.** Although it draws plenty of gay customers, Baja Betty's is popular with just about everyone in the Hillcrest area. It's a low-key but elegant space with chandeliers and soft lighting, and it stocks more than 100 brands of tequila and mixes plenty of fancy cocktails. ⊠ *1421 University Ave., Hillcrest* ☎ *619/269–8510.*

10

★ **Bourbon Street.** Locals stop by here to meet old friends or make new ones. The front area is a karaoke spot, and the outdoor courtyard draws crowds that gather to watch and comment on whatever's on the large-screen TV. Weekends, a back area known as the Stable Bar has DJs who turn the small room into a makeshift dance floor. ⊠ *4612 Park Blvd., University Heights* ☏ *619/291–0173.*

Flicks. A hip video bar that's popular with the see-and-be-seen crowd, Flicks plays music and comedy videos on four big screens. There are drink specials every night. ⊠ *1017 University Ave., Hillcrest* ☏ *619/297–2056.*

Lei Lounge. This fabulous tropical-theme lounge is like a minivacation, with cabanas, fire pits, palm trees, froufrou cocktails, tasty tapas, and DJ-spun music during Sunday brunch. It's paradise for an afternoon or evening—or both. ⊠ *4622 Park Blvd., University Heights* ☏ *619/813–2272.*

Martinis Above Fourth. This swank lounge presents live piano and cabaret on weekends to a friendly crowd. Swill cocktails inside or out on the patio, and consider a meal afterward—there's also a restaurant serving contemporary American fare. ⊠ *3940 4th Ave., 2nd fl., Hillcrest* ☏ *619/400–4500.*

Rich's. The dancing and music here are some of the best in the city, making Rich's popular not only with gay men but also plenty of lesbians and straight revelers. ⊠ *1051 University Ave., Hillcrest* ☏ *619/295–2195.*

★ **Top of the Park.** Held only on Friday evenings, this festive after-work cocktail party on the rooftop of the Park Manor Suites hotel is de rigueur with the locals. It's a great way to kick off the weekend, and the views of downtown and Balboa Park are stupendous. ⊠ *525 Spruce St., Hillcrest* ☏ *619/291–0999.*

Urban Mo's Bar and Grill. Mo's rounds up cowboys for line dancing and two-stepping on its wooden dance floor—but be forewarned, yee-hawers, it can get pretty wild on Western nights. There are also Latin and hip-hop nights and a drag revue, but the real allure is in the creative drinks ("Gone Fishing"—served in a fishbowl, for example) and the breezy patio where love (or something like it) is usually in the air. ⊠ *308 University Ave., Hillcrest* ☏ *619/491–0400.*

PIANO BARS

Inn at the Park. This lounge at the Park Manor Suites offers large booths to settle into as a piano player entertains Wednesday through Sunday, beginning at 7 pm. This venue is a nice place to relax after a day in Balboa Park. ⊠ *3167 5th Ave., Hillcrest* ☏ *619/296–0057.*

Red Fox Steak House. Typically referred to as Red Fox Room, this lounge is dearly loved by locals, and not just the seniors who flock here to sing Sinatra tunes to tickled ivories and the occasional impromptu horn section. At this dimly lit, old-school piano bar, a multigenerational crowd mingles happily and sometimes joins in the serenade. ⊠ *2223 El Cajon Blvd., North Park* ☏ *619/297–1313.*

Stop for happy hour drinks at Pacific Beach's sleek JRDN lounge.

MISSION BAY AND THE BEACHES

BARS

Bar West. The brainchild of the guys who opened the Gaslamp's successful Stingaree, Bar West brings downtown flavor to style-starved PB. Though clean-lined and attractive, the bar is packed with the usual suspects (collegiates, beach crowd), and the dance floor is a sweaty meat market on weekends. ⊠ *959 Hornblend St., Pacific Beach* ☎ *858/273–9378.*

Barefoot Bar and Grill. This beachfront watering hole and hotel bar with a tiki feel attracts flocks of singles, especially on summer weekends when there is live music in the afternoon. ■**TIP**➔ Make a splashy appearance and roll up in your boat—you can dock at the bar. ⊠ *Paradise Point Resort & Spa, 1404 W. Vacation Rd., Mission Bay* ☎ *858/581–5960.*

Firehouse PB. Firehouse PB goes for Miami chic in the heart of Pacific Beach. The late-night offerings are generic (oontz-oontz house music and run-of-the-mill food and drinks), but linger on the rooftop lounge for an on-fire happy hour with an ocean view. ⊠ *722 Grand Ave., Pacific Beach* ☎ *858/274–3100.*

★ **JRDN.** This contemporary lounge occupies the ground floor of Pacific Beach's chicest boutique hotel, Tower23. JRDN, pronounced "Jordan," captures both the laid-back personality of the neighborhood and the increasingly sophisticated sensibility of San Diego, with sleek walls of windows and an expansive patio overlooking the Pacific Beach boardwalk. ⊠ *723 Felspar St., Pacific Beach* ☎ *858/270–5736.*

Moondoggies. This relaxed hangout welcomes Gidget wannabes, as well as a mixed, laid-back crowd of people who don't mind shoulder bumps or beer spills. Large and airy, Moondoggies has a sports-bar feel heightened by the dozens of TVs in every available spot, many showing surf and skate videos that remind you that the beach is only two blocks away. A large, heated outdoor patio draws smokers. Local rock, funk, or reggae bands play here. ⊠ *832 Garnet Ave., Pacific Beach* ☏ *858/483–6550.*

Pacific Beach Bar & Grill. Only a block away from the beach, this popular nightspot has a huge outdoor patio, so you can enjoy star-filled skies as you party. The lines here on weekends are generally the longest of any club in Pacific Beach. There's plenty to see and do, from billiards and satellite TV sports to an interactive trivia game. The grill takes orders until 1 am, so it's a great place for a late-night snack. ⊠ *860 Garnet Ave., Pacific Beach* ☏ *858/272–4745.*

Pacific Shores. This bar isn't going for classy with its acid-trip mermaid mural, but hey, it's OB—a surf town populated by leftovers from the '60s, man. A laid-back but see-and-be-seen crowd congregates here for relatively inexpensive drinks (no beers on tap, though) and pop and rock tunes on the jukebox. ⊠ *4927 Newport Ave., Ocean Beach* ☏ *619/223–7549.*

RT's Longboard Grill. A young, tanned crowd comes to schmooze and booze under the indoor palapas that give this lively bar a south-of-the-border feel. ⊠ *1466 Garnet Ave., Pacific Beach* ☏ *858/270–4030.*

Tavern at the Beach. Drink specials and socializing draw fun-loving college students to this bar, although if you get bored you can always watch one of the dozens of TVs. ⊠ *1200 Garnet Ave., Pacific Beach* ☏ *858/272–6066.*

WINE BARS

The Vine. Alongside a small-plates food menu, this romantic little wine bar serves a solid selection of moderately priced wines by the glass. For a perfect afternoon, grab a seat on the patio, order a cheese plate, and raise a toast as your wine opens up in the tangy sea air. ⊠ *1851 Bacon St., Ocean Beach* ☏ *619/222–8463.*

COFFEEHOUSES

Zanzibar Coffee Bar and Gallery. This cozy, dimly lighted spot along Pacific Beach's main strip is a great place to mellow out and eavesdrop, or to just watch the club-hopping singles make their way down the street. ⊠ *976 Garnet Ave., Pacific Beach* ☏ *858/272–4762.*

NIGHT BAY CRUISES

Bahia Belle. This Mississippi-style stern-wheeler offers relaxing evening cruises along Mission Bay that include cocktails, dancing, and live music (these floating bars are known as booze cruises for a reason). Cruises run from Wednesday through Sunday in early summer, daily in July and August, and Friday and Saturday in winter (there are no cruises in December and January). The $10 fare is less than most nightclub covers. ⊠ *998 W. Mission Bay Dr., Mission Bay* ☏ *858/539–7779.*

ROCK, POP, HIP-HOP, FOLK, AND BLUES CLUBS

710 Beach Club. This surprisingly spacious beach bar hosts well-known local and, occasionally, national bands playing rock, reggae, and especially potent blues. This is a good place to enjoy a drink before or after a nice walk on the boardwalk or on Crystal Pier a few steps away. ✉ *710 Garnet Ave., Pacific Beach* ☎ *858/483–7844.*

LA JOLLA

BARS

Cafe Japengo. This is the post-work socializing spot for young La Jolla professionals. A sushi bar is one draw, but most come here for the singles scene that plays itself out nightly. ✉ *8960 University Center La., La Jolla* ☎ *858/450–3355.*

Jose's Court Room. Jose's Court Room is a hit with yuppies from La Jolla and other neighboring beach communities. This hole-in-the-wall's lack of space gives suave singles an excuse to get up close and personal. ✉ *1037 Prospect St., La Jolla* ☎ *858/454–7655.*

Karl Strauss Brewing Company. This microbrewery is a pleasantly casual escape from the more upscale offerings that dominate La Jolla. Strauss's seasonal and specialty beers don't hold up against creations by San Diego's other award-winning breweries, but the drafts are decent and the bar grub is satisfying. Expect a mix of post-work escapees and tourists. ✉ *1044 Wall St., La Jolla* ☎ *858/551–2739.*

COFFEEHOUSES

★ **Brockton Villa Restaurant.** This charming café overlooking La Jolla Cove has indoor and outdoor seating, as well as scrumptious desserts and coffee drinks; the beans are roasted in San Diego. It closes at 9 most nights. ✉ *1235 Coast Blvd., La Jolla* ☎ *858/454–7393.*

Pannikin. This bright coffeehouse with indoor and outdoor seating attracts folks who have been shopping and sightseeing in La Jolla's village. Several locations are scattered throughout the county. ✉ *7467 Girard Ave., La Jolla* ☎ *858/454–5453.*

COMEDY AND CABARET

★ **Comedy Store La Jolla.** Like its sister establishment in Hollywood, this club hosts some of the best national touring and local talent. Cover charges range from nothing on open-mic nights to $20 or more for national acts. A two-drink minimum applies for all shows. Seating is at bistro-style tables. ✉ *916 Pearl St., La Jolla* ☎ *858/454–9176.*

JAZZ CLUBS

Clay's La Jolla. Clay's is a new version of one of San Diego's most famous jazz venues, which closed in the mid-1990s, then returned five years later in a slightly different format. Perched on the top floor of the Hotel La Jolla, Clay's delivers an ocean view and a lineup of mostly jazz musicians (and the occasional small band) Thursday through Sunday. ✉ *7955 La Jolla Shores Dr., La Jolla* ☎ *858/459–0541.*

10

ROCK, POP, HIP-HOP, FOLK, AND BLUES CLUBS

Ché Café. This good old-fashioned bastion of counterculture at University of California at San Diego, presents some of the edgiest music around. The all-ages café is also home to a restaurant serving vegan and vegetarian food, and it hosts countless events, parties, and workshops related to leftist politics and activism. The crowd skews very young and the vibe is decidedly punk-rock, but that doesn't stop old fogeys (read: anyone over 25) from joining in the fun. ⊠ *Bldg. 161, UCSD campus, La Jolla* ☎.

POINT LOMA AND CORONADO

BARS

Brigantine. This is surely the most popular of the local chain's seven outposts. The newly redesigned restaurant offers scenic harbor views and a happy hour that can't be beat. Try the fish tacos—they're among the best in San Diego, and go particularly well with a frosty margarita. ⊠ *2725 Shelter Island Dr., Point Loma* ☎ *619/224–2871* ⊕ *www.brigantine.com.*

★ **The Pearl Hotel.** Step into late '60s Palm Springs, with shag carpet, clean lines, and lots of wood accents. The lobby bar is almost as fabulous as the outdoor pool area, where inflatable balls bob in illuminated water and vintage flicks show on a huge screen. And feel free to drink to excess. After 10 pm, when the bar closes, you can stay over at a discounted $79 "play and stay" rate if there are any rooms available. ⊠ *1410 Rosecrans St., Point Loma* ☎ *619/226–6100.*

WINE BARS

ENO at the Hotel Del Coronado. ENO at the Hotel Del Coronado, or the Hotel Del, is a stylish contemporary wine bar serving fine wines, artisanal cheeses, and gourmet chocolates. ⊠ *1500 Orange Ave., Coronado* ☎ *619/522–8490.*

COFFEEHOUSES

Living Room. This coffee shop is in an old house with creaky wooden floors and plenty of cubbyholes for the college students who are regulars here. Not far from the water, it's a great place to catch a caffeine buzz before walking along Shelter Island. There are several other locations, including popular branches in Old Town and La Jolla. ⊠ *1018 Rosecrans St., Point Loma* ☎ *619/222–6852.*

ROCK, POP, HIP-HOP, FOLK, AND BLUES CLUBS

Humphrey's by the Bay. Surrounded by water, Humphrey's is the summer stomping ground of musicians such as the Cowboy Junkies and Chris Isaak. From June through September this dining and drinking oasis hosts the city's best outdoor jazz, folk, and light-rock concert series. The rest of the year the music moves indoors and with a lineup that includes first-rate jazz and blues. ⊠ *2241 Shelter Island Dr., Shelter Island* ☎ *619/224–3577.*

Winston's. In a former bowling alley, this Ocean Beach rock club hosts local bands, reggae groups, and, occasionally, 1960s-style bands. The crowd, mostly locals, is typically mellow, but can get rowdy. ⊠ *1921 Bacon St., Ocean Beach* ☎ *619/222–6822.*

The Arts

WORD OF MOUTH

"I would really suggest going to Balboa Park . . . lots of artsy and cultural things going on and it's just plain beautiful. Also, there is an outdoor theater that sometimes hosts various free concerts where you can bring a picnic and wine and sit and enjoy the music & people watching. If you like theaters—there is the Globe theater."

—losangelestraveller

Updated by
AnnaMaria
Stephens

Locals like to gripe about the arts scene in San Diego. Some even believe that we're culturally anemic because of a countywide overdose on sunshine—who wants to sit inside and paint (or act or dance) when it's so beautiful out nearly every day? But the city does have a thriving arts scene, featuring both seasoned heavyweights and up-and-comers.

Step aside, New York City. San Diego's theater scene may be regional, but it's a breeding ground for Broadway-bound productions. Some of the more notable exports include *Jersey Boys,* The Who's *Tommy, Dirty Rotten Scoundrels,* and *Whisper House,* a 2010 rock musical by the Tony Award-winning composer Duncan Sheik and librettist Kyle Jarrow.

The world-class Old Globe Theatre, which recently expanded with its $22-million, state-of-the-art Conrad Prebys Theatre Center, stages everything from classic Shakespeare to Dr. Seuss's *How the Grinch Stole Christmas.* The La Jolla Playhouse, founded in 1947 by Gregory Peck, has hosted more than 40 world premieres, and marquee actors such as Neil Patrick Harris and Holly Hunter have stood in its spotlight.

San Diego's dance scene is nothing to scoff at, either. In addition to thoroughly respectable ballet troupes—City Ballet and San Diego Ballet—the city's modern movers are making waves. In 2009, Jean Isaacs celebrated its 35th anniversary, while Malashock performed at New York's prestigious Association of Performing Arts Presenters Conference.

In the visual arts arena, San Diego's stellar reputation is spreading regionally and beyond. Area galleries combine international artists with locally grown talent, while collectors from around the world get in on the buying action. Every year, the San Diego Art Prize gives a nod to a select group of established and emerging artists—some of international acclaim—while the Orchids and Onions doles out best of (and worst of) awards for architecture.

THE ARTS PLANNER

TICKETS

San Diego Art + Sol. You can scan arts listings and book tickets through San Diego Art + Sol, produced by a partnership of organizations, including the City of San Diego Commission for Arts and Culture and the San Diego Convention & Visitors Bureau. ⊕ *www.sandiego.org/artandsol.*

Book tickets well in advance, preferably at the same time you make hotel reservations. Outlets selling last-minute tickets do exist, but you risk paying top rates or getting less-than-choice seats—or both.

Arts Tix. You can buy advance tickets, many at half price, to theater, music, and dance events at Arts Tix. ⊠ *Horton Plaza, Gaslamp Quarter* ☎ *858/381–5595* ⊕ *www.sdartstix.com.*

Ticketmaster. Ticketmaster sells tickets to many performances. Service charges vary according to the event, and most tickets are nonrefundable. ☎ *800/745–3000* ⊕ *www.ticketmaster.com.*

GALLERY AND MUSEUM NIGHTS

Museums and galleries in San Diego host monthly nighttime events meant to lure the city's culturati—especially of the younger variety.

The San Diego Museum of Art hosts an occasional sundown series called **Culture & Cocktails** (☎ *619/232–7931* ⊕ *www.sdmart.org*) to coincide with major new exhibitions. For a $15 admission, visitors can enjoy cocktails and nibbles, DJs and live entertainment, and a cool artsy twenty- and thirtysomething crowd.

The San Diego Museum of Contemporary Art Downtown (⊕ *www.mcasd.org*) ups the artsy ante with its long-running Thursday Night Thing—aka **TNT**—a boisterous quarterly happening with drinks, live entertainment, and thematically related activities.

Oceanside Museum of Art (⊕ *www.oma-online.org*) has also gotten in on the nighttime action with **Art After Dark,** a now-and-again event for the North County set.

Up in Solana Beach, the third Thursday of the month brings **Cedros Gallery Nights.** Galleries and boutiques keep their doors open, and locals head out to mingle.

DANCE

Whether you fancy *rond du jambes* or jazz hands, San Diego's scene is *en pointe* for dance fans.

★ **California Ballet Company.** The company performs high-quality contemporary and classical works September through May.

Civic Theatre. The Nutcracker is staged annually at the Civic Theatre. ⊠ *3rd Ave. and B St., Downtown.*

Balboa Theatre. Other ballets are presented at Balboa Theatre. ⊠ *868 4th Ave., Downtown.*

City Ballet. The ballet holds performances at the **Spreckels Theatre** and other area venues from November through May. At Christmastime,

The Spreckels Organ Pavilion in Balboa Park hosts free Monday night concerts in the summer.

they dance a mean *Nutcracker*. ✉ *Spreckels Theatre, 121 Broadway, Downtown* ☎ *858/272–8663.*

Eveoke Dance Theater. San Diego's major avant-garde dance company performs a regular season of dance theater works, produces several special events, and presents community-focused classes and exhibitions. ✉ *2811-A University Ave., North Park* ☎ *619/238–1153.*

Jean Isaacs' San Diego Dance Theater. The company has earned serious kudos for its diverse company and provocative programming, which has included Mexican waltzes and modern jazz. Performances are held at different venues around the city. ☎ *619/225–1803.*

Malashock. The city's esteemed modern dance company, presents edgy, intriguing works at venues throughout the city; Malashock has often collaborated on performances with the San Diego Opera, the San Diego Symphony, and other major cultural institutions. ☎ *619/260–1622.*

San Diego Ballet. The ballet brings a vast repertory of classic and contemporary ballets to several venues countywide, as well as in-studio performances. ✉ *2650 Truxton Rd., Point Loma* ☎ *619/294–7378.*

FILM

Cinephiles will find plenty of options in San Diego, from free outdoor summer screenings to a late-fall film fest.

Landmark Theatres. Known for first-run foreign, art, American independent, and documentary offerings, Landmark operates three theaters in the San Diego area.

TOP ARTS EXPERIENCES

Arts free-for-all: Summertime means free concerts, movies, and theater throughout the county.

Puppet strings: Your kids might not care for Shakespeare at the Old Globe, but you can introduce them to great acting at Balboa Park's Marie Hitchcock Puppet Theatre.

Architectural walkabouts: Whether you fancy frilly Victorians or soaring Spanish Colonials, there's a walking tour for you at Urban Safaris (⊕ *www.walkingtoursofsandiego.com*)

Gallery gathering: Before you visit, scour gallery Web sites for upcoming openings, which usually include a spread of sips and snacks—and art, of course.

San Diego Film Festival: This five-day festival in September is a must for film lovers and celebrity spotters—a day pass will get you in to some of San Diego's most glamorous parties.

La Jolla Village Cinemas is a modern multiplex set in a shopping center. ⊠ *8879 Villa La Jolla Dr., La Jolla.*

Hillcrest Cinemas is a posh multiplex right in the middle of Uptown's action. ⊠ *3965 5th Ave., Hillcrest.*

Ken Cinema is considered by many to be the last bastion of true avant-garde film in San Diego. It plays a roster of art and revival films that changes almost every night (many programs are double bills). It publishes its listings in the Ken, a small newspaper distributed in nearly every coffeehouse and music store in the county. ⊠ *4061 Adams Ave., Kensington.*

Museum of Photographic Arts. In its 226-seat theater, the museum runs a regular film program that includes classic American and international cinema by prominent filmmakers, as well as the occasional cult film. Each MoPA screening is preceded by an informative introduction from the museum staff. ⊠ *1649 El Prado, Balboa Park* ☎ *619/238–7559.*

Reuben H. Fleet Science Center. Movies about space, science, and nature are shown on the IMAX screen here. ⊠ *1875 El Prado, Balboa Park* ☎ *619/238–1233.*

San Diego Film Festival. The festival screens local, national, and international entries at the **Gaslamp Theater** (⊠ *701 5th Ave., Gaslamp Quarter*). The city's glitterati—and some Hollywood celebs—rub shoulders at the fest's films, panels, and finale. It typically takes place in late September. ⊠ *10981 San Diego Mission Rd., Suite 112, Mission Valley* ☎ *619/582–2368* ⊕ *www.sdff.org.*

Sherwood Auditorium. The 500-seat auditorium at the Museum of Contemporary Art hosts foreign and classic film series and special cinema events. ⊠ *700 Prospect St., La Jolla* ☎ *858/454–3541.*

GALLERIES

Sure, surf art is popular 'round these parts, but you can also view (and purchase) world-class, cutting-edge collectibles.

The Art of Tim Cantor. The artist works in a private studio in the back of this gallery that showcases his intense, mysterious works in oil and sculpture. ⊠ *527 4th Ave., Gaslamp Quarter* ☎ *619/235–6990* ⊕ *www.timcantor.com.*

Chuck Jones' Studio Gallery. This gallery, often crowded at night with after-dinner strollers, is devoted to the extensive animation art of the late Chuck Jones, cartoon director at Warner Bros. from 1938 to 1962 and creator of the Road Runner and Wile E. Coyote, among other characters. ⊠ *232 5th Ave., Gaslamp Quarter* ☎ *619/294–9880.*

CJ Gallery. This gallery in the historic Whitney Building specializes in contemporary fine art. ⊠ *343 4th Ave., Gaslamp Quarter* ☎ *619/595–0048* ⊕ *www.cjartgallery.com.*

Kettner Arts Complex. Several fine-art galleries are in this building, including **Perry L. Meyer Fine Art** (☎ *619/358–9512* ⊕ *www.plmeyerfineart. com*). ⊠ *2400 Kettner Blvd., Little Italy.*

Michael J. Wolf Fine Arts. In the historic Brunswick Building, the Gaslamp's oldest art gallery presents the work of emerging contemporary artists. ⊠ *363 5th Ave., Suite 102, Gaslamp Quarter* ☎ *619/702–5388* ⊕ *www. mjwfinearts.com.*

Prospect Place Fine Art. Etchings and lithographs by 19th- and 20th-century masters include works by Miró, Matisse, Rufino Tamayo, and Chagall. ⊠ *1268 Prospect St., La Jolla* ☎ *858/459–1978.*

MUSIC

San Diego can rightfully toot its horn: the local symphony and opera are on par with the nation's top regional offerings.

Balboa Theatre. Reopened in 2008 after being shuttered for more than two decades, the renovated theater dates from the glamorous 1920s, and in addition to its architectural splendor, offers unsurpassed sound. ⊠ *868 4th Ave., Gaslamp Quarter* ☎ *619/570–1100.*

Fodor's Choice ★ **Copley Symphony Hall.** The great acoustics here are surpassed only by the incredible Spanish baroque interior. Not just the home of the San Diego Symphony Orchestra, the renovated 2,200-seat 1920s-era theater has also hosted major stars like Elvis Costello and Sting. ⊠ *750 B St., Downtown* ☎ *619/235–0804.*

Cricket Wireless Amphitheatre. The largest concert venue in town (and another victim of corporate-supporter renaming), the amphitheater can accommodate 20,000 concertgoers with reserved seats and lawn seating. It presents top-selling national and international acts during its late-spring to late-summer season. ⊠ *2050 Entertainment Cir., Chula Vista, California* ☎ *619/671–3500.*

★ **La Jolla Athenaeum Music & Arts Library.** The Athenaeum is a membership-supported, nonprofit library with an exceptional collection of books, periodicals, CDs, and other media related to arts and music. It also hosts

DID YOU KNOW?

Before reopening in 2008, the Balboa Theatre had many lives. Originally built in 1924 it screened films from Mexico as Teatro Balboa, then housed sailors during World War II.

jazz and chamber music concerts throughout the year. ⊠ *1008 Wall St., La Jolla* ☎ *858/454–5872.*

Open-Air Theatre. Top-name rock, reggae, and popular artists give summer concerts under the stars at this theater. ⊠ *San Diego State University, 5500 Campanile Dr., College Area* ☎ *619/594–6947.*

Orchestra Nova San Diego. From September to May, a 30-plus member ensemble performs classics, pop, and Handel's *Messiah* in a number of different venues, including St. Paul's Cathedral downtown, Sherwood Auditorium in La Jolla, and Qualcomm Hall in Sorrento Valley. ☎ *858/350–0290.*

★ **San Diego Opera.** Drawing international artists, the opera's season runs January–April. Past performances have included *Die Fledermaus, Faust, Idomeneo,* and *La Bohème,* plus concerts by such talents as the late Luciano Pavarotti. ⊠ *Civic Theatre, 3rd Ave. and B St., Downtown* ☎ *619/533–7000.*

San Diego Symphony Orchestra. The orchestra puts on special events year-round, including classical concerts and summer and winter pops. Nearly all concerts are held at Copley Symphony Hall; the Summer Pops series is held on the Embarcadero, beyond the San Diego Convention Center on North Harbor Drive. ⊠ *750 B St., Downtown* ☎ *619/235–0804.*

Sherwood Auditorium. A 500-seat venue in the Museum of Contemporary Art, the auditorium hosts classical and jazz events. ⊠ *700 Prospect St., La Jolla* ☎ *858/454–3541.*

★ **Spreckels Organ Pavilion.** This is the home of a giant outdoor pipe organ donated to the city in 1915 by sugar magnates John and Adolph Spreckels. The beautiful Spanish baroque pavilion hosts concerts by civic organist Carol Williams and guest organists on most Sunday afternoons and on most Monday evenings in summer. Local military bands, gospel groups, and barbershop quartets also perform here. All shows are free. ⊠ *Balboa Park* ☎ *619/702–8138.*

Spreckels Theatre. A landmark theater erected in 1912, the Spreckels hosts comedy, dance, theater, and concerts. Good acoustics and old-time elegance make this a favorite local venue. ⊠ *121 Broadway, Downtown* ☎ *619/235–9500.*

Valley View Casino Center. Big-name concerts are held here with room for 13,000-plus fans. ⊠ *3500 Sports Arena Blvd., Sports Arena* ☎ *619/224–4171.*

Viejas Arena. Formerly known as Cox Arena, the Viejas Arena attracts big acts to its 12,500-person facility. ⊠ *San Diego State University, 5500 Canyon Crest Dr., College Area* ☎ *619/594–6947.*

THEATER

With the Old Globe Theatre and the La Jolla Playhouse, San Diego's theater scene is a local star—and a major player for page-to-stage and Broadway-bound productions.

Coronado Playhouse. This cabaret-type theater near the Hotel Del Coronado stages regular dramatic and musical performances. ⊠ *1835 Strand Way, Coronado* ☎ *619/435–4856.*

The Lamb's Players Theater presented Tim Slover's *Joyful Noise*, about the creation of Handel's *Messiah*.

Diversionary Theatre. San Diego's premier gay and lesbian company presents a range of original works that focus on LGBT themes. ✉ *4545 Park Blvd., University Heights* ☎ *619/220–0097.*

Fodor's Choice ★ **La Jolla Playhouse.** The playhouse crafts exciting and innovative productions under the artistic direction of Christopher Ashley, May through March. Many Broadway shows, such as *Tommy* and *Jersey Boys*, have previewed here before heading for the East Coast. The playhouse has three stages: the Mandell Weiss Theatre has the main stage, the Mandell Weiss Forum is a thrust stage, and the Sheila and Hughes Potiker Theatre is a black-box theater. ✉ *University of California at San Diego, 2910 La Jolla Village Dr., La Jolla* ☎ *858/550–1010.*

★ **Lamb's Players Theatre.** The theater's regular season of five productions runs from February through November. It also stages a musical, *Festival of Christmas*, in December. *An American Christmas* is the company's dinner-theater show at the Hotel Del Coronado. ✉ *1142 Orange Ave., Coronado* ☎ *619/437–0600.*

Lynx Performance Theatre. This progressive theater space is known for presenting often controversial and edgy works. ✉ *2653-R Ariane Dr., California* ☎ *619/889–3190.*

Lyric Opera San Diego. A variety of operas, operettas, and other musical theater productions including several Gilbert and Sullivan works are performed by the company at the Stephen and Mary Birch North Park Theatre. ✉ *Birch North Park Theatre, 2891 University Ave., North Park* ☎ *619/239–8836.*

Marie Hitchcock Puppet Theatre. Amateur and professional puppeteers and ventriloquists entertain here five days a week. The cost is just a few dollars for adults and children alike. If you feel cramped in the 200-seat theater, don't worry; the shows rarely run longer than a half hour. ⊠ *2125 Park Blvd., Balboa Park* ☎ *619/544–9203.*

Fodor's Choice **Old Globe Theatre.** The oldest professional theater in California presents
★ classics, contemporary dramas, and experimental works. The Globe has two sister theaters: the intimate Cassius Carter Centre Stage and the outdoor Lowell Davies Festival Theater. The Old Globe also mounts a popular Shakespeare Festival every summer at Lowell Davies. The recently opened Conrad Prebys Theatre Center merges the flagship Old Globe Theatre with a new, state-of-the-art multilevel facility. ⊠ *1363 Old Globe Way, Balboa Park* ☎ *619/234–5623.*

Old Town Theatre. A 248-seat theater operated by Cygnet Theatre Company, this is one of the more interesting small San Diego theater groups. Catch local takes on edgy classics like *Sweeney Todd*. ⊠ *4040 Twiggs St., Old Town* ☎ *619/688–2494.*

San Diego Civic Theatre. In addition to being the home of the San Diego Opera, the theater presents musicals and other major Broadway-style productions throughout the year. ⊠ *3rd Ave. and B St., Downtown* ☎ *619/570–1100.*

San Diego Repertory Theatre. San Diego's first resident acting company performs contemporary works year-round. ⊠ *Lyceum Theatre, 79 Horton Plaza, Gaslamp Quarter* ☎ *619/231–3586.*

Starlight Musical Theatre. A summertime favorite, the Starlight performs a series of musicals performed in an outdoor amphitheater mid-June to early October. Because of the theater's proximity to the airport, actors often have to freeze midscene while a plane flies over. ⊠ *Starlight Bowl, 2005 Pan American Plaza, Balboa Park* ☎ *619/232–7827.*

Sushi Performance & Visual Art. This nationally acclaimed group provides an opportunity for well-known performance artists to do their thing at a variety of venues around town. ⊠ *390 11th Ave., East Village* ☎ *619/235–8466.*

Beaches

WORD OF MOUTH

"Everybody agrees that La Jolla is a wonderful place to spend a couple of hours. The beach is wide, sandy, excellent for a long barefoot walk. The cliffs have bizarre rocks, coves, amazing views, and a wide array of wildlife. There is the Children's Pool, a small sandy beach which is now occupied by a large horde of seals."

—Echnaton

SAN DIEGO'S BEST BEACHES

Step aside, Caribbean. Move over, Hawaii. San Diego is in the house! What makes this unique Southern California city stand out are its clean waters, its natural landscape, and its easygoing charm. There's strength and drama to its coastline, too, thanks to the high terrain that melds with the sea.

(above) Pacific Beach is the place to party. (lower right) Sea lions at the Children's Pool. (upper right) The U.S. Open Sandcastle Competition at Imperial Beach takes place annually in July or August.

With more than 50 mi of beach, there's bound to be a perfect stretch of sand for everyone. San Diego is a popular surfing area, but even nonsurfers appreciate the cool, refreshing waters and the intrigues of snorkeling. Most beaches are family-friendly, but some attract more specific crowds. Ocean Beach has a hipster feel, while Pacific Beach is a magnet for partiers. North County beaches have select surfing spots, and Black's Beach has at least a smattering of nudists. Each of the beaches has its charms, so be sure to check out more than one.

BEACH BONFIRE

Just because the sun went down doesn't mean its time to go home. Nothing compares to sitting around a crackling fire as the evening breeze brings in whiffs of the sea. Fires are allowed only in fire rings, which you can find at **Ocean Beach, Mission Beach, Pacific Beach,** and **La Jolla Shores**. The rings get claimed quickly in summer, so stake your claim early by putting your wood in the ring and your gear nearby.

12

BEST BEACHES FOR . . .

OCEAN VIEWS

The view at **Sunset Cliffs** in Point Loma is dramatic and heart-achingly beautiful. Look for the few picnic tables that are positioned near the edge of the cliffs. **Torrey Pines State Natural Reserve** also provides fantastic views from its 300-foot cliffs.

ROMANCE

For a beautiful secluded spot, head to the lone shacklike hut that's nestled among the rocks at La Jolla's **Windansea Beach**. At **Fletcher Cove** in Solana Beach, look for the single bench overlooking the sea at the beach entrance.

KIDS

Despite its name, the **Children's Pool** isn't a great spot to take your kids to swim, but they'll love watching the seals and sea lions that populate its waters. **La Jolla Shores** is popular for the gentle waves in its swimmer's section, and **Mission Bay**'s serene inlets make for shallow swimming pools.

OCEAN WALK

The Hotel Del Coronado on **Coronado Beach** makes the perfect backdrop to a walk along silky sand stretching into the horizon. **Silver Strand** and **Imperial Beach** are also lovely.

AFTER-BEACH DRINKS

Pacific Beach's Garnet Street is home to the neighborhood's liveliest bars. College students head to Garnet on Friday and Saturday nights; at other times, it's a laid-back scene. **Pacific Beach Bar and Grill** and **Moondoggies** attract a younger crowd, while the **Silver Fox** is the quintessential dive bar.

BEST BEACH EATS

Living Room. This eatery is within walking distance of La Jolla Cove. Look for a table in back, where an open window lets in the fresh ocean air. ⊠ *1010 Prospect St., La Jolla* ☎ *858/459–1187.*

Sbicca's. Not far from the shores of Del Mar, the upscale Sbicca's is famous for its roast chicken. ⊠ *215 15th St., Del Mar, California* ☎ *858/481–1001.*

Pizza Port. One of three branches, the Pizza Port in Solana Beach is prized by North County locals. They head to this combination pizzeria-brewery for original pies like the seafood-laden Pizza Solana as well as house-brewed stout and cream ales. ⊠ *135 N. Hwy. 101, Solana Beach, California* ☎ *858/481–7332.*

Las Olas. One of the best oceanfront Mexican restaurants in North County, Las Olas is right across the street from the beach. Grab a margarita or some grilled lobster before going to see surfers waiting for a sweet break. ⊠ *2655 S. Coast Hwy. 101, North County* ☎ *760/942–1860.*

LA JOLLA'S BEACHES AND BEYOND

La Jolla (pronounced La Hoya) means "the jewel" in Spanish and appropriately describes this small, affluent village and its beaches. Some of the area's most beautiful coastline can be found here, as well as an elegant upscale atmosphere.

(above) La Jolla is synonymous with beautiful vistas. (lower right) The view from Coast Highway 101 in Carlsbad is spectacular. (upper right) Hike down to the beach from Torrey Pines.

Conveniently located between North County and the Mission and South bays, La Jolla is easily accessible from downtown San Diego and North County. It's worth it to rent a car to be able to visit the different beaches along the coast. The town's trademark million-dollar homes won't disappoint either—their cliff-side locations make them an attractive backdrop to the brilliant views of the sea below. Downtown La Jolla is more commercialized, with high-end stores great for browsing. La Jolla Shores, a mi-long beach, is located in the more residential area to the north. Above all, the beach and cove are La Jolla's prime charms—the cove's seals and underwater kelp beds are big draws for kayakers and nature lovers.

IN THE BUFF

Let's face it, some people just don't like tan lines. Black's Beach is one of the largest clothing-optional beaches in the United States. The chances of running into naked beachgoers of all ages are higher at the north end, and Black's is properly secluded and difficult to get to. The Black's Beach Bares (⊕ *www.blacksbeach.org*) organization chronicles their free-spirited nudist tendencies on their Web site.

COAST HIGHWAY 101

The portion of Coast Highway 101 that runs from North County to La Jolla is one of San Diego's best drives. Start from South Carlsbad beach at Tamarack Avenue and continue south through Leucadia, Encinitas, Cardiff-by-the-Sea, Solana Beach, Del Mar, and, finally, La Jolla. Any turn west will take you toward the beach. The drive offers intermittent glimpses of the sea; views from Carlsbad and Cardiff are especially beautiful. The grand finale, however, is at Torrey Pines, where you'll see waves rolling toward the misty, high-bluffed beach.

12

THE CLIFFS AT TORREY PINES

The view of the ocean from the 300-foot-high sandstone cliffs at the top of Torrey Pines State Natural Reserve is exquisite and vast. To reach the cliffs and their spectacular views, hike along one of the short trails leading from the visitor center. Find a place to perch along the sandy edge, where you can sit and let your legs dangle. If you're lucky, you may see dolphins swimming along the shore or surfers riding a break.

SEALS AT THE CHILDREN'S POOL

In the last decade, much of La Jolla's harbor seal population has made itself at home at the Children's Pool beach, prompting concerns about water contamination due to the seals' waste. Swimmers were told to avoid the pools; in 2004, one irked swimmer took legal action, claiming that the pool is for children and snorkelers, who benefit from the shallow waters—not for the seals. Animal rights groups argued that the seals should be protected in their chosen natural habitat. After a prolonged court battle, a November 2009 ruling sided with the seals, citing a federal law that protects them. The debate continues, however, whether a rope barrier separating the seals from onlookers should be used year-round or only during the seals' five-month pupping season. A December 2010 ruling limited the permit to five months, but an appeal is expected.

LA JOLLA COVE WALK AND SHOP

If you're not keen on going into the water (or the sand for that matter) but still interested in taking in the sea air, the area surrounding La Jolla Cove is ideal for walking and shopping with a view. Park at any of the available metered spaces on Girard Avenue in downtown La Jolla and browse the Arcade Building, built in the Spanish Mission style. Make your way toward the cove by following signs, or simply walk toward any patches of ocean you see. Look for the gazebos that dot the edge of the cove; they make great photo ops.

WATER SPORTS

One of the most popular water activities is kayaking along the caves and snorkeling among the kelp beds near the cove at the Underwater Ecological Reserve. Kayak rental shops offer special outings that include midnight moonlight kayaking and a chance to dive among leopard sharks that roam La Jolla's waters. Don't worry; the sharks are harmless.

Updated by
Christine Pae

California's coast has a great deal to boast about, but the state's southernmost region stands apart when it comes to sand, surf, and sea. Step out of the car and onto the beach to immediately savor its allure: smell the fresh salty air, feel the plush sand at your feet, hear waves breaking enticingly from the shore, and see the often breathtaking vistas.

San Diego's sandstone bluffs offer spectacular views of the Pacific as a palette of blues and greens: there are distant indigo depths, emerald coves closer to shore, and finally, the mint-green swirls of the foamy surf. On land, the beach is silvery brown, etched with wisps of darker, charcoal-color sand and flecked with fool's gold.

San Diego's beaches have a different vibe from their northern counterparts in neighboring Orange County and glitzy Los Angeles farther up the coast. San Diego is more laid-back and relaxed and less of a scene. Cyclists on cruiser bikes whiz by as surfers saunter toward the waves and sunbathers bronze under the sun, be it July or November.

There is a lot of variety among the beaches. La Jolla Shores and Mission Bay both have gentle waves and shallow waters that provide safer swimming for kids; whereas the high swells at Black's and Tourmaline attract surfers worldwide. If you're looking for dramatic ocean views, Torrey Pines State Beach and Sunset Cliffs provide a desertlike chaparral backdrop, with craggy cliffs overlooking the ocean below. Beaches farther south in Coronado and Silver Strand have longer stretches of sand that are perfect for a contemplative stroll or a brisk jog. Then there are those secluded, sandy enclaves that you may happen upon on a scenic drive down Highway 101. Whether you're seeking a safe place to take the kids or a hot spot to work on your tan, there is something for everyone.

⇨ *Beach reviews are listed geographically from south to north.*

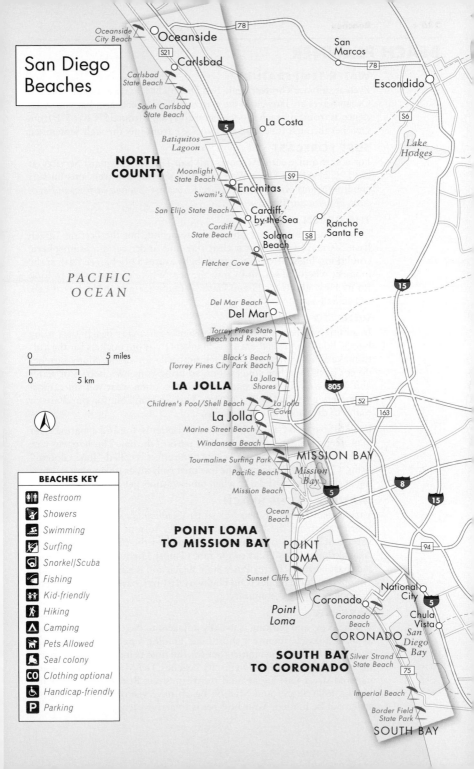

BEACH PLANNER

WATER TEMPERATURE

Even at summer's hottest peak, San Diego's beaches are cool and breezy. Ocean waves are large, and the water will be colder than what you experience at tropical beaches—temperatures range from 55°F to 65°F from October through June, and 65°F to 73°F from July through September.

SURF FORECAST

For a surf and weather report, call San Diego's Lifeguard Services at ☎ 619/221–8824. These Web sites also provide live webcams on surf conditions and water temperature forecasts: ⊕ *www.surfingsandiego. com,* ⊕ *www.surfline.com.*

THE GREEN FLASH

Some people think it's a phony phenomenon, but the fleeting "green flash" is real, if rare. On a clear day and under certain atmospheric conditions, higher-frequency green light causes a brief green flash at the moment when the sun sinks into the sea. Where's a good spot to look for it? How about the Green Flash restaurant, right on the boardwalk in Pacific Beach.

WHAT TO BRING

In addition to beach essentials like sunscreen, many beachgoers bring boogie boards to ride the waves, blankets to lie on, buckets for the kids to make sand castles, and a beach umbrella for shade. Many beaches do not have shoreline concessions, so bring your own bottles of water and snacks. While surfers and bodysurfers often wear wet suits, most swimmers go without in summer. They're available for purchase or rental in the shops in beach towns.

Despite Southern California's famous balminess, fog and a marine layer may creep in unexpectedly at various parts of the day. This happens particularly often in early summer, when the effect is called "June Gloom." Bring a light sweater in case the fine mist rolls in, or if you plan on staying at the beach until dark, when temperatures get cooler.

GETTING TO THE BEACH

Various San Diego Transit bus stops (⊕ *www.sdcommute.com*) are a short walk from the beach, but it's better to rent a car to explore a variety of beaches on your own. Driving to the beach on the scenic coastal routes is also part of the fun. County Highway S21 runs along the coast between Torrey Pines State Beach and Reserve and Oceanside, although its local names (Old Highway 101 or Coast Highway 101, for example) vary by community.

PARKING

Beach access and parking is usually adjacent to beaches but some, such as Black's Beach, require a short hike. Finding a parking spot near the ocean can be hard in summer, but for the time being, unmetered parking is available at all San Diego city beaches. Del Mar has a pay lot and metered street parking around the 15th Street Beach. Larger beaches like La Jolla Shores and Mission Beach have visitor parking lots, but space can be limited. Your best bet is to arrive early.

BEACH RULES

Pay attention to signs listing illegal activities; undercover police often patrol the beaches. Smoking and alcoholic beverages are completely banned on city beaches. Drinking in beach parking lots, on board-walks, and in landscaped areas is also illegal. Certain beaches also prohibit skateboarding. Fires are allowed only in fire rings or elevated barbecue grills. Although it may be tempting to take a sea creature as a souvenir from a tide pool, it may upset the delicate ecological balance and it's illegal, too.

SAFETY

Lifeguards are stationed at city beaches from Sunset Cliffs up to Black's Beach in the summertime, but coverage in winter is provided by roving patrols only. When swimming in the ocean be aware of rip currents, which are common in California shores. If you are caught in one, don't panic. Swim parallel to the shore until you can reach land without resistance. To be safe, go swimming near lifeguard posts where you will be visible. Few beaches have lockers to keep your belongings secure. If you're going to the beach solo and plan on going in the water, leave your wallet in the trunk of your car.

POLLUTION

San Diego's beaches are well maintained and very clean during summertime, when rainfall is infrequent. Beaches along San Diego County's northern cities are typically cleaner than ones farther south. Pollution is generally worse near river mouths and storm-drain outlets, especially after heavy rainfall. Call San Diego's Lifeguard Services at ☎ *619/221–8824* for a recorded message that includes pollution reports along with surfing and diving conditions. The Heal the Bay organization (⊕ *www.healthebay.org*) monitors and grades California coastal water conditions yearly.

BEACH CAMPING

Overnight camping is not allowed on any San Diego city beach, but there are campgrounds at some state beaches (☎ *800/444–7275 for reservations* ⊕ *www.reserveamerica.com*) throughout the county.

DOG BEACHES

Leashed dogs are permitted on most San Diego beaches and adjacent parks from 6 pm to 9 am; they can run unleashed anytime at Dog Beach at the north end of Ocean Beach and, from the day after Labor Day through June 14, at Rivermouth in Del Mar. It's rarely a problem, however, to take your pet to isolated beaches in winter.

RED TIDE

When sporadic algae blooms turn coastal waters a reddish-brown hue, San Diegans know the "red tide" has arrived. Environmentalists may see it as a bane to healthy ocean life, but the phenomenon is welcomed as a chance to witness ocean phosphorescence. The phytoplankton that causes the discoloration is unsightly only until nightfall. After dark, the algae-rich waters crash against the sand, inciting bioluminescent plankton to emit a bluish-green neon light. The result is a marvelous display of glow-in-the-dark waves.

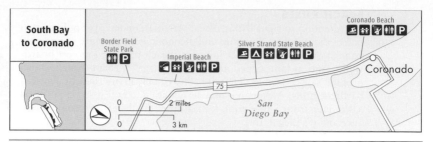

BEACHES BY NEIGHBORHOOD

SOUTH BAY TO CORONADO

SOUTH BAY

Border Field State Park. This southernmost San Diego beach is different from most California beaches; there are no lifeguards, and the fence marking off the south end of the parking lot also marks the U.S.–Mexican border. The beach is part of Border Field State Park, a marshy area with chaparral and wildflowers that's a favorite among horseback riders and hikers. The park contains much of the Tijuana River estuary, a haven for migrating birds. Access to the park is often closed to motor vehicles because of lack of manpower; you can park about a mile away at the entrance to the state beach and walk along the salt flats. When open, the park has barbecue grills, plentiful parking, and restrooms. Beware: in winter the grounds are often posted with contamination signs because of sewer runoff from Tijuana. **Best for:** bird-watching, horseback riding, solitude. **Amenities:** grills, parking at Monument Mesa, picnic tables, toilets. ⊠ *Exit I–5 at Dairy Mart Rd. and head west along Monument Rd., South Bay.*

Imperial Beach. In July or early August this classic Southern California beach is the site of the U.S. Open Sandcastle Competition (⊕ *www.usopensandcastle.com*). The rest of the year, this laid-back beach is a great place for long walks away from crowds. The beach break here is often excellent, but sewage contamination can be a problem, especially in winter and after heavy rains. There are lifeguards, restrooms, parking, and plenty of eateries nearby. A walk on the pier (with its own seafood restaurant), the southernmost in California, allows views of Mexico to the south and Point Loma to the north. A walk on the beach south toward Border Field State Park or north toward Coronado is a great way to experience a quiet, uncrowded shore—not always an easy thing to do. **Best for:** families, fishing pier, long walks. **Amenities:** lifeguard year-round, picnic tables, playground, showers, toilets. ⊠ *Take Palm Ave. west from I–5 until it hits water, South Bay.*

CORONADO

Silver Strand State Beach. This quiet Coronado beach is ideal for families. The water is relatively calm, lifeguards and rangers are on duty year-round, and there are places to rollerblade or ride bikes. Three day-use parking lots provide room for more than 1,000 cars. RV sites at a state

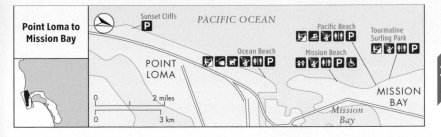

12

campground ($50 by the beach, $35 inland) are available by reservation (☎ *800/444–7275* ⊕ *www.reserveamerica.com*). Foot tunnels under Route 75 lead to a bay-side beach that has great views of the San Diego skyline. Across from the beach are the Coronado Cays, an exclusive community popular with yacht owners and celebrities, and the Loews Coronado Bay Resort. **Best for:** camping, families, long walks, swimming. **Amenities:** lifeguard year-round, camping facilities, food concessions open in summer, grills/fire pits, parking ($10), picnic tables, showers, toilets. ⊠ *From San Diego–Coronado Bridge, turn left onto Orange Ave., which becomes Rte. 75, and follow signs, Coronado* ☎ *619/435–5184.*

☺ **Coronado Beach.** With the famous Hotel Del Coronado as a backdrop,
★ this stretch of sandy beach is one of San Diego County's largest and most picturesque. It's perfect for sunbathing, people-watching, or Frisbee. Exercisers include Navy SEAL teams as well as the occasional Marine Recon unit, who do training runs on the beaches in and around Coronado. Parking can be difficult on the busiest days. There are plenty of restrooms and service facilities, as well as fire rings on the north end. **Best for:** families, long walks, swimming. **Amenities:** lifeguard year-round, grills/fire pits at north end, parking (free on street), picnic tables, playground, showers, toilets. ⊠ *From the San Diego–Coronado bridge, turn left onto Orange Ave. and follow signs, Coronado.*

POINT LOMA, MISSION BAY, AND LA JOLLA

POINT LOMA

Sunset Cliffs. One of the more secluded beaches in the area, Sunset Cliffs is popular with surfers and locals. A few miles long, it lies beneath the jagged cliffs on the west side of the Point Loma peninsula. At the south end of the peninsula, near Cabrillo Point, tide pools teeming with small sea creatures are revealed at low tide. Farther north the waves lure surfers and the lonely coves attract sunbathers. Stairs at the foot of Pescadero and Bermuda avenues provide beach access, as do some cliff trails, which are treacherous at points. There are few facilities. A visit here is more enjoyable at low tide; check the local newspaper for tide schedules. **Best for:** couples/romance, scenic drives, scenic views, tide pools. **Amenities:** parking in lots and on street, picnic tables. ⊠ *Take I–8 west to Sunset Cliffs Blvd. and head west, Point Loma.*

Ocean Beach. Much of this mile-long beach is a haven for volleyball players, sunbathers, and swimmers. The area around the municipal pier at the south end is a hangout for surfers and transients. The pier itself is

The grassy palm-lined park above La Jolla Cove is great for picnics.

open to the public 24 hours a day for fishing and walking, and there's a restaurant midpier. The beach is south of the channel entrance to Mission Bay. You'll find fire rings as well as plenty of casual places to grab a snack on adjoining streets. Swimmers should beware of strong rip currents around the main lifeguard tower. There's a dog beach at the north end where Fido can run leash-free. During the summer there can be as many as 100 dogs running in the sand. For picnic areas and a paved path, check out Ocean Beach Park across from Dog Beach. **Best for:** dogs, fishing pier, sunbathing, surfing, volley ball. **Amenities:** lifeguard year-round, grills/fire pits, parking in lots and on street, picnic tables, showers, toilets. ⊠ *Take I–8 west to Sunset Cliffs Blvd. and head west; a right turn off Sunset Cliffs Blvd. takes you to the water, Point Loma.*

MISSION BAY

Mission Beach. San Diego's most popular beach draws huge crowds on hot summer days, but it's lively year-round. The 2-mi-long stretch extends from the north entrance of Mission Bay to Pacific Beach. A wide boardwalk paralleling the beach is popular with walkers, joggers, roller skaters, rollerbladers, and bicyclists. Surfers, swimmers, and volleyball players congregate at the south end. Scantily clad volleyball players practice on Cohasset Court year-round. Toward its north end, near the Belmont Park roller coaster, the beach narrows and the water becomes rougher. The crowds grow thicker and somewhat rougher as well. For parking, you can try for a spot on the street, but your best bets are the two big lots at Belmont Park. **Best for:** accessibility, bicycling, boardwalk, families, volleyball. **Amenities:** lifeguard year-round, grills/fire pits, parking widely available at Belmont Park, picnic tables,

showers, toilets. ⊠ *Exit I–5 at Grand Ave. and head west to Mission Blvd.; turn south and look for parking near roller coaster at West Mission Bay Dr., Mission Bay.*

Pacific Beach/North Pacific Beach. The boardwalk of Mission Beach turns into a sidewalk here, but there are still bike paths and picnic tables along the beach. Pacific Beach runs from the north end of Mission Beach to Crystal Pier. North Pacific Beach extends from the pier north. The scene here is particularly lively on weekends. There are designated surfing areas, and fire rings are available. Parking can be a challenge, but there are plenty of restrooms, showers, and restaurants in the area. **Best for:** couples/romance, nightlife, singles scene, surfing, swimming. **Amenities:** lifeguard year-round, grills/fire pits, parking in lots and on street, picnic tables, showers, toilets. ⊠ *Exit I–5 at Grand Ave. and head west to Mission Blvd. Turn north and look for parking, Mission Bay.*

Tourmaline Surfing Park. Year-round, this is one of the area's most popular beaches for surfing and sailboarding. Separate areas designated for swimmers and surfers are strictly enforced. There's a 175-space parking lot at the foot of Tourmaline Street that normally fills to capacity by midday. **Best for:** boating, surfing. **Amenities:** lifeguard year-round, parking in lots and on street, picnic tables, showers, toilets. ⊠ *Take Mission Blvd. north (it turns into La Jolla Blvd.) and turn west on Tourmaline St., Mission Bay.*

LA JOLLA

Windansea Beach. Named for a hotel that burned down in the late 1940s, Windansea Beach has increasingly gained notoriety due to its association with surfers. If the scenery here seems familiar, it's because Windansea and its habitués were the inspiration for Tom Wolfe's article "The Pump House Gang," about a group of surfers who protect their surf turf from outsiders. The reef break here forms an unusual A-frame wave, making this beach one the most popular (and crowded) surf spots in San Diego County. Just below the parking lot is a palm-covered surf shack, constructed in 1946 and named a historical landmark in 1998. With its incredible views and secluded sunbathing spots set among sandstone rocks, Windansea

SNACK TIP

Trader Joe's. On your way to Pacific Beach? Head to Trader Joe's for picnic supplies including sandwich fixings, chips, dried fruit, nuts, wine, and good cheese. ⊠ *1211 Garnet Ave., Pacific Beach* ☎ *858/272-7235.*

is also one of the most romantic of West Coast beaches, especially at sunset. You can usually find nearby street parking. **Best for:** couples/romance, sunsets, surfing, solitude, tide pools. **Amenities:** lifeguard in summer, street parking. ⊠ *Take Mission Blvd. north (it turns into La Jolla Blvd.) and turn west on Nautilus St., La Jolla.*

WORD OF MOUTH

"Windansea is about five minutes south of downtown La Jolla off Nautilus Street and is a famous surfing beach. I also love Coronado. It has a world-class beach—it stretches for about a mile or more, and is also in a lovely town."
—nanabee

Marine Street Beach. Wide and sandy, this strand often teems with sunbathers, swimmers, walkers, and joggers. The water is known as a great spot for bodysurfing, although the waves break in extremely shallow water and you'll need to watch out for riptides. **Best for:** body boarding, solitude, swimming. **Amenities:** lifeguard, street parking, picnic tables, showers and toilets near cove. ⊠ *Accessible from Marine St., off La Jolla Blvd., La Jolla.*

Children's Pool. Because of the pool's location at the tip of the La Jolla peninsula, you can actually look east to get unmatched panoramic views of the coastline and ocean. This shallow cove, protected by a seawall, has small waves and no riptide. The area just outside the pool is popular with scuba divers, who explore the offshore reef when the surf is calm. Groups of harbor seals hang out along the beach, claiming it as their own during the winter pupping season. At this rate, it may have to be renamed the "Seals' Pool." While kids love to watch the seals and sea lions, swimming is not advised. **Best for:** families, scenic views, seal-watching. **Amenities:** lifeguard year-round, limited street parking, picnic tables, showers, toilets. ⊠ *Follow La Jolla Blvd. north, when it forks, stay to left, then turn right onto Coast Blvd., La Jolla.*

Shell Beach. North of Children's Pool is a small cove, accessible by stairs, with a relatively secluded beach. The exposed rocks off the coast have been designated a protected habitat for sea lions; you can watch them sun themselves and frolic in the water. **Best for:** sea lion–watching, tide pools. **Amenities:** lifeguard, street parking, picnic tables, showers and toilets available near the cove. ⊠ *Continue along Coast Blvd. north from Children's Pool, La Jolla.*

Fodor's Choice ★
La Jolla Cove. This shimmering blue inlet is what first attracted everyone to La Jolla, from Native Americans to the glitterati; it's the secret to the village's enduring cachet. You'll find "the Cove"—as locals refer to it, as though it were the only one in San Diego—beyond where Girard Avenue dead-ends into Coast Boulevard, marked by towering palms that line a promenade where people strolling in designer clothes are as common as Frisbee throwers. A palm-lined park sits on top of cliffs formed by the incessant pounding of the waves. At low tide the pools and cliff caves are a destination for explorers. Divers, snorkelers, and kayakers can check out the underwater delights of the **San Diego–La Jolla Underwater Park Ecological Reserve.** The cove is also a favorite of rough-water swimmers. **Best for:** diving, long walks, scenic views,

snorkeling, tide pools. **Amenities:** lifeguard year-round (reduced hours in winter), parking on side streets, picnic tables, showers, toilets. ✉ *Follow Coast Blvd. north to signs, or take La Jolla Village Dr. exit from I–5, head west to Torrey Pines Rd., turn left, and drive downhill to Girard Ave.; turn right and follow signs, La Jolla.*

12

☺ **La Jolla Shores.** This is one of San Diego's most popular beaches, so get ★ here early on summer weekends. The lures are an incredible view of La Jolla peninsula, a wide sandy beach, an adjoining grassy park, and the gentlest waves in San Diego. In fact, several surf schools teach here, and kayak rentals are nearby. A concrete boardwalk parallels the beach. Arrive early to get a parking spot in the lot at the foot of Calle Frescota. **Best for:** boogie boarding, families, long walks, sunbathing, surfing, swimming. **Amenities:** lifeguard year-round, grills/fire pits, parking in lots and on side streets, picnic tables, playground, showers, toilets. ✉ *8200 Camino del Oro, From I–5 take La Jolla Village Dr. west and turn left onto La Jolla Shores Dr.; head west to Camino del Oro or Vallecitos St., turn right, La Jolla.*

★ **Black's Beach.** The powerful waves at this beach, which is officially known as Torrey Pines City Park beach, attract world-class surfers, and its relative isolation appeals to nudist nature lovers (although by law nudity is prohibited) as well as gays and lesbians. Backed by cliffs whose colors change with the angle of the sun, Black's can be accessed from Torrey Pines State Beach to the north, or by a narrow path descending the cliffs from Torrey Pines Glider Port. Access to parts of the shore coincides with low tide. There are no lifeguards on permanent duty, although they do patrol the area between spring break and mid-October. Strong rip currents are common—only experienced swimmers should take the plunge. Storms have weakened the cliffs in the past few years; they're dangerous to climb and should be avoided. Part of the fun here is watching hang gliders and paragliders ascend from the Torrey Pines Glider Port atop the cliffs. **Best for:** solitude, sunbathing (nude), surfing. **Amenities:** lifeguard sometimes, parking available at the Torrey Pines Glider Port and La Jolla Farms. ✉ *Take Genesee Ave. west from I–5 and follow signs to Torrey Pines Glider Port; easier access, via a paved path, available on La Jolla Farms Rd., but parking is limited to 2 hrs., La Jolla.*

★ **Torrey Pines State Beach and Reserve.** One of San Diego's best beaches encompasses 2,000 acres of bluffs and bird-filled marshes. A network of meandering trails leads to the sandy shoreline below. Along the way enjoy the rare Torrey pine trees, found only here and on Santa Rosa Island, offshore. Guided tours of the nature preserve are offered on weekends. Torrey Pines tends to get crowded in summer, but you'll find more isolated spots heading south under the cliffs leading to Black's Beach. **Best for:** families, hiking, scenic views, sunbathing, swimming. **Amenities:** lifeguard year-round (reduced hours in winter), parking in two small lots, showers, toilets. ✉ *Take Carmel Valley Rd. exit west from I–5, turn left on Rte. S21, Del Mar* ☎ *858/755–2063* ⊕ *www. torreypine.org* 🅿 *Parking $10.*

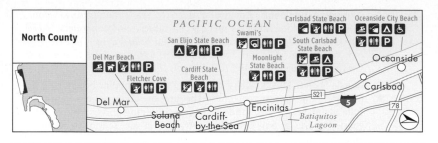

NORTH COUNTY BEACHES

DEL MAR

Del Mar Beach. The numbered streets of Del Mar, from 15th north to 29th, end at a wide beach popular with volleyball players, surfers, and sunbathers. Parking can be a problem in town; there's metered parking along the beach, making it challenging to stay for more than a few hours. The portion of Del Mar south of 15th Street is lined with cliffs and rarely crowded. Leashed dogs are permitted on most sections of the beach year-round; from the day after Labor Day through June 14, dogs may run free at Rivermouth, Del Mar's northernmost beach. During the annual summer meeting of the Del Mar Thoroughbred Club, horse bettors sit on the beach in the morning, working on the *Daily Racing Form* before heading across the street to the track. Food, hotels, and shopping are all within an easy walk of the beach. Because parking is at a premium, it's a great idea to bring a bike to cruise around the city before or after the beach. **Best for:** dogs, families, picnicking, swimming. **Amenities:** lifeguard year-round (reduced hours in winter), food concession at 17th Street, metered parking on streets, picnic tables, playground, showers, toilets. ⊠ *Take Via de la Valle exit from I–5 west to Rte. S21 (also known as Camino del Mar in Del Mar) and turn left, Del Mar.*

SOLANA BEACH

Fletcher Cove. Most of the beaches in the little city of Solana Beach are nestled under cliffs, and access is limited to private stairways. However, at the west end of Lomas Santa Fe Drive you'll find access to a small beach, known locally as Fletcher Cove. Also here are restrooms and a parking lot. During low tide it's an easy walk under the cliffs to nearby beaches. High tide can make some of the beach impassable. There's also a pay lot with restrooms and easy beach access at the north end of town. Tides and surf conditions are posted at a kiosk by the parking lot. **Best for:** couples/romance, families, picnicking, solitude, swimming, tide pools. **Amenities:** lifeguard year-round (reduced hours in winter), parking in lot and on street, picnic tables, playground, showers, toilets. ⊠ *From I–5 take Lomas Santa Fe Dr. west, Solana Beach.*

CARDIFF-BY-THE-SEA

Cardiff State Beach. This beach, popularly known as George's, begins at the parking lot immediately north of the cliffs at Solana Beach. A reef break draws surfers, although this stony beach is not particularly appealing otherwise. However, a walk south gives you great access to some of the secluded coves of Solana Beach. Pay attention to the

Check out the scene along Carlsbad State Beach's pedestrian walkway.

incoming tide or you may have to wade or swim back to the parking lot. **Best for:** surfing, swimming. **Amenities:** lifeguard, parking at small lot and on street, showers, toilets. ⊠ *From I–5 turn west on Lomas Santa Fe Dr. to Rte. S21 (Old Hwy. 101) and turn right, Cardiff-by-the-Sea* 🕾 *760/753–5091* 🚗 *Parking $10.*

San Elijo State Beach. There are campsites (🕾 *800/444–7275* ⊕ *www. parks.ca.gov for reservations*) atop a scenic bluff at this park, which also has a store and shower facilities plus beach access for swimmers and surfers. Sites run $35 for inland and $50 for ocean lots. **Best for:** camping, families, surfing. **Amenities:** lifeguard year-round, parking, grills/fire pits, picnic tables, showers, toilets. ⊠ *From I–5 exit at Encinitas Blvd. head west. Turn left (south) on S. Coast Hwy. for about 2 mi, Cardiff-by-the-Sea* 🕾 *760/753–5091* 🚗 *Parking $10 per car, or park free nearby on U.S. 101.*

ENCINITAS

★ **Swami's.** The palms and the golden lotus-flower domes of the nearby Self-Realization Center temple and ashram earned this picturesque beach its name. Extreme low tides expose tide pools that harbor anemones, starfish, and other sea life. Remember to look but don't touch; all sea life here is protected. The beach is also a top surfing spot; the only access is by a long stairway leading down from the cliff-top Seaside Roadside Park, where there's free parking. On big winter swells, the bluffs are lined with gawkers watching the area's best surfers take on, and be taken down by, some of the best big waves in the county. Offshore, divers do their thing at North County's only underwater park, Encinitas Marine Life Refuge. **Best for:** diving, surfing, tide pools.

Amenities: lifeguard year-round, parking, picnic tables, toilets. ⊠ *Follow Rte. S21 north from Cardiff, or Exit I–5 at Encinitas Blvd., go west to Rte. S21, and turn left, Encinitas.*

Moonlight State Beach. Large parking areas and lots of facilities make this beach, tucked into a break in the cliffs, an easy getaway. To counterbalance erosion, sand is trucked in every year. The volleyball courts on the north end attract many competent players, including a few professionals who live in the area. It's easily accessible from the Encinitas Coaster train station. **Best for:** families, solitude, surfing, swimming. **Amenities:** lifeguard year-round (reduced hours in winter), food concessions in summer, grills/fire pits, parking in lot and on street, picnic tables, playground, showers, toilets. ⊠ *Take Encinitas Blvd. exit from I–5 and head west to 3rd St., turn left; parking lot is on your right at top of hill, Encinitas.*

CARLSBAD

South Carlsbad State Beach/Carlsbad State Beach. Erosion from winter storms has made the southern Carlsbad beaches rockier than most beaches in Southern California. This is particularly true of South Carlsbad, a stretch of which is named in honor of Robert C. Frazee, a local politician and civic booster. Still, it's a good swimming spot, there are fine street- and beach-level promenades outside downtown Carlsbad, and for self-contained RVs there's overnight camping (☎ *800/444–7275*). No overnight camping is allowed at Carlsbad State Beach, farther to the north, but there's a fishing area and a parking lot. A cement walkway borders the beach and continues into downtown Carlsbad, too. The south swell here means good summer surf when other San Diego beaches are bereft. The beach has separate swimming and surfing sections. **Best for:** camping, jogging, long walks, sunbathing. **Amenities:** lifeguard year-round, camping facilities, grills/fire pits, parking in lots and on street, picnic tables, showers, toilets. ⊠ *Exit I–5 at La Costa Ave. and head west to Rte. S21, turn north and follow coastline, Carlsbad* ☎ *760/438–3143.*

OCEANSIDE

Oceanside City Beach. Swimmers, surfers, and U.S. Marines (from nearby Camp Pendleton) often come to play here. The surf is good around the Oceanside Pier near the foot of Mission Avenue and on either side of the two jetties. Self-serve RV camping is permitted in the parking lot at the northernmost end of Harbor Beach. There's no tent camping. There are plenty of pay lots and meters around the pier and also in the Oceanside Harbor area. **Best for:** accessibility, long walks, fishing pier, swimming. **Amenities:** lifeguard year-round, RV camping facilities, food concessions, grills/fire pits, parking, picnic tables, playground, showers, toilets. ⊠ *Take Vista Way west from I–5 to Rte. S21 (Coast Hwy.) and turn right; best access points are from Cassidy St., Oceanside Pier, and Oceanside Harbor area, Oceanside.*

Sports and the Outdoors

WORD OF MOUTH

"If you are adventuresome, my two favorite recommendations are [first,] kayaking in La Jolla Cove. You are likely to see and maybe even be surrounded by leopard sharks, which are completely harmless. It is a stunning experience. [Second,] hiking at the Torrey Pines State Park. My favorite is the beach hike."

—ncounty

SURFING SAN DIEGO

Head to a San Diego beach on any given day and chances are you'll see a group of surfers in the water, patiently waiting to ride a memorable break. Spectators as well as surfers agree that catching a perfect wave is an unforgettable experience.

(above) La Jolla Shores is a good beach for beginner surfers. (lower right) Surfer at the end of a good ride. (upper right) Instructors at Surf Diva Surf School cater to women.

Surfing may have originated in Hawaii, but modern surfing culture is inextricably linked to the Southern California lifestyle. From the Malibu setting of *Gidget* to the surf-city sounds of Jan and Dean and the Beach Boys, and TV's *Laguna Beach* and *The OC*, the entertainment industry brought a California version of surfing to the landlocked, and in the process created an enduring mystique.

San Diego surfing in particular is unique. Underwater kelp beds help keep waves intact, preventing the choppiness that surfers bemoan. Santa Ana winds that begin to arrive in fall and throughout early winter bring coveted offshore winds that contribute to morning and evening "glass" (the stillness of the water that encourages smooth waves).

BEST TIME TO GO

In San Diego the biggest swells usually occur in winter, although good-size waves can form year-round. Generally, swells come from a northerly direction in winter and from the south in summer. Certain surf spots are better on different swells. In winter, try beaches like Swami's or Black's Beach. Summer spots are La Jolla's Windansea and nearby Tourmaline Surfing Park.

TYPES OF BREAKS

Beach break: Waves that break over sandbars and the sea-floor and are usually tamer and consistently long, thus typically the best type for beginners, with the exception of Black's Beach, which is legendary for its uniquely large beach breaks. **La Jolla Shores, Mission Beach,** and **Pacific Beach** are destinations for gentler, more forgiving waves.

Point break: Created as waves hit a point jutting into the ocean. Surfers then peel down the swell it creates. With the right conditions, this can create very consistent waves. **Swami's** has an excellent point break.

Reef break: Waves break as they hit reef. It can create great (but dangerous) surf. There's a good chance of getting smashed and scraped over extremely sharp coral or rocks. Many of San Diego's best breaks occur thanks to underwater reefs, as at **San Elijo, La Jolla Cove,** and **Windansea.**

SAN DIEGO SURF FINDER

Get a closer view of surfers doing their thing from any municipal pier, such as at **Oceanside, Pacific,** and **Mission beaches.** The high bluffs of **Black's Beach** are also excellent points to watch surfers.

Swami's: Famous for its point break and beautiful waters.

Black's Beach: This is where to go for beach breaks. Serious surfers carry their boards and take a hike to reach the beach.

Windansea Beach: A dual beach for surf and romance. Known for its reef breaks.

Tourmaline Surfing Park: Windsurfers and surfers share Tourmaline's smooth waves.

La Jolla Shores: First-timers head here for more modest waves.

SURF SLANG

13

Barrel: The area created when a wave breaks onto itself in a curl.

Close out: When a wave breaks all at once, rather than breaking steadily in one direction.

Cutback: The most basic turn in surfing; executed to maintain position close to the barrel.

Dropping in: A severe breach of etiquette wherein a second surfer joins the wave later and cuts off the original rider.

Goofy foot: Having a right-foot-forward stance on the surfboard. The opposite is known as natural.

Grom: An affectionate term for those sun-bleached kids with tiny surfboards.

Hollow: Not all barrels create hollows, which are barrels big enough to create a tube that a surfer can ride within—also called the green room.

Lineup: A group of surfers waiting beyond the breakers for waves to come in.

Turtle roll: A maneuver in which the surfer rolls over on the surfboard, going underwater and holding the board upside down.

Updated by
Christine Pae

Evidence of San Diego's outdoorsy spirit is apparent everywhere; you'll find an occasional hot-air balloon floating into the sunset like a piece of candy in the sky, groups of surfers bobbing in the water at dawn, hang gliders swooping off sandstone cliffs, and white sails gliding gracefully along the shore. They are as much a part of San Diego's landscape as the sea, sand, and hills.

As you'd expect, the ocean is one of San Diego's most popular natural attractions. Surfers, swimmers, kayakers, divers, snorkelers, and sailboarders have 70 mi of shorefront to explore. You can rent equipment and take lessons in these sports, or head out on a fishing or whale-watching excursion aboard a charter boat. Even if you're inclined to do no more than sightsee, you can take a low-impact sunset stroll on a wide, sandy beach or explore secluded coves at low tide. At the end of the day at any beach in the county, you'll see a local ritual, as everyone stops what they're doing to watch the sun's orange orb slip silently into the blue-gray Pacific.

SPORTS AND THE OUTDOORS PLANNER

SAN DIEGO BY THE SEASONS

San Diego has miles of beaches and bays, numerous lakes, mountains, and deserts to explore. With balmy average temperatures and less than a foot of rain per year, the lure to go play outside is hard to resist. That said, Southern California isn't as seasonless as some claim. While the weather is generally mild and sunny year-round, the seasons do bring different outdoor activities.

Summer is the best time to plan your trip from an outdoor activities point of view (this is peak tourist season for a reason). San Diego's proximity to the ocean offers an almost endless selection of water activities. Rent kayaks at La Jolla Cove, take a charter boat off Point Loma for deep-sea tuna fishing, or simply hit the beach and go for a swim. The

TOP OUTDOOR EXPERIENCES

Kayak La Jolla's caves: Join a tour to explore the seven caves off La Jolla Cove; you'll see lots of wildlife, including seals, sea lions, and maybe leopard sharks and dolphin.

Rollerblading on the boardwalk: Rent Rollerblades and skim along the Mission Bay boardwalk. You'll be in good company among the scene-making muscle men and babes in bikinis.

Catch a wave: Surf La Jolla Cove's famous reef breaks or watch the surfers at Swami's beach from the Self-Realization Foundation's meditation gardens on the cliffs above.

Frisbee golf: Check out this local sport at Balboa Park's Morley Field. It's like golf, but with Frisbees.

Glorious golf: With so many courses in San Diego, there's sure to be something for every golfer. Add to that the perfect weather and sweeping views of the ocean and it's tee time.

13

Bahia Resort at Mission Bay offers Jet Ski and sailboat rentals to help you enjoy the shimmering bay.

The temperature begins to cool down for winter, but before it does, Santa Ana winds usher a warm dry spell throughout Southern California through the **fall**. It's the perfect time to shoot 18 holes at the Park Hyatt Aviara in Carlsbad, or take a hike at the Bayside Trail at Cabrillo National Monument—fall's cloudless skies allow for a crisp, clear vision of the Pacific. And although the foliage in San Diego doesn't turn into burnished reds and golds, you can appreciate the rare species of evergreen at Torrey Pines State Reserve.

Winter in California is hardly bitter or harsh, but the weather certainly gets too cold for water sports. Serious surfers love the breaks best in winter, when the swells are high. Black's Beach continues to be one of the most challenging surfing beaches in San Diego. Winter is also when gray whales migrate to warmer waters. Charter boats offer whale-watching trips between December and March. View the whales with San Diego Harbor Excursion or with the more intimate Whakapono Sailing Charter, based in Mission Bay.

In **spring,** wildflowers begin to appear at Anza-Borrego Desert Park. At peak months, the desert terrain blooms with vibrant colors. If you want more, take in the colorful, roselike ranunculus at the Flower Fields in Carlsbad. If you're interested in something sportier, Escondido's lakes are filled with bass, bluegill, and catfish waiting to be hooked.

PARTICIPATION SPORTS

BALLOONING

Enjoy views of the Pacific Ocean, the mountains, and the coastline south to Mexico and north to San Clemente from a hot-air balloon at sunrise or sunset; most excursions include beverages and snacks, too. The conditions are perfect: wide-open spaces and just enough wind to breeze you through them.

California Dreamin'. Turn here for hot-air balloon and biplane rides, specializing in Temecula wine country flights and Del Mar sunset coastal excursions. ⊠ *33133 Vista del Monte Rd., Temecula* ☎ *800/373–3359* ⊕ *www.californiadreamin.com.*

> ### THE GREAT WIDE OPEN
>
> An $8.50 round-trip ferry ride transports you and your bike from downtown San Diego to hyper-flat, super-cruisable Coronado, with a wide, flat beach, the historic Hotel Del Coronado (an unbeatable background for photos), and the beautifully manicured gardens of its many residential streets.

Skysurfer Balloon Company. Lift off from one of several locations for a one-hour flight in North County or Temecula. ⊠ *2658 Del Mar Heights Rd., Del Mar* ☎ *858/481–6800* ⊕ *www.sandiegohotairballoons.com.*

BICYCLING

BIKE PATHS

Route S21. On any given summer day, Route S21 (or Old Highway 101) from La Jolla to Oceanside looks like a freeway for cyclists. It's easily the most popular and scenic bike route around, never straying more than a quarter mile from the beach. Although the terrain is fairly easy, the long, steep Torrey Pines grade is world famous for weeding out the weak. Another Darwinian challenge along this route is dodging slow-moving pedestrians and cars pulling over to park in towns like Encinitas, Del Mar, and Oceanside.

Kearny BMX. For those who want to take their biking experience to the extreme, the Kearny BMX has a dirt track where BMXers rip it up, racing three times a week, with time for practice beforehand. ⊠ *3170 Armstrong St.* ☎ *619/561–3824* ⊕ *www.kearnybmx.com.*

Lomas Santa Fe Drive. Experienced cyclists follow this route in Solana Beach east into Rancho Santa Fe, perhaps even continuing east on Del Dios Highway, past Lake Hodges, to Escondido. These roads can be narrow and winding in spots.

Mission Bay. For a leisurely ride, try Mission Bay. It has miles and miles of cement paths bordering big green lawns, children's playgrounds, and picnic spots.

Mission Beach Boardwalk. Take in this classic California scene, with babes on blades and bikes—in bikinis, of course—often slowing foot and bike traffic to a crawl.

Coast Highway 101 is a haven for bicyclists from Oceanside down to La Jolla.

San Diego Harbor. Pedal past big boats and cruise ships at scenic San Diego Harbor.

BIKE TOURS AND RENTALS

Hike Bike Kayak San Diego. This outfitter offers a wide range of guided bike tours, from easy excursions around Mission Bay and Coronado Island to slightly more rigorous trips through coastal La Jolla. Mountain-biking tours are also available, and the company also rents bikes of all types (and can van-deliver them to your hotel). ⊠ *2246 Ave. de la Playa, La Jolla, San Diego* ☎ *858/551–9510, 866/425–2925* ⊕ *www.hikebikekayak.com.*

Cheap Rentals Mission Beach. Right on the boardwalk, this place has good daily and weekly prices for bike rentals, which include beach cruisers, tandems, hybrids, and two-wheeled baby carriers. ⊠ *3689 Mission Blvd., Mission Beach, San Diego* ☎ *858/488–9070, 800/941–7761* ⊕ *www.cheap-rentals.com.*

Holland's Bicycles. This great rental source on Coronado Island has a sister store (**Bikes and Beyond** ☎ *619/435–7180)* located at the ferry landing, so you can jump on your bike as soon as you cross the harbor from downtown San Diego. ⊠ *977 Orange Ave., Coronado, San Diego* ☎ *619/435–3153* ⊕ *www.hollandsbicycles.com.*

Wheel Fun Rentals. At the downtown Holiday Inn, Wheel Fun rents surreys, cruisers, mountain bikes, tandems, and electric bicycles, among other two-, three-, and four-wheeled contraptions. They have a number of other locations around San Diego; call or visit the website for details. ⊠ *1355 N. Harbor Dr., Downtown, San Diego* ☎ *619/239–3347* ⊕ *www.wheelfunrentals.com.*

BULLFIGHTING

California Academy of Tauromaquia. The academy opened in 1997 as the first bullfighting school in the United States. Year-round, the school offers a weeklong (Tuesday through Saturday) course in San Diego that finishes with a trip to a working bull ranch in northern Baja California. An intensive (12 hours of instruction) weekend course, beginning on Friday in San Diego and moving to the bull ranch in Baja on Saturday, takes place once or twice monthly year-round. A weekend intensive course in central Mexico and one or two annual field trips to Spain are also part of the syllabus. ✉ *Point Loma, San Diego* ☎ *619/709–0664* ⊕ *www.bullfightschool.com.*

DIVING AND SNORKELING

San Diego City Lifeguard Service. For recorded diving information, contact the San Diego City Lifeguard Service. ☎ *619/221–8824.*

DIVE SITES

Mission Beach. The HMCS *Yukon*, a decommissioned Canadian warship, was intentionally sunk off Mission Beach to create a diving destination. A mishap caused it to settle on its side, creating a surreal, M.C. Escher–esque diving environment. This is a technical dive and should be attempted only by experienced divers; even diving instructors have become disoriented inside the wreck.

Fodor'sChoice ★ **San Diego–La Jolla Underwater Park Ecological Preserve.** Enthusiasts the world over come to San Diego to snorkel and scuba dive off La Jolla and Point Loma. Because all sea life is protected here, this 6,000-acre preserve is the best place to see large lobster, sea bass, and sculpin (scorpion fish), as well as numerous golden garibaldi damselfish, the state marine fish. It's common to see hundreds of beautiful (and harmless) leopard sharks schooling at the north end of the cove, near La Jolla Shores, especially in summer.

Scripps Canyon. Off the south end of Black's Beach, the rim of Scripps Canyon lies in about 60 feet of water. The canyon plummets more than 900 feet in some sections.

Sunset Cliffs. Another popular diving spot is Sunset Cliffs in Point Loma, where the sea life and flora are relatively close to shore. Strong rip currents make it an area best enjoyed by experienced divers, who mostly prefer to make their dives from boats. Farther offshore, the Point Loma kelp beds harbor a nice variety of both plants and animals. It's illegal to take any wildlife from the ecological preserves in La Jolla or near Cabrillo Point. Spearfishing requires a license (available at most dive stores), and it's illegal to take out-of-season lobster and game fish.

DIVE TOURS AND OUTFITTERS

Ocean Enterprises Scuba Diving. Stop in for everything you need to plan a diving adventure, including equipment, advice, and instruction. ✉ *7710 Balboa Ave., Suite 101, Clairemont Mesa, San Diego* ☎ *858/565–6054* ⊕ *www.oceanenterprises.com.*

Scuba San Diego. This center is well regarded for its top-notch instruction and certification programs, as well as for guided dive tours of kelp reefs in La Jolla Cove, night diving at La Jolla Canyon, and unguided charter boat trips to Mission Bay's Wreck Alley or to the Coronado Islands (in Mexico, just south of San Diego). ⊠ *Located at the San Diego Hilton Hotel, 1775 E. Mission Bay Dr., Mission Bay, San Diego* ☎ *619/260–1880* ⊕ *www. scubasandiego.com.*

GO FISH

The California Department of Fish and Game (⊕ *www.dfg.ca.gov*) issues "Fishing Passports" showing 150 different species of fresh and saltwater fish and shellfish found throughout the state. Fishing aficionados can catch (and hopefully, release) in San Diego County many of the species listed, receiving a stamp for each species caught.

13

FISHING

San Diego's waters are home to many game species; you never know what you'll hook. Depending on the season, a half- or full-day ocean charter trip could bring in a yellowfin, dorado, sea bass, or halibut. Longer trips to Mexican waters can net you bigger game like a marlin or a bigeye tuna. Pier fishing doesn't offer as much potential excitement, but it's the cheapest ocean fishing option available. No license is required to fish from a public pier, which includes those at Ocean Beach, Imperial Beach, and Oceanside.

Public lakes are frequently stocked with a variety of trout and large-mouth bass, but also have resident populations of bluegill and catfish.

California Department of Fish and Game. A fishing license, available at most bait-and-tackle and sporting-goods stores, is required for fishing from the shoreline. Nonresidents can purchase an annual license or a 10-day, 2-day, or 1-day short-term license. Licenses can also be purchased online through the Department's website or at the San Diego headquarters. Children under 16 do not need a license.

Note that city reservoirs no longer sell snacks, drinks, bait, or fishing licenses, nor do they rent pedal boats or electric motors. Make sure to obtain your fishing license in advance. They accept cash only for day-use fees. ⊠ *4949 Viewridge Ave., Kearny Mesa, San Diego* ☎ *858/467–4201* ⊕ *www.dfg.ca.gov.*

FRESHWATER FISHING

Lake Jennings. County-operated Lake Jennings is stocked with trout in winter and catfish during the summer; it's a popular fly-fishing spot. ⊠ *10108 Bass Rd., Lakeside* ☎ *619/443–2510* ⊕ *www.lakejennings.org.*

Lake Morena. This lake is a popular spot both for fishing and camping. ⊠ *2550 Lake Morena Dr.* ☎ *619/478–5473* ⊕ *www.lakemorena.com.*

Sutherland. This city-operated reservoir, open March through September on weekends, is a good spot for catching bluegill and bass. ⊠ *22850 Sutherland Dam Rd., Ramona* ☎ *619/668–2050.*

Dixon, Hodges, and Wohlford. These three freshwater lakes surround the North County city of Escondido.

Oakvale RV Park. Visitors to the lake's south shore will find Oakvale RV Park. There's a supply store, and camping is allowed. ☎ 760/749–2895.

Lake Wohlford Resort. Anglers can rent motor-home lots here, on the lake's north shore. ☎ 760/749–2755.

Lake Wohlford Cafe. Stop in for live worms (not on the menu, of course) and other fishing supplies. The café also rents out rowboats and motorboats. ☎ 760/749–6585.

Dixon Lake Campground. This city-administered campground offers amenities similar to those of Lake Wohlford. ☎ 760/741–3328, 760/839–4680 *ranger station.*

SALTWATER FISHING

Fisherman's Landing. You can book space on a fleet of luxury vessels from 57 feet to 124 feet long. From here you can go on multiday trips in search of yellowfin tuna, yellowtail, and other deep-water fish. Whale-watching trips are also available. ✉ *2838 Garrison St., Point Loma, San Diego* ☎ *619/221–8500* ⊕ *www.fishermanslanding.com.*

H&M Landing. Join up for fishing trips, plus whale-watching excursions from December through March. ✉ *2803 Emerson St., Point Loma, San Diego* ☎ *619/222–1144* ⊕ *www.hmlanding.com.*

Helgren's Sportfishing. Your best bet in North County, Helgren's offers a full assortment of trips from Oceanside Harbor. ✉ *315 Harbor Dr. S, Oceanside* ☎ *760/722–2133* ⊕ *www.helgrensportfishing.com.*

Seaforth Boat Rentals. Call here to arrange a charter for an ocean adventure or to rent a sailboat, powerboat, or skiff from their Mission Bay, Coronado, or downtown San Diego locations. ✉ *1641 Quivira Rd., Mission Bay, San Diego* ☎ *619/223–1681, 888/834–2628 reservations* ⊕ *www.seaforthboatrental.com.*

FRISBEE GOLF

Morley Field Disc Golf Course. Like golf, except with Frisbees, disc golf is a popular local sport. The Morley Field Disc Golf Course, in Balboa Park, is open daily from dawn to dusk. Frisbees are available to rent for a small fee, and there's also a small fee for using the course (it's first come, first served). Rules are posted for those new to the sport. ☎ ⊕ *www.morleyfield.com.*

GOLF

San Diego's climate—generally sunny, without a lot of wind—is perfect for golf, and there are some 90 courses in the area, appealing to every level of expertise. Experienced golfers can play the same greens as PGA-tournament participants, and beginners or rusty players can book a week at a golf resort and benefit from expert instruction. You'd also be hard-pressed to find a locale that has more scenic courses—everything from sweeping views of the ocean to verdant hills inland.

During busy vacation seasons it can be difficult to get a good tee-off time. Call in advance to see if it's possible to make a reservation. You don't necessarily have to stay at a resort to play its course; check if the one you're interested in is open to nonguests. Most public courses in the area provide a list of fees for all San Diego courses.

Southern California Golf Association. Search their website for detailed and valuable information on all clubs. ☎ *818/980–3630* ⊕ *www.scga.org.*

COURSES

Below are some of the best courses to play in the area. The adult public's green fees for an 18-hole game are included for each course, as well as the courses' championship (blue) yardage; carts (in some cases mandatory), instruction, and other costs are additional. Rates go down during twilight hours, and San Diego residents may be able to get a better deal. Prices change regularly, so check with courses for up-to-date green fees and deals.

★ **Arrowood Golf Course.** Sited next to a nature preserve, this peaceful coastal links in Oceanside is one of the most scenic new layouts in the region (it opened in 2005). ✉ *5201 Village Dr., Oceanside* ☎ *760/967–8400* ⊕ *www.arrowoodgolf.com* 🏌 *18 holes. 6721 yds. Par 71. Green Fee: $85/$110* ⌢ *Facilities: Driving range, putting green, pitching area, golf carts, rental clubs, pro shop, golf academy/lessons, restaurant, bar.*

Balboa Park Municipal Golf Course. Because it's in the heart of Balboa Park, this links is convenient for downtown visitors. ✉ *2600 Golf Course Dr., Balboa Park, San Diego* ☎ *619/235–1184* ⊕ *www.balboaparkgolf.com* 🏌 *18 holes. 6267 yds. Par 72. Green Fee: $40/$50* ⌢ *Facilities: Driving range, putting green, pitching area, golf carts, pull carts, rental clubs, pro shop, golf academy/lessons, restaurant, bar.*

★ **Coronado Municipal Golf Course.** Views of San Diego Bay and the Coronado Bridge from the front 9 make this course popular—it's difficult to get on unless you reserve a tee time, 8 to 14 days in advance, for an additional $60. ✉ *2000 Visalia Row, Coronado, San Diego* ☎ *619/435–3121* ⊕ *www.golfcoronado.com* 🏌 *18 holes. 6590 yds. Par 72. Green Fee: $30/$35. Reservations essential* ⌢ *Facilities: Driving range, putting green, pitching area, golf carts, pull carts, rental clubs, pro shop, golf academy/lessons, restaurant, bar.*

★ **Cottonwood at Rancho San Diego Golf Club.** If it's your birthday, you can play for free at Cottonwood, which has two courses. The Lakes (which has 10 lakes) and Ivanhoe are both good walking courses, with nice practice putting greens. On weekend mornings tee times include mandatory cart rental. ✉ *3121 Willow Glen Rd., El Cajon* ☎ *619/442–9891, 800/455–1902* ⊕ *www.cottonwoodgolf.com* 🏌 *36 holes. Ivanhoe: 6831 yds., Lakes: 6610 yds. Ivanhoe: Par 72, Lakes: Par 71. Green Fee: $35/$59. Reservations essential* ⌢ *Facilities: Driving range, putting green, pitching area, golf carts, pull carts, rental clubs, pro shop, golf academy/lessons, restaurant, bar.*

Encinitas Ranch. Tucked away in the former flower fields of coastal North County, Encinitas is a hilly course that provides beautiful views of the Pacific as you play its championship holes. ✉ *1275 Quail Gardens Dr., Encinitas* ☎ *760/944–1936* ⊕ *www.jcgolf.com* 🏌 *18 holes. 6587 yds. Par 72. Green Fee: $67/$89. Reservations essential* ⌢ *Facilities: Driving range, putting green, golf carts, pull carts, rental clubs, pro shop, golf academy/lessons, restaurant, bar.*

Torrey Pines Golf Course has fantastic views to go along with its challenging holes.

Mission Bay Golf Course. A not-very-challenging executive course with par 3 and 4 holes, Mission Bay is lighted for night play (the final tee time is at 7:45 pm for 9 holes). ⊠ *2702 N. Mission Bay Dr., Mission Bay, San Diego* ☎ *858/581–7880* ⊕ *www.sandiego.gov* ⛳ *18 holes. 2719 yds. Par 58. Green Fee: $29/$36 for 18 holes* ☞ *Facilities: Driving range, putting green, pitching area, golf carts, pull carts, rental clubs, lessons.*

Riverwalk Golf Clubs. Near the Fashion Valley shopping center, this course has a combination of three different 9-hole courses, which means less waiting. ⊠ *1150 Fashion Valley Rd., Fashion Valley, San Diego* ☎ *619/296–4653* ⊕ *www.riverwalkgc.com* ⛳ *27 holes. Presidio: 3397 yds. Mission: 3153 yds. Friars: 3230 yds. Par 72. Green Fee: $99/$125* ☞ *Facilities: Driving range, putting green, golf carts, rental clubs, pro shop, golf academy/lessons, restaurant, bar.*

Fodor's Choice ★ **Torrey Pines Golf Course.** One of the best public golf courses in the United States, Torrey Pines was the site of the 2008 U.S. Open and has been the home of the Buick Invitational (now the Farmers Insurance Open) since 1968. The par-72 South Course receives rave reviews from the touring pros. Redesigned by Rees Jones in 2001, it's longer, more challenging, and more expensive than the North Course. Tee times may be booked from 8 to 90 days in advance at ☎ *877/581–7171* and are subject to an advance booking fee ($43). A full-day or half-day instructional package includes cart, green fee, and a golf-pro escort for the first 9 holes. ⊠ *11480 N. Torrey Pines Rd., La Jolla, San Diego* ☎ *858/452–3226, 800/985–4653* ⊕ *www.torreypinesgolfcourse.com* ⛳ *36 holes. South: 7227 yds., North: 6874 yds. North and South: Par 72. Green Fee: South: $183/$229, North: $100/$125* ☞ *Facilities: Driving range,* *putting green, pitching area, golf carts, pull carts, caddies upon request in advance, rental clubs, pro shop, golf academy/lessons, restaurant, bar.*

RESORTS

Barona Creek. Hilly terrain and regular winds add to the challenge at this East County resort course. Fast greens will test your finesse. If your game is on, you can always see if your luck holds in the adjacent casino. ⊠ *1932 Wildcat Canyon Rd., Lakeside* ☎ *619/387–7018* ⊕ *www.barona.com* ⅄ *18 holes. Approx. 7000 yds. Par 72. Green Fee: $120/$160. Reservations essential* ☞ *Facilities: Driving range, putting green, pitching area, golf carts, rental clubs, pro shop, lessons, snack bar.*

★ **Carlton Oaks Lodge and Country Club.** Lots of local qualifying tournaments are held at this difficult course, designed by Pete Dye to include many trees and water hazards. ⊠ *9200 Inwood Dr., Santee* ☎ *619/448–4242* ⊕ *www. carltonoaksgolf.com* ⅄ *18 holes. 6700 yds. Par 72. Green Fee: $65/$85. Reservations essential* ☞ *Facilities: Driving range, putting green, pitching area, golf carts, rental clubs, pro shop, lessons, restaurant, bar.*

Doubletree Golf Resort San Diego. This fairly hilly inland North County course is well maintained. ⊠ *14455 Peñasquitos Dr.* ☎ *858/672–9100* ⊕ *www.doubletreegolf.com* ⅄ *18 holes. 6428 yds. Par 72. Green Fee: $45/$69* ☞ *Facilities: Putting green, pitching area, golf carts, rental clubs, pro shop, golf academy/lessons, restaurant, bar.*

★ **La Costa Resort and Spa.** There's an excellent golf school at this verdant location, which is one of the premier golf resorts in Southern California. After a full day on the links you can wind down with a massage, steam bath, and dinner at the resort. ⊠ *2100 Costa del Mar Rd., Carlsbad* ☎ *760/438– 9111* ⊕ *www.lacosta.com* ⅄ *36 holes. North: 6608 yds., South: 6524 yds. North and South: Par 72. Green Fee: $195/$205. Reservations essential* ☞ *Facilities: Driving range, putting green, pitching area, golf carts, caddies, rental clubs, pro shop, golf academy/lessons, restaurant, bar.*

Morgan Run Resort and Club. The 27 holes of this very popular walking course, which can be played in three combinations of 9, are open only to members, guests of members, and resort guests. ⊠ *5690 Cancha de Golf, Rancho Santa Fe* ☎ *858/756–2471* ⊕ *www.morganrun.com* ⅄ *27 holes. East: 3173 yds., North: 3113 yds., South: 3380 yds. East: Par 36, North: Par 35, South: Par 36. Green Fee: $100/$120. Reservations essential* ☞ *Facilities: Driving range, putting green, pitching area, golf carts, pull carts, rental clubs, pro shop, golf academy/lessons, restaurant, bar.*

Fodor'sChoice **Park Hyatt Aviara Golf Club.** Designed by Arnold Palmer, this top-quality
★ course includes views of the protected adjacent Batiquitos Lagoon and the Pacific Ocean. The carts, which are fitted with GPS systems that tell you the distance to the pin, are included in the cost. ⊠ *7447 Batiquitos Dr., Carlsbad* ☎ *760/603–6900* ⊕ *www.golfaviara.com* ⅄ *18 holes. 7007 yds. Par 72. Green Fee: $215/$235* ☞ *Facilities: Driving range, putting green, pitching area, golf carts, rental clubs, pro shop, golf academy/lessons, restaurant, bar.*

★ **Rancho Bernardo Inn and Country Club.** The course management here is JC Golf, which has a golf school as well as several other respected courses throughout Southern California that are open to guests of the Rancho Bernardo Inn. The restaurant here, El Bizcocho, serves one of the best Sunday brunches in the county. ⊠ *17550 Bernardo Oaks Dr., Rancho Bernardo* ☎ *858/675–8470* ⊕ *www.ranchobernardoinn.com* ⚑ *18 holes. 6631 yds. Par 72. Green Fee: $100/$135* ⚐ *Facilities: Driving range, putting green, golf carts, rental clubs, pro shop, golf academy/lessons, restaurant, bar.*

Redhawk. This challenging course is good enough to have earned a four-star rating from *Golf Digest* and a top 10 ranking from *California Golf Magazine.* ⊠ *45100 Redhawk Pkwy., Temecula* ☎ *951/302–3850* ⊕ *www.redhawkgolfcourse.com* ⚑ *18 holes. 7110 yds. Par 72. Green Fee: $70/$90* ⚐ *Facilities: Driving range, putting green, pitching area, golf carts, pull carts, rental clubs, pro shop, golf academy/lessons, restaurant, bar.*

★ **Sycuan Resort & Casino.** A *Golf Digest* favorite, this course also comes highly recommended by anyone who's played here. Hackers will love the executive par-3 course; seasoned golfers can play the championship courses. ⊠ *3007 Dehesa Rd., El Cajon* ☎ *619/219–6028, 800/457–5568* ⊕ *www.sycuanresort.com* ⚑ *54 holes. Willow: 6687 yds., Oak: 6682 yds., Pine: 2508 yds. Willow and Oak: Par 72, Pine: Par 54. Green Fee: Willow and Oak $57/$79, Pine $19/$26* ⚐ *Facilities: Driving range, putting green, pitching area, golf carts, pull carts, rental clubs, pro shop, golf academy/lessons, restaurant, bar.*

HANG GLIDING AND PARAGLIDING

Torrey Pines Gliderport. Perched on the cliffs overlooking the ocean north of La Jolla, this is one of the most spectacular spots to hang glide in the world. It's for experienced pilots only, but hang-gliding and paragliding lessons and tandem rides for inexperienced gliders are available. Those who'd rather just watch can grab a bite at the snack shop after parking in the large dirt lot, but barriers keep them from looking right over the cliff, which would give better views of their airborne fellows. ⊠ *2800 Torrey Pines Scenic Dr., La Jolla, San Diego* ☎ *858/452–9858* ⊕ *www.flytorrey.com.*

HIKING AND NATURE TRAILS

From beachside bluffs and waterfront estuaries to the foothills and trails of the nearby Laguna Mountains and the desert beyond, San Diego County has several vegetation and climate zones—and plenty of open space for hiking. Even if you lack the time to explore the outskirts, a day hike through the canyons and gardens of Balboa Park or the canyons and hills of Mission Trails Park is a great way to escape to nature without leaving the city. A list of scheduled walks appears in the *Reader* (⊕ *www.sandiegoreader.com*), where you can also read articles by local hiking outdoors expert, Jerry Schad.

Guided hikes are conducted regularly through Los Peñasquitos Canyon Preserve and the Torrey Pines State Beach and Reserve.

HIKING

Fodor's Choice
★
Bayside Trail at Cabrillo National Monument. Driving here is a treat in itself, as a vast view of the Pacific unfolds before you. The view is equally enjoyable on Bayside Trail (2 mi round-trip), which is home to the same coastal sagebrush that Juan Rodriguez Cabrillo saw when he first

discovered the California coast in the 16th century. After the hike, you can explore nearby tide pools, the monument statue, and the Old Point Loma Lighthouse. ⊠ *1800 Cabrillo Memorial Dr., from I–5, take the Rosecrans exit and turn right on Canon St. then left on Catalina Blvd.; continue following signs to the park, Point Loma, San Diego* ☎ *619/557–5450* ⊕ *www.nps.gov.*

Hike Bike Kayak San Diego. Join guided treks through Torrey Pines State Beach and Reserve, and Mission Trails Regional Park, the latter including Cowles Mountain and Fortuna Mountain. ⊠ *2246 Ave. de la Playa, La Jolla, San Diego* ☎ *858/551–9510, 866/425–2925* ⊕ *www. hikebikekayak.com.*

Los Peñasquitos Canyon Preserve. At this inland park north of Mira Mesa, San Diegans don't need the coast to take scenic hikes. The trails, which extend 5–7 mi in one direction, accommodate equestrians, runners, walkers, and cyclists as well as leashed dogs. Look at maps for trails specific to bikes and horses. A small waterfall among large volcanic rock boulders is one of the park's most popular sites—it's an unexpected oasis amid the arid valley landscape. ⊠ *12020 Black Mountain Rd., from I–15, exit Mercy Rd,. and head west to Black Mountain Rd.; turn right then left at first light; follow road to Ranch House parking lot, Rancho Peñasquitos, San Diego* ☎ *858/484–7504* ⊕ *www.sandiego.gov.*

Mission Trails Regional Park. This park 8 mi northeast of downtown encompasses nearly 5,800 acres of wooded hillsides, grasslands, chaparral, and streams. Trails range from easy to difficult; they include one with an impressive view of the city from Cowles Mountain and another along a historic missionary path. Lake Murray is at the southern edge of the park, off Highway 8. ⊠ *1 Father Junípero Serra Trail, Mission Valley, San Diego* ☎ *619/668–3281* ⊕ *www.mtrp.org.*

★ **Torrey Pines State Reserve.** Hiking aficionados will appreciate this park's many winning features: a number of modest trails that descend to the sea, an unparalleled view of the Pacific, and a chance to see the Torrey pine tree, one of the rarest pine breeds in the United States. The reserve hosts guided nature walks as well. All food is prohibited at the reserve, so save the picnic until you reach the beach below. Parking is $10. ⊠ *12600 N. Torrey Pines Rd., from I–5, exit Carmel Valley Rd. and head west toward Coast Hwy. 101 until you reach Torrey Pines State Beach; turn left, La Jolla, San Diego* ☎ *858/755–2063* ⊕ *www. torreypine.org.*

WORD OF MOUTH

"You will find plenty to see at Anza-Borrego if you have never been to the desert before. There are some interesting pictographs, *morteros* [shallow bowl-like indentations on large stone formations used to ground seeds and nuts], fan-palm-studded oases, and varied topography…the desert scenery is best at daybreak and dusk."

—Binthair

13

DID YOU KNOW?

You don't have to know how to paraglide to launch off the cliffs at Torrey Pines Glider-port. With a tandem flight, a trained instructor does all the work, leaving you free to shout with glee.

NATURE TRAILS

Anza-Borrego Desert State Park. At more than 600,000 acres, this is the largest state park in California. There are 500 mi of dirt roads and countless trails for hiking. Visits here are especially popular during the two-week desert wildflower bloom, which happens between early February and late April. The exact timing depends on winter rains, so it's best to call the park ahead of time for advice. The park is about a two-hour drive east of downtown San Diego, at the far eastern end of San Diego County. ✉ *200 Palm Canyon Dr., Borrego Springs* ☎ *760/767–5311* ⊕ *www.parks.ca.gov.*

Tijuana Estuary. Mostly contained within Border Field State Park, this estuary is one of the last riparian environments in Southern California. The freshwater and saltwater marshes shelter migrant and resident waterfowl. Horse-riding trails fringe the south end of the Tijuana Estuary in Border Field State Park. The visitor center is open Wednesday through Sunday. ✉ *301 Caspian Way, exit I–5 at Coronado Ave., head west to 3rd St., turn left onto Caspian, which leads into estuary parking lot, Imperial Beach* ☎ *619/575–3613* ⊕ *www.tijuanaestuary.com.*

HORSEBACK RIDING

Bright Valley Farms. Take riding lessons or join a trail ride on the winding paths of the Sweetwater River valley. ✉ *12310 Campo Rd., Spring Valley* ☎ *619/670–1861* ⊕ *www.brightvalleyfarms.com.*

Sweet Water Farms. Join the farm's guides for trail rides through the stunning nature trails of inland San Diego County's Bonita area. They offer horse camping as well. ✉ *3051 Equitation La., Bonita* ☎ *619/475–3134* ⊕ *www.sweetwaterhorses.com.*

JET SKIING

Jet Skis can be launched from most ocean beaches, although you must ride beyond surf lines, and some beaches have special regulations governing their use.

El Capitan Reservoir. The only freshwater lake that allows Jet Skis is El Capitan Reservoir, 30 mi northeast of the city near Lake Jennings. Take I–8 north to Lake Jennings Park Road, head east on El Monte Road, and follow signs; there's a day-use fee of $10 per person.

San Diego Jet Ski Rentals. The shop is open daily in spring, summer, and fall; in winter, call ahead for a reservation. ✉ *1636 Grand Ave., Pacific Beach, San Diego* ☎ *858/272–6161.*

Seaforth Boat Rentals. You can rent Yamaha WaveRunners here for two or three people. ✉ *1715 Strand Way, Coronado, San Diego* ☎ *619/437–1514, 888/834–2628.*

Snug Harbor Marina. Waveless Mission Bay and the small Snug Harbor Marina, east of the intersection of Tamarack Avenue and I–5 in Carlsbad, are favorite spots. ✉ *4215 Harrison St., Carlsbad* ☎ *760/434–3089.*

JOGGING

Embarcadero. The most popular run downtown is along the Embarcadero, which stretches for 2 mi around the bay.

Balboa Park. There are uncongested sidewalks all through the area, but the alternative in the downtown area is to head east to Balboa Park, where trails snake through the canyons. Joggers can start out from any parking lot, but it's probably easiest to start anywhere along the 6th Avenue side. Entry to the numerous lots is best where Laurel Street connects with 6th Avenue. There's also a fitness circuit course in the park's **Morley Field** area.

Del Mar. Park your car near 15th Street and run south along the cliffs for a gorgeous view of the ocean.

Mission Bay. This area is popular with joggers for its wide sidewalks and basically flat landscape. Trails head west around Fiesta Island, providing distance as well as a scenic route.

13

OVER-THE-LINE

A giant beach party as much as a sport, Over-the-Line is a form of beach softball played with two teams of just three people each. Every July, over two weekends that include wild beer drinking and partying, the world championships are held on Fiesta Island. (The district's councilman pulled some strings to exempt OTL tournament from the city's beach booze ban.) Admission is free, but parking is impossible, and traffic around Mission Bay can become unbearable (shuttle buses are available). Check the Old Mission Beach Athletic Club's Web site (⊕ www.ombac.org) for more information.

Mission Beach boardwalk. This is a great place to run while soaking up the scenery and beach culture. Organized runs occur almost every weekend. They're listed in *Competitor* magazine, which is available for free at bike and running shops.

Roadrunner Sports. Stop in at Roadrunner for all the supplies and information you'll need for running in San Diego. ⊠ *5553 Copley Dr.* ☎ *858/974–4475* ⊕ *www.roadrunnersports.com.*

KAYAKING

There are several places to kayak throughout San Diego, but by far the best choice is an afternoon spent exploring the seven caves off La Jolla Cove. The caves are a cool place to explore and you can often see seals, sea lions, and sometimes dolphin.

Hike Bike Kayak San Diego. This shop offers several kayak tours, from easy excursions in Mission Bay that are well suited to families and beginners on to more advanced jaunts. Tours include kayaking the caves off La Jolla coast, whale-watching (from a safe distance) December through March, moonlight and sunset trips, and a cruise into the bay to see SeaWorld's impressive fireworks shows over the water in the summer. Tours last two to three hours and cost between $35 and $60 per person; cost includes kayak, paddle, life vest, and guide. ⊠ *2246 Ave. de la Playa, La Jolla, San Diego* ☎ *858/551–9510, 866/425–2925* ⊕ *www.hikebikekayak.com.*

A kayak trip is the best way to experience the sea caves off La Jolla Cove.

ROLLERBLADING AND ROLLER-SKATING

Cheap Rentals Mission Beach. Come here for good prices on Rollerblades, especially for the full day; rental comes with helmet and knee and elbow pads. ⊠ *3689 Mission Blvd., Mission Beach, San Diego* ☏ *858/488–9070, 800/941–7761* ⊕ *www.cheap-rentals.com.*

Holland's Bicycles. This is the place to go to rent skates, blades, and bikes to cruise the beachwalk of Coronado. ⊠ *977 Orange Ave., Coronado, San Diego* ☏ *619/435–3153.*

Skateworld. This facility has several public sessions daily on weekends, with adults-only skating on Tuesday evenings. In addition to private group sessions for bladers and skaters, the San Diego Roller Derby is based here. ⊠ *6907 Linda Vista Rd., Linda Vista, San Diego* ☏ *858/560–9349* ⊕ *www.sandiegoskateworld.com.*

SAILING AND BOATING

★ The city's history is full of seafarers, from the ships of the 1542 Cabrillo expedition to the America's Cup that once had a home here. Winds in San Diego are fairly consistent, especially in winter. You can rent a slip at one of several marinas if you're bringing your own boat. If not, you can rent vessels of various sizes and shapes—from small paddleboats and kayaks to Hobie Cats—from various vendors. In addition, most bayside resorts rent equipment for on-the-water adventures. Kayaks are one of the most popular boat rentals, especially in La Jolla, where people kayak around the Underwater Park and Ecological Reserve at the cove. Most of what's available from these outlets is not intended for the open ocean—a dangerous place for the inexperienced.

For information, including tips on overnight anchoring, contact the **Port of San Diego Mooring Office** (☎ *619/686–6227* ⊕ *www.portofsandiego.org*).

For additional information contact the **San Diego Harbor Police** (☎ *619/686–6272*).

BOAT RENTALS

Seaforth Boat Rentals. You can book charter tours and rent kayaks, Jet Skis, fishing skiffs, and powerboats from 10 feet to 20 feet long, as well as sailboats from 16 to 36 feet here. They also can hook you up with a skipper for a deep-sea fishing trip. ⊠ *1715 Strand Way, Coronado, San Diego* ☎ *619/437–1514, 888/834–2628.*

Bahia Resort Hotel. This facility and its sister location, the **Catamaran Resort Hotel,** rent paddleboats, kayaks, powerboats, and sailboats from 14 to 22 feet. The Bahia also rents out a ski boat. ⊠ *998 W. Mission Bay Dr., Mission Bay, San Diego* ☎ *858/488–2582* ⊕ *www.bahiahotel.com.*

Catamaran Resort Hotel. ⊠ *3999 Mission Blvd., Mission Beach, San Diego* ☎ *858/488–2582.*

Carlsbad Paddle Sports. This shop handles kayak sales, rentals, and instruction for coastal North County. ⊠ *2002 S. Coast Hwy., Oceanside* ☎ *760/434–8686* ⊕ *www.carlsbadpaddle.com.*

BOAT CHARTERS

California Cruisin'. Contact California Cruisin' for yachting charter excursions and dinner cruises. ⊠ *1450 Harbor Island Dr., Downtown, San Diego* ☎ *619/296–8000, 800/449–2248* ⊕ *www.californiacruisin.com.*

Harbor Sailboats. You can rent sailboats from 22 to 41 feet long here for open-ocean adventures. The company also offers skippered charter boats for whale-watching, sunset sails, and bay tours. ⊠ *2040 Harbor Island Dr., Harbor Island, San Diego* ☎ *619/291–9568, 800/854–6625* ⊕ *www.harborsailboats.com.*

Hornblower Cruises and Events. This outfit operates harbor cruises, sunset cocktail and dining cruises, whale-watching excursions, and yacht charters. ⊠ *1066 N. Harbor Dr., Embarcadero, San Diego* ☎ *619/686–8700, 888/467–6256* ⊕ *www.hornblower.com.*

★ **Whakapono Sailing Charter.** For more intimate sails book time on Whakapono's 30-foot sailboat for sunset cruises in summer or daytime sightseeing (whale-watching in winter). Call to make reservations with the captain in advance. ⊠ *939 Winston Dr., Mission Bay, San Diego* ☎ *619/988–9644, 800/659–0141* ⊕ *www.whakapono.us.*

SKATEBOARD PARKS

Skateboarding culture has always thrived in San Diego, and recent changes in liability laws have encouraged a jump in the number of skate parks. A good number of top pro skateboarders live in San Diego and often practice and perfect new moves at local skate parks. Pads and helmets (always a good idea) are required at all parks.

Escondido Sports Center. This 22,000-square-foot skate park includes a miniramp, street course, and vertical ramp. ⊠ *3315 Bear Valley Pkwy., Escondido* ☎ *760/839–5425* ⊕ *www.escondido.org/sportscenter.*

Magdalena Ecke Family YMCA. This YMCA is very popular among the many pros in the area. It has a competition street course, two cement pools, and a classic vertical ramp. ⊠ *200 Saxony Rd., Encinitas* ☎ *760/942–9622.*

> **GREAT LEAP**
>
> San Diego skateboarder Danny Way, who already held world records for distance and height on a skateboard, set a new world record on July 9, 2005, when he became the first person to jump over the Great Wall of China without the use of a motorized vehicle, and live to tell the tale.

Ocean Beach Skatepark at Robb Field. The largest skatepark in the city, this has a huge street plaza, bowls, ledges, grind rails, and quarter-pipes. ⊠ *2525 Bacon St., Ocean Beach, San Diego* ☎ *619/525–8486.*

SURFING

If you're a beginner, consider paddling in the waves off Mission Beach, Pacific Beach, Tourmaline Surfing Park, La Jolla Shores, Del Mar, or Oceanside. More experienced surfers usually head for Sunset Cliffs, La Jolla reef breaks, Black's Beach, or Swami's in Encinitas. All necessary equipment is included in the cost of all surfing schools. Beach-area Y's offer surf lessons and surf camp in the summer months and during spring break.

★ **Hike Bike Kayak San Diego.** Sign up for group and private lessons in La Jolla, year round. If you know what you're doing but didn't bring your stick, they rent boards, too. ⊠ *2246 Ave. de la Playa, La Jolla, San Diego* ☎ *858/551–9510, 866/425–2925* ⊕ *www.hikebikekayak.com.*

Kahuna Bob's Surf School. This surf school conducts two-hour lessons in coastal North County seven days a week; in summer there's surf camp for kids. ☎ *760/721–7700, 800/524–8627* ⊕ *www.kahunabob.com.*

San Diego Surfing Academy. Choose from private and group lessons and customizable surf camps for teens, kids, and adults. Instructional videos are also available online. The academy, which has been running since 1995, is based near South Carlsbad State Beach and meets for lessons at Seapointe Resort in Carlsbad. ☎ *760/230–1474, 800/447–7873* ⊕ *www.surfingacademy.com.*

★ **Surf Diva Surf School.** Check out clinics, surf camps, surf trips, and private lessons especially formulated for girls and women. Clinics and trips are for women only, but guys can book private lessons from the nationally recognized staff. ⊠ *2160 Ave. de la Playa, La Jolla, San Diego* ☎ *858/454–8273* ⊕ *www.surfdiva.com.*

SURF SHOPS

Cheap Rentals Mission Beach. Many local surf shops rent both surf and bodyboards. Cheap Rentals Mission Beach is right on the boardwalk, just steps from the waves. They rent wet suits, bodyboards, and skimboards in addition to soft surfboards and long and short fiberglass rides.

CLOSE UP

Longboarding vs. Shortboarding

Longboarders tend to ride boards more than 8 feet long with rounded noses. Shortboarders ride lightweight, high-performance boards from 5 to 7 feet long with pointed noses. (Funboards are a little longer than shortboards, with broad, round noses and tails that make them good for beginners who want something more maneuverable than a longboard.) A great longboarder will have a smooth, fluid style and will shuffle up and down the board, maybe even riding on the nose with the toes of both feet on the very edge ("hanging 10"). Shortboarders tend to surf faster and more aggressively. The best shortboarders surf perpendicular to the wave face and may even break free of the wave—known as "aerials" or "catching air." Nonsurfers are often most impressed and amused by the mistakes. "Wipeouts," the sometimes spectacular falls, inevitably happen to all surfers.

13

⊠ *3689 Mission Blvd., Mission Beach, San Diego* ☎ *858/488–9070, 800/941–7761* ⊕ *www.cheap-rentals.com.*

Hansen's. A short walk from Swami's beach, Hansen's is one of San Diego's oldest and most popular surf shops. It has an extensive selection of boards, wet suits, and clothing for sale, and a rental department as well. ⊠ *1105 S. Coast Hwy. 101, Encinitas* ☎ *760/753–6595, 800/480–4754* ⊕ *www.hansensurf.com.*

TENNIS

Most of the more than 1,300 courts around the county are in private clubs, but a few are public.

Balboa Tennis Club at Morley Field. Practice your backhand at one of the 25 courts, 19 of them lighted. The Tennis Cafe serves snacks, soups, and sandwiches. Courts are available on a first-come, first-served basis for a daily $5-per-person fee. Heaviest use is 9 am–11 am and after 5 pm; at other times you can usually arrive and begin playing. Pros offer clinics and classes. ⊠ *2221 Morley Field Dr., Balboa Park, San Diego* ☎ *619/295–9278* ⊕ *www.balboatennis.com.*

La Costa Resort and Spa. This tennis complex has 17 hard and clay courts, 7 of them lighted, plus professional instruction, clinics, and workouts. ⊠ *2100 Costa Del Mar Rd., Carlsbad* ☎ *760/931–7501* ⊕ *www. lacosta.com.*

La Jolla Tennis Club. This club has nine public courts near downtown; five are lighted; the daily fee is $10. The club has a reservations system (call from 12 to 72 hours ahead to reserve a court) for members only. ⊠ *7632 Draper Ave., La Jolla, San Diego* ☎ *858/454–4434* ⊕ *www.ljtc.org.*

Peninsula Tennis Club. The 12 lighted courts at the privately owned Peninsula Tennis Club are available to the public for $5 per person daily. ⊠ *2525 Bacon St., at Robb Field, Ocean Beach, San Diego* ☎ *619/226–3407.*

Several San Diego resorts have top-notch tennis programs staffed by big-name professional instructors.

Rancho Valencia Resort. Among the top tennis resorts in the nation, this has 18 hard courts and several instruction programs. Tennis shoes and tennis attire (no T-shirts) are required. ⊠ *5921 Valencia Circle, Rancho Santa Fe* ☎ *858/759–6224* ⊕ *www.ranchovalencia.com.*

VOLLEYBALL

San Diego Volleyball Club. Ocean Beach, South Mission Beach, Del Mar Beach, Moonlight Beach, and the western edge of Balboa Park are major congregating points for volleyball enthusiasts. These are also the best places to find a pickup game. Contact the San Diego Volleyball Club to find out about organized games and tournaments. ☎ *858/385–1855* ⊕ *www.sdvbc.org.*

WATERSKIING

Mission Bay is popular for waterskiing, although the bay is often polluted, especially after a heavy rain. As a general rule, it's best to get out early, when the water is smooth and the crowds are thin.

Seaforth Boat Rentals. Boats and equipment can be rented from Seaforth Boat Rentals. ⊠ *1715 Strand Way, Coronado, San Diego* ☎ *619/437–1514, 888/834–2628 reservations.*

WHALE-WATCHING CRUISES

Whale-watching season peaks in January and February, when thousands of gray whales migrate south to the warm weather, where they give birth to their calves. Head to Cabrillo National Monument's Whale Overlook to see the whales pass through Point Loma. If you want a closer look, charter boats and cruises host whale-watching excursions.

Hornblower Cruises and Events. Hornblower has yachts to take passengers to catch a glimpse of gray whales and perhaps an occasional school of dolphins. Rates are $34 on weekdays and $39 on weekends. ⊠ *1066 N. Harbor Dr., Embarcadero, San Diego* ☎ *619/686–8700, 888/467–6256* ⊕ *www.hornblower.com.*

WINDSURFING

Also known as sailboarding, windsurfing is a sport best practiced on smooth waters, such as Mission Bay. More experienced windsurfers will enjoy taking a board out on the ocean. Wave jumping is especially popular at the Tourmaline Surfing Park in La Jolla and in the Del Mar area, where you can also occasionally see kiteboarders practice their variation on the theme.

Bahia Resort Hotel. Sailboard rentals and instruction are available at the Bahia Resort Hotel. ⊠ *998 W. Mission Bay Dr., Mission Bay, San Diego* ☎ *858/488–2582* ⊕ *www.bahiahotel.com.*

A kiteboarder joins the surfers waiting for a wave at Pacific Beach.

Catamaran Resort Hotel. The Catamaran Resort Hotel, a sister location of the Bahia Resort Hotel, offers similar services. ⊠ *3999 Mission Blvd., Mission Beach, San Diego* ☎ *858/488–1081.*

Mission Bay Aquatic Center. As the world's largest instructional waterfront facility, Mission Bay Aquatic offers lessons in wakeboarding, sailing, surfing, waterskiing, rowing, kayaking, and windsurfing. Equipment rental is also available here, but the emphasis is on instruction, and most rentals require a minimum two-hour orientation lesson before you can set out on your own. Reservations are recommended, particularly during the summer. Skippered keelboats and boats for waterskiing or wakeboarding are available for hire with reservations. Free parking is also available. ⊠ *1001 Santa Clara Pl., Mission Beach, San Diego* ☎ *858/488–1000* ⊕ *www.missionbayaquaticcenter.com* ⊙ *Sept.—May, Tues.–Sun. 8–5, June–Aug., daily 8–7.*

SPECTATOR SPORTS

BASEBALL

Fodor's Choice
★ Long a favorite spectator sport in San Diego, where games are rarely rained out, baseball gained even more popularity in 2004 with the opening of PETCO Park, a stunning 42,000-seat facility in the heart of downtown. In March 2006, the semifinals and the final game of the first-ever World Baseball Classic, scheduled to be a quadrennial event fielding teams from around the world, took place here.

San Diego Padres. The Padres slug it out for bragging rights in the National League West from April into October—they won the division in 2005 and 2006. Tickets are usually available on game day, but games with such rivals as the Los Angeles Dodgers and the San Francisco Giants often sell out quickly. For an inexpensive day at the ballpark, go for the $5 park pass (available for purchase at the park only) and have a picnic on the grass, while watching the play on one of several giant-screen TVs. ⊠ *100 Park Blvd., Downtown, San Diego* ☎ *619/795–5000, 877/374–2784* ⊕ *www.sandiegopadres.com.*

> **PETCO PARK TOURS**
>
> Most San Diegans love the PETCO baseball park, but it wasn't always so. After voters narrowly approved the project, more than a dozen lawsuits stalled construction for years. Issues were traffic, downtown congestion, and the fact that San Diego already had a perfectly serviceable baseball stadium. Take a tour before any home game and see whether the $450-million-plus price tag was worth it.

BASKETBALL

Although there have been a few attempts to bring pro and semipro basketball to San Diego, no team has endured. Die-hard basketball fans instead rely on college teams to give them their fix.

San Diego State University Aztecs. The Aztecs compete from November through March in the Western Athletic Conference with such powers as the University of Utah and Brigham Young University. ⊠ *Viejas Arena, College Ave. exit off I–8, College Area, San Diego* ☎ *619/283–7378* ⊕ *www.goaztecs.com.*

University of San Diego Toreros. The Toreros take on West Coast Conference opponents that include Pepperdine University, the University of San Francisco, and the University of California at Santa Barbara. ⊠ *Jenny Craig Pavilion, 5998 Alcalá Park, Linda Vista, San Diego* ☎ *619/260–4803* ⊕ *www.usdtoreros.com.*

FOOTBALL

San Diego Chargers. The Chargers fill Qualcomm Stadium from August through December and sometimes as late as January. Games with AFC West rivals the Oakland Raiders are particularly intense. ⊠ *9449 Friars Rd., Mission Valley, San Diego* ☎ *858/874–4500 Charger Park, 877/242–7437 season tickets* ⊕ *www.chargers.com.*

★ **San Diego State University Aztecs.** The Aztecs compete in the Mountain West Conference and attract the most loyal fans in town, with attendance rivaling that for the Chargers. The biggest game of the year is always a showdown with Brigham Young University. Like the Chargers, the Aztecs also play their home games at Qualcomm Stadium. ☎ *619/283–7378, 877/737–8039 ticket office* ⊕ *www.goaztecs.com.*

Holiday Bowl. One of college football's most-watched playoff games, this takes place in Qualcomm Stadium around the end of December. ☎ *619/283–5808.*

Shopping

WORD OF MOUTH

"Coronado is a must! Check out the Hotel Del for high tea. Walk behind the hotel along the amazing beach. A few blocks away are a bunch of shops and restaurants on the ocean side of the city."

—TMP

SEAPORT VILLAGE AND CORONADO

Seaport Village along the Embarcadero's waterfront has more than 50 stores. Coronado, across San Diego Bay, is a charming beach community perfect for strolling and window-shopping. Whether you have two hours or a whole day to browse, there's plenty of bounty on both sides of the bay.

(above) Four mi of cobblestone pathways wind through the 54 shops of Seaport Village. (right) A 15-minute ferry ride will take you from Downtown to Ferry Landing Marketplace in Coronado.

Begin your shopping tour at the 14-acre Seaport Village, where you'll find stores stocking seashells and collectibles, trendy surfwear and jewelry. Then head down to the Broadway Pier, and take the 15-minute ferry ride to Coronado; you can also drive or take the Old Town Trolley Tour over the San Diego–Coronado Bridge. The postcard view of the skyline and the magnificent bridge is well worth the trip. Ferry Landing Marketplace in Coronado has a dozen browse-worthy shops, as well as several good food options, including some with amazing views. The Coronado Shuttle takes passengers from Ferry Landing to Orange Avenue, the city's main drag for shopping, dining, and people-watching.

BEST TIME TO GO

Both Seaport Village and Coronado attract hordes of visitors on weekends, so opt for a weekday visit or arrive before noon. Ferries ($4.25 each way) from Seaport Village's Broadway Pier depart hourly on weekdays from 9 to 9, and until 10 on weekends.

BEST BOOKS

Upstart Crow and **Bay Books** offer independent bookstore charm.

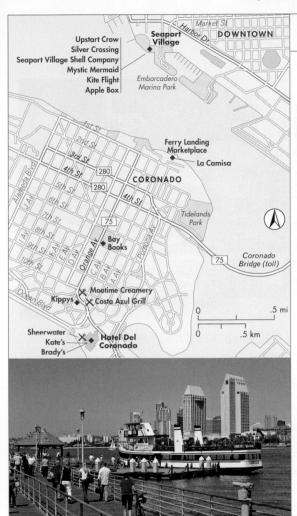

REFUELING IN CORONADO

Stop in at **Mootime Creamery** for a handcrafted ice-cream creation. Mandy Moore, Jason Alexander, and Cuba Gooding Jr. have all been spotted enjoying a Mootime treat.

Relax with a cocktail or fruit smoothie on the patio of the breezy **Sheerwater** restaurant at the Hotel Del Coronado. You can also drink in the view of the spectacular beach.

For a tasty lunch alfresco, the **Costa Azul Grill** serves great nachos and fish tacos.

WHAT YOU'LL WANT

CLOTHES

Brady's. You'll find European-designed menswear and sexy leather jackets here.

Kate's. The flirty frocks here will dazzle dinner mates.

Kippys. For the rock-star look, check out the fabulous beaded belts.

JEWELRY

Mystic Mermaid. This store offers bracelets made from typewriter keys and handmade beaded, silver, and ceramic earrings.

Silver Crossing. One of the standout shops in Seaport Village, the rings, earrings, charms, and pendants here won't blow your budget.

KIDS' STUFF

Apple Box. Pick up a personalized wooden toy from a collection of more than 1,500 battery-free playthings here.

Kite Flite. You can try out the amazing collection of high-flying toys before you buy just outside their door.

UNIQUE SOUVENIRS

La Camisa. You'll find everything from San Diego Chargers hoodies to Coronado Bridge snow globes.

Seaport Village Shell Company. Shop for seashell jewelry, ornaments, and carved wooden fish.

14

OLD TOWN

Within this 1½-mi area of Old Town, you'll find gifts, art, crafts, and clothes that are hard to find in other parts of the city, and many of the retail shops also brim over with San Diego souvenirs—key chains, snow globes, T-shirts, and banners supporting the Chargers and Padres.

(above) Don't miss Old Town Saturday Market every Saturday from 9 to 4. (right) Old Town Trolley Tours stop at Old Town San Diego State Historic Park.

Old Town Historic State Park has more than a dozen sites that pay homage to San Diego's early California past (from 1821 to 1872). For those who don't have the time to venture south of the border, the shops are a chance to browse through handcrafted wares from local and regional Mexican artists, while also soaking up the festive atmosphere. Bazaar del Mundo, Old Town Market, and Fiesta de Reyes are the major shopping areas, but you'll also find unique shops along San Diego Avenue that alternate with the numerous Mexican restaurants there. Old Town is easily reachable by car or via the San Diego Trolley and bus system.

BEST TIME TO GO

Plan to visit any day but Sunday, when crowds are at their peak. Keep in mind that many of the shops close early weekdays, so try to wrap up your shopping before 5 pm. If you're there on Saturday, be sure to check out Old Town Saturday Market.

BEST FOR KIDS

For a sugar rush, head to **Cousin's Old Town Candy Shop.**

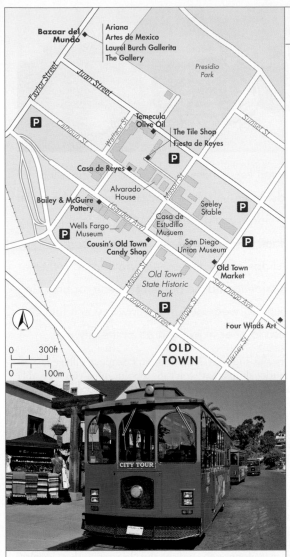

Bazaar del Mundo

Ariana
Artes de Mexico
Laurel Burch Gallerita
The Gallery

Presidio Park

Taylor Street
Juan Street
Calhoun St.
Wallace St.

Temecula Olive Oil

The Tile Shop
Fiesta de Reyes

Sunset St.

Casa de Reyes

Alvarado House

Bailey & McGuire Pottery

Garden Ave.
Mason St.

Seeley Stable

Wells Fargo Museum

Casa de Estudillo Museum

Cousin's Old Town Candy Shop

San Diego Union Museum

Old Town State Historic Park

Mason St.
Congress Street
Twiggs St.

Old Town Market

San Diego Ave.

Four Winds Art

Harney St.

OLD TOWN

0   300ft
0   100m

REFUELING

A midafternoon margarita and savory plate of nachos at the festive **Casa de Reyes,** inside Old Town State Historic Park, will lift your spirits. For lunch or dinner, try the homemade tamales, sizzling fajitas, or one of the massive combination plates. Blazing fire pits, strolling live musicians, and waitresses in colorful Mexican dresses add to the party feel.

WHAT YOU'LL WANT

CLOTHING AND ACCESSORIES

Ariana. You'll find fiesta skirts, peasant blouses, woven shawls, and unique jewelry at this local favorite.

HOME DECOR

Bailey & McGuire Pottery. Affordably priced pottery, baskets, and crafts from around the world.

Four Winds Art. Native American art, gourds, beadwork, weavings, and folk art for casual buyers and serious collectors.

The Tile Shop. Spiff up your home with hand-painted tile house numbers in wrought-iron frames.

MEXICAN WARES

Artes de Mexico. The best stop for Mexican folk art, with hand-carved boxes, ceramic masks, and silver jewelry.

Fiesta de Reyes. You'll find mini sombreros, piñatas, and Day of the Dead figurines.

Old Town Market. Free music performances plus 18 carts and specialty shops with wares from Mexico and South America.

14

Updated
by Amanda
Knoles

San Diego's retail venues are as diverse as the city's vibrant neighborhoods. From La Jolla's tony boutiques to the outlet malls at San Ysidro, you'll find stores that appeal to every taste and budget. Enjoy near-perfect weather year-round as you explore shops along the scenic waterfront. Whether you're on a mission to find the perfect souvenir, or browsing for a sharp outfit to wear out on the town, you'll find San Diego has much to offer in every area of the city.

Into kitschy gifts and souvenirs? Downtown's Seaport Village has an abundance of quirky shops that won't disappoint, plus you'll be able to enjoy the coastal breezes while you shop for that Coronado Bridge snow globe.

The Gaslamp Quarter, downtown's trendy hot spot, is where you'll find independent shops selling urban apparel, unique home decor, and vintage treasures. If you can't find it in the boutiques, head for Westfield Horton Plaza, the downtown mall with more than 130 stores and 26 eateries. Nearby, Little Italy is the place to find contemporary art and home decor.

Old Town is a must for pottery, ceramics, jewelry, and handcrafted baskets. Uptown is known for its mélange of funky bookstores, offbeat gift shops, and nostalgic collectibles, and the beach towns have the best swimwear and sandals. La Jolla's chic boutiques offer a more intimate shopping experience along with some of the classiest clothes, jewelry, and shoes in the county.

Trendsetters will have no trouble finding must-have handbags and designer apparel at the world-class Fashion Valley mall in Mission Valley, a haven for luxury brands such as Hermès, Jimmy Choo, and Carolina Herrera.

Most malls have free parking in a lot or garage, and parking is not usually a problem. Westfield Horton Plaza and some of the shops in the Gaslamp Quarter offer validated parking or valet parking.

SHOPPING PLANNER

OPENING HOURS

Shops near tourist attractions and the major shopping malls tend to open early and close late. Standard hours are typically 10–9 on weekdays and 10–10 on weekends. Smaller shops may close as early as 5 on weekdays and Sunday, however. It's best to call ahead for hours if you have your heart set on visiting a particular shop.

STEALS AND DEALS

Visit ⊕ *www.sandiego.citysearch.com* and ⊕ *www.signonsandiego. com* for details on local shops and sales. The *San Diego Union-Tribune* (⊕ *www.signonsandiego.com*) and the *San Diego Reader* (⊕ *www. sandiegoreader.com*) frequently offer coupons. Most hotels have brochure and magazine racks where you can pick up flyers from shops around town and directories for the major shopping malls. Some shops also give discounts to AARP and AAA members as well as military personnel.

SNAG A BARGAIN AT OUTLET MALLS

Some hotels offer free shuttles to shopping centers, outlet malls, and nearby casinos. Check with the concierge for schedules.

Carlsbad Premium Outlets. Carlsbad Premium Outlets, a 40-minute drive north of downtown San Diego, features 90 outlet stores, including Barneys New York, Anne Klein, Kenneth Cole, Michael Kors, Oakley, Juicy Couture, and True Religion. ⊠ *5620 Paseo del Norte, Suite 100, Carlsbad* ☎ *760/804–9000* ⊕ *www.premiumoutlets.com.*

Las Americas Premium Outlets. Situated in San Ysidro, just north of the border from Mexico, this mall has two duty-free shops and 120 outlet stores, including Neiman Marcus Last Call and a Nike Factory Store. Las Americas can be reached via the San Diego Trolley. By car take the Camino de la Plaza exit off I–5. ⊠ *4211 Camino de la Plaza, San Ysidro* ☎ *619/934–8400* ⊕ *www.premiumoutlets.com.*

Viejas Outlet Center. This mall, in the East County foothills off I–8, is directly across the street from Viejas Casino. Stores include Coach, Ralph Lauren/Polo, Jones New York, Nine West, Osh Kosh, and Guess. In the summer months Viejas hosts a free outdoor concert series on the parklike grounds. ⊠ *5005 Willows Rd., Alpine* ☎ *619/659–2070* ⊕ *www.shopviejas.com.*

SHOPPING BY NEIGHBORHOOD

DOWNTOWN

The city's ever-changing downtown offers a variety of shopping venues including the open-air Horton Plaza mall, the eclectic shops of the Gaslamp Quarter, and Seaport Village, a complex of diverse waterfront stores. Offering a plethora of edgy boutiques, warehouses converted to retail, and antique shops within easy walking distance of the Convention Center and downtown hotels, the area is a shopper's delight.

TOP SHOPPING EXPERIENCES

Fashion Valley: Bloomingdale's, Nordstrom, Saks, Neiman Marcus, and haute boutiques are all under one roof.

Gaslamp Quarter: Transform yourself from tourist to hipster in no time with finds from the Gaslamp's trendy boutiques.

La Jolla: At the ocean-side enclave of the rich and famous, prices might leave your credit card reeling...but browsing is free.

Old Town: No need for a passport, Mexico's finest crafts, artwork, and jewelry are all here north of the border.

Seaport Village: Souvenir central offers something for all ages.

EMBARCADERO

Spanning 14 acres and offering more than 50 shops and 17 restaurants, Embarcadero's Seaport Village is the most popular destination in this marina neighborhood. The picturesque shopping center caters to tourists with a heavy concentration of souvenir shops, but you'll also find toys, art, jewelry, clothes for the whole family, and nostalgic collectibles.

SHOPPING CENTERS

★ **Seaport Village.** Quintessentially San Diego, this waterfront complex of more than 50 shops and restaurants has sweeping bay views, fresh breezes, and great strolling paths. Horse and carriage rides, an 1895 Looff carousel, and frequent public entertainment are side attractions. The Seaport is within walking distance of hotels, the San Diego Convention Center, and the San Diego Trolley, and there's also an easily accessible parking lot with two hours free with purchase validation.

Apple Box. This shop features a delightful selection of battery-free wooden toys for all ages. ☎ *619/230–1818.*

Discover Nature. Discover Nature is where you can find gifts for the office, plus wind chimes and jewelry. ☎ *619/231–1299.*

Kite Flite. Peruse this huge inventory of kites in every size, shape, and price range; they'll let you try before you buy. ☎ *619/234–KITE.*

Latitudes. Latitudes sells beachwear for men and women. ☎ *619/235–0220.*

Mystic Mermaid. Check out a terrific selection of hand-dyed silk scarves, unique jewelry, and fashions for women. ☎ *619/233–0321.*

San Diego Surf Co. Stop in for all the top brands in beachwear and surf apparel. ☎ *619/696–8967.*

Seaport Village Shell Company. Browse a wide assortment of shells, coral, jewelry, and craft items. ☎ *619/234–1004.*

Silver Crossing. Treat yourself to affordable sterling silver rings, charms, and chains plus jewelry designs combining glass, marcasite, and gemstones. ☎ *619/325–4925.*

Upstart Crow. This shop carries a terrific selection of books, journals, gifts, and greeting cards. The outdoor coffee bar is great for people-watching while you grab a snack. ☎ *619/232–4855.*

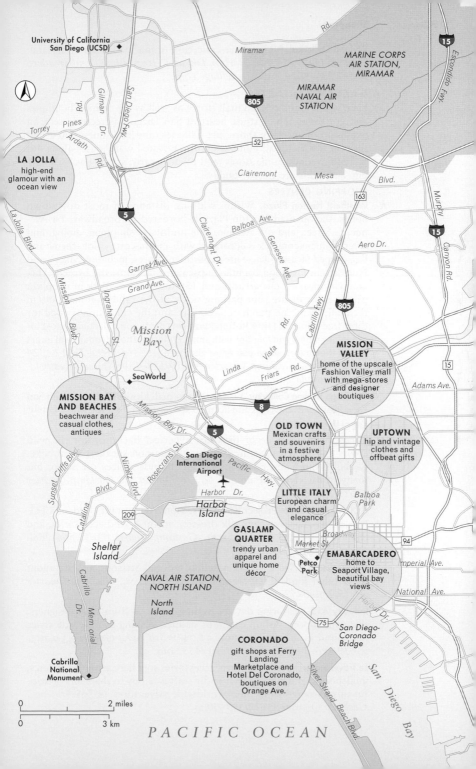

University of California
San Diego (UCSD) ◆

LA JOLLA
high-end
glamour with an
ocean view

MARINE CORPS
AIR STATION,
MIRAMAR

MIRAMAR
NAVAL AIR
STATION

Miramar

Clairemont   Mesa   Blvd.

MISSION VALLEY
home of the upscale
Fashion Valley mall
with mega-stores
and designer
boutiques

*Mission
Bay*

SeaWorld ●

**MISSION BAY
AND BEACHES**
beachwear and
casual clothes,
antiques

OLD TOWN
Mexican crafts
and souvenirs
in a festive
atmosphere

UPTOWN
hip and vintage
clothes and
offbeat gifts

San Diego
International
Airport

Pacific Hwy.

Harbor Dr.

*Harbor
Island*

LITTLE ITALY
European charm
and casual
elegance

*Balboa
Park*

*Shelter
Island*

**GASLAMP
QUARTER**
trendy urban
apparel and
unique home décor

EMBARCADERO
home to
Seaport Village,
beautiful bay
views

Petco
Park ◆

*NAVAL AIR STATION,
NORTH ISLAND*

*North
Island*

Cabrillo
National
Monument ▲

CORONADO
gift shops at Ferry
Landing
Marketplace and
Hotel Del Coronado,
boutiques on
Orange Ave.

San
Diego
Bay

San Diego-
Coronado
Bridge

0 ├──────┤ 2 miles
0 ├──────┤ 3 km

PACIFIC OCEAN

Wyland Galleries. Add to your collection of marine-life art at Wyland. ☎ 619/544–9995 ✉ *W. Harbor Dr. at Kettner Blvd., Embarcadero* ☎ 619/235–4014 ⊕ *www.spvillage.com.*

GASLAMP QUARTER

Here you'll find the usual mall stores as well as hip fashion boutiques and gift shops. The historic heart of San Diego has recently seen an explosion of specialty shops, art galleries, and boutiques; you'll find them in the Victorian buildings and renovated warehouses along 4th and 5th avenues. Some stores tend to close early, starting as early as 5 pm, and many are closed Sunday.

SHOPPING CENTERS

★ **Westfield Horton Plaza.** Within walking distance of most downtown hotels, the open-air Horton Plaza is bordered by Broadway, 1st Avenue, G Street, and 4th Avenue. The multilevel shopping, dining, and entertainment complex is decorated with a terra-cotta color scheme and flag-draped facades. There are department stores, including Macy's and Nordstrom; fast-food counters; upscale restaurants; the Lyceum Theater; cinemas; a game arcade; and 130 other stores. Park in the plaza garage and validate your parking ticket at the validation machines in the mall; there's no purchase necessary and the validation is good for three free hours. ■ **TIP➜** Horton Plaza sets aside some parking spaces for expectant moms and families with small children. The attendant will direct you to the spaces when you enter the garage. ☎ *619/696–7111* ✉ *324 Horton Plaza, Gaslamp Quarter* ☎ *619/238–1596* ⊕ *www.westfield. com/hortonplaza.*

San Diego Trading Company. Visit their two mall kiosks brimming with San Diego–inspired souvenirs and licensed sports apparel for the whole family.

SPECIALTY STORES

CLOTHING AND ACCESSORIES **Blends.** Minimalist decor provides a perfect backdrop for the wild colors and patterns featured on limited-edition sneakers from Nike, Reebok, Vans, and other in-demand brands. Prices are steep, but many of the styles are unique. ✉ *726 Market St., Gaslamp Quarter* ☎ *619/233–6126.*

GOGA by Gordana. Project Runway season 6 contestant Gordana Gehlhausen specializes in sexy silk dresses, one-of-a-kind accessories, and chic casual wear. ✉ *401 Market St., Gaslamp Quarter* ☎ *619/564–7660* ⊕ *www.shopgoga.com.*

Hat Works. Hat Works has been selling fedoras, Stetsons, and just about every other kind of hat since 1922. ✉ *433 E St., Gaslamp Quarter* ☎ *619/234–0457.*

Industry 453. Featuring day to evening fashions from local designers, this contemporary shop caters to women seeking avant-garde styles not found in department stores. ✉ *449 5th Ave., Gaslamp Quarter* ☎ *619/696–3459* ⊕ *www.industry453.com.*

Le Travel Store. Among the travel accessories sold here are luggage, totes, guidebooks, and maps. The friendly staff is happy to share lots of helpful tips garnered from their worldwide adventures. ✉ *745 4th Ave., Gaslamp Quarter* ☎ *619/544–0005.*

DID YOU KNOW?

Seaport Village has 13 casual eateries and four nicer restaurants. Whether you're craving ice cream or seared tuna, you'll find it there.

Lucky Brand Jeans. Shop here for women's, men's, kids', and even babies' jeans, as well as hip fashions. ⊠ *621 5th Ave., Gaslamp Quarter* ☎ *619/230–9260.*

Pink Zone. This boutique is popular with teens, college students, and young working women on the prowl for trendy tops, pants, and dresses at budget prices. ⊠ *440 5th Ave., Gaslamp Quarter* ☎ *619/236–0148.*

Puma. Friendly and knowledgeable sales associates will help you find stylish athletic shoes or a colorful hoodie with the trademark feline logo at this sporty store. ⊠ *410 5th Ave., Gaslamp Quarter* ☎ *619/338–9601* ⊕ *www.puma.com.*

Quiksilver Boardriders Club. This shop features Quiksilver's full line of surf clothing, accessories, and their famous surfboards. ⊠ *402 5th Ave., Gaslamp Quarter* ☎ *619/234–3125.*

Ron Stuart. Sharp-dressed men flock to this men's shop for Manzoni suits, Tommy Bahama shirts, and expert tailoring on-site. ⊠ *225 A St., Gaslamp Quarter* ☎ *619/232–8850* ⊕ *www.ronstuartmensclothing. com* ✹ *Closed Sun.*

Urban Outfitters. You'll find street-vibe fashions, accessories, and shoes for men and women, plus home decor and whimsical gift items. ⊠ *665 5th Ave., Gaslamp Quarter* ☎ *619/231–0102* ⊕ *www.urbanoutfitters.com.*

HOME ACCESSORIES AND GIFTS

Bubbles Boutique. You'll find stuff for use beyond the bathtub, although the selection of handcrafted soaps and bath treats is pleasingly broad. There are also sugar and salt body scrubs, body moisturizers, and manly shaving gels, pajamas, robes, and slippers. ⊠ *226 5th Ave., Gaslamp Quarter* ☎ *866/236–9003* ⊕ *www.bubblesboutique.com.*

Cuban Cigar Factory. This cigar store and lounge, popular with San Diego Padres fans, offers aficionados a comfy spot to savor a fine smoke with a beer or glass of wine. Tobacco grown from Cuban seed in the Dominican Republic, Central America, and elsewhere goes into the cigars, sold in boxes of 10 and 25, along with accessories such as humidors. ⊠ *551 5th Ave., Gaslamp Quarter* ☎ *619/238–2496* ⊕ *www. cubancigarfactory.com.*

Vitreum. Admire handcrafted home decor and unique glassware at this gallerylike shop owned by Japanese artist Takao. ⊠ *619 West Fir St., Little Italy* ☎ *619/237–9810* ⊕ *www.vitreum-us.com* ✹ *Closed Sun.*

LITTLE ITALY

With more than 33,500 square feet of retail, Little Italy is an especially fun place to visit during holiday celebrations and special events like Art-Walk in April and Chalk la Strada in June. Many shops have a strong European ambience, and shoppers will find enticing wares that include colorful ceramics, handblown glassware, modern home accents, and designer shoes. The stretch along Kettner Boulevard and India Street from Laurel to Date Street is the Art and Design District.

SPECIALTY STORES

CLOTHING AND ACCESSORIES

Carol Gardyne Boutique. Shop here for hand-painted silk scarves, accessories, wall hangings, and stylish women's clothing. ⊠ *1840 Columbia St, Little Italy* ☎ *619/233–8066* ⊕ *www.carolgardyne.com.*

SAN DIEGO'S EAST VILLAGE

Just a hop, skip, and a jump from the Gaslamp Quarter, the up-and-coming East Village offers a variety of shops that cater to local hipsters and visitors looking for edgy streetwear, novelty tees, and unique accessories. Look for them in stores from 8th to 10th avenues between Broadway and J Street. Here are some of our favorites.

Five and a Dime. This popular hangout features labels like Crooks & Castles, Brixton, Stussy, Hellz Bellz, and Alphanumeric. Choose from a fun selection of hats, shoes, sweaters, and tees for guys and gals, and be sure to check out the sunglasses and jewelry. ⊠ *701 8th Ave., East Village* ☎ *619/236–0364* ⊕ *www.5andadime.com.*

Unsteady. Shop for attention-getting tees, skate shoes, hoodies, dresses, hats, and accessories from labels like Nudie, Evil Doers, Beta Unit, and Mishka. ⊠ *744 8th Ave., East Village* ☎ *619/800–8439* ⊕ *www.shopunsteadyboutique.com.*

■**TIP→** During "Evenings in the East Village" (⊕ *www.sdeastvillage. com*), merchants, restaurants, and galleries invite residents and visitors to stroll the area and enjoy art, music, and food. Visit the website for upcoming dates.

Kapreeza. Owner Renata Carlseen stocks her elegant boutique with upscale lingerie and sexy swimwear from European designers. ⊠ *2400 Kettner Blvd., #253, Little Italy* ☎ *619/702–6355* ⊕ *www.kapreeza. com* ⏾ *Closed Sun. and Mon.*

Rosamariposa. This charming jewelry shop specializes in necklaces, earrings, and bracelets crafted by Indonesian artists using natural fibers, wood, seeds, and recycled glass. ⊠ *611 West Fir St., Little Italy* ☎ *619/237–8064* ⊕ *www.rosamariposasd.com.*

HOME ACCESSORIES AND GIFTS

Bella Stanza. The elegant Italian handmade gifts for the home include a large collection of colorful ceramics, glass, and art pieces. ⊠ *1501 India St., Suite 120, Little Italy* ☎ *619/239–2929* ⊕ *www.bellastanzagifts. com* ⏾ *Closed Sun. and Mon.*

Blick Art Materials. Besides supplying local artists with their tools, Blick Art Materials also carries fine stationery, beautiful leather-bound journals, and a fine selection of art books. ⊠ *1844 India St., Little Italy* ☎ *619/687–0050* ⊕ *www.dickblick.com.*

Boomerang for Modern. Thoroughly mid-20th-century modern design is celebrated here. Aficionados will discover now-classic furniture and accessories produced by Charles and Ray Eames and George Nelson. Small exhibitions showcase vintage and recent works in the modernist spirit, many by local artists. ⊠ *2475 Kettner Blvd., Little Italy* ☎ *619/239–2040* ⊕ *www.boomerangformodern.com* ⏾ *Closed Sun.*

French Garden Shoppe. Specializing in European home furnishings, this inviting store also offers great gift items like pottery, cookware, candles, and imported gourmet foods. ⊠ *2307 India St., Little Italy* ☎ *619/238–4700* ⊕ *www.frenchgardenshoppe.com.*

Masquerade Art of Living. Masquerade's collections include fine art and wearable art, as well as mirrors, lamps, and other home accessories, and gifts. ⊠ *1608 India St., Little Italy* 🕾 *619/235–6564* ☾ *Closed Mon.*

Mixture. Housed in a 1940s brick warehouse, Mixture blends art and high design for the home. You'll find high-style bedding, rugs, glassware, and bath and body products here, along with original art and sculpture. ⊠ *2210 Kettner Blvd., Little Italy* 🕾 *619/239–4788* ⊕ *www. mixturehome.com* ☾ *Closed Mon.*

OLD TOWN

Located north of downtown off I–5, Old Town is tourist-focused, but the festival-like ambience and plethora of Mexican restaurants also makes it a popular destination for locals. At Old Town Historic Park, you'll feel like a time traveler as you visit shops housed in restored adobe buildings. Farther down the street you'll find stores selling Mexican blankets, piñatas, and glassware. Old Town Market offers live entertainment, local artists selling their wares from carts, and a market crammed with unique apparel, home decor, toys, jewelry, and food. Dozens of stores sell San Diego logo merchandise and T-shirts at discounted prices, and you'll find great deals on handcrafted jewelry, art, and leather accessories.

SHOPPING CENTERS

Fodor's Choice
★

Bazaar del Mundo Shops. An arcade with a Mexican villa theme shares the corner of Taylor and Juan with the Guadalajara Restaurant and offers a variety of riotously colorful gift shops such as **Ariana,** for ethnic and artsy women's fashions; **Artes de Mexico,** which has a fine array of handmade Latin American crafts and Guatemalan weavings; and **The Gallery,** which has handmade jewelry, Native American crafts, collectible glass, and original serigraphs by John August Swanson. The **Laurel Burch Galleria** carries the complete collection of this northern California artist's signature jewelry, accessories, and totes. ⊠ *4133 Taylor St., Old Town* 🕾 *619/296–3161* ⊕ *www.bazaardelmundo.com.*

Fiesta de Reyes. Within the Old Town San Diego State Historic Park, the Fiesta de Reyes has the easy feel of Old California. Friendly shopkeepers dressed as Californios host a collection of boutiques and eateries around a flower-filled square, which has been designed in keeping with Old Town's early days, from the 1850s, and many of the shops stock items reminiscent of that era. Stroll through the **Fiesta Cocina** for festive kitchenware, **Temecula Olive Oil** for local olive oils and artisan foods, **Hot Licks** for gourmet hot sauces, and **Hacienda de Las Rosas** for wine and tastings. The **Tile Shop** carries hand-painted Mexican tiles, **Geppetto's** specializes in classic wooden toys, and **La Panaderia** offers baked goods made using early Mexican cooking methods. Two restaurants, **Casa de Reyes** and the period **Barra Barra Saloon,** serve Mexican food. Shops are open daily 10–9 June–November. ⊠ *2754 Calhoun St., Old Town* 🕾 *866/378–2943* ⊕ *fiestadereyes.com.*

Old Town Market. Featuring a variety of Latin-inspired shops, carts, and local artisans, this eclectic market offers everything from silver jewelry to dolls, gourmet foods, home decor, and apparel. ⊠ *4010 Twiggs St., Old Town* ☎ *619/278–0955.*

★ **Old Town Saturday Market.** San Diego's largest artisan market features live music and local artists selling jewelry, paintings, photography, hand-blown glass, apparel, pottery, and decorative items. It's open every Saturday from 9 to 4, and admission is free. To get here, take the San Diego Trolley to the Old Town stop and walk two blocks south. ⊠ *3950– 3999 Harney St., west of San Diego Ave., Old Town* ☎ *858/272–7054* ⊕ *www.oldtownsaturdaymarket.com* 🖺 *Free* ☉ *Sat. 9–4.*

OFF THE BEATEN PATH

Kobey's Swap Meet. Not far from Old Town, San Diego's premier flea market seems to expand every week. Sellers display everything from futons to fresh strawberries at the open-air event. The back section, with secondhand goods, is great for bargain hunters. The swap meet is open Friday–Sunday 7–3; admission is 50¢ on Friday and $1 on weekends, children under 11 free; parking is free. ⊠ *Valley View Casino Center parking lot, 3500 Sports Arena Blvd., Sports Arena* ☎ *619/226–0650* ⊕ *www.kobeyswap.com.*

SPECIALTY STORES

HOME ACCESSORIES AND GIFTS

Bailey & McGuire Pottery. Inside a historic adobe building, this shop sells authentic Mexican pottery and also carries some crafts from international artists. ⊠ *2769 San Diego Ave., Old Town* ☎ *619/295–0306.*

★ **Cousin's Candy Shop.** Sample taffy made on-site and choose from 16 flavors of homemade fudge. The old-time candies in nostalgic tins make thoughtful gifts. ⊠ *2711 San Diego Ave., Old Town* ☎ *877/226–3977* ⊕ *www.cousinscandy.com.*

Del Sol of San Diego. Unique tees, sweatshirts, hats, tote bags, and jewelry at this fun shop change color when exposed to sunlight. There is a second location in Seaport Village. ⊠ *2448 San Diego Ave., Old Town* ☎ *619/299–6965* ⊕ *www.delsolsandiego.com.*

The Diamond Source. Specializing in fashionable diamond and precious gemstone jewelry, this shop features unique designs from master jeweler Marco Levy. ⊠ *2474 San Diego Ave., Old Town* ☎ *619/299–6900* ⊕ *www.thediamondsource.com* ☉ *Closed Mon.*

Four Winds Art. The selection of excellent arts and crafts here includes paintings, pottery, dolls, handcrafted jewelry, and rugs created by Native Americans. ⊠ *2448 San Diego Ave., Old Town* ☎ *619/692–0466* ⊕ *www.4windsart.com.*

Variations Imports. Shop here for wall decor, clocks, candleholders, Asian figurines, and unusual imports from around the world. ⊠ *3975 Twiggs St., Old Town* ☎ *619/260–1008* ⊕ *www.variationsimports.com.*

Ye Olde Soap Shoppe. This shop carries hand-fashioned soaps, as well as a full line of soap-making supplies, including kits, herbs, and vegetable bases. ⊠ *2497 San Diego Ave., Old Town* ☎ *619/543–1300* ⊕ *www. soapmaking.com.*

14

Old Town is the place to go for colorful Mexican wares.

UPTOWN

Hillcrest has many avant-garde apparel shops alongside gift, book, and music stores. North Park, east of Hillcrest, is a retro buff's paradise with resale shops, trendy boutiques, and stores that sell a mix of old and new. University Avenue is good for affordable furniture, gift, and specialty stores appealing to college students, singles, and young families. South Park's 30th, Juniper, and Fern streets have everything from the hottest new denim lines to baby gear and craft supplies. The shops and art galleries in Mission Hills, west of Hillcrest, have a modern and sophisticated ambience that suits the well-heeled residents.

SPECIALTY STORES

BOOKS

Obelisk. The shelves here hold a bounty of gay and lesbian literature, cards, and gifts. ⊠ *1029 University Ave., Hillcrest* ☎ *619/297–4171.*

CLOTHING AND ACCESSORIES

Le Bel Age Boutique. Owner Valeri designs some of the jewelry sold at this charming contemporary clothing boutique, in business since the '80s. ⊠ *1607 W. Lewis St., Mission Hills* ☎ *619/297–7080* ☉ *Closed Sun. and Mon.*

Mimi & Red Boutique. Laid-back ambience, friendly service, and racks full of moderate to high-end women's fashions have made this shop a favorite with cool San Diegans. Rebecca Beeson and Betsey Johnson are here, along with RVCA, Nu Collective, and accessories by Amy Kathryn. The store also has a location in La Jolla. ⊠ *3032 University Ave., North Park* ☎ *619/298–7933* ⊕ *www.mimiandred.com.*

Mint. Affordably priced ballet flats and wild stilettos share space with urban sneakers, retro boots, and colorful espadrilles. ⊠ *525 University Ave., Hillcrest* ☏ *619/291–6468.*

NYLA Kensington. Offering upscale quality at affordable prices, this women's boutique features hot brands like Saint Grace, Mac & Jac, Kenzie Girl, and Michael Stars. Splurge on sundresses, jeans, jewelry, bags, and shoes. ⊠ *4095 Adams Ave., Kensington* ☏ *619/280–5300* ⊕ *www. nylakensington.com* ⊘ *Closed Mon.*

RUFSKIN. The flagship boutique for the namesake denim line features sexy jeans, casual and dress shirts for men, swimwear, bold accessories, and a custom leather collection. ⊠ *3944 30th St., North Park* ☏ *619/341–2660* ⊕ *www.rufskin.com* ⊘ *Closed Sun.*

FOOD   **Henry's Marketplace.** Head to this San Diego original for fresh produce, bulk grains, nuts, snacks, dried fruits, and health foods. ⊠ *4175 Park Blvd., North Park* ☏ *619/291–8287.*

HOME   **Babette Schwartz.** This zany pop-culture store sells toys, books, T-shirts,
ACCESSORIES   and magnets. ⊠ *421 University Ave., Hillcrest* ☏ *619/220–7048*
AND GIFTS   ⊕ *www.babette.com.*

California Fleurish. This perfumery has lots of extras: silk scarves, delicate Japanese pottery, beeswax candles, and fine vinegars and soaps. ⊠ *4011 Goldfinch St., Mission Hills* ☏ *619/291–4755* ⊕ *www.californiafleurish.com.*

Cathedral. Voted the "Best Place to Smell" in a local poll, this store is definitely worth a sniff around. It specializes in uniquely designed candles, fragrant oils, home decor, and bath goods. ⊠ *435 University Ave., Hillcrest* ☏ *619/296–4046* ⊕ *www.shopcathedral.com.*

The Grove. Crafters stock up on beads, fabric trims, pattern books, and knitting and crochet supplies at this popular shop, which also offers instruction classes and wares from a variety of vendors. Find paintings from local artists, organic clothing, children's apparel, books, toys, and home decor. ⊠ *3010 Juniper St., South Park* ☏ *619/284–7684* ⊕ *www. thegrovesandiego.com* ⊘ *Closed Mon.*

Ink by Kymberli Parker. Find high-quality paper items, pens, cards, and unique gifts. Custom invitations and personalized stationery are also available. ⊠ *127 W. University Ave., Hillcrest* ☏ *619/233–4203* ⊕ *www. indiainkpapers.com* ⊘ *Closed Sun. and Mon.*

Maison en Provence. The French proprietors Pascal and Marielle Giai sell sunny fabrics and pottery from Provence. There are also fine soaps, antique postcards, and Laguiole cutlery. ⊠ *820 Ft. Stockton Dr., Mission Hills* ☏ *619/298–5318* ⊕ *www.everythingprovence.com* ⊘ *Closed Sun. and Mon.*

★   **Mingei International Museum Store.** Featuring an international collection of textiles, jewelry, apparel, and home decor, this museum shop also offers a rotating gallery of artworks and a nice selection of books on crafts and folk art. ⊠ *1439 El Prado, Balboa Park* ☏ *619/239–0003* ⊕ *www.mingei.org* ⊘ *Closed Mon.*

Taboo Studio. A rotating roster of artists display and sell handcrafted jewelry at this upscale gallery featuring limited-edition pieces designed with precious metals and gemstones. ⊠ *1615½ W. Lewis St, Mission Hills* ☏ *619/692–0099* ⊕ *www.taboostudio.com* ⊘ *Closed Sun. and Mon.*

14

MISSION BAY AND THE BEACHES

Mission, Grand, and Garnet are the big shopping avenues in the beach towns. Souvenir shops are scattered up and down the boardwalk, and along Mission Boulevard you'll find surf, skate, and bike shops, bikini boutiques, and stores selling hip T-shirts, jeans, sandals, and casual apparel. Garnet Avenue is the hot spot for resale boutiques, thrift stores, and pawn shops. The Ocean Beach Antique District in the 4800 block of Newport Avenue invites browsing with several buildings housing multiple dealers under one roof. Independent stores showcase everything from vintage watches and pottery to linens and retro posters.

SPECIALTY STORES

CLOTHING **Men's Fashion Depot.** San Diego insiders head for this warehouse-style men's store for discounted suits and affordable tuxedos. Speedy alterations are available. ⊠ *3730 Sports Arena Blvd., Point Loma* ☎ *619/222–9570* ⊕ *www.mensfashiondepot.net.*

Pilar's Beach Wear. Browse Southern California's largest selection of major-label swimsuits, including the sexy styles featured in *Sports Illustrated*'s swimsuit issue. ⊠ *3745 Mission Blvd., Mission Beach* ☎ *858/488–3056* ⊕ *www.pilarsbeachwear.com.*

Raw Clothing. A local favorite since 1992, this beachside shop offers hip casual wear for the whole family. Find styles by Frankie B and Juicy Couture, Indah, and hot denim from Joe's Jeans. ⊠ *940 Garnet Ave., Pacific Beach* ☎ *858/483–9111* ⊕ *www.rawclothing.com.*

FOOD **Trader Joe's.** Snacks on the beach are as necessary as sunscreen, so stop here for treats that include dried fruits and nuts, and for wine and cheese for the evening. ⊠ *1211 Garnet Ave., Pacific Beach* ☎ *858/272–7235.*

HOME ACCESSORIES AND GIFTS **Cottage Antiques.** Part of the Ocean Beach antiques district, this charming shop features vintage home and garden decor in a cozy cottage setting. ⊠ *4873 Newport Ave., Ocean Beach* ☎ *619/222–1967* ⊕ *cottageantiques.biz.*

Great News Discount Cookware. Cooks drool over the bakeware, cutlery, tools, and gadgets sold here. There's a cooking school in the back, an extensive selection of cookbooks, and excellent customer service. ⊠ *1788 Garnet Ave., Pacific Beach* ☎ *858/270–1582* ⊕ *www.great-news.com.*

Ocean Gifts and Shells. This huge beach-theme store is filled with seashells of every size and shape, nautical decor, wind chimes, swimwear, toys, and souvenirs. ⊠ *4934 Newport Ave., Mission Bay* ☎ *619/269–3981* ⊕ *oceangiftsandshells.com.*

LA JOLLA

Known as San Diego's Rodeo Drive, La Jolla has chic boutiques, art galleries, and gift shops lining narrow, twisty streets that are often celebrity-soaked. Prospect Street and Girard Avenue are the primary shopping stretches, and North Prospect is chockablock with art galleries (⇨ *see Chapter 11: The Arts, for information on art galleries).* The Upper Girard Design District stocks home decor accessories and luxury furnishings. Parking is tight in the village, and store hours vary widely, so it's wise to call in advance. Most shops on Prospect Street stay open until 10 pm on weeknights to accommodate evening strollers. On the east side of I–5, office buildings surround the Westfield UTC mall, where you'll find department and chain stores. UTC has undertaken a $900 million revitalization project that aims to make it one of the greenest shopping centers in the country. Other planned improvements include a state-of-the-art movie theater, additional parking, and a more contemporary exterior with lush gardens.

SHOPPING CENTERS

Westfield UTC. This popular outdoor mall east of La Jolla village has more than 150 shops and 27 eateries, plus an ice-skating rink. Department stores include Nordstrom, Macy's, and Sears.

Charles David. Complete your look here with high-fashion women's shoes. ☎ 858/625–0275.

Chuao Chocolatier. Pronounced "chew-wow," this artisanal chocolate factory is named after a region in Venezuela that produces the world's most highly prized cacao beans. ☎ 858/546–1463 ⊕ www. chuaochocolatier.com.

Naartjie. Stylish clothing and accessories for babies and children are available at this boutique. ☎ 858/625–0940.

Papyrus. Stop in for a wide selection of San Diego postcards, whimsical note cards, gifts, and fine stationery. ☎ 858/458–1399.

Toys, Etc. Children of all ages will delight in this huge selection of educational toys, dolls, train sets, and games. ☎ 858/459–5104 ✉ 4545 La Jolla Village Dr., between I–5 and I–805, La Jolla ☎ 858/546–8858 ⊕ www.westfield.com/utc.

OFF THE BEATEN PATH

Del Mar Plaza. Del Mar Plaza is worth a side trip if you plan to visit Del Mar and its racetrack. The piazza-style center includes three floors of upscale shops, ocean-view restaurants, and free underground parking. ✉ 1555 Camino del Mar, at Hwy. 101 and 15th St., Del Mar ⊕ www. delmarplaza.com.

★ **Coast Walk Plaza.** This seaside shopping area has breathtaking views, great paths for strolling, and benches perfect for people-watching

Miss Trendy. This high-end fashion boutique carries cutting-edge clothing, shoes, and jewelry from the region's hottest designers. ☎ 858/456–2621.

Gaia Oasis Day Spa. Stock up here with tempting organic lotions and potions perfect for pampering facials and body treatments at home. Brands include Gaia, Sacred Earth, Aqua Dessa, and Sonoma Lavender. Aromatherapy candles, pillows, robes, and inspirational books and CDs are also available. ☎ 858/456–8797.

Suzan's Silver and Amber Jewelry. This shop specializes in affordably priced contemporary jewelry handcrafted from sterling silver and semiprecious stones. ☎ 858/454–9808 ✉ 1298 Prospect, at Roslyn La. and Coast Blvd. S, La Jolla.

14

Stores on Prospect Street in La Jolla buzz with activity until late in the evening.

SPECIALTY STORES

BOOKS

Warwick's. An upscale bookstore and a La Jolla fixture since 1896, Warwick's often hosts big-name author signings. ✉ *7812 Girard Ave., La Jolla* ☎ *858/454–0347.*

CLOTHING AND ACCESSORIES

Ascot Shop. The classic Ivy League look is king in this traditional haberdashery that sells menswear by Andrew J, Ike Behar, and Reyn Spooner. The small women's section offers designs from Audrey Talbott and Zanella. ✉ *7750 Girard Ave., La Jolla* ☎ *858/454–4222* ⊘ *Closed Sun.*

Encore. This go-to resale emporium for many sharp-dressed women and men features gently used clothing and accessories from labels like Chanel, Dolce & Gabbana, Versace, and Gucci. All items in the popular upstairs clearance area are priced below $199. ✉ *7655 Girard Ave, La Jolla* ☎ *858/454–7540* ⊕ *www.encorelajolla.com.*

La Jolla Surf Systems. One block from La Jolla Shores Beach, this La Jolla institution for vivid California beach and resort wear has been in business since 1979. Tame the waves with surfboards by Olas or Tuberville and boogie boards by BZ and Morey. This shop also rents surfboards, beach chairs, umbrellas, and snorkel gear. ✉ *2132 Ave. de la Playa, La Jolla* ☎ *858/456–2777.*

Let's Go La Jolla. Boasting an upscale fashion collection spread over two levels, this trend-savvy store offers top name designs in denim, casual, and formal wear for men and women. ✉ *7863 Girard Ave., La Jolla* ☎ *858/459–2337* ⊕ *www.letsgoclothing.com.*

Nicole Miller. A favorite of San Diego's best-dressed women, this chic boutique is a great place to spot vacationing celebrities. Give your wardrobe a boost with figure-flattering dresses and tops, tailored trousers, and sexy evening frocks. ✉ *1275 Prospect St., La Jolla* ☎ *858/454–3434* ⊕ *www.nicolemiller.com.*

Rangoni of Florence. This boutique carries its own house brand as well as other, medium-price European men's and women's footwear brands including Amalfi, Icon, and Pele Moda, mostly fashioned in Italy. ✉ *7870 Girard Ave., La Jolla* ☎ *858/459–4469.*

14

HOME
ACCESSORIES
AND GIFTS

Africa and Beyond. This gallery carries Shona stone sculpture, textiles, crafts, masks, and jewelry. ✉ *1250 Prospect St., La Jolla* ☎ *858/454–9983* ⊕ *www.africaandbeyond.com.*

Alexander Perfumes and Cosmetics. Products rarely seen in the United States are available in this European-style perfumery, which claims to have the largest selection of fragrances in California. Its cosmetic lines include Lancaster, Darphin, and Orlane. ✉ *7914 Girard Ave., La Jolla* ☎ *858/454–2292.*

The Artful Soul. There are jewelry, handbags, and gifts by more than 130 contemporary crafts artists here, many of whom are local. ✉ *7660-A Fay Ave., La Jolla* ☎ *858/459–2009* ⊕ *www.artfulsoul.com.*

Burns Drugs. You almost expect to see the Happy Days gang at this '50s-era store. It's a great place to buy inexpensive postcards, souvenirs, and sunscreen, and the gift section features everything from whimsical figurines and novelty socks to trendy purses and kitchen decor. ✉ *7824 Girard Ave., between Silverado and Wall Sts., La Jolla* ☎ *858/459–4285.*

Everett Stunz. This store stocks the finest in luxury home linens, robes, and sleepwear in cashmere, silk, and Swiss cotton. ✉ *7616 Girard Ave., La Jolla* ☎ *800/883–3305.*

★ **La Mano.** Save yourself a trip to Venice and explore the wide selection of delightful papier-mâché and ceramic Carnival masks, many handmade. You'll also find the traditional Carnival costumes, including black hooded capes, for rent. ✉ *1298 Prospect St., La Jolla* ☎ *858/454–7732* ⊕ *www.lamanomasks.com.*

Muttropolis. Dogs will love the very chic chew toys (a Chewy Vuitton purse, a Cosmo-paw-litan). They'll also love the accessories, such as high-fashion coats and hoodies for strutting La Jolla's sun-splashed streets. There's haute cat-ture for felines here as well, and lots of catnip toys. ✉ *7755 Girard Ave., La Jolla* ☎ *858/459–9663* ⊕ *www.shop.muttropolis.com.*

JEWELRY

Philippe Charriol Boutique. Charriol's U.S. flagship store features watches, necklaces, and bracelets in the Swiss brand's stainless-steel and Celtic cable designs. There are fine leather goods and pens as well. ✉ *1227 Prospect St., La Jolla* ☎ *858/551–4933, 800/872–0172.*

Pomegranate. Contemporary and antique jewelry is paired here with fashions by American, European, and Asian designers. ✉ *1152 Prospect St., La Jolla* ☎ *858/459–0629.*

CORONADO

Coronado's resort hotels attract tourists in droves, but somehow the town has managed to avoid being overtaken by chain stores. Instead, shoppers can browse a variety of family-owned shops and dine at sidewalk cafés along Orange Avenue, stroll through the arcade at the historic Hotel Del Coronado, or take in the specialty shops at the Ferry Landing Marketplace.

SHOPPING CENTERS

Fodor'sChoice ★ **Ferry Landing Marketplace.** A staggering view of San Diego's downtown skyline across the bay, a dozen boutiques, and a variety of restaurants all make a delightful place to shop while waiting for a ferry. Shops are open daily from 10 to 7. A **farmers' market** takes place on Tuesday from 2:30 to 6 pm, and several of the restaurants feature daily happy hours, with live music on Friday.

> ### LIKE A RHINESTONE COWGIRL
>
> If you've ever envied the studded and bejeweled belts worn by rock and country music stars, **Kippys** will help you custom-design your very own. Choose from a rainbow of Swarovski crystals to adorn your choice of belt styles and patterns. Prices range from $110 to $300 and up, and belts are ready in two to three weeks.

La Camisa. This is a fun place to pick up kitschy souvenirs, T-shirts, fleece jackets, and postcards. ☎ 619/435–8009.

Scottish Treasures. Get in touch with your Celtic roots with imported apparel, gifts, tableware, and jewelry from Ireland, Scotland, England, and Wales. You can even order a custom-made kilt. ☎ 619/435–1880.

Men's Island Sportswear. Complete your seaside getaway with hats, tropical sportswear, and accessories here. ☎ 619/437–4696 ⊠ 1201 1st St., at B Ave., Coronado ☎ 619/435–8895 ⊕ www.coronadoferrylanding.com.

Fodor'sChoice ★ **Hotel Del Coronado.** At the dozen gift shops within the peninsula's main historic attraction, you can purchase sportswear, designer handbags, jewelry, and antiques. **Babcock & Story Emporium** (☎ Ext. 7265) carries an amazing selection of home decor, garden accessories, and classy gifts. The **Toy Castle** (☎ Ext. 7330) has a hard-to-resist collection of stuffed animals, toys, and games. **Spreckels Sweets & Treats** (☎ Ext. 7627) offers old-time candies, freshly made fudge, and decadent truffles. Women will appreciate the stylish fashions and accessories at **Kate's** (☎ Ext. 7601) and **IsabelB** (☎ Ext. 7384), while well-dressed men can't go wrong with a shirt or jacket from **Brady's** (☎ Ext. 7339). For those celebrating a special occasion, **Del Coronado Jewels** (☎ Ext. 7340) features vintage, traditional and modern jewelry. ⊠ 1500 Orange Ave., Coronado ☎ 619/435–6611 plus extension ⊕ www.hoteldel.com/shopping.

SPECIALTY STORES

Orange Avenue. Friendly shopkeepers make the boutiques lining Orange Avenue, Coronado's main drag, a good place to browse for clothes, home decor, gift items, and gourmet foods.

BOOKS ★ **Bay Books.** This old-fashioned bookstore is the spot to sit, read, and sip coffee on an overcast day by the sea. International travelers should look for the large selection of foreign-language magazines and newspapers,

You can rent bikes at Coronado's Ferry Landing Marketplace to tour around Coronado.

and there's a section in the back devoted to children's books and games. There are plenty of secluded reading nooks and a sidewalk reading area with a coffee bar. ⊠ *1029 Orange Ave., Coronado* ☎ *619/435–0070* ⊕ *www.baybookscoronado.com.*

CLOTHING AND ACCESSORIES

Dale's Swim Shop. All things beachy catch your eye in this shop crammed with swimsuits, hats, sunglasses, and sunscreen. ⊠ *1150 Orange Ave., Coronado* ☎ *619/435–1757.*

Island Birkenstock. Do your feet a favor and check out the comfy sandals and walking shoes sold here. All the latest Birkenstock styles are available in sizes to fit men, women, and children. ⊠ *1350 Orange Ave, Coronado* ☎ *619/435–1071.*

Kippys. Madonna and Liz Hurley have been photographed in the high-quality leather belts manufactured by Kippys. The company's fringed suede vests, sexy leather pants, and beaded denim are all here. ⊠ *1114 Orange Ave., Coronado* ☎ *619/435–6218* ⊕ *www.kippys.com.*

Orange Blossoms Boutique. The shop's casual wear for women and babies includes embellished tees, frilly tops, and colorful handmade sweaters. ⊠ *952 Orange Ave., Coronado* ☎ *619/437–8399* ⊕ *www. orangeblossomsboutique.com.*

FOOD

In Good Taste. Come here for smooth-as-silk chocolates and fudge, specialty cheeses, wine, truffles, and fresh bread. ⊠ *1146 Orange Ave., Coronado* ☎ *619/435–8356.*

HOME ACCESSORIES AND GIFTS

The Attic. White-painted cottage furniture, quilts, linens, and lots of Victoriana are available in this store. ⊠ *1112 10th St., Coronado* ☎ *619/435–5614.*

Seaside Papery. This sister store of Seaside Home in La Jolla carries high-end wedding invitations, greeting cards, wrapping papers, and luxury personal stationery. ⊠ *1162 Orange Ave., Coronado* ☎ *619/435–5565* ⊕ *www.seasidepapery.com.*

MISSION VALLEY

Northeast of downtown near I–8 and Route 163, Mission Valley boasts two major shopping centers and a few smaller strip malls. Fashion Valley features an impressive roster of high-end department stores and luxury boutiques. It's one of only three shopping malls in the world to have Neiman Marcus, Saks Fifth Avenue, Nordstrom, and Bloomingdale's under one roof. At Westfield Mission Valley, mainstream mainstays like Macy's and Old Navy, plus bargain-hunter favorites like Marshall's and Nordstrom Rack, abound. The San Diego Trolley and city buses make stops at both centers.

SHOPPING CENTERS

Fodor's Choice
★

Fashion Valley. San Diego's best and most upscale mall has a contemporary Mission theme, lush landscaping, and more than 200 shops and restaurants. Acclaimed retailers like Bloomingdale's, Neiman Marcus, and Tiffany are here, along with boutiques from fashion darlings like Michael Kors, Jimmy Choo, Tory Burch, and James Perse. Barneys NY CO-OP is a favorite of fashionistas in search of labels that are edgier and smaller than those at most other stores. ⊠ *7007 Friars Rd., Mission Valley* ☎ *619/688–9113* ⊕ *www.shopfashionvalleymall.com.*

Na Hoku. This Hawaiian jewelry store has Tahitian black pearls and pendants fashioned as exotic flowers. ☎ *619/294–7811.*

Park in the Valley. This U-shape mall is across the street from Westfield Mission Valley. ⊠ *1750 Camino de la Reina, Mission Valley.*

OFF 5th. Stop here to score bargain-price fashions by Ralph Lauren, Armani, and Burberry seen at Saks last season. ☎ *619/296–4896*

Westfield Mission Valley. The discount stores at San Diego's largest outdoor mall sometimes reward shoppers with the same merchandise as that sold in Fashion Valley, the mall up the road, but at lower prices. Shops include Macy's; American Eagle Outfitters; Bed Bath & Beyond; Ann Taylor Loft; Charlotte Russe; and Victoria's Secret. The Family Lounge is a lifesaver for parents shopping with kids. Along with private nursing areas, baby-changing stations, and bottle warmers, the lounge has a TV with DVD player, and children's books and toys. It's near the restrooms by the food court. ⊠ *1640 Camino del Rio, Mission Valley* ☎ *619/296–6375* ⊕ *www.westfield.com/missionvalley.*

North County and Environs

WITH TIJUANA

WORD OF MOUTH

"We took our son to San Diego when he was 12 years old. We visited the Zoo and the Wild Animal Park and he loved them both. We also went to LEGOLAND because our son was always a huge LEGO fan. While he might have been a little old for LEGOLAND, we still had a fun day. The LEGO structures were impressive."

—mikesmom

WELCOME TO NORTH COUNTY AND ENVIRONS

TOP REASONS TO GO

★ **Talk to the animals:** Get almost nose to nose with giraffes, lions, antelope, and gazelle at the San Diego Zoo Safari Park in Escondido.

★ **Build a dream at LEGOLAND California Resort:** Explore model cities including New Orleans, Washington, D.C., and New York City built with LEGO bricks.

★ **Beach bumming:** Surf Swami's for towering blue-water break, tiptoe through the sand at Moonlight Beach, cruise the coast in a sailboat, or spot a whale spouting.

★ **Winery touring SoCal style:** There's more than a drop to drink while winery touring in Temecula, home to more than 30 wineries producing red and white wines, boutique lodging, and classy restaurants.

★ **Discover the desert wilderness:** Anza-Borrego Desert State Park encompasses more than 600,000 acres, most of it wilderness. Springtime, when the wildflowers are in full bloom, is glorious.

1 **North Coast.** From Del Mar to Oceanside are the quintessential beach towns marching north along I-5. These coastal cities have grown up recently and offer sophisticated shopping, art galleries, dining, and accommodations, but you'll still find great beaches where you can watch surfers testing the breaks in winter. LEGOLAND California Resort and other attractions are just east of I-5.

2 **Inland North County and Temecula.** Historically this is the citrus- and avocado- growing belt of San Diego County. Since the opening of the San Diego Zoo Safari Park in Escondido and expansion of the winemaking industry in Temecula Valley more than 20 years ago, visitors have added inland North County to their must-see lists.

3 **The Backcountry and Julian.** The backcountry consists of the mountain ranges that separate metropolitan San Diego and the North Coast from the desert. It's where San Diegans go to hike, commune with nature, share a picnic, and study the night sky. Julian, the only real community within these mountains, is famous for its apple pies.

4 **The Desert.** The Anza-Borrego Desert is desert at its best: vast mostly untracked wilderness where you can wander and camp where you wish; a huge repository of prehistoric beasts; and the best wildflower display in Southern California in the springtime.

5 **Tijuana.** Less than 20 mi from downtown, TJ is still a popular day trip for "yanqui" tourists, despite a spike in gang-related crime. The trick is to stay safely on the beaten path. Instead of heading south of the border solo, sign up for a guided bus tour. You'll get the best of Baja without all the worry.

GETTING ORIENTED

San Diego's North County, encompassing the portion of San Diego County that lies north of the metro area from the ocean to the desert, has some of the same attractions of the city to the south: perpetual sunshine, great beaches, and entertainment, including the ever-growing LEGOLAND Resort complex and the San Diego Zoo's Safari Park. A visit to North County offers a chance to escape the metro area and find a little quiet in the backcountry, serious wine tasting and good eating in Temecula, several luxury resorts and golf courses, two world-class destination spas, art and historic centers, a bit of gold-rush era history, and a more laid-back lifestyle.

15

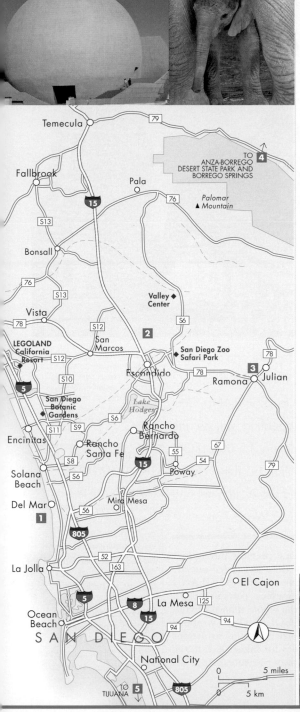

Temecula — 79
TO
ANZA-BORREGO
DESERT STATE PARK AND
BORREGO SPRINGS — **4**
Fallbrook
Pala
76
Palomar
▲ Mountain
15
S13
Bonsall
76
S13
Valley ◆
Center
Vista
S12
S6
78
2
LEGOLAND
California
Resort
San
Marcos
San Diego Zoo
◆ Safari Park
78
S12
S10
Escondido
78
3
Julian
5
Ramona
San Diego
Botanic
Gardens
Lake
Hodges
S11
S9
S6
Rancho
Bernardo
Encinitas
Rancho
Santa Fe
55
67
S8
15
54
79
Solana
Beach
S6
Poway
Del Mar
Mira Mesa
1
56
805
52
163
La Jolla
El Cajon
125
8
La Mesa
15
Ocean
Beach
94
94
S A N   D I E G O
National City
TO
TIJUANA **5**
805
0 ——— 5 miles
0 ——— 5 km

LEGOLAND CALIFORNIA RESORT

What opened more than a decade ago as a 128-acre theme park based on the popular LEGO bricks has now evolved into LEGOLAND California Resort with three appealing venues: the original LEGOLAND containing 15,000 LEGO models crafted from 35 million brightly colored bricks, the shark-infested Sea Life Aquarium, and the splash-around LEGOLAND Water Park.

(above) A builder puts the finishing touches on Miniland's San Francisco model. (lower right) The model of New York City includes the new Freedom Tower, which has yet to be built. (upper right) LEGOLAND entrance.

The LEGO-building-block theme prevails throughout the three venues. However, SeaLife is located outside the main gates, and both SeaLife and the LEGOLAND Water Park have separate entrance fees. You can spend a day visiting all three or spend the whole time at LEGOLAND. The attractions at LEGOLAND are wrapped around a lagoon with toddler-size rides and attractions to the left as you enter and rides for bigger kids to the right. Kids of any age love the water features.

SERVICE INFORMATION

✉ *1 LEGOLAND Dr. Exit I–5 at Cannon Rd. and follow signs east ¼ mi*
☎ *760/918-5346*
⊕ *www.legolandca.com*
🎫 *$69 adults, $59 kids; SeaLife $20 adults, $13 kids; Water Park $12; 1-day Hopper $89 adults, $79 kids; 2-day Hopper $10 more; additional fees for some rides, parking $12, $15 for campers/RVs*
☾ *Closed Tues.–Wed., call for information.*

THE BEST OF LEGOLAND RESORT

Most LEGOLAND attractions appeal to specific age groups. Plan to organize your visit around the attractions that will most appeal to the kids you have in tow. If you have very small kids, expect to spend a lot of time in **Fun Town** and exploring **Castle Hill,** where they can drive miniature cars and joust astride mechanical horses, respectively. Kids may want to take the same ride over and over again; allow time for it, especially if there are long lines. Water features at **Pirate Shores** and rides in the **Land of Adventure** appeal to all ages; kids need to meet height requirements (generally 34"–36") in both areas.

School-age kids enjoy the Fun Town rides such as the free-fall sense they get on the **Kid Power Towers,** learning to drive at **Driving School,** and navigating the waterway at the **Skipper School.** The closest thing to a thrill ride is the **Knight's Tournament,** a robo-coaster that twists and turns upside down over a pond at **Castle Hill.**

LEGOLAND'S centerpiece, **Miniland USA** may amaze adults more than the kids with its animated depictions of New York, Washington, D.C., New Orleans, and the California coastline constructed from 24 million LEGO blocks.

Sea Life Aquarium (requires a separate ticket), opened in 2008, offers a quiet educational diversion from the theme park. You can spend a couple of hours walking through the displays that include an underwater acrylic tunnel through a 200,000 gallon tank with sharks, stingrays, and tropical fish. You'll also get eyeball to eyeball with rays, eels, a giant Pacific octopus, and seahorses. The animals are most active during feeding time, check the Web site for feeding schedule.

LEGOLAND Water Park (requires a separate ticket), opened in 2010, may be the place to go on a hot summer day to splash down waterslides, build a LEGO raft, cruise down a lazy river, get soaked under a splash tower, and even go wading at a sandy beach.

TIPS

■ Bring swimsuits—you'll get wet at **Pirate Shores,** riding the **Bionicle** or **Aquazone,** and at the **Water Works.** Lockers are at the entrance and at Pirate Shores.

■ Little kids up to 10 or 12 years love LEGOLAND, but your older children will probably find it a bit juvenile or may want to spend the whole time in the Water Park.

■ The best ticket value is one of the **Hopper tickets** that give you one admission to LEGOLAND plus Sea Life and the Water Park.

■ Crowds are much lighter midweek.

■ The **Model Mom Care Center** is a comfortable nook to feed and change your baby. It holds a rocking chair, refrigerator, and changing station.

■ Be sure to try Granny's Apple Fries, Castle Burgers, and Pizza Mania for pizzas and salads. The Market near the entrance has excellent coffee, fresh fruit, and yogurt.

15

SAN DIEGO ZOO SAFARI PARK

The San Diego Zoo Safari Park, an 1,800-acre preserve set in the hills outside Escondido, offers a fabulous peek into the lives of wild animals largely unconfined and free to move about as they would in their native habitat.

(above) An African rhinoceros greets a guest at the Safari Park. (lower right) A giraffe is on view for the Journey Into Africa tour. (upper right) Campers at the Roar and Snore Sleepover.

Originally created to protect and breed endangered animals in the 1970s, the Safari Park has become a living laboratory of species protection and recovery. A visit to the preserve will show you how the animals live in natural surroundings, interact with other species, give birth, and raise their young. More than 3,500 animals of more than 400 species roam or fly above the expansive grounds. The park is a part of the San Diego Zoo, but quite apart from it in many ways. Located in the San Pasqual Valley 35 mi north of the zoo, it has expansive enclosures where animals can roam and a large collection of botanical gardens. The park is dedicated to conservation and has operated a very successful breeding program that is bringing back many endangered species.

SERVICE INFORMATION

✉ *15500 San Pasqual Valley Rd. Take I-15 north to Via Rancho Pkwy. and follow signs, 6 mi* ☎ *760/747-8702* ⊕ *www.sdzsafaripark.org* ☟ *$40 includes Journey into Africa tour and Conservation Carousel; $76 two-visit pass includes a 1-day pass to the zoo and safari park or two 1-day passes to either; parking $10* ☉ *Daily 9–dusk, later in summer (call ahead for closing time)* ⊟ *D, MC, V.*

THE BEST OF SAN DIEGO ZOO SAFARI PARK

The best way to see these preserves is to take the 45-minute, **Journey into Africa** bus tour. As you pass in front of the large, naturally landscaped enclosures, you can see animals bounding across prairies and mesas as they would in the wild. Predators are separated from prey by deep moats, but only the elephants, tigers, lions, and cheetahs are kept in isolation. Photographers with zoom lenses can get spectacular shots of zebras, gazelles, and rhinos. In summer, when the park stays open late, the trip is especially enjoyable in the early evening, when the heat has subsided and the animals are active and feeding. When the bus travels through the park after dark, sodium-vapor lamps illuminate the active animals.

At the heart of the park, **Nairobi Village** holds things to see and do. Animals in the **Petting Kraal** here affectionately tolerate tugs and pats and are quite adept at posing for pictures with toddlers. At the **Congo River Village** 10,000 gallons of water pour each minute over a huge waterfall into a large lagoon.

Hidden Jungle, an 8,800-square-foot greenhouse, is a habitat for creatures that creep, flutter, or just hang out in the tropics. Gigantic cockroaches and bird-eating spiders share the turf with colorful butterflies and hummingbirds and oh-so-slow-moving two-toed sloths.

Lorikeet Landing, simulating the Australian rain forest, holds 75 of the loud and colorful small parrots—you can buy a cup of nectar at the aviary entrance to induce them to land on your hand.

The **Lion Camp** gives you a close-up view of the king of beasts in a slice of African wilderness. As you walk through this exhibit, you can watch the giant cats lounging around through a 40-foot-long window. The last stop is a research station where you can see them all around you through glass panels.

TIPS

■ Kids can feed animals at the **Petting Kraal,** check out the baby animals at the **Animal Care Center,** and ride the **Conservation Carousel**.

■ Take the **Savanna Safari** ($40) guided tour for the best value. You can also soar above it all on the **Flightline** zip line ($70) or scoot around on a **Segway Safari** ($80).

■ Stroll the 2-mi **Kilimanjaro Safari Walk** into the **Heart of Africa.** Along the way you'll pass lowland gorillas, the Lion Camp, cheetahs, and the elephant overlook.

■ Find the best views at Baja Garden, Elephant Overlook, Great Rift Lift Deck, and Kilmia Point.

■ Rental camcorders, strollers, and wheelchairs are available. Serious shutterbugs might consider joining one of the special **Photo Caravan** tours ($90–$150).

■ You can stay overnight in the park in summer on a **Roar and Snore Sleepover** (adults $140–$220, kids 8–11 $120–$160).

15

SPAS SAN DIEGO STYLE

Personal pampering rules at San Diego area spas. San Diego can claim one of the largest concentrations of destination spas in the United States as well as many elegant resort spas.

(above) La Costa Resort's Spanish colonial style is chic yet inviting. (lower right) The beautiful Mediterranean garden pool at La Costa Resort. (upper right) Couples' massage room at Devine spa.

At destination spas, a treatment program including meals, exercise classes, and recreation is developed especially for you based on your needs. Prices are steep, but the stay is all-inclusive except for tax and tips. Check spa Web sites for reduced rate weeks. Before you visit a destination spa, you'll fill out a form about your health and fitness levels and goals. Meals are healthy and delicious and cater to your weight goals. You also receive a spa wardrobe to wear during your stay.

Resort spas are adjunct to other resort facilities. Many resorts have special treatment facilities for couples; they also typically offer elegant lounges, fitness facilities, and locker rooms. Resort spas are open to nonguests, but reservations are essential. Spa customers can sometimes use other facilities such as the restaurant, pool, or gym. Each spa has its own personality and signature treatments, so look for the one that best suits your needs and budget.

SPA KNOW-HOW

Tipping: If you're unsure of the spa's policy on gratuities, ask. The total of your tips should add up to between 15% and 20% of the total cost of your treatment.

Chilling: You can have a glass of your favorite wine or a cocktail while being rubbed and scrubbed at most resorts.

Modesty: Some resort spas have coed lounges, so be sure to don your robe.

DESTINATION SPAS

Celebrities like Julia Roberts and Oprah Winfrey have stayed at **Cal-a-Vie,** and so can you. **Signature experience:** The yin/yang of romping through the hillsides and then cooling off in your antiques-filled villa and being rubbed and wrapped. **Price:** $8,095 to $8,595 per week, $5,595 for four days, and $4,195 for three days. Upgrade to one of seven recently added suites for an additional fee. ⊠ *29402 Spa Havens Way, Vista* ☎ *760/945-2055 or 866/772-4283* ⊕ *www.cal-a-vie.com.*

Considered by many to be the world's best destination spa, the venerable **Golden Door** occupies a serene canyon. **Signature experience:** The serenity of your surroundings will awaken your soul. Explore it from your Honjin inn–inspired room where you have a traditional private shrine, secluded garden, and deck. **Price:** $7,495–$7,750 per week, $4,725 for four days, and $3,625 for three days. Check the website for special Gold Saver Weeks, offering discounted rates. ⊠ *777 Deer Springs Rd., San Marcos* ☎ *760/744-5777 or 800/424-0777* ⊕ *www.goldendoor.com.*

RESORT SPAS

Bring your swimsuit to **La Costa Resort and Spa**. Join friends in the picture-perfect Mediterranean garden where you can swim, sun, and shower. **Signature experience:** The shoulder-pounding Roman water massage. **Price:** Body treatments $155–$310; ayurvedic treatment at the Chopra Center $205–$395; day spa $325–$455. ⊠ *2100 Costa Del Mar Rd., Carlsbad* ☎ *800/854-5000* ⊕ *www.lacosta.com.*

Devine spa beckons couples to retreat at **Rancho Valencia Resort** for relaxation, romance, and renewal. **Signature experience:** Bergamont Bliss couple's treatment—take a plunge in the secluded pool, polish your partner with a bergamont sea salt scrub, then relax with a citrus massage. **Price:** Body treatments $150–$290; spa fusion $210–$450; couples $380–$650; day spa $795. ⊠ *5921 Rancho Valencia Sr., Rancho Santa Fe* ☎ *858/759-6490* ⊕ *www.ranchovalencia.com.*

SPA GLOSSARY

Ayurveda: Refers to Indian techniques including massage, oils, herbs, and diet to encourage perfect body balance.

Hot stone massage: A massage that employs hot smooth stones either rested on the body on applied to the skin with pressure.

Reflexology: Massage on the pressure points of feet, hands, and ears.

Shiatsu: Japanese massage applied with fingers, elbows, feet, and hands.

Swedish massage: A technique that relaxes muscles through stroking, kneading, and tapping.

Swiss shower: A multijet bath that alternates hot and cold water, frequently used after body treatments and mud wraps.

Vichy shower: A body treatment in which a person lies on a cushioned waterproof mat and is showered by overhead jets.

Watsu: A treatment conducted in a warm pool involving gentle massage and stretches.

15

Updated by
Bobbi Zane

A whole world of scenic grandeur, fascinating history, and scientific wonder lies just beyond San Diego's city limits. If you travel north along the coast, you'll encounter the great beaches for which the region is famous, along with some sophisticated towns holding fine restaurants, great galleries, and museums.

Learn about sea creatures and the history of music in Carlsbad, home of LEGOLAND and Sea Life Aquarium. If you travel east, you'll find fresh art hubs in Escondido, home of the San Diego Zoo Safari Park, a pair of world-class destination spas, a selection of challenging golf courses, and nightlife in bucolic settings. Inspiring mountain scenery plus beautiful places to picnic and hike can be found in the Cuyamaca Mountains, the historic gold-rush-era town of Julian (now known far and wide for its apple pies), and Palomar Mountain. The vast wilderness of the Anza-Borrego Desert holds a repository of ancient fossils like no other, and is also home to one of the most colorful displays of native spring flowers. Just beyond the county limits in Temecula you can savor Southern California's only developed wine country, where more than three dozen wineries offer tastings and tours.

NORTH COUNTY AND ENVIRONS PLANNER

GETTING HERE AND AROUND
BUS AND TRAIN TRAVEL
The Metropolitan Transit System covers the city of San Diego up to Del Mar.

Buses and trains operated by North County Transit District serve all coastal communities in San Diego County, going as far east as Escondido. Routes are coordinated with other transit agencies serving San Diego County. Amtrak stops in Solana Beach and Oceanside.

Coaster operates commuter rail service between San Diego and Oceanside, stopping in Old Town, Sorrento Valley, Solana Beach, Encinitas, and Carlsbad en route. The last Coaster train leaves San Diego at about

7 each night. The North County Transit District Sprinter runs a commuter service between Oceanside and Escondido.

Bus and Train Contacts Metropolitan Transit System (☏ *619/233–3004* ⊕ *www.sdcommute.com*). **North County Transit District** (☏ *619/233–3004* ⊕ *www.sdcommute.com*). **Amtrak** (☏ *760/722–4622 in Oceanside; 800/872–7245* ⊕ *www.amtrakcalifornia.com*). **Coaster** (☏ *800/262–7837* ⊕ *www.sdcommute.com*).

CAR TRAVEL

Interstate 5 is the main freeway artery connecting San Diego to Los Angeles, passing just east of the beach cities from Oceanside south to Del Mar. Running parallel west of I–5 is Route S21, also known and sometimes indicated as Highway 101, Old Highway 101, or Coast Highway 101, which never strays too far from the ocean. An alternate, especially from Orange and Riverside counties, is I–15, the inland route through Temecula, Escondido, and eastern San Diego.

A loop drive beginning and ending in San Diego is a good way to explore the backcountry and Julian area. You can take the S1, the Sunrise National Scenic Byway (sometimes icy in winter) from I–8 to Route 79 and return through Cuyamaca Rancho State Park (also icy in winter). If you're only going to Julian (a 75-minute trip from San Diego in light traffic), take either the Sunrise Byway or Route 79, and return to San Diego via Route 78 past Santa Ysabel to Ramona and Route 67; from here I–8 heads west to downtown.

Escondido sits at the intersection of Route 78, which heads east from Oceanside, and I–15, the inland freeway connecting San Diego to Riverside, which is 30 minutes north of Escondido. Route 76, which connects with I–15 north of Escondido, veers east to Palomar Mountain. Interstate 15 continues north to Fallbrook and Temecula.

To reach the desert from downtown San Diego, take I–8 east to Highway 79 north, to Highway 78 east, to Routes S2 and S22 east.

RESTAURANTS

Dining in the North County tends to reflect the land where the restaurant is located. Along the coast, for example, you'll find one luxury fine-dining spot after another. Most have dramatic water views and offer platters of exquisite fare created by graduates of the best culinary schools. Right next door you can wander into a typical beach shack or diner for the best hamburger you've ever tasted. You'll find locally sourced food at restaurants throughout the area, although a few chefs have adopted molecular gastronomic techniques. Backcountry cuisine is generally served in huge portions and tends toward home cooking, steak and potatoes, burgers, and anything fried.

HOTELS

Like the restaurants, hotels in the North County reflect the geography and attractions where they are set. There are a number of luxury resorts that offer golf, tennis, entertainment, and classy service. For those who want the ultimate pampered vacation, the North County holds two world-class spas: Cal-a-Vie and the Golden Door. Along the beach, there are quite a few stand-alone lodgings that attract the beach crowd;

15

they may lack in appeal and service but charge a big price in summer. Lodgings in the Carlsbad area are very family-friendly, some with their own water parks. In Temecula, some of the best and most delightful lodgings are tied to wineries; they offer a whole experience: accommodations, spa, dining, and wine. One-of-a-kind bed-and-breakfasts are the rule in the Julian area.

WHAT IT COSTS					
	¢	$	$$	$$$	$$$$
Restaurants	under $10	$10–$17	$18–$27	$28–$35	over $35
Hotels	under $90	$90–$160	$161–$230	$231–$300	over $300

Restaurant prices are for a main course at dinner, excluding 8.75% tax. Hotel prices are for a standard double room in high (summer) season, excluding 9% to 10.5% tax.

VISITOR INFORMATION
San Diego Convention and Visitors Bureau (☎ 800/848–3336 ⊕ www. sandiego.org).

NORTH COAST: DEL MAR TO OCEANSIDE

Once upon a time, to say that the North Coast of San Diego County was different from the city of San Diego would have been an understatement. From the northern tip of La Jolla up to Oceanside, a half dozen small communities developed separately from urban San Diego—and from one another. Del Mar, because of its 2½ mi of wide beaches, splendid views, and Thoroughbred horse-racing complex, was the playground of the rich and famous. Up the road, agriculture played a major role in the development of Solana Beach and Encinitas.

Carlsbad, too, rooted in the old Mexican rancheros, has agriculture in its past, as well as the entrepreneurial instinct of a late-19th-century resident, John Frazier, who promoted the area's water as a cure for common ailments and constructed a replica of a European mineral-springs resort. Oceanside was a beachside getaway for inland families in the 19th century; its economic fortunes changed considerably with the construction of Camp Pendleton as a Marine Corps training base during World War II. Marines still train at the huge base today.

What these towns shared was at least a half-century's worth of Southern California beach culture—think Woodies (wood-bodied cars), surfing, the Beach Boys, alternate lifestyles—and the road that connected them. That was U.S. Highway 101, which nearly passed into oblivion when I–5 was extended from Los Angeles to the Mexican border.

Then began an explosion of development in the 1980s, and the coast north of San Diego has come to resemble a suburban extension of the city itself. Once-lovely hillsides and canyons have been bulldozed and leveled to make room for bedroom communities in Oceanside, Carlsbad, and even such high-price areas as Rancho Santa Fe and La Jolla.

If you venture off the freeway and head for the ocean, you'll discover remnants of the old beach culture surviving in the sophisticated towns of Del Mar, Solana Beach, Cardiff-by-the-Sea, Encinitas, Leucadia, Carlsbad, and Oceanside, where the arts, fine dining, and elegant lodgings also now rule. As suburbanization continues, the towns are reinventing themselves—Carlsbad, for instance, is morphing from a farming community into a tourist destination with LEGOLAND California, several museums, and an upscale outlet shopping complex. Oceanside, home of one of the longest wooden piers on the West Coast (its first pier was built in the 1880s), promotes its beach culture with a yacht harbor, and beachside resort hotel construction is underway.

DEL MAR

23 mi north of downtown San Diego on I–5, 9 mi north of La Jolla on Rte. S21.

Del Mar comprises two sections: the small historic village adjacent to the beach west of I–5 and a growing business center surrounded by multimillion-dollar tract housing east of the freeway. Tiny Del Mar village, the smallest incorporated city in San Diego County, holds a population of 4,500 tucked into a 2.1-square-mi beachfront. It's known for its quaint half-timbered Tudor-style architecture, 2 mi of accessible beaches, and the Del Mar racetrack and San Diego County Fairgrounds complex. The village attracted rich and famous visitors from the beginning; they still come for seclusion and to watch the horses run. Its new face is the Del Mar Gateway business complex with high-rise hotels and fast-food outlets east of the interstate at the entrance to Carmel Valley. Both Del Mars, old and new, hold expensive homes belonging to staff and scientists who work in the biotech industry and at UC San Diego in adjacent La Jolla. Access to Del Mar's beaches is from the streets that run east–west off Coast Boulevard; access to the business complex is via Highway 56.

TOUR OPTIONS

Civic Helicopters gives whirlybird tours of the area along the beaches. The cost varies according to the model of helicopter and the number of passengers so call for pricing. Biplane, Air Combat and Warbird Adventures conducts excursions aboard restored 1920s-vintage open-cockpit biplanes and military-style Top Dog air combat flights on prop-driven Varga VG-21s. Flights are from Montgomery Field and start at $199 per couple for 20 minutes.

Tour Contacts Biplane, Air Combat and Warbird Adventures (☎ 760/438–7680 or 800/759–5667 ⊕ www.barnstorming.com). **Civic Helicopters** (☎ 760/438–8424 ⊕ www.civichelicopters.com).

EXPLORING

Del Mar Fairgrounds. The Spanish Mission–style fairground is the home of the **Del Mar Thoroughbred Club** (☎ 858/755–1141 ⊕ *www.dmtc. com*). Crooner Bing Crosby and his Hollywood buddies—Pat O'Brien, Gary Cooper, and Oliver Hardy, among others—organized the club in the 1930s, primarily because Crosby wanted a track near his Rancho Santa Fe home. Even now the racing season here (usually July–September, Wednesday–Monday, post time 2 pm) is one of the most fashionable

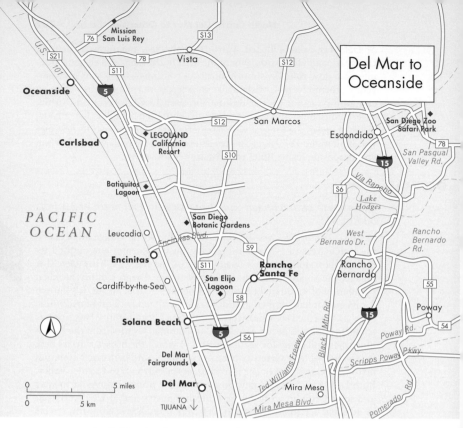

in California. If you're new to horse racing, stop by the Plaza de Mexico where you'll find staff who can explain how to place a bet on a horse. The track also hosts free Four O'Clock Friday concerts following the races. Del Mar Fairgrounds hosts more than 100 different events each year, including the Del Mar Fair (San Diego County), which draws more than a million visitors annually, plus a number of horse shows. ⊠ *2260 Jimmy Durante Blvd.* ☎ *858/793–5555* ⊕ *www.sdfair.com.*

Del Mar Plaza. Along with its collection of shops, the plaza contains outstanding restaurants and landscaped plazas and gardens with Pacific views. The shops and restaurants are pricey, but the view—best enjoyed from the upper-level benches and chairs—is free. ⊠ *1555 Camino del Mar* ⊕ *www.delmarplaza.com.*

🕑 **Freeflight.** This small exotic-bird training aviary adjacent to the Del Mar Fairgrounds is open to the public. You're allowed to handle the birds—a guaranteed child pleaser. ⊠ *2132 Jimmy Durante Blvd.* ☎ *858/481–3148* ⊠ *$5* ☉ *Thurs.–Tues. 10–4, Wed. 10–2.*

Seagrove Park. Summer evening concerts take place at the west end of this small stretch of grass overlooking the ocean. ⊠ *15th St.*

WHERE TO EAT

$$$$
FRENCH
Fodor's Choice
★

✕ Addison. Sophisticated and stylish, Addison challenges many ideas about what fine dining is all about. The dining room and adjacent bar feel Italian and clubby, with intricately carved dark-wood motifs, heavy arches, and marble and wood floors. The tables, by contrast, are pure white adorned with a single flower. William Bradley, one of San Diego's most acclaimed rising star chefs, serves up explosive flavors in his four-course prix-fixe dinners, such as Prince Edward Island mussels with champagne sabayon and lemon verbena jus or foie gras de canard with Le Puy lentils, port wine, and smoked bacon mousse. Entrées include spring lamb *persille* (parsely and garlic topping) with pistachio pâté brisée and caramelized garlic puree or perfectly cooked wild Scottish salmon with sauce *vin jaune* (white wine from the Jura region of France), roasted eggplant stick, and pine nuts. Acclaimed for its extensive wine collection, Addison challenges vino lovers with a 160-page wine list. ✉ *5200 Grand Del Mar Way* ☎ *858/314–1900* ⊕ *www.addisondelmar.com* ⌖ *Reservations essential* ☽ *Closed Sun. and Mon. No lunch.*

> **DID YOU KNOW?**
>
> San Diego County consists of 18 incorporated cities and several unincorporated communities, and is about the same size as the state of Connecticut.

$
AMERICAN

✕ Elijah's Delicatessen. San Diegans are known to complain about the scarcity of decent, East Coast–type delicatessens. Well, this comfortable, no-frills establishment, tucked into a corner of a shopping center, fits the bill. The vast menu extends to all the Jewish deli classics, including blintzes, chopped liver, smoked fish platters, skyscraping sandwiches, and baked beef brisket with potato pancakes. As a plus—this is Del Mar, after all—you can be served on a pleasant outdoor terrace. ✉ *2638 Del Mar Heights Rd.* ☎ *858/259–4880* ⊕ *www.elijahsrestaurant.com.*

$
VIETNAMESE

✕ Le Bambou. Small, carefully decorated, and more elegant than any Vietnamese restaurant in San Diego proper, Le Bambou snuggles into the corner of a neighborhood shopping center and is easy to overlook. Those in the know, however, seek it out for authoritative versions of such classics as ground shrimp grilled on sugarcane; Imperial rolls generously stuffed with shrimp and noodles; and make-your-own meat wraps at the table. ✉ *2634 Del Mar Heights Rd.* ☎ *858/259–8138* ☽ *Closed Mon. No lunch weekends.*

$$$
AMERICAN
Fodor's Choice
★

✕ Market Restaurant + Bar. Carl Schroeder—one of San Diego's hottest young chefs—makes his debut with a restaurant that combines casual mod decor with creative and fun New California fare. The menu changes regularly depending upon what's fresh. The well-heeled foodie crowd digs Schroeder's seasonally inspired dishes that have a playful spirit, whether it's a blue cheese soufflé with seasonal fruit, a Maine lobster salad with mango, or a local black cod with soba noodles. A well-edited wine list offers food-friendly wines by the best and brightest young winemakers around the world. Desserts are exquisite, such as the lemon soufflé tart with buttermilk ice cream or the milk chocolate panna cotta with espresso caramel. ✉ *3702 Via de la Valle* ☎ *858/523–0007* ⊕ *www.marketdelmar.com* ☽ *No lunch.*

15

$$$ ✕ **Pacifica Del Mar.** The view of the shimmering Pacific from this lovely
SEAFOOD restaurant perched atop Del Mar Plaza is one of the best along the
★ coast, and complements the simply prepared, beautifully presented sea-
food. The highly innovative menu is frequently rewritten to show off
such creations as barbecue sugar-spice salmon with mustard sauce, and
mustard catfish with Yukon Gold potato–corn succotash. The crowd
ranges from young hipsters at the bar to well-dressed businesspeople
on the outdoor terrace overlooking the surf where glass screens block
any hint of a chilly breeze. ✉ *Del Mar Plaza, 1555 Camino del Mar*
☎ *858/792–0476* ⊕ *www.pacificadelmar.com.*

WHERE TO STAY
For expanded hotel reviews, visit Fodors.com.

$$$$ ⊞ **Grand Del Mar.** Mind-blowing indulgence in serene surroundings
Fodor'sChoice sets the Grand Del Mar apart from any other luxury hotel in the San
★ Diego area. **Pros:** ultimate luxury; secluded, on-site golf course. **Cons:**
service can be slow; hotel is not on the beach. ✉ *5200 Grand Del Mar
Ct.* ☎ *858/314–2000 or 888/314–2030* ⊕ *www.thegranddelmar.com*
⤵ *218 rooms, 31 suites* ⚲ *In-room: safe, Internet, Wi-Fi. In-hotel: 6
restaurants, bars, golf course, pools, tennis courts, gym, spa, children's
programs, business center, parking, some pets allowed.*

$$$$ ⊞ **L'Auberge Del Mar Resort and Spa.** A boutique hotel occupying a cov-
★ eted corner in Del Mar, L'Auberge is just steps from restaurants, shop-
ping, and the beach. **Pros:** sunset views from the Waterfall Terrace;
excellent service; walk to the beach. **Cons:** even with good sound-
proofing the Amtrak train can be heard as it roars through town;
adult atmosphere; ground-level rooms surrounding the terrace are very
public. ✉ *1540 Camino del Mar* ☎ *858/259–1515 or 866/893–4389*
⊕ *www.laubergedelmar.com* ⤵ *112 rooms, 8 suites* ⚲ *In-room: safe,
Wi-Fi. In-hotel: 2 restaurants, bars, pools, tennis courts, gym, spa,
business center, parking.*

$$ ⊞ **San Diego Marriott Del Mar.** Within walking distance of AMN Health-
care, Peregrine, Fair Isaacs, and other companies in the Carmel Valley
Corporate Center, this is convenient for business travelers. **Pros:** friendly
ambience in public areas; lots of wonderful art. **Cons:** noisy in outside
public areas; rooms are on the small side. ✉ *11966 El Camino Real*
☎ *858/523–1700* ⊕ *www.marriott.com* ⤵ *281 rooms, 3 suites* ⚲ *In-
room: Internet, Wi-Fi. In-hotel: restaurant, bar, pool, gym, parking.*

SHOPPING
The tiered, Mediterranean-style **Del Mar Plaza** (✉ *1555 Camino Del
Mar* ⊕ *www.delmarplaza.com*) has flower-filled courtyards, fountains,
a spectacular view of the Pacific, and some fine restaurants. Some businesses validate parking, which is underground. **Georgiou** (☎ *858/481–
1964*) specializes in designer women's fashions.

The San Diego County Fair comes to Del Mar Fairgrounds every June to July.

SOLANA BEACH

1 mi north of Del Mar on Rte. S21, 25 mi north of downtown San Diego on I–5 to Lomas Santa Fe Dr. west.

Once-quiet Solana Beach is *the* place to look for antiques, collectibles, and contemporary fashions and artwork. The Cedros Design District, occupying four blocks south of the Amtrak station, contains shops, galleries, designers' studios, restaurants, and a popular jazz and contemporary music venue, the Belly Up Tavern. The town is known for its excellent restaurants, but most area lodging (excluding a Holiday Inn) is in adjacent Del Mar and Encinitas. Solana Beach was the first city in California to ban smoking on its beaches. Now most cities in San Diego have followed suit.

WHERE TO EAT

$

MEXICAN

✗ **Don Chuy.** Family-run and utterly charming, Don Chuy serves authentic Mexican cuisine to Southern Californians who, before dining here, may have tasted only a pale version of the real thing. The flavors are savory and convincing, and the portions sufficient to banish hunger until the following day. For something straight from the soul of Mexican home cooking, try the *nopales con chorizo y huevos*, a scramble of tender cactus leaves, crumbled spicy sausage, and eggs; this is served with piles of rice and beans as well as a warm tortilla and the palate-warming house salsa. ✉ *650 Valley Ave.* ☎ *858/794–0535* ⊕ *www. donchuymexicanrestaurant.com.*

$ ✕ **The Fish Market.** There's no ocean view at the North County branch of
SEAFOOD   downtown's waterfront restaurant, but this eatery remains popular with
🕒   residents and tourists for its simple preparations of very fresh fish and
★   shellfish from a menu that changes daily. The oyster bar here is popular.
The scene is lively, crowded, and noisy—a great place to bring the kids.
✉ *640 Via de la Valle* ☎ *858/755–2277* ⊕ *www.thefishmarket.com.*

$$ ✕ **Pacific Coast Grill.** This casual beach-town eatery offers seasonal
AMERICAN   Pacific Coast fare that reflects California's Mexican and Asian influ-
ences. Lunch in the spacious dining room or the dog-friendly sunny
patio brings excellent crispy popcorn shrimp, a Brie-stuffed burger with
port wine sauce, or perfect fried fish tacos washed down with a Gold
Margarita that sings with fresh lime and lemon juice. The funky decor
includes a dog motif hidden in the mosaic tile floor and unique objets
d'art. Evenings are a scene, as attractive beachy types sip microbrews
and well-priced wines, especially during the daily happy hour from 4 to
7 pm. Don't miss the Hawaiian barbecue glazed salmon, lobster tacos,
or the ancho chile-crusted ahi tuna with eggplant. ✉ *437 S. Hwy. 101*
☎ *858/794–4632* ⊕ *www.pacificcoastgrill.com.*

$$$$ ✕ **Pamplemousse Grille.** Justly celebrated as one of North County's best
FRENCH   restaurants, the "Grapefruit Grill," across the street from the race-
★   track, offers casual French-country dining California style. Chef-pro-
prietor Jeffrey Strauss brings a caterer's sensibilities to the details, like
a mix-or-match selection of sauces—such as wild mushroom, grain
mustard, or peppercorn—to complement the simple but absolutely
top-quality grilled meats and seafood. Appetizers can be very clever,
like the Kim Chee seafood martini. Whatever you do, save room for
dessert; you can watch the pastry chef build it for you at the demon-
stration area in the dining room. Popular sweet endings include pear
tart tatin, roasted pineapple cake, and chocolate peanut-butter bombe.
The comfortable rooms are painted with murals of bucolic country
scenes, and the service is quiet and professional. ✉ *514 Via de la Valle*
☎ *858/792–9090* ⊕ *www.pgrille.com* ⚏ *Reservations essential* ⊘ *No
lunch Sat.–Thurs.*

$ ✕ **Pizza Port.** Local families flock to the casual Port for its great pizza
PIZZA   and handcrafted brews. Pick a spot at one of the long picnic-type tables,
choose traditional or whole-grain beer crust for your pie and any origi-
nal topping—such as the Monterey, with pepperoni, onions, mush-
rooms, and artichoke hearts—and tip back a brew from one of the
longest boutique lists in San Diego. Even dessert reeks of hops: stout
floats with homemade ice cream for the over-21 set, or made with root
beer for everyone else. ✉ *135 N. Hwy. 101* ☎ *858/481–7332* ⊕ *www.
pizzaport.com* ⚏ *Reservations not accepted.*

$$$$ ✕ **Red Tracton's.** Across the street from the Del Mar racetrack, this deluxe
STEAK   old-fashioned steak and seafood house is a high-roller's heaven. Every-
one from the bar pianist to the exceptional waitresses is well aware that
smiles and prompt service can result in tips as generously sized as the
gigantic Australian lobster tails that the menu demurely lists at "market
price." Tracton's serves simple but good food, and the menu highlights
roasted prime rib in addition to prime New York sirloin, top-grade
pork back ribs, panfried scallops, and such starters as lobster bisque

and "jumbo" shrimp on ice. ☒ *550 Via de la Valle* ☏ *858/755–6600* ⊕ *www.redtractonssteakhouse.com* ⌖ *Reservations essential* ⊙ *Sun. lunch late summer only.*

NIGHTLIFE

Belly Up Tavern (☒ *143 S. Cedros Ave.* ☏ *858/481–8140* ⊕ *www.bellyup. com*), a fixture on local papers' "best of" lists, has been drawing crowds of all ages since it opened in the mid-'70s. The BUT's longevity attests to the quality of the eclectic entertainment on its stage. Within converted Quonset huts, critically acclaimed artists play everything from reggae and folk to—well, you name it.

SHOPPING

★ **Antique Warehouse** (☒ *212 S. Cedros Ave.* ☏ *858/755–5156*) holds more than 100 booths that carry American and European antiquities, art, books, glass, dolls, and jewelry.

Birdcage (☒ *143 S. Cedros Ave., Suite J* ☏ *858/793–6262*) specializes in unusual home accessories.

The **Cedros Design District** (⊕ *www.cedrosdesigndistrict.net*) is a collection of more than 85 shops that specialize in interior design and gifts.

Cool accessories such as designer beds and totes for haute dogs and cats are at **Muttropolis** (☒ *227 S. Cedros Ave.* ☏ *858/755–3647*).

Trios Gallery (☒ *404 N. Cedros Ave.* ☏ *858/793–6040*) showcases the work of local artists, including James Hubbell, plus art glass, Judaica, and designer jewelry.

15

RANCHO SANTA FE

4 mi east of Solana Beach on Rte. S8, Lomas Santa Fe Dr., 29 mi north of downtown San Diego on I–5 to Rte. S8 east.

Groves of huge, drooping eucalyptus trees cover the hills and valleys of this affluent and exclusive town east of I–5. Rancho Santa Fe and the areas surrounding it are primarily residential, where you'll see mansions at every turn in the road. It's also common to see entire families riding horses on the many trails that crisscross the hillsides.

Modeled after a Spanish village, the town was designed by Lilian Rice, one of the first women to graduate with a degree in architecture from the University of California. Her first structure, a 12-room house built in 1922, evolved into the Inn at Rancho Santa Fe, which became a gathering spot for celebrities such as Bette Davis, Errol Flynn, and Bing Crosby. The challenging Rancho Santa Fe Golf Course, the original site of the Bing Crosby Pro-Am and considered one of the best courses in Southern California, is open only to members of the Rancho Santa Fe community and guests of the inn. A wildfire ripped through this tranquil community in the fall of 2007, but thankfully most of the little village was saved.

WHERE TO EAT AND STAY

For expanded hotel reviews, visit Fodors.com.

$$$$ ✗ **Mille Fleurs.** Mille Fleurs is a winner, from its location in the heart of
FRENCH wealthy, horsey Rancho Santa Fe to the warm Gallic welcome extended

by proprietor Bertrand Hug and the talents of chef Martin Woesle. The quiet dining rooms are decorated like a French villa. Menus are written daily to reflect the market and Woesle's mood, so you'll find some interesting seasonal choices such as antelope with peppercorn-cacao sauce, chino's farm brussels sprouts, hazelnut spätzle and roasted pear. Other selections include a duck salad done three ways (confit, prosciutto, and foie gras) with endive-apple slaw and bourbon barrel–aged maple syrup dressing; or Maine lobster risotto with saffron, spring garlic, pea tendrils, Parmesan, and a light sorrel–champagne sauce. Finish the evening with a decadent dessert such as the Rancho Santa Fe Orange Delight, a blood-orange gratin served with cinnamon ice cream, candied orange peel, and chocolate–orange truffles. ☒ *Country Squire Courtyard, 6009 Paseo Delicias* ☎ *858/756–3085* ⚖ *Reservations essential* ☻ *No lunch Sat.–Mon.*

$$$ ✕ **Restaurant at Rancho Valencia.** It always feels like spring when dining
FRENCH   in the garden room at the Restaurant at Rancho Valencia. Bouquets
★   of fresh flowers are everywhere, potted plants fill nooks and crannies, and rattan furnishings complete the mood. This is a serious restaurant, however, where you're likely to dine on Baja grouper with chorizo and saffron, veal ribeye with sweetbreads, or a pork chop with brussel sprouts and sweet potato confit. And that's just dinner. The restaurant serves a selection of entrée salads and sandwiches at lunch and a full breakfast. The restaurant is refined without being stuffy; service is beyond attentive. ☒ *5921 Valencia Circle* ☎ *858/756–1123* ⊕ *www. ranchovalencia.com.*

$$$ ⌂ **Inn at Rancho Santa Fe.** Understated elegance is the theme of this genteel
★   old resort, designed in 1924 by Lilian Rice. **Pros:** historic hotel; excellent service. **Cons:** cottages spread out around grounds. ☒ *5951 Linea del Cielo* ☎ *858/756–1131 or 800/843–4661* ⊕ *www.theinnatrsf.com* ⌦ *75 rooms, 12 suites* ⚹ *In-room: safe, kitchen (some), Wi-Fi. In-hotel: restaurant, bar, pool, tennis court, gym, spa, business center, parking.*

$$$$ ⌂ **Rancho Valencia Resort and Spa.** One of Southern California's hid-
Fodor'sChoice   den treasures has luxurious accommodations in Spanish-style casitas
★   scattered on 40 acres of landscaped grounds. **Pros:** gorgeous surroundings; impeccable service; large rooms. **Cons:** secluded; expensive. ☒ *5921 Valencia Circle* ✉ *Box 9126, Rancho Santa Fe 92067* ☎ *858/756–1123 or 800/548–3664* ⊕ *www.ranchovalencia.com* ⌦ *49 suites* ⚹ *In-room: safe, Wi-Fi. In-hotel: restaurant, bar, pools, tennis courts, gym, spa, parking.*

SHOPPING

Country Friends (☒ *6030 El Tordo* ☎ *858/756–1192*) is a great place for unusual gifts. Operated by a nonprofit foundation, it carries collectibles, silver, and antiques donated or consigned by the community's residents.

The **Vegetable Shop** (☒ *6123 Calzada del Bosque* ☎ *858/756–3184*) is the place to buy the same premium (and very expensive) fruits and rare baby vegetables that the Chino Family Farm grows for many of San Diego's upscale restaurants, and for such famed California eateries as Chez Panisse in Berkeley and Spago in Los Angeles.

ENCINITAS

6 mi north of Solana Beach on Rte. S21, 7 mi west of Rancho Santa Fe on Rte. S9, 28 mi north of downtown San Diego on I–5.

Flower breeding and growing has been the major industry in Encinitas since the early part of the 20th century; the town now calls itself the Flower Capital of the World, thanks to the large number of nurseries operating here. The city, which encompasses the coastal towns of Cardiff-by-the-Sea and Leucadia as well as inland Olivenhain, is home to Paul Ecke Poinsettias (open only to the trade), which tamed the wild poinsettia in the 1920s and today is the largest producer and breeder of the Christmas blossom in the world. During the spring blooming season some commercial nurseries east of I–5 are open to the public. The palms and the golden domes of the Self-Realization Fellowship Retreat mark the southern entrance to downtown Encinitas.

U.S. 101—now Route S21—was the main route connecting all the beach towns between southern Orange County and San Diego before the I–5 freeway was constructed to the east of Encinitas. Local civic efforts are bringing back the historic California–U.S. 101 signs and restoring the boulevard's historic character.

GETTING HERE AND AROUND

From San Diego, head north on I–5. If you're already on the coast, drive along Route S21. You'll find lodgings, restaurants, and the beach along Route S21 (Old Highway 101) west of the freeway. The San Diego Botanic Gardens and commercial plant nurseries lie to the east of the freeway.

EXPLORING

San Diego Botanic Gardens. More than 4,000 rare, exotic, and endangered plants are on display on 35 landscaped acres. Displays include plants from Central America, Africa, Australia, the Middle East, the Mediterranean, the Himalayas, Madagascar, and more; the most diverse collection of bamboo in North America; California native plants; and subtropical fruits. The park opened the largest interactive children's garden on the West Coast in 2009. Kids can roll around in the Seeds of Wonder garden, explore a baby dinosaur forest, discover a secret garden, or play in a playhouse. An Under the Sea Garden displays rocks and succulents that uncannily mimic an underwater environment. ⊠ *230 Quail Gardens Dr.* ☎ *760/436–3036* ⊕ *www.sdbgarden. org* ☒ *$12* ☉ *Daily 9–5.*

San Elijo Lagoon Conservancy. Between Solana Beach and Encinitas, this is the most complex of the estuary systems in San Diego North County. A 7-mi network of trails surrounds the 1,000-acre park, where more than 700 species of plants, fish, and birds (many of them migratory) live. Be sure to stop by the LEED-certified gold New San Elijo Lagoon Native Centre, which debuted in early 2009. The center, open 9 to 5 daily, offers museum-quality exhibits about the region and a viewing deck overlooking the estuary. Docents offer free public walks every Saturday from 10 to 11 am. ⊠ *2710 Manchester Ave., Cardiff-by-the-Sea* ☎ *760/436–3944* ⊕ *www.sanelijo.org* ☒ *Free* ☉ *Daily dawn–dusk.*

15

Self-Realization Fellowship Retreat. Founded in 1936 as a retreat and place of worship, the retreat center also offers one of the best views along the Pacific Coast, a sweeping seascape extending north and south as far as the eye can see. Paramahansa Yogananda, author of the classic *Autobiography of a Yogi*, created two beautiful meditation gardens that are open to the public. The gardens are planted with flowering shrubs and trees and contain a series of ponds connected by miniature waterfalls populated by tropical fish. Swami's Point at the south end of the gardens is a popular surfer's break. ⊠ *215 K St.* ☏ *760/753–1811* ⊕ *www.encinitastemple.org* ✉ *Free* ⊙ *Tues.–Sat. 9–5, Sun. 11–5.*

WHERE TO EAT

¢   ✕ **Bubby's Gelato.** A hardworking French couple makes the region's best
CAFÉ gelato and sorbets in this unassuming little shop tucked away in the Lumberyard Shopping Center. Each flavor is clear and intense, with a dense creaminess. Sit on the sunny patio whiling away the afternoon as flavors of honey-lavender, green tea, or roasted banana wash over you. The rainbow of flavors ranges from chocolate-hazelnut to vanilla tinged with rose. On the lighter side, try the sunset-color apricot sorbet or the deep-red raspberry. Bubby's also serves an assortment of tasty sandwiches. ⊠ *937 S. Coast Hwy. 101* ☏ *760/436–3563* ▭ *No credit cards.*

$ ✕ **Ki's Restaurant.** Veggies with a view could be the subtitle for this
VEGETARIAN venerable Cardiff-by-the-Sea restaurant that grew from a simple juice shack. Ki's is well known for heart-healthy, locally sourced, ovo-lacto, vegetarian-friendly dishes like huevos rancheros, filling tofu scrambles, egg salad wraps, chopped salads with feta and nuts, watermelon juice, and carrot ice-ream smoothies. The menu also includes turkey wraps piled on wheat bread and dinner entrées such as pork chops with apple amaretto glaze and spicy seafood stew, all prepared with minimal fat. Get a table up top for incomparable ocean views, but be prepared for a wait, as service is rather poor. ⊠ *2591 S. Coast Hwy. 101, Cardiff -by-the-Sea* ☏ *760/436–5236.*

¢   ✕ **La Especial Norte.** Casual to the point of funkiness, this Mexican café
MEXICAN is a great hit with locals who flock here to slurp up large bowls of delicious homemade soups. Try the chicken, beans, and rice, or the Seven Seas fish soup accompanied by tortillas and a dish of cabbage salad. You can also order renditions of the standard burrito, enchilada, and taco, and premium margaritas. ⊠ *644 N. Coast Hwy. 101* ☏ *760/942–1040.*

WHERE TO STAY

For expanded hotel reviews, visit Fodors.com.

$–$$ ⊞ **Moonlight Beach Motel.** This folksy, laid-back motel just steps from the surf looks better on the outside than inside. **Pros:** within walking distance of the beach; great ocean views; public barbecues. **Cons:** plain motel; small rooms. ⊠ *233 2nd St.* ☏ *760/753–0623 or 800/323–1259* ⊕ *www.moonlightbeachmotel.com* ⤴ *24 rooms* ⚭ *In-room: kitchen. In-hotel: parking.*

¢   ⊞ **Ocean Inn Hotel.** Across from the train tracks on the main drag through the north end of Leucadia, this basic motel is apt to be somewhat noisy. **Pros:** basic motel; close to beach. **Cons:** on busy highway. ⊠ *1444 N. Coast Hwy. 101* ☏ *760/436–1988 or 800/546–1598*

⊕ *www.oceaninnhotel.com* ⇆ *50 rooms* ♿ *In-room: Wi-Fi. In-hotel: laundry facilities, parking* ⏀ *Breakfast.*

SHOPPING

Souvenir items are sold at shops along U.S. 101 and in the Lumberyard Shopping Center. Encinitas also abounds in commercial plant nurseries where you can pick up a bit of San Diego to take home.

Anderson's La Costa Nursery (⊠ *400 La Costa Ave.* ☎ *760/753–3153* ⊕ *www.andersonslacostanursery.com*) offers rare and hard-to-find orchids, bromeliads, cactus, and succulents.

Hansen's (⊠ *1105 S. Coast Hwy. 101* ☎ *800/480–4754* ⊕ *www.hansensurf.com*), one of San Diego's oldest surfboard manufacturers, is owned by Don Hansen, surfboard shaper extraordinaire, who came here from Hawaii in 1962. The store also stocks a full line of recreational clothing and casual wear.

Weideners' Gardens (⊠ *695 Normandy Rd.* ☎ *760/436–2194*) carries begonias, fuchsias, and other flowers. It's closed sporadically in fall and winter; call for hours.

15

CARLSBAD

6 mi from Encinitas on Rte. S21, 36 mi north of downtown San Diego on I–5.

Once-sleepy, Carlsbad, lying astride I–5 at the north end of a string of beach towns extending from San Diego to Oceanside, has long been popular with beachgoers and sunseekers. On a clear day in this village you can take in sweeping ocean views that stretch from La Jolla to Oceanside by walking the 2-mi-long sea walk running between the Encina power plant and Pine Street. En route, you'll find several stairways leading to the beach and quite a few benches. More recently, however, much of the attention of visitors to the area has shifted inland, east of I–5, to LEGOLAND California and other attractions in its vicinity—two of the San Diego area's most luxurious resort hotels, one of the last remaining wetlands along the Southern California coast, a discount shopping mall, golf courses, the cattle ranch built by movie star Leo Carrillo, and colorful spring-blooming Flower Fields at Carlsbad Ranch. Until the mid-20th century, when suburban development began to sprout on the hillsides, farming was the main industry in Carlsbad, with truckloads of vegetables shipped out year-round. Some agriculture remains. Area farmers develop and grow new varieties of flowers, including the ranunculus that transform a hillside into a rainbow each spring, and Carlsbad strawberries are among the sweetest you'll find in Southern California; in spring you can pick them yourself in fields on both sides of I–5.

GETTING HERE AND AROUND

LEGOLAND California Resort, off Cannon Road east of I–5, is surrounded by the Flower Fields, hotels, and the Museum of Making Music. On the west side of the freeway you'll find beach access at several points and quaint Carlsbad village shops.

ESSENTIALS

Visitor Information Carlsbad Convention and Visitors Bureau (✉ *400 Carlsbad Village Dr., Carlsbad* ☎ *760/434–6093 or 800/227–5722* ⊕ *visitcarlsbad.com*).

EXPLORING

Batiquitos Lagoon. Development has destroyed many of the lagoons and saltwater marsh wildlife habitats that used to punctuate the North County coastline, but the 610-acre lagoon has been restored to support fish and bird populations. A stroll along the 2-mi trail from the Batiquitos Lagoon Foundation Nature Center along the north shore of the lagoon reveals nesting sites of the red-winged blackbird; lagoon birds such as the great blue heron, the great egret, and the snowy egret; and life in the mud flats. This is a

quiet spot for contemplation or a picnic. Free docent tours are offered on weekends; visit the Web site or call for updated schedules. Take the Poinsettia Lane exit off I–5, go east, and turn right onto Batiquitos Drive, then right again onto Gabbiano Lane. ✉ *7380 Gabbiano La.* ☎ *760/931–0800* ⊕ *www.batiquitosfoundation.org* ☉ *Weekdays 9–12:30, weekends 9–3 (4 in summer).*

Carlsbad Mineral Water Spa. Remnants from late 1800s, including the original well dug by John Frazier and a monument to Frazier, are found here. The elaborately decorated stone building houses a small day spa and the Carlsbad Water Company, a 21st-century version of Frazier's waterworks, where the Carlsbad water is still sold. ✉ *2802 Carlsbad Blvd.* ☎ *760/434–1887* ⊕ *www.carlsbadmineralspa.com.*

☺
Fodor'sChoice
★

Flower Fields at Carlsbad Ranch. In spring the hillsides are abloom on this, the largest bulb production farm in Southern California. Here, from mid-March through mid-May, you can walk through fields planted with thousands of Giant Tecolote ranunculus—a stunning 50-acre display of color against the backdrop of the blue Pacific Ocean. Also to be seen are the rose gardens—including the miniature rose garden and the Walk of Fame garden, lined with examples of every All-American Rose Selection award-winner since 1940—and demonstration gardens created by artists who normally work with paint and easel. You can walk through a sweet-pea maze and a historical display of Paul Ecke poinsettias that were bred by the Ecke Nursery. Family activities include an open-air wagon drawn by an antique tractor ($5), LEGO Flower Garden, and kids' playground. The unusually large and well-stocked Armstrong Garden Center at the exit carries plants, garden accessories, and ranunculus

The spring blooms at the Flower Fields at Carlsbad Ranch are not to be missed.

bulbs. ✉ *5704 Paseo del Norte, east of I–5* ☎ *760/431–0352* ⊕ *www. theflowerfields.com* 🎫 *$10* 🕐 *Mar.–May, daily 9–6.*

🕐 **LEGOLAND California Resort.**

Fodor's Choice
★ ⇨ *See the highlighted listing in this chapter.*

Leo Carrillo Ranch Historic Park. This was a real working ranch with 600 head of cattle owned by actor Leo Carrillo, who played Pancho in the *Cisco Kid* television series in the 1950s. Before Carrillo bought the spread, known as Rancho de Los Kiotes, in 1937, the rancho, occupying portions of a Spanish land grant, was the home of a band of Luiseno Indians. Carrillo's hacienda and other buildings have been restored to reflect the life of the star when he hosted his Hollywood friends for long weekends in the country. Four miles of trails take visitors through colorful native gardens to the cantina, washhouse, pool and cabana, barn, and stable that Carrillo used. You can see the insides of these buildings on weekends when guided tours are offered. After Carrillo's death in 1961, the ranch remained in the family until 1979, when part of the acreage was acquired by the city for a park. ✉ *6200 Flying Leo Carrillo La.* ☎ *760/476–1042* ⊕ *www.leocarrilloranch.org* 🎫 *Free* 🕐 *Tues.–Sat. 9–5, Sun. 11–5.*

🕐 **Museum of Making Music.** Take an interactive journey through 100 years of popular music that displays more than 500 vintage instruments and samples of memorable tunes from the past century. Hands-on activities include playing a digital piano, drums, guitar, and electric violin. ✉ *5790 Armada Dr., east of I–5* ☎ *760/438—5996* ⊕ *www. museumofmakingmusic.org* 🎫 *$7* 🕐 *Tues.–Sun. 10–5.*

WHERE TO EAT

$$
AMERICAN

✕ **Bistro West.** This busy spot, part of the West Inn complex, might be called the boisterous bistro, especially if you get there during happy hour when it appears that all of Carlsbad is tipping back a few. The bistro specializes in comfort food; a huge chicken potpie tops the list that also includes meat loaf, several burger variations, pastas, and pizza. You can select from a long wine list of mostly California products at fair prices; many are available by the glass. ✉ *4960 Av. Encinas* ☎ *760/930–8008* ⊕ *www. bistrowest.com* ⌧ *Reservations essential.*

$$$
MEDITERRANEAN
Fodor'sChoice
★

✕ **BlueFire Grill.** Starting with the setting and concluding with a dinner, fire and water drama defines this signature restaurant that's part of La Costa resort complex. The centerpiece of the resort's entrance plaza, the grill holds an outdoor patio with fire pits, fountains, and a year-round floral display. Inside is a contemporary Mission-style room surrounding a green bottle glass fountain that extends the length of the main dining room. The menu features local seafood and vegetables combined in exciting ways. As a starter, try the Carlsbad mussels and Manila clams in a Riesling broth, followed by a prime flatiron steak with white truffle and lobster mac and cheese. Tantalizing desserts include luscious Carlsbad strawberries marinated in balsamic and lemon herb crème brûlée. ✉ *2100 Costa Del Mar Rd.* ☎ *760/929–6306* ⊕ *www.dinebluefire.com* ⌧ *Reservations essential* ⊙ *Closed Sun.–Tues. No lunch.*

WHERE TO STAY

For expanded hotel reviews, visit Fodors.com.

$
☾

⌂ **Carlsbad Inn Beach Resort.** Gable roofs, half-timber walls, and stone supports are among the noteworthy architectural elements at this sprawling inn and time-share condominium complex with direct access to the beach. **Pros:** walk to the beach; warm ambience. **Cons:** lots of kids; on the main drag. ✉ *3075 Carlsbad Blvd.* ☎ *760/434–7020 or 800/235–3939* ⊕ *www.carlsbadinn.com* ⌫ *54 rooms, 7 suites* ⌂ *In-room: safe, kitchen (some), Internet, Wi-Fi. In-hotel: restaurant, pool, gym, water sports, children's programs, laundry facilities, business center, parking.*

$$
☾

⌂ **Grand Pacific Palisades Resort & Hotel.** It's all about the LEGO at the Grand Pacific, where a rotating cast of LEGO creations preside over the lobby. **Pros:** close walk to LEGOLAND; gorgeous adult pool with Pacific view; kid area and pool. **Cons:** small rooms; tiny closets. ✉ *5805 Armada Dr.* ☎ *800/725–4723* ⊕ *www.grandpacificpalisades.com* ⌫ *90 rooms, 162 time-share villas* ⌂ *In-room: kitchen (some), Wi-Fi. In-hotel: pools, gym, laundry facilities, business center, parking.*

$$$$ ⊞ **La Costa Resort and Spa.** A major transformation turned the legendary
☾ '50s-style resort into a chic Spanish colonial oasis with dark wood, open-
beam ceilings, paneling, crystal chandeliers, and leather and wrought-
iron furnishings. **Pros:** huge glamorous spa; excellent kids' facilities;
popular restaurant. **Cons:** very spread out, making long walks necessary;
lots of kids. ⊠ *2100 Costa del Mar Rd.* ☎ *760/438–9111 or 800/854–*
5000 ⊕ *www.lacosta.com* ⇆ *610 rooms, 120 villas* ᴋ *In-room: safe,*
Internet, Wi-Fi. In-hotel: 6 restaurants, bars, golf courses, pools, tennis
courts, gym, spa, children's programs, business center, parking.

$ ⊞ **Pelican Cove Inn.** Two blocks from the beach and surrounded by palm
trees and mature colorful gardens with secluded nooks, this two-story
bed-and-breakfast has spacious rooms with gas fireplaces, canopied
feather beds, and private entrances. **Pros:** welcoming host; attractive
rooms. **Cons:** limited facilities; located on a side street away from downtown. ⊠ *320 Walnut Ave.* ☎ *888/735–2683* ⊕ *www.pelican-cove.com*
⇆ *10 rooms* ᴋ *In-room: no a/c, Internet, Wi-Fi. In-hotel: parking*
⑩ *Breakfast.*

$$ ⊞ **Sheraton Carlsbad Resort & Spa.** If location is everything, this Sheraton
has it two ways: you can walk right into LEGOLAND's Castle Hill
through a private back entrance directly from the hotel, or you can
walk to the Crossings at Carlsbad golf course. **Pros:** private entrance to
LEGOLAND; lovely views from many rooms. **Cons:** high noise level in
public areas. ⊠ *5480 Grand Pacific Dr.* ☎ *760/827–2400 or 800/444–*
3515 ⊕ *www.sheratoncarlsbadresort.com* ⇆ *250 rooms* ᴋ *In-room:*
safe, Internet, Wi-Fi. In-hotel: restaurant, bar, pool, tennis court, gym,
spa, business center, parking, some pets allowed.

$$ ⊞ **West Inn and Suites.** Warm and friendly defines this boutique hotel,
★ located on the west side of I–5, closer to the beaches than to LEGO-
LAND. **Pros:** family- and pet-friendly; full breakfast; organized activities. **Cons:** adjacent to railroad tracks and freeway. ⊠ *4970 Av. Encinas*
☎ *760/448–4500 or 866/431–9378* ⊕ *www.westinnandsuites.com*
⇆ *86 rooms, 36 suites* ᴋ *In-room: safe, Internet, Wi-Fi. In-hotel: 2*
restaurants, bars, pool, gym, laundry facilities, business center, parking,
some pets allowed ⑩ *Breakfast.*

SHOPPING

★ **Carlsbad Premium Outlets** (⊠ *5620 Paseo Del Norte* ☎ *760/804–9000*
or 888/790–7467 ⊕ *www.premiumoutlets.com/carlsbad*) is the only
upscale designer factory outlet in the San Diego area. Within this attrac-
tively landscaped complex you can find Salvatore Ferragamo, Le Creu-
set, and Polo Ralph Lauren. **Barney's New York** (☎ *760/929–9600*)
carries a large selection of designer women's and men's fashions. You
can find home accessories at the **Crate and Barrel Outlet** (☎ *760/692–*
2100). **Dooney & Bourke** (☎ *760/476–1049*) sells their popular handbags and accessories at discounted prices.

15

OCEANSIDE

8 mi north of Carlsbad on Rte. S21, 37 mi north of downtown San Diego on I–5.

The beach culture is alive and well in Oceanside despite redevelopment activities that are changing the face of the waterfront. Mixed-use hotels and residences are under construction to enhance the beach culture and make it more accessible. Visitors to this part of downtown Oceanside can stay within walking distance of the city's best swimming and surfing beaches: Harbor Beach, brimming with beach activities and fun, and Buccaneer Beach, where you'll find some of the best surfing in North County. Many who have been in the military link Oceanside with Camp Pendleton, the huge U.S. Marine base that lies at the north end of the city. Until recently the military was Oceanside's main industry, now being eclipsed by tourism; proximity to the base still has its benefits, as most businesspeople offer discounts to active military personnel and their families. Also home to the largest and one of the best-preserved California missions, Mission San Luis Rey, Oceanside's history extends back to the 1700s, when the Spanish friars walked along the California coast founding missions as they went. Today Oceanside celebrates its historic culture with the regionally exciting Oceanside Museum of Art, displaying the works of San Diego area artists. Residents and visitors gather weekly at the farmers' market and Sunset Market, where shopping for fresh-picked produce is a pleasant pastime.

GETTING HERE AND AROUND

The northernmost of the beach towns, Oceanside lies 8 mi north of Carlsbad via I–5; exit the freeway on Mission Avenue. If you go west you'll come to the redeveloped downtown and harbor where you'll find most of the restaurants, lodgings, and attractions. Downtown Oceanside is quite walkable from the Transportation Center, where Amtrak, the Coaster, and Sprinter stop. Buses and taxis are also available at the Transportation Center.

ESSENTIALS

Visitor Information Oceanside Welcome Center (✉ *928 N. Coast Hwy., Oceanside* ☎ *760/721–1101 or 800/350–7873* ⊕ *www.californiawelcomecenter. org* ⊙ *Daily 9–5*).

EXPLORING

TOP ATTRACTIONS

California Surf Museum. A large collection of surfing memorabilia, photos, vintage boards, apparel, and accessories are on display here. ✉ *312 Pier View Way* ☎ *760/721–6876* ⊕ *www.surfmuseum.org* ◀ *$3* ⊙ *Daily 10–4, until 8 Thurs.*

Camp Pendleton. The nation's largest amphibious military training complex encompasses 17 mi of Pacific shoreline. It's not unusual to see herds of tanks and flocks of helicopters maneuvering through the dunes and brush alongside I–5. You may also see herds of sheep keeping the bushland down and fertile fields growing next to the Pacific coastline.

Mission San Luis Rey. Known as the King of the Missions, it was built in 1798 by Franciscan friars under the direction of Father Fermin Lasuen to help educate and convert local Native Americans. Once a location for filming Disney's *Zorro* TV series, the well-preserved mission, still owned by the Franciscans, was the 18th and largest and most prosperous of California's missions. The *sala* (parlor), the kitchen, a friar's bedroom, a weaving room, and a collection of religious art convey much about early mission life. Retreats are still held here, but a picnic area, a gift shop, and a museum (which has the most extensive collection of old Spanish vestments in the United States) are also on the grounds, as are sunken gardens and the *lavanderia*, the original open-air laundry area. Tours are generally self-guided, although docent-led tours can be arranged in advance. The mission's retreat center has limited, inexpensive dormitory-style overnight accommodations. ⊠ *4050 Mission Ave.* ☎ *760/757–3651* ⊕ *www.sanluisrey.org* ⊑ *$4* ☉ *Daily 9-5.*

Fodor's Choice ★

Oceanside Pier. South of Oceanside Harbor, at 1,942 feet, this is one of the longest piers on the West Coast. The water surrounding it is known for its surf breaks and good fishing. A restaurant, Ruby's Diner, stands at the end of the wooden pier's long promenade.

15

WORTH NOTING

Helgren's Sportfishing. You can schedule daily ocean fishing trips and whale-watching coastal excursions here. ⊠ *315 Harbor Dr. S* ☎ *888/206–3241* ⊕ *www.helgrensportfishing.com.*

Oceanside Harbor. With 900 slips, this is North County's fishing, sailing, and water-sports center. There's a small dining and retail area at the north end of the harbor where you can linger and watch the boats coming and going. ⊠ *1540 Harbor Dr. N* ☎ *760/435–4000.*

Oceanside Museum of Art. Housed in side-by-side buildings designed by two Southern California modernist architects—the old City Hall designed by Irving Gill and the Central Pavilion designed by Frederick Fisher—the museum showcases works by San Diego area artists, including paintings and photography. ⊠ *704 Pier View Way* ☎ *760/435–3720* ⊕ *www.oma-online.org* ⊑ *$8* ☉ *Tues.–Sat. 10–4, Sun. 1–4.*

Wave Waterpark. A 3-acre water park run by the city of Vista, it's also one of the few places in the country with a flow-rider, a type of standing wave that allows riders on bodyboards to turn, carve, and slash almost as though they were surfing on a real wave. If you haven't learned how to do that, you can tube down the park's own river or slip down the 35-foot waterslide. ⊠ *101 Wave Dr., Vista* ☎ *760/940–9283* ⊕ *www. thewavewaterpark.com* ⊑ *$17* ☉ *Memorial Day–Labor Day, Mon.– Fri. 10–4, Weekends 12–6; Labor Day–end Sept., weekends 12–5.*

WHERE TO EAT

¢ ✕ **101 Cafe.** A diner dating back to 1928, this is both a local hangout and the headquarters of the historic Highway 101 movement. You'll find all kinds of Highway 101 memorabilia here along with breakfast, lunch, and dinner. The menu lists burgers, sandwiches, and salads for lunch, and chicken-fried steak, spaghetti, and meat loaf for dinner. ⊠ *631 S. Coast Hwy.* ☎ *760/722–5220* ⌇ *Reservations not accepted* ▭ *No credit cards.*

AMERICAN

¢–$ ✕ **Harbor Fish & Chips**. Pick up a basket of fresh-cooked fish-and-chips
SEAFOOD   at this dive and you're in for a treat. The shop has been serving the
combo—and clam chowder, shrimp cocktail, and fish sandwiches—to
boaters and visitors for more than 40 years. It looks like it, too, with fish
trophies hung on walls and from the ceiling. Outdoor tables offer terrific
views of the Oceanside Marina. ⊠ *276 S. Harbor Dr.* ☎ *760/722–4977.*

WHERE TO STAY

For expanded hotel reviews, visit Fodors.com.

$$$ ⊡ **Oceanside Marina Suites**. Of all the oceanfront lodgings in North
★   County towns, this hotel occupies the best location—a spit of land sur-
rounded by water and cool ocean breezes on all sides. **Pros:** best sunsets
in Oceanside; spacious rooms; free parking. **Cons:** marina location apt
to be busy on weekends. ⊠ *2008 Harbor Dr. N* ☎ *760/722–1561 or
800/252–2033* ⊕ *www.omihotel.com* ⟿ *6 rooms, 51 suites* ⚲ *In-room:
no a/c, kitchen, Internet, Wi-Fi. In-hotel: pool, laundry facilities, busi-
ness center, parking* ⦾ *Breakfast.*

$$ ⊡ **Wyndham Oceanside Pier Resort**. Located just steps from the beach and
Oceanside Pier, this family-friendly resort is the first of several set to
open along the Oceanside beachfront, featuring a combination of hotel
rooms and condo rentals. **Pros:** beachfront location; family-friendly.
Cons: no spa; limited hotel rooms. ⊠ *333 N. Myers* ☎ *760/901–1200*
⊕ *www.extraholidays.com* ⟿ *24 rooms, 132 suites* ⚲ *In-room: safe,
kitchen (some), Internet, Wi-Fi (some). In-hotel: 2 restaurants, bar,
pool, gym, beach, children's programs, business center, parking.*

SHOPPING

Oceanside Photo & Telescope (⊠ *918 Mission Ave.* ☎ *800/483–6287*
⊕ *www.optcorp.com*) is the place to pick up a telescope or binoculars
for viewing San Diego County's dazzling night sky. Call for information
about stargazing parties the store holds regularly in the San Diego area.

INLAND NORTH COUNTY AND TEMECULA

Long regarded as San Diego's beautiful backyard, replete with green
hills, quiet lakes, and citrus and avocado groves, inland San Diego
County and the Temecula wine country are among the fastest-growing
areas in Southern California. Subdivisions, many containing palatial
homes, now fill the hills and canyons around Escondido and Rancho
Bernardo. At the northern edge of this region, Fallbrook (longtime
self-proclaimed Avocado Capital of the World) has morphed into an
emerging arts community. Beyond Fallbrook is Temecula, the premium
wine-making area of southern Riverside County. Growth notwithstand-
ing, inland San Diego County still has such natural settings as the San
Diego Zoo Safari Park, Rancho Bernardo, and the Welk Resort. The
region is also home to a number of San Diego County's Indian casinos,
among them Pala, Harrah's Rincon, Valley View, and Pauma. Pachenga
lies just over the county line near Temecula.

RANCHO BERNARDO

23 mi northeast of downtown San Diego on I–15.

Rancho Bernardo straddles a stretch of I–15 between San Diego and Escondido and is technically a neighborhood of San Diego. Originally sheep- and cattle-grazing land, it was transformed in the early 1960s into a planned suburban community, one of the first, and a place where many wealthy retirees settled down. It's now home to a number of high-tech companies, the most notable of which is Sony. If you want to spend some time at the nearby Safari Park, this community, home of the world-class Rancho Bernardo resort, makes a convenient and comfortable headquarters for a multiday visit.

WHERE TO EAT

$$ ✕ **Bernard'O**. Intimate despite its shopping-center location, Bernard'O is
FRENCH the choice for a romantic dinner. Sit fireside in the small dining room, dine by candlelight, and savor contemporary versions of classic rack of lamb or grilled Scottish salmon with asparagus. An extensive wine list includes rare old vintages from California and France along with well-priced newer bottles. ⊠ *12457 Rancho Bernardo Rd.* ☎ *858/487–7171* ⊙ *Closed Sun. No lunch Sat.–Mon.*

$ ✕ **Chin's Szechwan Cuisine**. Locals pick Chin's for special occasions. It
CHINESE feels rich, with dark-red walls, blooming orchids everywhere, and heavy wooden furnishings. The extensive menu lists popular items such as Kung Pao chicken, sizzling beef and scallops, and tangerine crispy beef. ⊠ *15721 Bernardo Heights Pkwy.* ☎ *858/676–0166* ⊕ *www. govisitchins.com.*

$$$ ✕ **El Bizcocho**. Wealthy locals rate this restaurant at the Rancho Ber-
FRENCH nardo Inn tops for style and cuisine. Candlelit tables, plush banquettes, and quiet, live piano music make for a tranquil setting. The ever-changing menu might feature day-boat scallops prepared four ways, Hudson Valley roasted duck, and a selection of certified Angus beef. The wine list has more than 1,500 wines, including rare vintages, although the by-the-glass selection is limited. ⊠ *Rancho Bernardo Inn, 17550 Bernardo Oaks Pkwy.* ☎ *858/675–8550* ⊕ *www.ranchobernardoinn. com/bizcocho* ⚠ *Reservations essential* ⊙ *Dinner Tues.–Sat. Brunch Sun. Closed Mon.*

$$ ✕ **French Market Grille**. The Grille's flower-decked dark-wood din-
FRENCH ing room and patio with twinkling lights will help you forget that you're eating in a shopping center. The French fare changes with the seasons; typical entrées include rack of lamb, oven-roasted swordfish and lobster with vermouth, or Pacific Coast bouillabaise. If you love French desserts, save room for one of the classics offered here, apple tarte tatin, crêpes suzette, and crème brûlée. However, there have been recent complaints about slow service. ⊠ *15717 Bernardo Heights Pkwy.* ☎ *858/485–8055* ⊕ *www.frenchmarketgrille.com.*

15

WHERE TO STAY

For expanded hotel reviews, visit Fodors.com.

$$$ ⛱ **Rancho Bernardo Inn Resort and Spa.** On 265 oak-shaded acres sur-
☾ rounded by a well-established residential community, the resort's
★ two-story, red-roof adobe buildings are complemented by bougain-
villea-decked courtyards adorned with original art. **Pros:** gorgeous
flower-decked grounds; excellent service; spa. **Cons:** walking required
in spacious grounds; distance from most visitor attractions. ✉ *17550
Bernardo Oaks Dr.* ☎ *858/675–8500 or 877/517–9340* ⊕ *www.
ranchobernardoinn.com* ⤳ *287 rooms, 15 suites* ⬥ *In-room: safe,
Internet, Wi-Fi. In-hotel: 3 restaurants, bars, golf courses, pools, ten-
nis courts, gym, spa, children's programs.*

SHOPPING

A trip to **Bernardo Winery** (✉ *13330 Paseo Del Verano Norte* ☎ *858/487–
1866* ⊕ *www.bernardowinery.com*) feels like traveling back to early
California days; some of the vines on the former Spanish land-grant
property have been producing grapes for more than 100 years. The old-
est operating winery in Southern California, Bernardo was founded in
1889 and has been operated by the Rizzo family since 1928. Most of the
grapes come from other wine-growing regions. Besides the wine-tasting
room and shop selling cold-pressed olive oil and other gourmet good-
ies, restaurant Cafe Merlot serves lunch daily except Monday. About
a dozen shops offer apparel, home-decor items, and arts and crafts. If
you're lucky, the glassblowing artist will be working at the outdoor
furnace. The winery is open daily 9–5 weekdays and 10–6 weekends;
the shops are open Tuesday–Sunday 10–5.

ESCONDIDO

*8 mi north of Rancho Bernardo on I–15, 31 mi northeast of downtown
San Diego on I–15.*

Escondido and the lovely rolling hills around it were originally a land
grant bestowed by the governor of Mexico on Juan Bautista Alvarado
in 1843. The Battle of San Pasqual, a bloody milestone in California's
march to statehood, took place just east of the city. For a century and a
half, these hills supported citrus and avocado trees, plus large vineyards.
The rural character of the area began to change when the San Diego
Zoo established its Safari Park in the San Pasqual Valley east of town
in the 1970s. By the late 1990s suburban development had begun to
transform the hills into housing tracts. The California Center for the
Arts, opened in 1993, now stands as the downtown centerpiece of a
burgeoning arts community that includes a collection of art galleries
along Grand Avenue. Despite its urbanization, Escondido still supports
several pristine open-space preserves that attract nature lovers, hikers,
and mountain bikers.

ESSENTIALS

Visitor Information Escondido Chamber of Commerce (✉ *720 N. Broadway,
Escondido* ☎ *760/745–2125* ⊕ *www.escondidochamber.org*).

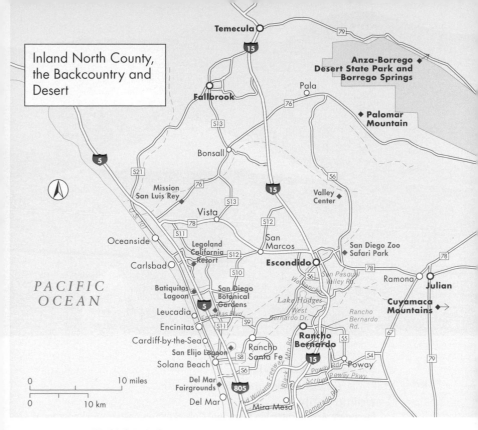

Inland North County,
the Backcountry and
Desert

Temecula

Anza-Borrego
Desert State Park and
Borrego Springs

Pala

Fallbrook

Palomar
Mountain

Bonsall

Mission
San Luis Rey

Valley
Center

Vista

Oceanside

Legoland
California
Resort

San
Marcos

Escondido

San Diego Zoo
Safari Park

Carlsbad

Ramona

Julian

PACIFIC
OCEAN

Batiquitos
Lagoon

San Diego
Botanical
Gardens

Lake Hodges

Rancho
Bernardo
Rd.

Cuyamaca
Mountains

Leucadia

West
Bernardo Dr.

Encinitas

Cardiff-by-the-Sea

San Elijo Lagoon

Rancho
Santa Fe

Rancho
Bernardo

Solana Beach

Poway

0   10 miles

0   10 km

Del Mar
Fairgrounds

Del Mar

Mira Mesa

EXPLORING
TOP ATTRACTIONS

California Center for the Arts. An entertainment complex with two theaters,
an art museum, and a conference center, the center presents operas,
musicals, plays, dance performances, and symphony and chamber-music
concerts. Performers conduct free workshops for children; check the
Web site for dates. The museum, which focuses on 20th-century art,
occasionally presents blockbuster exhibits such as the glass art of Dale
Chihuly or photos by Ansel Adams, making a side trip here worthwhile.
⊠ *340 N. Escondido Blvd.* ☎ *800/988–4253 box office; 760/839–4120*
museum ⊕ *www.artcenter.org* ⊠ *$5* ☉ *Tues.–Sat. 10–4, Sun. 1–5.*

Daley Ranch. A 3,058-acre conservation area and historic ranch site, it
holds over 20 mi of multipurpose trails for hikers, mountain bikers,
and equestrians. The 2.4-mi Boulder Loop affords sweeping views of
Escondido, and the 2.5-mi Ranch House Loop passes two small ponds,
the Daley family ranch house built in 1928, and the site of the original log cabin. Private cars are prohibited on the ranch, but a Sunday
shuttle service is provided from the parking area to the entrance. Free
naturalist-guided hikes are offered on a regular basis; call for schedule. ⊠ *3024 La Honda Dr.* ☎ *760/839–4680* ⊕ *www.ci.escondido.ca.us*
⊠ *Free* ☉ *Daily dawn–dusk.*

Enjoying the wine at Orfila Vineyards in Escondido.

⚓ **San Diego Zoo Safari Park.**

Fodor's Choice ★ ⇨ *See the highlighted listing in this chapter.*

WORTH NOTING

Escondido Arts Partnership Municipal Gallery. Showcasing works by local artists, the gallery has regular exhibitions and year-round special events. ✉ *262 E. Grand Ave.* ☎ *760/480–4101* ⊙ *Tues.–Sat. 11–4.*

Escondido History Center. The outdoor center is adjacent to the California Center for the Arts, in Grape Day Park. The museum consists of several historic buildings moved here to illustrate local development from the late 1800s, when grape growing and gold mining supported the economy. Exhibits include the 1888 Santa Fe Depot, Escondido's first library, the Bandy Blacksmith shop, a furnished 1890 Victorian house, and other 19th-century buildings. ✉ *321 N. Broadway* ☎ *760/743–8207* ⊕ *www. escondidohistory.org* 🎟 *$3 suggested donation* ⊙ *Tues.–Sat. 1–4.*

Orfila Vineyards. This vineyard offers tours and tastings of award-winning Syrah, Sangiovese, and Viognier produced from grapes harvested from the 10,000-acre vineyard. The Rose Arbor has a picnic area, and there's a gift shop with wine-related merchandise. ✉ *13455 San Pasqual Rd.* ☎ *760/738–6500* ⊕ *www.orfila.com* ⊙ *Daily 10–6, guided tours at noon.*

⚓ **Queen Califia's Magical Circle.** The last work by sculptor Niki de Saint Phalle (1930–2002), this sculpture garden consists of nine totemic figures up to 21 feet tall. Adorned with stylized monsters, animals, protective deities, geometric symbols, and crests, they evoke ancient tales and legends. Saint Phalle designed the garden for the entertainment of children, who can scramble around and on the giant fanciful figures.

✉ *Kit Carson Park, Bear Valley Pkwy. and Mary La.* ☎ *760/839–4691* ⊕ *www.queencalifia.org* ✉ *Free* ☉ *Tues.–Sun., daily 8–dusk except when raining.*

San Dieguito River Park. The park maintains several hiking and walking trails in the Escondido area. These are part of an intended 55-mi-long Coast to Crest Trail that will eventually link the San Dieguito Lagoon near Del Mar with the river's source on Volcan Mountain, north of Julian. Among the existing trails are three that circle Lake Hodges: the **North Shore Lake Hodges Trail;** the **Piedras Pintadas Trail,** which informs about native American Kumeyaay lifestyles and uses for native plants; and the **Highland Valley Trail,** the first mile of which is the Ruth Merrill Children's Walk. Three trails in **Clevenger Canyon** lead to sweeping views of the San Pasqual Valley. Visit the Web site for a list of upcoming guided hikes. ✉ *14103 Highland Valley Rd.* ☎ *858/674–2270* ⊕ *www.sdrp.org* ✉ *Free* ☉ *Daily dawn–dusk*.

OFF THE BEATEN PATH

Keys Creek Lavender Farm. In spring a visit to this organic lavender farm is worth a detour. A self-guided walking tour takes you through 6 acres planted with 28 varieties of lavender and to an area where plants are distilled into essential oils. A gift shop sells lavender products and plants. ✉ *12460 Keys Creek Rd., Valley Center* ☎ *760/742–3844 or 877/358–0444* ⊕ *www.keyscreeklavenderfarm.com* ✉ *Free* ☉ *May and June, Fri.–Sun. 10–5.*

WHERE TO EAT AND STAY

For expanded hotel reviews, visit Fodors.com.

With the exception of the Welk Resort, which is now primarily a time-share property, Escondido has little to offer in the way of accommodations.

$$$
FRENCH

✗ **Vincent's on Grand**. Here's an excellent choice for dining before attending an event at the nearby California Center for the Arts. Original paintings decorate the walls, and crisp white tablecloths cover the tables, adorned with fresh flowers. The menu changes frequently; offerings might include tournedos Merlot, sweet potato ravioli, beef Wellington, or duck à l'orange. The wine list is serious, as are the desserts. The service is friendly and attentive. ✉ *113 W. Grand Ave.* ☎ *760/745–3835* ☉ *Closed Sun. and Mon. No lunch weekends.*

$$$

🏨 **Welk Resort**. Sprawling over 600 acres of rugged, oak-studded hillside, this resort, built by bandleader Lawrence Welk in the 1960s, is now a time-share property. **Pros:** nicely appointed spacious rooms; excellent theater; popular golf course. **Cons:** located outside the city; very spread-out; rooms may not always be available due to time-share. ✉ *8860 Lawrence Welk Dr.* ☎ *760/749–3000 or 800/932–9355* ⊕ *www.welkresort.com/sandiego* ↺ *574 suites* ⚑ *In-room: kitchen, Wi-Fi. In-hotel: restaurant, bar, golf courses, pools, tennis courts, gym, laundry facilities, parking.*

SHOPPING

Although farmland began to give way to suburbs in the 1990s, and the area's fruit, nut, and vegetable bounty has diminished, you can still find overflowing farm stands in the San Pasqual Valley and in Valley Center, just east of the city. These days Escondido has begun to look to the arts to sustain its economy. The downtown streets surrounding the California Center for the Arts are getting makeovers, attracting mid- to high-end art galleries and restaurants to replace the thrift stores and diners.

🔄 **Bates Nut Farm** (✉ *15954 Woods Valley Rd., Valley Center* ☎ *760/749–3333* ⊕ *www.batesnutfarm.biz*) is the home of San Diego's largest pumpkin patch in fall, where you might find 200-pound squash. The 100-acre farm, in the Bates family for five generations, sells locally grown pecans, macadamia nuts, and almonds. There's a petting zoo holding farm animals, a picnic area, and a gift shop.

Canterbury Gardens (✉ *2402 S. Escondido Blvd.* ☎ *760/746–1400* ⊕ *www.canterburygardens.com*), occupying an old winery, specializes in giftware and seasonal decorative accessories for the home, plus a year-round selection of Christmas ornaments and collectibles by Christopher Radko, Mark Robert's Fairies, and Department 56.

FALLBROOK

19 mi northwest of Escondido on I–15 to Mission Rd., Rte. S13, to Mission Dr.

A quick 5-mi detour off I–15 between Temecula and San Diego, Fallbrook bills itself as the Avocado Capital of the World. Avocado orchards fill the surrounding hillsides, and guacamole is served in just about every eatery. You can even pig out on avocado ice cream at the annual Avocado Festival in April. But this small agricultural town is also morphing into an interesting arts center. The art and cultural center showcases the work of local and regional painters, sculptors, and fiber artists. The National Gourd and Fiber Show in June draws lovers of this art from all over Southern California. You'll find several intriguing galleries displaying antiques, jewelry, watercolors, and photography on Main Avenue. Innovative restaurants now supplement the staple fast-food joints, and the Fallbrook Winery is making a name for itself in the South Coast wine region.

EXPLORING

Blue Heron Gallery. You'll find tons of interesting stuff in this storefront gallery/antiques shop, operated by Robert Sommers, whose own photographic images are quite dramatic. Other images are from Native American collections by Edward Curtis and George Wharton James. If you're into antiques, try some of the mid-century or earlier Craftsman furnishings or pick up some antique silver. ✉ *113 N. Main Ave.* ☎ *760/731–9355.*

Brandon Gallery. This Fallbrook art institution that has been showing works of regional emerging and professional artists for more than 30 years is the place to find excellent quality watercolors, ceramics, jewelry, and baskets. It's a cooperative in which all work shown is judged and artists showing are members. ✉ *105 N. Main Ave.* ☎ *760/723–1330* ⊕ *www.fallbrookbrandongallery.org.*

Fallbrook Art Center. Housed in a typical midcentury modern building that served as the Rexall Pharmacy for 30 years, the spacious center hosts more than a dozen local and regional art shows yearly, including the annual Gourd and Fiber Fine Art Show, and also lures a number of national touring art shows, among them the National Watercolor Society Show and Reflections of Nature. The Café des Artistes, tucked into a back corner of the center, serves salads and sandwiches. ⊠ *103 S. Main St.* ☎ *760/728–1414* ⊕ *www.fallbrookartcenter.org* ⊡ *$5* ⊙ *Mon.–Sat. 10–4, Sun. noon–3; occasionally closed between shows. Café: Closed Sun. No dinner.*

Fallbrook Winery. It's worth visiting this winery, perched on a lovely hillside outside Fallbrook, where winemakers Duncan Williams and Vernon Kindred produce bottles that bring back medals from state and national competitions. They make wine from grapes grown on 36 hilly acres surrounding the winery and from other areas in California. Try the estate-bottled Rosato Sangiovese rosé, fruity sauvignon blanc reserve, or the big Syrah special selection. ⊠ *2554 Via Rancheros* ☎ *760/728–0156* ⊕ *www.fallbrookwinery.com* ⊡ *$7 tasting fee* ⊙ *Open by appointment only.*

WHERE TO EAT AND STAY

For expanded hotel reviews, visit Fodors.com.

$$–$$$
SEAFOOD
✕ **AquaTerra.** A pleasant room in the Pala Mesa Golf Resort, AquaTerra is locally popular. Most come for the seafood selections on the wide-ranging menu that lists cherry crusted salmon with saffron butter, seabass in a ginger soy marinade, and Parmesan halibut, or the expertly made items on the sushi bar menu. Tables here offer good golf-course views, and in warm weather you can dine outside on the patio. The restaurant serves breakfast, lunch, and dinner. ⊠ *2001 Old Hwy. 395* ☎ *760/728–5881* ⊕ *www.palamesa.com.*

$–$$
MEDITERRANEAN
✕ **Brothers Bistro.** Everything from sauces to breads is made in-house at this cozy bistro that's tucked into a back corner of the Major Market Shopping Center. Owner/chef Ron Nusser has a New York touch with Italian specialties such as Alla Diana Pasta, an antipasto-like Monterey seafood salad, and roasted halibut. But the most popular item on the menu is homemade lasagna, nearly a pound per serving with house-made marinara and three cheeses. Eat in the small dining room, where huge paintings adorn every wall, or on the tree-shaded patio outdoors. There's an extensive list of California wines, many available by the glass. ⊠ *835 S. Main St., Suite A* ☎ *760/731–9761* ⊕ *www. brothersbistro.net* ⊙ *No lunch weekends.*

$
MEXICAN
✕ **La Caseta.** La Caseta, or little cottage, serves up small surprises. The casual cottage with wraparound windows and colorful murals is bright and cheerful. You can dine indoors or in good weather outside on the patio. Chef Delos Eyer brings traditional Mexican fare up to date with options including grilled chicken wrap with achiote sauce and savory black beans, San Filipe fish tacos, charbroiled shrimp diablo, and meatless black bean quesadillas. Don't miss the fabulous Xango, a banana caramel cheesecake chimichanga with vanilla ice cream, and Death by Chocolate, a tower of chocolate ice cream perched on a huge chocolate walnut cookie. ⊠ *111 N. Vine St.* ☎ *760/728–9737* ⊕ *www. lacasetafinemexicanfood.com* ⊙ *Closed Sun.*

$
⊡ **Pala Casino Resort Spa.** More than most casino resorts tucked into the San Diego County backcountry, the Pala resort pampers guests with

15

lovely spacious rooms and suites, a big selection of dining options, a tranquil spa, and an enticing entertainment schedule. **Pros:** classy ambience; cabanas at pool. **Cons:** remote location; challenging drive from I–15. ⊠ *11154 Hwy. 76* ☎ *760/510–5100 or 877/725–2766* ⊕ *www.palacasino.com* ⇨ *425 rooms, 82 suites* ⚹ *In-room: safe, Internet. In-hotel: 10 restaurants, bars, gym, spa, parking.*

$$ ⛳ **Pala Mesa Golf Resort.** This friendly two-story resort, tucked into a
★   canyon right off the I–15 midway between Temecula and Escondido, offers excellent value and is popular with convention groups and golf enthusiasts. **Pros:** attractive grounds; spacious rooms; dog-friendly. **Cons:** adjacent to freeway; resort's age is showing. ⊠ *2001 Old Hwy. 395* ☎ *760/728–5881 or 800/722–4700* ⊕ *www.palamesa.com* ⇨ *133 rooms* ⚹ *In-room: Internet. In-hotel: restaurant, bar, golf course, pool, tennis courts, gym, parking, some pets allowed.*

TEMECULA

29 mi from Escondido, 60 mi from San Diego on I–15 north to Rancho California Rd. east.

Once an important stop on the Butterfield Overland Stagecoach route and a market town for the huge cattle ranches surrounding it, Temecula (pronounced teh-*mec*-yoo-la) is now a developed wine region, part of the South Coast region, which also includes some wineries in San Diego County. Known for its gently rolling hills, the region is studded with ancient oak trees and vernal pools, and with premium wineries whose winemakers are experimenting with a number of European varietals such as Roussanne, Nebbiolo, and Viognier with fragrant and flavorful results. Most of the wineries that line both sides of Rancho California Road as it snakes east from downtown offer tours and tastings (for a fee) daily and have creatively stocked boutiques, picnic facilities, and restaurants on the premises. Lately, visitors will also find that the wineries have been joined by luxury boutique lodgings. Meanwhile, local developers have created an Old Town along historic Front Street on the west side of I–15. This section is home to boutique shops, good restaurants, a children's museum, and a theater. In addition to its visitor appeal, Temecula is also a suburban bedroom community for many who work in San Diego North County.

TOUR OPTIONS

Several companies offer individual and group tours of the Temecula wine country with departures from San Diego and Temecula. Some include lunch or refreshments as part of the package.

Limousine Tours Destination Temecula (☎ *951/695–1232 or 800/584–8162* ⊕ *www.destem.com*).

Grapeline Wine Country Shuttle (☎ *951/693–5755 or 888/894-6379* ⊕ *www.gogrape.com*).

ESSENTIALS

Visitor Information Temecula Valley Visitor Center (⊠ *28690 Mercedes St., Suite A, Temecula* ☎ *951/506–0056* ⊕ *www.visittemecula.org*).

EXPLORING

Pennypickle's Workshop: Temecula Children's Museum. This is the imaginary home of Professor Phineas Pennypickle, where kids accompanied by parents enter a time machine that carries them through six rooms of interactive exhibits demonstrating perception and illusion, music making, flight and aviation, chemistry and physics, plus power and electricity. The shop stocks an array of educational toys, games, and books. ⊠ *42081 Main St.* ☎ *951/308–6370* ⊑ *$4.50* ⊙ *2-hr sessions Tues.–Sat. at 10, 12:30, and 3; Fri., also at 5:30; Sun. at 12:30 and 3.*

Old Town Temecula. Once a hangout for cowboys, Old Town has been updated and expanded while retaining its Old West appearance. A walking tour put together by the **Temecula Valley Historical Society,** starting at the Temecula Valley Museum, covers some of the old buildings; most are identified with bronze plaques.

Santa Rosa Plateau Ecological Reserve. This preserve provides a glimpse of what this countryside was like before the developers took over with trails winding through oak forests and past vernal pools and rolling grassland. A visitor and operations center has interpretive displays and maps; some of the reserve's hiking trails begin here. There are designated trails for leashed dogs, horses, and mountain bikers. Take I–15 south to Clinton Keith Road exit and head west 5 mi. ⊠ *39400 Clinton Keith Rd., Murrieta* ☎ *951/677–6951* ⊕ *www.santarosaplateau.org* ⊑ *$2* ⊙ *Daily dawn–dusk; visitor center daily 9–5.*

Temecula Valley Museum. Adjacent to Sam Hicks Monument Park, this museum focuses on Temecula Valley history, including early Native American life, Butterfield stage routes, and the ranchero period. A hands-on interactive area for children holds a general store, photographer's studio, and ride-a-pony station. Outside there's a playground and picnic area. ⊠ *28314 Mercedes St.* ☎ *951/694–6450* ⊑ *$2 suggested donation* ⊙ *Tues.–Sat. 10–4, Sun. 1–4.*

WHERE TO EAT

$$
CONTINENTAL

✕ **Baily's.** A genteel clientele and attentive service mark this fine-dining restaurant on the second floor of Baily's Old Town Dining establishment (downstairs is the Front Street Bar & Grill). Tall windows draped in red frame a town-and-country view. Contemporary cuisine leans heavily on fresh interpretations of classics such as rack of lamb, ribeye, and salmon Wellington. The menu changes frequently to take advantage of locally grown produce. The restaurant offers a four-course dining option for just $5 plus the cost of your entrée selection. There's an impressive wine list. ⊠ *28699 Old Town Front St.* ☎ *951/676–9567* ⊕ *www.oldtowndining.com* ⌅ *Reservations essential.*

$$$
ECLECTIC

✕ **Café Champagne.** The Thornton Winery's airy country restaurant, whose big windows overlook the vineyards, serves serious contemporary cuisine flavored with the winery's own products. On the seasonal menu, you may find warm Brie en croute with honey-walnut sauce, pan-roasted duck with pomegranate reduction, and smoked filet mignon in a cabernet-merlot demi-glace. ⊠ *32575 Rancho California Rd.* ☎ *951/699–0088* ⊕ *www.thorntonwine.com* ⌅ *Reservations essential.*

$
SOUTHERN

✕**Front Street Bar & Grill.** Having fun is the rule here, where you can dine in a big indoor room or outside on a quiet patio. The easy-on-the-budget menu lists eight gourmet burgers, chipotle-braised barbecued ribs, chili-stuffed chicken, and jambalaya. You can also nosh on Irish nachos and jalapeno calamari tempura. This can be a noisy place as there's entertainment weekend nights. ✉ *28699 Old Town Front St.* ☎ *951/676–9567* ⊕ *www.oldtowndining.com* ⚠ *Reservations not accepted.*

$$$
CONTINENTAL
☼

✕**Vineyard Rose.** Big and barnlike, the Vineyard Rose is a good choice for Mediterranean-style family dining, one that will give the kids a chance to sample some excellent cooking. Consider seared sea bass and sea scallops with risotto or Shelton Farms chicken. The restaurant, part of the South Coast Winery complex, serves three meals daily. ✉ *34843 Rancho California Rd.* ☎ *951/587–9463 or 866/994–6379* ⊕ *www. wineresort.com* ⚠ *Reservations essential.*

WHERE TO STAY
For expanded hotel reviews, visit Fodors.com.

$$–$$$

🏨 **South Coast Winery Resort & Spa.** The Temecula wine country's most luxurious resort offers richly appointed rooms surrounded by 38 acres of vineyards. **Pros:** elegantly appointed rooms; full-service resort; good value. **Cons:** spread out property requires lots of walking; $15 resort fee. ✉ *34843 Rancho California Rd.* ☎ *951/587–9463 or 866/994–6379* ⊕ *www.wineresort.com* ⤴ *76 rooms, 2 suites* ⚐ *In-room: safe, Wi-Fi. In-hotel: restaurant, bar, pool, gym, spa, parking* ⦿*Breakfast.*

$$

🏨 **Temecula Creek Inn.** This upscale golf resort occupies a hillside adjacent to I–15 a short distance from the winery-touring area. **Pros:** golf; convenient for winery touring; popular restaurant on-site. **Cons:** some rooms are noisy. ✉ *44501 Rainbow Canyon Rd.* ☎ *951/694–1000 or 877/517–1823* ⊕ *www.temeculacreekinn.com* ⤴ *130 rooms, 1 guesthouse* ⚐ *In-room: safe, Internet, Wi-Fi. In-hotel: restaurant, bar, golf course, pool, tennis courts, gym, business center, parking.*

SPORTS AND THE OUTDOORS
A Grape Escape Balloon Adventure (☎ *951/699–9987 or 800/965–2122* ⊕ *www.hotairtours.com*) has morning hot-air balloon lift-offs from Wilson Creek Winery.

Temecula draws thousands of people to its **Balloon and Wine Festival** held in late spring. Hot-air balloon excursions are a good choice year-round.

California Dreamin' (☎ *800/373–3359* ⊕ *www.californiadreamin.com*) schedules hot-air balloon rides from a private Temecula vineyard.

SHOPPING
Tastings of locally pressed olive oil are offered at the **Temecula Olive Oil Company** (✉ *28653 Old Town Front St.* ☎ *951/693–0607* ⊕ *www. temeculaoliveoil.com*), where you can find a selection of oils seasoned with garlic, herbs, and citrus. This Old Town shop has dipping and cooking oils, locally crafted oil-based soaps and bath products, and a selection of preserved and stuffed olives.

Ready for lift-off at Temecula's Balloon and Wine Festival.

THE BACKCOUNTRY AND JULIAN

The Cuyamaca and Laguna mountains to the east of Escondido—sometimes referred to as the backcountry by county residents—are favorite weekend destinations for hikers, nature lovers, stargazers, and apple-pie fanatics. Most of the latter group head to Julian, a historic mining town now better known for apple pie than for the gold once extracted from its hills. Nearby Cuyamaca Rancho State Park, once a luscious ancient oak and pine forest, was temporarily closed after it burned in a 2003 fire. While evidence of the fire is still visible in some areas, many of the park's ancient oak trees have come back to life, hiking and horse trails have been repaired, and most campgrounds are open with new facilities.

CUYAMACA MOUNTAINS

The Cuyamaca and Laguna mountains separate coastal and inland San Diego from the desert. Abundant winter rainfall produces thick oak and pine forests, year-round streams, and sparkling waterfalls here. The mountains were also home to a small gold rush in the 1870s, remnants of which can be seen throughout the region. Wildlife including deer, coyotes, and mountain lions is abundant.

Cuyamaca Rancho State Park. Spread over more than 25,000 acres of open meadows, oak woodlands, and mountains and rising to 6,512 feet at Cuyamaca Peak, much of the park, including its infrastructure, burned during a wildfire in 2003. Local volunteers continue to reconstruct the 120 mi of hiking and nature trails, picnic areas, campgrounds, and museum, and much has been completed. However, even nine years

CLOSE UP

Casino Country

San Diego County, along with the Temecula area, is the Indian gaming capital of California, with more than 13 tribes currently operating casinos in the region's rural backcountry. The casinos range from resorts, with headliner entertainment and golf courses, to small rooms tucked away on rural crossroads with slot machines and cards. Although the gaming options may resemble what you might find in Las Vegas, the action is definitely different. The casinos stand alone on back roads, so it's not practical to travel from one to another. The big casinos—Viejas, Barona, Sycuan, Rincon, Pala, and Pachenga—are popular with local seniors and some Asian visitors. Many casinos offer bus transport, so call before visiting and save on gas. Gambling age is 18 years, 21 in some casinos.

Viejas Casino (⌧ *5000 Willows Rd., Alpine* ☎ *619/445–5400 or 800/847–6537* ⊕ *www.viejas.com*) is a massive Native American–theme entertainment and shopping complex. Viejas has more than 2,500 slot machines, plus blackjack, poker, bingo, pai gow, and off-track wagering. There are six restaurants and a cocktail lounge, plus a high-end bar and VIP lounge. The Viejas Outlet Center, a factory outlet mall across from the casino, has more than 50 shops, restaurants, and a landscaped amphitheater.

Barona Valley Ranch Resort and Casino (⌧ *1932 Wildcat Canyon Rd., Lakeside* ☎ *619/443–2300 or 888/722–7662* ⊕ *www.barona.com*) is an all-in-one Western-style destination with gaming, hotel, restaurants, and golf course. In the casino you can find 2,000 slots, over 80 gaming tables including blackjack, a poker room, and off-track betting. The 400-room Barona Valley Ranch hotel has a fitness center, day spa, and pool.

More compact than other area casinos, **Sycuan Casino** (⌧ *5469 Casino Way, El Cajon* ☎ *619/320–6078 or 866/364–8262* ⊕ *www.sycuan.com*) has 2,000 slot machines; table games such as blackjack, poker, and pai gow; and a bingo parlor. Portions of the casino are smoke-free. The tribe also owns the nearby Sycuan Resort.

Harrah's Rincon Casino & Resort (⌧ *777 Harrah's Rincon Way, Valley Center* ☎ *760/751–3100* ⊕ *www. harrahs.com*) lies in the shadow of Palomar Mountain. The resort has 662 rooms and five entertainment venues. The casino holds 2,000 slot machines and 60 table games. It also hosts World Series of Poker events. There are seven restaurants, plus a spa, pool, and gym.

Pechanga Resort & Casino (⌧ *45000 Pechanga Pkwy., Temecula* ☎ *951/693–1819* ⊕ *www.pechanga. com*) has some of the best accommodations. The resort hotel holds 517 rooms, seven restaurants and a food court, a gym, sauna, swimming pool, spa, and golf course. The casino has 3,000 slot machines, more than 132 table games, a high-limit gaming area with VIP lounge, and no-smoking poker room. Live championship boxing matches are held in the Grand Ballroom, and there is a rooftop lounge offering sweeping evening views.

—Bobbi Zane

later a drive through the park will reveal nature's healing processes, as abundant seasonal wildflowers and other native plants emerge from the earth in a breathtaking display. For an inspirational desert view, stop at the lookout about 2 mi south of Julian on Route 79; on a clear day you can see several mountain ranges in hues ranging from pink to amber stepped back behind the Salton Sea. ✉ *13652 Hwy. 79, Julian* ☎ *760/765–3020* ⊕ *www.parks.ca.gov.*

☁ **Lake Cuyamaca.** Behind a dam constructed in 1888 the 110-acre lake offers fishing, boating, picnicking, nature hikes, and wildlife-watching. Anglers regularly catch trout, smallmouth bass, and sturgeon. A shaded picnic area occupies the lakeshore. Families can rent small motorboats, rowboats, and paddleboats by the hour. Free fishing classes for adults and kids are held Saturday at 10 am. Fishing licenses and advice are available at the tackle shop. Two rental condominiums, three sleeping cabins, 19 RV campsites with hookups, and 21 tent sites are available with reservations (call Monday through Thursday). ✉ *15027 Hwy. 79, Julian* ☎ *760/765–0515 or 877/581–9904* ⊕ *www.lakecuyamaca.org* 🎫 *$6 per vehicle for picnic area* ⊙ *Daily dawn–dusk.*

Sunrise National Scenic Byway. In the Cleveland National Forest, this is the most dramatic approach to Julian—its turns and curves reveal amazing views of the desert from the Salton Sea all the way to Mexico. You can spend an entire day roaming these mountains; an early-morning hike to the top of Garnet Peak (mile marker 27.8) is the best way to catch the view. Springtime wildflower displays are spectacular, particularly along Big Laguna Trail from Laguna Campground. There are picnic areas along the highway at Desert View and Pioneer Mail.

15

WHERE TO EAT

$ ✕ **Franz's Lake Cuyamaca Restaurant.** This tidy, lace-curtained lakefront

AUSTRIAN café specializes in Austrian fare, highlights of which include a selection of schnitzels and wursts, plus several chicken and steak entrées. Austrian beers are on tap. The restaurant, as well as the adjacent food market, is popular with anglers and locals. ✉ *15027 Hwy. 79, Julian* ☎ *760/765–0700.*

JULIAN

62 mi from San Diego to Julian, east on I-8 and north on Rte. 79.

Gold was discovered in the Julian area in 1869, and gold-bearing quartz a year later. More than $15 million worth of gold was taken from local mines in the 1870s. Many of the buildings along Julian's Main Street and the side streets today date back to the gold-rush period; others are reproductions.

When gold and quartz became scarce, the locals turned to growing apples and pears. During the fall harvest season you can buy fruit, sip cider, eat apple pie, and shop for local original art, antiques, and collectibles. But spring is equally enchanting (and less congested), as the hillsides explode with wildflowers—thousands of daffodils, lilacs, and peonies. More than 50 artists have studios tucked away in the hills surrounding Julian; they often show their work in local shops and galleries.

Try Julian's famous apple pies at Mom's Pie House on 2119 Main Street.

The Julian area comprises three small crossroads communities: Santa Ysabel, Wynola, and historic Julian. You can find bits of history, shops, and dining options in each community. Most visitors come to spend a day in town, but the hillsides support many small bed-and-breakfast establishments for those who want to linger longer.

ESSENTIALS

Visitor Information Julian Chamber of Commerce (✉ *2129 Main St., Julian* ☎ *760/765–1857* ⊕ *www.julianca.com*).

EXPLORING

TOP ATTRACTIONS

Ⓒ ★ **California Wolf Center.** This center, just outside Julian, is one of the few places in North America where you can get an up-close view of the gray wolves that once roamed much of the continent. Dedicated to the preservation of the endangered North American gray wolf, the center participates in breeding programs, and houses several captive packs, including some rare Mexican grays, a subspecies of the North American gray wolf that came within seven individuals of extinction in the 1970s. The animals are kept secluded from public view in 3-acre pens, but some may be seen by visitors during weekly educational tours. Private tours are by appointment. ✉ *Hwy. 79 at KQ Ranch Rd.* ☎ *619/234– 9653* ⊕ *www.californiawolfcenter.org* 🎫 *$10–25, reservations required* ⊙ *Tour Sat. 2 pm, Sun. 10 am. (call for additional seasonal tour times).*

Ⓒ **Julian Pioneer Museum.** When the gold mines in Julian played out, the mobs of gold miners who had invaded it left, leaving behind discarded mining tools and empty houses. Today the Julian Pioneer Museum, a 19th-century brewery, displays remnants of that time, including pioneer clothing, a collection of old lace, and old photographs of the town's historic buildings and mining structures. ✉ *2811 Washington St.* ☎ *760/765–0227* 🖃 *$3* ⊙ *Apr.–Dec., Thurs.–Sun. 10–4; Jan.–Mar., weekends 10–4.*

Observer's Inn. One of the best ways to see Julian's star-filled summer sky is by taking a sky-tour here, where Mike and Caroline Leigh have set up an observatory with research-grade telescopes where they conduct sky tours on dark nights. The hosts guide you through the star clusters and galaxies, pointing out planets and nebulae. They recently started offering daytime solar tours as well. It's also an inn, if you wish to stay the night. ✉ *3535 Hwy. 79* ☎ *760/765–0088* ⊕ *www.observersinn.com* ⚓ *Reservations essential* 🖃 *$20 per person.*

Volcan Mountain Wilderness Preserve. The 1¼ -mi trail through the preserve passes through Engelmann oak forest, native manzanita, and rolling mountain meadows to a viewpoint where the panorama extends north all the way to Palomar Mountain. On a clear day you can see Point Loma in San Diego. At the entrance you pass through gates designed by James Hubbell, a local artist known for his ironwork, wood carving, and stained glass. Hikes are offered weekends in summer. ✉ *From Julian take Farmer Rd. to Wynola Rd., go east a few yards, and then north on continuation of Farmer Rd.* ☎ *760/765–4098* ⊕ *www. volcanmt.org* 🖃 *Free* ⊙ *Daily dawn–dusk.*

WORTH NOTING

Banner Queen Trading Post Gallery. A step inside what was the mine superintendent's home in the run-down-looking remnant of an old gold mine dug into a hillside on Banner Grade, 5 mi east of Julian, reveals a wealth of contemporary art. Five rooms are filled with paintings, photos, sculpture, ceramics, stained glass (even some fire glass), and woven pieces by Julian artists. Prices range from $30 or less for photos and pottery to hundreds for paintings and sculptures by widely recognized artists such as James Hubbell and Bob Verdugo. ✉ *36766 Hwy. 78* ☎ *760/765–2168* ⊙ *Fri.–Sun. 1–5.*

Eagle Mining Company. Five blocks east of the center of Julian, you can take an hour-long tour of an authentic Julian gold mine. A small rock shop and gold-mining museum are also on the premises. ✉ *C St.* ☎ *760/765–0036* 🖃 *$10* ⊙ *Daily 10–4, weather permitting.*

Mission Santa Ysabel. West of Santa Ysabel, this tiny late-19th-century adobe mission continues to serve several local Native American communities. A small museum on the premises (⊙ *Daily 8–3*) holds memorabilia from local families, Native Americans, and the parish. ✉ *23013 Hwy. 79* ☎ *760/765–0810.*

Santa Ysabel Valley. Three Native American tribes live in this valley which looks pretty much the way the backcountry appeared a century ago, with sweeping meadows surrounded by oak-studded hillsides. The tribes operate small farms and run cattle here, although the valley's beautiful pasturelands have been threatened by development in recent years. However, in 2000 the Nature Conservancy acquired large portions of the valley to set aside as a nature preserve. The village of **Santa Ysabel,** 7 mi west of Julian, has several interesting shops.

15

WHERE TO EAT

$$
AMERICAN

✕**Julian Grille.** The menu at this casual restaurant inside one of Julian's historic homes appeals to a variety of tastes, including vegetarian. Chicken dishes and steaks are popular. Lunch options include good burgers, whopping sandwiches, and soups. There's a tree-shaded dining area that is heated on cool evenings. Beware, service can be hit or miss. ✉ *2224 Main St.* ☎ *760/765–0173* ◷ *No dinner Mon.*

$
AMERICAN
★

✕**Julian Pie Company.** The apple pies that made Julian famous come from the Smothers family bakery in a one-story house on Main Street. In pleasant weather you can sit on the front patio and watch the world go by while savoring a slice of hot pie—from Dutch apple to apple mountain berry crumb—topped with homemade cinnamon ice cream. The Smothers family has been making pies in Julian since 1986; by 1989 they had bought their own orchard, and by 1992 they had built a larger bakery in Santa Ysabel. At lunchtime the Julian location also serves soup and sandwiches. The Santa Ysabel bakery just makes pies. ✉ *2225 Main St.* ☎ *760/765–2449* ✉ *21976 Hwy. 79, Santa Ysabel* ☎ *760/765–2400* ⊕ *www.julianpie.com.*

$
CAFÉ
☺

✕**Julian Tea and Cottage Arts.** Sample finger sandwiches, scones topped with whipped cream, and lavish sweets during afternoon tea inside the Clarence King House, built by Will Bosnell in 1898. Regular sandwiches, soups, salads, and a children's tea are also available. Victorian teas are presented during the holiday season. ✉ *2124 3rd St.* ☎ *760/765–0832 or 866/765–0832* ⊕ *www.juliantea.com* ⚶ *Reservations essential* for designated seating times ◷ *Closed Tues. and Wed. No dinner.*

$$
ITALIAN

✕**Romano's Dodge House.** You can gorge on huge portions of antipasto, pizza, pasta, sausage sandwiches, and seafood in a cozy old house. Specialties include pork Juliana simmered in apple cider, pasta Pacifica, and brasciole. This is a casual, red-checked-tablecloth kind of place, where you can dine outside in good weather. Recent reviews have complained about food quality and price. ✉ *2718 B St.* ☎ *760/765–1003* ⊕ *www. romanosjulian.com* ◷ *Closed Tues.*

$
PIZZA

✕**Wynola Pizza Express.** Locals come to this quaint and casual indoor-outdoor restaurant for delicious, single-portion pizzas such as pesto pizza, Thai chicken pizza, vegan pizza, and tostada pizza. Other items include chili, lasagna, seared Cajun salmon, and a killer fire-roasted artichoke dip served with homemade buffalo crackers. Entertainers usually perform on weekends in the adjacent Red Barn or, in fine weather, outdoors. ✉ *4355 Hwy. 78, Santa Ysabel* ☎ *760/765–1004* ⊕ *www. wynolapizzaexpress.com.*

JULIAN'S BLACK HISTORY

According to local history and old photos, the Julian area had a large population of African-Americans in the years following the Civil War. Indeed, it was a black man, Fred Coleman, who discovered gold in Julian, and the Julian Hotel was founded and operated by Albert and Margaret Robinson, also black. Headstones recognizing the contributions of Julian's black pioneers continue to be placed in the old section of the Pioneer Cemetery.

WHERE TO STAY

For expanded hotel reviews, visit Fodors.com.

$$ ⊞ **Butterfield Bed and Breakfast.** Built in the 1930s, this inn on a 3-acre hilltop is cordial and romantic with knotty-pine ceilings, Laura Ashley accents, and a gazebo in the backyard. **Pros:** great food; interesting hosts; secluded. **Cons:** very quiet; no room phone. ✉ *2284 Sunset Dr.* ☎ *760/765–2179 or 800/379–4262* ⊕ *www.butterfieldbandb.com* ⤳ *5 rooms* ♿ *In-room: Wi-Fi. In-hotel: parking* ❑ *Breakfast.*

$ ⊞ **Julian Gold Rush Hotel.** Built in 1897 by freed slave Albert Robinson and his wife, Margaret, this more than 100-year-old hotel is Julian's only designated national landmark. **Pros:** genuine historic hotel; convivial atmosphere. **Cons:** small rooms; no TV. ✉ *2032 Main St.* ☎ *760/765–0201 or 800/734–5854* ⊕ *www.julianhotel.com* ⤳ *14 rooms, 2 suites* ♿ *In-room: no TV, Wi-Fi* ❑ *Breakfast.*

$ ⊞ **Julian Lodge.** A replica of a late-19th-century Julian hotel, this two-story lodge calls itself a bed-and-breakfast. **Pros:** in-town location; free parking. **Cons:** limited facilities; simple appointments. ✉ *2720 C St.* ☎ *760/765–1420 or 800/542–1420* ⊕ *www.julianlodge.com* ⤳ *23 rooms* ♿ *In-hotel: parking* ❑ *Breakfast.*

$$$–$$$$ ★ ⊞ **Orchard Hill Country Inn.** On a hill above town, this lodge and five Craftsman-style cottages have a sweeping view of the countryside. **Pros:** most luxurious digs in Julian; good food. **Cons:** limited amenities. ✉ *2502 Washington St.* ☎ *760/765–1700 or 800/716–7242* ⊕ *www.orchardhill.com* ⤳ *10 rooms, 12 suites* ♿ *In-room: Wi-Fi. In-hotel: bar, parking* ❑ *Breakfast.*

$$ ⊞ **Wikiup Bed and Breakfast.** Best known for its herd of llamas, Wikiup appeals to animal lovers. **Pros:** private entrances; fireplaces in all rooms. **Cons:** limited facilities. ✉ *1645 Whispering Pines Dr.* ☎ *760/765–1890 or 800/694–5487* ⊕ *www.wikiupbnb.com* ⤳ *5 rooms* ♿ *In-hotel: parking* ❑ *Breakfast.*

SHOPPING

The Julian area has a number of unique shops that are open weekends, but midweek hours vary considerably. In autumn locally grown apples, pears, nuts, and cider are available in town and at a few roadside stands. The best apple variety produced here is a Jonagold, a hybrid of Jonathan and Golden Delicious.

The **Birdwatcher** (✉ *2775 B St.* ☎ *760/765–1817*) offers items for wild-bird lovers, including birdhouses, birdseed, hummingbird feeders, plus bird-theme accessories such as jewelry, apparel, novelties, and guide-books for serious birders.

The **Falcon Gallery** (✉ *2015A Main St.* ☎ *760/765–1509*), in a replica of one of Julian's original hotels, has works by local artists, books about area history including Native American history, and a small but tantalizing collection of books and art and science kits for kids.

Mountain Gypsy (✉ *2007 Main St.* ☎ *760/765–0643*) is popular area-wide for an extensive collection of jewelry and trendy apparel in petite and plus sizes.

15

Santa Ysabel Art Gallery (⊠ *Rte. 78 and Rte. 79, Santa Ysabel* 🖀 *760/765–1676*) shows watercolors, stained glass, sculptures, and other creations by local artists.

PALOMAR MOUNTAIN

35 mi northeast of Escondido on I–15 to Rte. 76 to Rte. S6, 66 mi northeast of downtown San Diego on Rte. 163 to I–15 to Rte. 76 to Rte. S6.

Palomar Mountain, at an altitude of 6,140 feet and with an average of 300 clear nights per year, has the distinction of being the home of one of the world's most significant astronomical observation sites, the Hale 200-inch telescope installed at the Palomar Observatory in 1947. Before that, the mountain played a role in San Diego County's rich African-American history and culture. One of many who migrated to the area in the mid-19th century was Nathan Harrison, a former slave who owned a large swath of property on the mountain where he farmed and raised cattle, the importance of which is just being revealed through archaeological excavations conducted by local university students. According to local historians, Harrison and other former slaves made up a major segment of the backcountry population until about 1900. A devastating fire burned most of the lower slopes of Palomar Mountain in 2007, but the top of the mountain (home to the telescope, campgrounds, and a little settlement) remained untouched.

EXPLORING

🕲 **Mission San Antonio de Pala.** A living remnant of the mission era, this mission, built in 1816 to serve Native American Indians, still ministers to the Native American community. It is the only original Spanish mission still serving its initial purpose. The old jail and cemetery are part of the original mission. ⊠ *Pala Mission Rd. off Rte. 76, 6 mi east of I–15, Pala* 🖀 *760/742–3317* 🎟 *$2* ⊙ *Museum and gift shop Tues 10–4, Wed.–Fri. 9–4, Sat. 9–5, Sun. 9–2.*

🕲 **Palomar Mountain State Park.** One of the few areas in Southern California with a Sierra-like atmosphere, the park holds a forest of pines, cedars, western dogwood, native azalea, and other plants. Wildflower viewing is good in spring. **Boucher Lookout,** on one of several nature/hiking trails, affords a sweeping view to the west. There's trout fishing in Doane Pond. The Doane Valley campground offers 31 sites with tables, fire pits, and flush toilets. From May to October, reservations are strongly recommended, and can be made seven months in advance. ⊠ *Off Hwy. S6 at Hwy. S7, Palomar Mountain* 🖀 *760/742–3462 ranger station; 800/444–7275 campsite reservations* ⊕ *www.parks.ca.gov* (reservations taken April–October only; the rest of the year it's first-come, first-serve.) 🎟 *$8, camping $30.*

Palomar Observatory. Atop Palomar Mountain, the observatory is owned and operated by the California Institute of Technology, whose astronomy faculty conducts research here. The observatory houses the Hale Telescope, as well as 60-inch, 48-inch, 24-inch, 18-inch, and Snoop telescopes. Some of the most important astronomical discoveries of the 20th century were made here, and already in this century scientists using the observatory's 48-inch telescope have detected a 10th planet. For the time being, this most distant known object in the solar system, a body larger than fellow dwarf-planet Pluto, has been named Eris. The small museum contains photos of some of these discoveries, as well as photos taken by NASA's Hubble Space Telescope and from recent

WORD OF MOUTH

"Anza-Borrego is great. There is a wonderful hike that you can take that will take you up to an oasis. If you are really lucky, you might see bighorn sheep."

—cferrb

NASA–European Space Agency missions to Mars and Saturn. A park with picnic areas surrounds the observatory. ⊠ *Rte. S6 north of Rte. 76, east of I–15, Palomar Mountain* ☎ *760/742–2119* ⊕ *www.astro. caltech.edu/palomar* ⊠ *Free, $8 guided tours* ☉ *Observatory for self-guided tours daily 9–4 during daylight saving time; 9–3 during standard time. Public guided tours weekends Apr.–Oct. at 11:30, 1:30, and 2:30.*

15

WHERE TO EAT

¢ ✗ **Mother's Kitchen.** This popular stop for motorcyclists (the road up there is the most popular biker route in Southern California) serves up huge portions of vegetarian fare, including mountain chili, Boca tacos, and lasagna. Sides include steaming-hot soup, nachos, and quesadillas. The atmosphere is mountain casual, with open-beam ceilings, knotty-pine tables, and fresh flowers everywhere. Waitresses are friendly, and local musicians entertain on weekends. ⊠ *Junction of Hwys. S6 and S7, Palomar Mountain* ☎ *760/742–4233* ⊕ *www.motherskitchenpalomar.com* ☉ *Closed Mon.–Wed. Labor Day–Memorial Day. No dinner.*

VEGETARIAN

THE DESERT

In most spring seasons the stark desert landscape east of the Cuyamaca Mountains explodes with colorful wildflowers. The beauty of this spectacle, as well as the natural quiet and blazing climate, lures many tourists and natives each year to Anza-Borrego Desert State Park, about a two-hour drive from central San Diego.

For hundreds of years the only humans to linger here were Native Americans of the Cahuilla and Kumeyaay tribes, who made their winter homes in the desert. It was not until 1774, when Mexican explorer Captain Juan Bautista de Anza first blazed a trail through the area seeking a shortcut from Sonora, Mexico, to San Francisco, that Europeans had their first glimpse of the oddly enchanting terrain.

The desert is best visited from October through May to avoid the extreme summer temperatures. Winter temperatures are comfortable, but nights (and sometimes days) are cold, so bring a warm jacket.

ANZA-BORREGO DESERT STATE PARK

88 mi from downtown San Diego (to park border due west of Borrego Springs).

GETTING HERE AND AROUND

You'll need a car to visit the Anza-Borrego Desert and Borrego Springs, which is totally surrounded by wilderness. The trip from San Diego is about 90 scenic mi, and it takes about two hours. Once there be prepared to drive on dusty roads as there is no public transportation. The best route to Borrego Springs is via I–8 east out of San Diego; exit east on Highway 79 and take the scenic drive through the Cuyamaca Mountains to Julian, where Highway 79 intersects with Highway 78 going east. Follow Highway 78 into the desert to Yaqui Pass Road, turn left and follow the signs to Borrego Springs Christmas Circle. Take Borrego Palm Canyon west to reach the Anza-Borrego Desert State Park headquarters.

TOUR OPTIONS

California Overland Excursions offers day tours and overnight excursions into hard-to-reach scenic desert destinations using open-air, military-transport vehicles. Typical destinations include Font's Point, the Badlands, and 17-Palm Oasis.

Tour Information **California Overland Excursions** (✉ *1233 Palm Canyon Dr., Borrego Springs* ☎ *760/767–1232 or 866/639–7567* ⊕ *www.californiaoverland.com*).

ESSENTIALS

Visitor Information **Anza-Borrego Desert State Park** (✉ *200 Palm Canyon Dr., Borrego Springs* ☎ *760/767–4205* ⊕ *www.parks.ca.gov*). **State Park Reservations** (☎ *800/444–7275* ⊕ *www.reserveamerica.com*). **Wildflower Hotline** (☎ *760/767–4684*).

EXPLORING

Anza-Borrego State Park. Today more than 1,000 square mi of desert and mountain country are included in the Anza-Borrego Desert State Park, one of the few parks in the country where you can follow a trail and pitch a tent wherever you like. No campsite is necessary, although there is a developed campground. Rangers and displays at an excellent **Visitor Information Center** (✉ *200 Palm Canyon Dr., Borrego Springs* ☎ *760/767–4205; 760/767–4684 wildflower hotline* ⊕ *www.parks. ca.gov* ☉ *Oct.–Apr. daily 9–5; May–Sept. weekends 9–5*) can point you in the right direction. Most of the desert plants can also be seen in the demonstration desert garden at the visitor center.

Five hundred miles of paved and dirt roads traverse the park, and you are required to stay on them so as not to disturb its ecological balance. There are also 110 mi of hiking and riding trails that allow you to explore canyons, capture scenic vistas, and tiptoe through fields of wildflowers in spring. The park is also home to rare Peninsula bighorn sheep, mountain lions, coyotes, black-tailed jackrabbit, and roadrunners. State Highway 78, which runs north and south through the park, has been designated the Juan Bautista de Anza National Historic Trail, marking portions of the route of the Anza Colonizing Expedition of 1775–76 that went from northern Mexico to the San Francisco Bay area. In addition, 28,000 acres have been set aside in the eastern part of

CLOSE UP

Spring Wildflowers

Southern California's famous warm, sunny climate has blessed this corner of the continent with an ever-changing, year-round palette of natural color. It's hard to find a spot anywhere around the globe that produces as spectacular a scene as San Diego does in spring—from the native plant gardens found tucked away in mountain canyons and streambeds to the carpets of wildflowers on the desert floor. You'll have to see it yourself to believe just how alive the deceptively barren desert really is.

WHEN TO GO
Spring debuts in **late February or early March.** Heavy winter rains always precede the best bloom seasons. And good blooms also bring even more beauty—a bounty of butterflies. A further boon: here in this generally temperate climate, the bloom season lasts nearly all year.

Some drought-tolerant plants rely on fire to germinate, and the years following wildfires generally produce a profusion of plant life not normally seen. Although wildfires in the Cuyamaca and Laguna mountains in 2002 and 2003 destroyed much of the ancient forest, subsequent years saw brilliant and unusual wildflower displays as a result.

WHAT TO SEE
Look for rare western redbud trees erupting into a profusion of crimson flowers, sometimes starting as early as February. Native California lilacs (ceanothus) blanket the hillsides throughout the backcountry with fragrant blue-and-white blossoms starting in May and showing until August.

Native varieties of familiar names show up in the mountain canyons and streambeds. A beautiful white western azalea would be the star in anyone's garden. A pink California rose blooms along streambeds in spring and summer. Throughout the year three varieties of native dogwood show off white blooms and beautiful crimson fall foliage. The **Cuyamaca Mountains** usually put on a display of fall color as the native oaks turn gold and red. By winter the rare toyon, known as the California Christmas tree, lights up the roadside with its red berries.

You can get a good introduction to mountain wildflowers by visiting **Julian** in early May, when the Women's Club puts on its annual **Wildflower Show.** For more than seven decades members have collected and displayed native plants and flowers from hillsides, meadows, and streambeds surrounding the mountain town. For information on exact dates call the Julian Chamber of Commerce (☎ 760/765–1857).

Farther east in the **Anza-Borrego Desert State Park,** the spring wildflower display can be spectacular: carpets of pink, purple, white, and yellow verbena and desert primrose as far as the eye can see. Rocky slopes yield clumps of beavertail cactus topped with showy pink blossoms, clumps of yellow brittlebush tucked among the rocks, and crimson-tip ocotillo trees. For a good introduction to desert vegetation, explore the visitor center demonstration garden, adjacent to the park's underground headquarters.

For a vivid view of both the mountain and desert spring flora, take I-8 east to Route 79, go north to Julian, and then east on Route 78 into Anza-Borrego park.

15

the desert near Ocotillo Wells for off-road enthusiasts. General George S. Patton conducted field training in the Ocotillo area to prepare for the World War II invasion of North Africa.

Many of the park's sites can be seen from paved roads, but some require driving on dirt roads, where it's easy to sink up to your wheel covers in dry sand. Rangers recommend using four-wheel-drive vehicles on the dirt roads. Carry the appropriate supplies: shovel and other tools, flares, blankets, and plenty of water. Canyons are susceptible to flash flooding; inquire about weather conditions before entering.

Wildflowers, which typically begin to bloom in January and are at their peak in mid-March, attract thousands of visitors each spring. A variety of factors including rainfall and winds determine how extensive the bloom will be in a particular year. However, good displays of low-growing sand verbena and white evening primrose can usually be found along Airport Road and DiGeorgio Road. Following wet winters, spectacular displays fill the dry washes in Coyote Canyon and along Henderson Canyon Road. The best light for photography is in early morning or late afternoon.

Narrows Earth Trail, off Route 78 east of Tamarisk Grove, is a short walk that reveals the many geologic processes involved in forming the desert canyons. Water, wind, and faulting created the commanding vistas along **Erosion Road,** a self-guided, 18-mi auto tour along Route S22. The **Southern Emigrant Trail** follows the route of the Butterfield Stage Overland Mail through the desert.

At **Borrego Palm Canyon,** a few minutes west of the visitor information center, a 1½-mi trail leads to a small oasis with a waterfall and palms. The Borrego Palm Canyon campground is the only developed campground with flush toilets and showers in the park. (Day use is $8 and camping is $25 in high season, $35 with hookup.)

Geology students from all over the world visit the Fish Creek area of Anza-Borrego to explore a famous canyon known as **Split Mountain** (⊠ *Split Mountain Rd. south from Rte. 78 at Ocotillo Wells*), a narrow gorge with 600-foot perpendicular walls that was formed by an ancestral stream. Fossils in this area indicate that a sea covered the desert floor at one time. A 2-mi nature trail west of Split Mountain rewards hikers with a good view of shallow caves created by erosion.

BORREGO SPRINGS

31 mi from Julian, east on Rte. 78 and Yaqui Pass Rd., and north on Rte. S3.

A quiet town with a handful of year-round residents, Borrego Springs is set in the heart of the Anza-Borrego Desert State Park and is emerging as a destination for desert lovers. From September through June, temperatures hover in the 80s and 90s, and you can enjoy activities such as hiking, nature study, golf, tennis, horseback riding, and mountain-bike riding. Even during the busier winter season, Borrego Springs feels quiet. There are four golf resorts, two bed-and-breakfast inns, and a growing community of winter residents, but the laid-back vibe prevails. If winter rains cooperate, Borrego Springs puts on some of the best wildflower displays in the low desert.

ESSENTIALS

Visitor Information Borrego Springs Chamber of Commerce (✉ 786 *Palm Canyon Dr., Borrego Springs* ☎ 760/767–5555 or 800/559–5524 ⊕ *www.borregospringschamber.com*).

EXPLORING

Galleta Meadows. Flowers aren't the only thing popping up from the earth in Borrego Springs: camels, llamas, saber-toothed tigers, tortoises, and monumental gomphotherium (a sort of ancient elephant) appear to roam the earth again at Galleta Meadows. These life-size bronze figures are of prehistoric animals whose fossils can be found in the Borrego Badlands. The col-

> ### UNBURIED TREASURE
>
> The Anza-Borrego Desert is one of the most geologically active spots in North America and a repository of geologic and paleontological treasure. Beneath its surface are fossil-bearing sediments containing the record of 7 million years of climate change, tectonic activity, upthrust, and subsidence—the richest fossil deposits in North America. Reading the fossil record, scientists have revealed that the badlands were once a wonderland of green, the home of saber-toothed tigers, flamingos, zebras, camels, the largest known mammoths, and a flying bird with a 16-foot wingspan.

15

lection, currently more than 50 sets of animals and growing, is the project of a wealthy Borrego Springs resident who is installing the works of art on property he owns for the entertainment of locals and visitors. Maps are available from Borrego Springs Chamber of Commerce. ✉ *Borrego Springs Rd. from Christmas Circle to Henderson Canyon* ☎ *760/767–5555* ⊕ *www.galletameadows.com* 🏷 *Free.*

WHERE TO EAT

$ ✕ **The Arches.** Set right on the edge of the Borrego Springs Golf Course, AMERICAN this is one of the most pleasant dining options in the area. There's indoor and outdoor seating, and the offerings are surprisingly good: try the chicken potpie for dinner. Service can be super casual. The Arches is open for breakfast as well. ✉ *1112 Tilting T Dr.* ☎ *760/767–5700* ◷ *Summer hrs vary; call ahead.*

$ ✕ **Carlee's Bar & Grill.** The local watering hole that seems to collect characters ranging from hippies to mountain men, Carlee's is the place to AMERICAN go any night of the week. A large, dimly lighted room holds both bar and dining tables. The menu lists pasta and pizza in addition to old-fashioned entrées such as liver and onions and mixed grill. Dinners come with soup or salad. ✉ *660 Palm Canyon Dr.* ☎ *760/767–3262.*

$ ✕ **Carmelita's Mexican Grill and Cantina.** A friendly family-run eatery MEXICAN tucked into a back corner of what is called "The Mall," Carmelita's draws locals and visitors all day whether it's for a hearty breakfast, a cooked-to-order enchilada or burrito, or to tip back a brew at the bar. The menu lists typical combination plates (enchiladas, burritos, tamales, and tacos). Salsas have a bit of zing, masas are tasty and tender. ✉ *575 Palm Canyon Dr.* ☎ *760/767–5666.*

$$
AMERICAN

✕**Krazy Coyote Bar & Grill/Red Ocotillo.** Two popular restaurants have combined at the Palms at Indianhead. The Krazy Coyote is a trendy mid-'50s-style café, with dark red walls adorned with movie posters and other memorabilia. The Red Ocotillo has inexpensive comfort food including sandwiches, burgers, and chicken-fried steak. Fare at the Krazy Coyote is more substantial and includes filet mignon and salmon. ✉ *2220 Hoberg Rd.* ☎ *760/767–7788* ⚖ *Reservations essential* ☺ *No lunch in Krazy Coyote; call for hrs in summer.*

WHERE TO STAY
For expanded hotel reviews, visit Fodors.com.

$

⌂ **Borrego Springs Resort and Country Club.** A popular choice for families who want to have fun, play a little golf, and hang out at the pool, this casual resort has the ambience of a country club (which it is) but none of the snooty trappings. **Pros:** good value; relaxed ambience. **Cons:** plain Jane as it can be; rooms around pool apt to be noisy; perfunctory service. ✉ *1112 Tilting T Dr.* ☎ *760/767–5700 or 888/826–7734* ⊕ *www.borregospringsresort.com* ⇝ *66 rooms, 34 suites* ♿ *In-room: kitchen (some), Wi-Fi (some). In-hotel: restaurant, bar, golf course, pools, tennis courts, gym, laundry facilities, parking, some pets allowed.*

$$–$$$
★

⌂ **Borrego Valley Inn.** Desert gardens of mesquite, ocotillo, and creosote surround the adobe buildings of this Southwestern-style inn. **Pros:** room to move around inside and out; lovely desert gardens; extremely private. **Cons:** very quiet; not for families. ✉ *405 Palm Canyon Dr.* ☎ *760/767–0311 or 800/333–5810* ⊕ *www.borregovalleyinn.com* ⇝ *15 rooms, 1 suite* ♿ *In-room: kitchen (some), Wi-Fi. In-hotel: pools, parking, not recommended for children under 14* ⦿ *Breakfast.*

$$

⌂ **The Palms at Indian Head.** Spectacular desert views can be had from this small hotel. **Pros:** midcentury modern ambience; star connection; great views. **Cons:** somewhat remote location; simple decor. ✉ *2220 Hoberg Rd.* ☎ *760/767–7788 or 800/519–2624* ⊕ *www.thepalmsatindianhead.com* ⇝ *12 rooms* ♿ *In-hotel: restaurant, bar, pool, some age restrictions* ⦿ *Breakfast.*

SPORTS AND THE OUTDOORS
The 27-hole course at **Borrego Springs Resort and Country Club** (☎ 760/767–3330) is open to the public. The green fees range from $40 to $65, including mandatory cart; discounts may be available to foursomes midweek.

The **Roadrunner Club** (☎ 760/767–5373) has an 18-hole par-3 golf course. Green fees are $35 riding, $30 walking.

Smoketree Arabian Horse Ranch (☎ 760/574–2537) offers a variety of equine encounters—guided desert rides on Arabian or quarter horses and a nonriding human-to-horse communication experience similar to horse whispering. The ranch also provides bed and breakfast accommodations for guests and their horses.

OFF THE BEATEN PATH

Ocotillo Wells State Vehicular Recreation Area. The sand dunes and rock formations at this 80,000-plus acre haven for off-road enthusiasts are fun and challenging. Camping is permitted throughout the area, but water is not available. The only facilities are in the small town (really

If you think the desert is just a sandy wasteland, the stark beauty of the Anza-Borrego Desert will shock you.

no more than a corner) of Ocotillo Wells. ✉ *Rte. 78, 18 mi east from Borrego Springs Rd.* ☎ *760/767–5391.*

TIJUANA

18 mi (29 km) south of San Diego.

Over the course of the 20th century, Tijuana grew from a ranch populated by a few hundred Mexicans into a Prohibition retreat for boozing and gambling. Then it morphed yet again into an industrial giant infamous for its proliferation of *maquiladoras* (sweatshops). With a documented population of 1.2 million (informal estimates run as high as 2 million), Tijuana has surpassed Ciudad Juárez to become the country's sixth-largest city. Whether the legendary sleazefest is now primary or secondary to Tijuana's economy, the place certainly hasn't shaken its bawdy image; tell someone you're going to Tijuana, and you'll still elicit knowing chuckles all around. In addition, recent drug-related crime along the border makes Tijuana an increasingly dangerous place to visit.

Tijuana is a popular spot for young Californians in search of the sort of fun not allowed back home, like a lower drinking age, and perhaps some souvenirs, like duty-free tequila, overpriced trinkets, marked-down medicines, and Polaroid photos taken with donkeys painted as zebras (which, we kid you not, are readily available on Avenida Revolución). Even amid the high-profile hotels, casual dining chains, art museums, and Omni movies that have swooped into the city's swankier Zona Río in the last decade, much of Tijuana still represents border culture at its most bleakly opportunistic, from corrupt cops to pharmacies loudly advertising volume discounts on 100mg Viagra tablets (about enough for a horse).

Meanwhile, as the population has mushroomed, driven largely by the maquiladoras, the government has struggled to keep up with the growth and demand for services; thousands live without electricity, running water, or adequate housing in villages along the border. And nowhere in Mexico are the realities of commercial sex laid out more starkly. Open prostitution is everywhere: in the Zona Norte, streetwalkers accost passersby as they sidestep pools of vomit; strip bars like Casa Adelita and Chicago Club also function as giant, multifloor brothels—every dancer is for sale. Maybe that's why they sell the Viagra in such ludicrous doses.

Now, tourists also have to worry about drug-related crime and violence. Military checkpoints have increased near the border, but robbery, gang violence, and even kidnapping is still happening frequently. If you must make Tijuana part of your trip, use extreme caution. ■ TIP➔ The safest way to travel to Tijuana is on a guided tour.

GETTING HERE AND AROUND

Getting to Tijuana from San Diego takes about an hour. When you go to Tijuana, it's preferable not to be burdened with a car in the city. In that case, you'll want to either drive to the border at San Ysidro and leave your car in a parking lot on the U.S. side, or take the San Diego Trolley (or a taxi) to San Ysidro, which will leave you at the border. At that point, you'll either walk across the border through the turnstiles (where you'll have the option of continuing into downtown Tijuana on foot or catching a Tijuana taxi to your destination in the city), or take a shuttle bus from the trolley station or parking lot to downtown Tijuana. However, due to safety issues we do not recommend traveling alone to Tijuana; opt for a guided tour instead.

ESSENTIALS

BANKS AND MONEY

Because of the ubiquity of U.S. dollars as an accepted currency, the money situation is a bit different in Baja Norte than elsewhere in Mexico. It is possible to spend your entire vacation in Baja Norte without changing your money into pesos, and because the U.S. currency is so universal, you won't usually be shortchanged on the exchange rate if you pay in dollars, as you might farther south. Many, or even most, establishments quote prices in both dollars and pesos. Sometimes, it can be advantageous to pay in dollars as opposed to pesos—be prepared to do a lot of quick arithmetic in your head.

If you do get pesos—and it's always a good idea, regardless, to get some—as elsewhere in Mexico, use ATMs rather than exchange booths. The former tend to have better exchange rates, and they're absolutely everywhere in Tijuana.

EMERGENCIES

In an emergency, dial 066. The operators speak at least a bit of English. For tourist assistance with legal problems, accidents, or other incidents dial the Visitor Assistance hotline at 078. The hotline is available 24/7 in English. If you need serious hospital treatment, you are well advised to head back to San Diego for treatment.

CLOSE UP

Seeing Tijuana Safely

Tijuana tourism has taken a hit in recent years as drug-related crime continues to escalate along the border. There are real dangers here including robbery, kidnapping, and gang violence. It's not recommended to travel to Tijuana on your own, but if you do, cross the border on foot and stick to popular, crowded areas. Pay close attention to your surroundings and keep cash and travel documents hidden.

It is much safer to cross into Tijuana with an English-speaking guide. We recommend **San Diego Scenic Tours** (☎ *858/273–8687* ⊕ *sandiegoscenic-tours.com*), which runs daily out of San Diego.

The **U.S. Consulate of Tijuana**'s Web site (⊕ *tijuana.usconsulate.gov*) lists important travel tips and emergency contacts. Also check the **U.S. State Department**'s Web site (⊕ *www.state. gov*), which lists entry requirements and safety warnings.

15

ENTRY REQUIREMENTS

Under new legislation, all U.S. citizens, including minor children, must show a passport or enhanced driver's license to enter or reenter the United States from Mexico. Minors traveling alone need notarized permission from the parents or a legal guardian. Mexico has a very strict policy about children entering the country. It is recommended to have a passport available at all times.

Citizens of the United States, Canada, Australia, and New Zealand do not need visas to visit Mexico. However, if you're going to be staying in Mexico for more than 72 hours or traveling more than 20–30 km (12–19 mi) from the border, make sure you get and keep a tourist card, *tarjeta de turista*, which you may be asked for if, for example, you take a domestic flight in Mexico.

TOUR OPTIONS

Five Star Tours runs a private Tijuana shuttle upon request and has several regularly scheduled tours. Among the Five Star's tours are Tijuana City Tour (operates Wed. and Fri. 11–5, $43), which includes the River and Casino Zones, Avenida Revolucion and Downtown. Five Star's Baja Wine Tour (Sat. 9–7, $93) visits two wineries in the Guadalupe Valley, stops in Ensenada for lunch and shopping. San Diego Scenic Tours offers half-day and full-day bus tours of Tijuana ($36 and $52). Sites include the Cultural Center, Agua Caliente Race Track, Avenue of Heroes with time allowed for shopping and dining.

Information Five Star Tours (✉ *1050 Kettner Blvd., San Diego* ☎ *619/232–5049* ⊕ *www.sdsuntours.com*). **San Diego Scenic Tours** (✉ *2255 Garnet Ave., San Diego* ☎ *858/273–8687* ⊕ *www.sandiegoscenictours.com*).

VISITOR INFORMATION

Mexican auto insurance, a quarterly newsletter, and discounts are available through Discover Baja, a San Diego–based membership club for Baja travelers. In Baja, tourism offices in the larger cities are usually open weekdays 9–7 (although some may close in early afternoon for

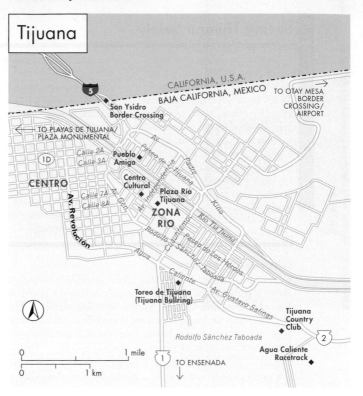

Tijuana

lunch) and weekends 9–1. Some of the smaller areas don't have offices. In Tijuana, tourist information offices, which distribute maps and other useful information, are positioned both at the border and downtown on Avenida Revolución; Tijuana also has a Baja California State Secretariat of Tourism office, which distributes more information about Baja generally. Visitors should pick up a brochure, Baja California State Map and Safety Tips, at the Port of Entry. Printed in English, it offers good advice on how to get the most out of your trip to Tijuana as well as how to handle most unfamiliar situations from public transit to sightseeing safely.

Tijuana Information Tijuana Convention and Visitors Bureau (✉ *Paseo de los Héroes 9365-201, Zona Río* ☎ *664/684-0537* ✉ *Ave. Revolución* ☎ *664/685-2210* ⊕ *www.tijuanaonline.org/EN* ✉ *Av. Revolución between Calles 3 and 4, Centro* ✉ *San Ysidro Pedestrian Border Crossing* ☎ *664/683-1405).*

Baja Information State Secretariat of Tourism of Baja California (✉ *1572 Juan Ruiz de Alarcon St., 3rd fl., Zona Rio, Tijuana* ☎ *664/682-3367* ⊕ *www.discoverbajacalifornia.com).*

Discover Baja (✉ *3264 Governor Dr., San Diego* ☎ *619/275-4225 or 800/727-2252* ⊕ *www.discoverbaja.com).*

Mercado Hidalgo has rows of produce and an amazing selection of piñatas.

EXPLORING

Avenida Revolución. This infamous strip, lined with shops and restaurants that cater to uninhibited travelers, has long been Tijuana's main tourism zone, even if the classier side of things has moved over to the Zona Río. Shopkeepers call out from doorways, offering low prices for garish souvenirs and genuine folk-art treasures. Many shopping arcades open onto Avenida Revolución; inside their front doors are mazes of stands with low-priced pottery and other crafts.

Centro Cultural (CECUT). The cultural center's stark, low-slung, tan buildings and globelike Omnimax Theater are beloved landmarks. The center's Museo de las Californias provides an excellent overview of Baja's history and natural profile, while the Omnimax shows a variety of exciting films exploring everything from our oceans to our skies. ⊠ *Paseo de los Héroes No. 9350, at Av. Mina, Zona Río* ☎ *664/687–9600* ⊕ *www.cecut.gob.mx* ⊠ *Museum $2, museum and Omnimax Theater $4* ⊙ *Tues.–Sun. 10–6; call or check website for films and showtimes.*

Pueblo Amigo. This entertainment center resembles a colonial village, with stucco facades and tree-lined paths leading to a domed gazebo. The complex includes a hotel, several restaurants and clubs, a huge grocery store, and a large branch of the Caliente Race Book, where gambling on televised sporting events is legal. Things get lively at night. ⊠ *Paseo de Tijuana between Puente Mexico and Calz. Independencia, Zona Río.*

San Ysidro Border Crossing. Locals and tourists jostle each other along the pedestrian walkway through the Viva Tijuana dining and shopping center and into the center of town. Artisans' stands line the walkway and adjoining streets, offering a quick overview of the wares to be found all over town.

SHOPPING

From the moment you cross the border, people will approach you or call out and insist that you look at their wares. Bargaining is expected in the streets and arcades, but not in the finer shops. If you drive, workers will run out from auto-body shops to place bids on new paint or upholstery for your car.

All along **Avenida Revolución** and its side streets, stores sell everything from tequila to Tiffany-style lamps. This shopping area spreads across Calle 2 to a pedestrian walkway leading from the border. Begin by checking out the stands along this walkway. Beware of fake goods, and above all, beware of higher prices offered to gringos. You may find that the best bargains are closer to the border; you can pick up your piñatas and sarapes on your way out of town. Between Calles 1 and 8, Avenida Revolución is lined with establishments stuffed with crafts and curios.

★ The **Mercado Hidalgo** (✉ *Calz. Independencia at Blvd. Sánchez Taboada, 5 blocks east of Av. Revolución, Zona Río*) is Tijuana's municipal market, with rows of fresh produce, some souvenirs, and Baja's best selection of piñatas.

Travel Smart
San Diego

WORD OF MOUTH

"From almost anywhere downtown (Gaslamp, Seaport Village-area, Embarcadero) you can walk to the ferry to Coronado. From the Gaslamp area you can take a bus to Balboa Park and its zoo, or go the 2–3 miles by cab at minimal cost. La Jolla is only 13 or so miles away but a long trip by bus."
—d_claude_bear

GETTING HERE AND AROUND

When traveling in the San Diego area, consider the big picture to avoid getting lost. Water lies to the west of the city. To the east and north, mountains separate the urban areas from the desert. If you keep going south, you'll end up in Mexico.

Downtown San Diego is made up of several smaller communities, including the Gaslamp Quarter and Balboa Park, that you can easily explore by walking, driving, riding the bus or trolley, or taking a taxi. In the heart of the city, numbered streets run west to east and lettered streets run north to south. The business district around the Civic Center, at 1st Avenue and C Street, is dedicated to local government and commerce.

■ AIR TRAVEL

Flying time to San Diego is 5 hours from New York, 3½ hours from Chicago, 3½ hours from Dallas, and 45 minutes from Los Angeles.

Major Airlines AeroMexico (☎ 800/237-6639 ⊕ www.aeromexico.com). **Air Canada** (☎ 888/247-2262 ⊕ www.aircanada.com). **AirTran Airways** (☎ 800/247-8726 ⊕ www.airtran.com). **Allegiant Air** (☎ 702/505-8888 ⊕ www.allegiantair.com). **Alaska Airlines** (☎ 800/252-7522 ⊕ www.alaskaair.com). **American Airlines** (☎ 800/433-7300 ⊕ www.aa.com). **Continental Airlines** (☎ 800/525-0280 ⊕ www.continental.com). **Delta Airlines** (☎ 800/221-1212 ⊕ www.delta.com). **Hawaiian Airlines** (☎ 800/367-5320 ⊕ www.hawaiianair.com). **JetBlue** (☎ 800/538-2583 ⊕ www.jetblue.com). **Southwest Airlines** (☎ 800/435-9792 ⊕ www.southwest.com). **United Airlines** (☎ 800/864-8331 ⊕ www.united.com). **USAirways** (☎ 800/428-4322 ⊕ www.usairways.com). **Virgin America** (☎ 877/359-8474 ⊕ www.virginamerica.com).

Regional Airlines Frontier Airlines (☎ 800/432-1359 ⊕ www.frontierairlines.com). **Sun Country Airlines** (☎ 800/359-6786 ⊕ www.suncountry.com). **WestJet** (☎ 888/937-8538 ⊕ www.westjet.com).

Airline Security Issues Transportation Security Administration (⊕ www.tsa.gov).

AIRPORT

The major airport is San Diego International Airport (SAN), called Lindbergh Field locally. Major airlines depart and arrive at Terminal 1 and Terminal 2; commuter flights identified on your ticket with a 3000-sequence flight number depart from a third commuter terminal. A red shuttle bus provides free transportation between terminals.

With only one runway serving two main terminals, San Diego's airport is too small to accommodate the heavy traffic of busy travel periods. Small problems including fog and rain can cause congested terminals and flight delays. Delays of 20–30 minutes in baggage claim aren't unusual.

Major construction started at the airport in 2010. Expect delays, road closures, and detours for the next several years. The result will be improved traffic flow and 10 additional gates at Terminal 2. Flight delays don't necessarily mean hours of boredom. The airport's Cultural Exhibits Program in Terminal 2 showcases a variety of stimulating and educational exhibits that highlight the city's culture and history. Exhibits change several times per year. Terminal 2 also features a performing arts series between 7 pm and 9:15 pm on the second Friday of each month. In addition, if you have a flight delay, consider catching a 10-minute cab ride downtown to go shopping or take one last stroll around the city.

If you need travel assistance at the airport, there are two Travelers Aid information booths, one in Terminal 1 and one in Terminal 2, open daily 6 am–11 pm.

Airlines and Airports Airline and Airport Links.com (⊕ www.airlineandairportlinks.

com). **San Diego International Airport**
(☎ 619/400–2400 ⊕ www.san.org).

GROUND TRANSPORTATION

San Diego International Airport is 3 mi from downtown. Shuttle vans, buses, and taxis run from the Transportation Plaza, reached via the skybridges from Terminals 1 and 2. The cheapest and sometimes most convenient shuttle is the Metropolitan Transit System's Flycr Route 992, red-and-blue-stripe buses that serve the terminals at 10- to 15-minute intervals between 5 am and 11 pm. These buses have luggage racks and make a loop from the airport to downtown along Broadway to 9th Avenue and back, stopping frequently within walking distance of many hotels; they also connect with the San Diego Trolley and Amtrak. The $2.25 fare includes transfer to local transit buses and the trolley, and you should have exact fare (in coins or bills) handy. Information about the Metropolitan Transit System's shuttles and buses, the San Diego Trolley, and Coaster commuter train can all be found on the San Diego Transit Web site.

If you're heading to North County, the Flyer can drop you off at the Santa Fe Depot, where you can take the Coaster commuter train as far north as Oceanside for $4–$5.50.

Of the various airport shuttles, only Cloud 9 Shuttle/SuperShuttle has tiedowns for wheelchairs; however, Access Shuttle can provide curbside service if requested in advance.

Ground shuttle service is available between LAX and San Diego, but can be prohibitively expensive, with rates for the two-hour trip starting at $200 (it can be a more-affordable option for groups, however). All of the shuttles listed at the end of this section offer the service.

Taxis departing from the airport are subject to regulated fares—all companies charge the same rate ($2.50 initial fee, $2.70 for each additional mile). Taxi fare is about $12 plus tip to most downtown hotels. The fare to Coronado runs about $20 plus tip. Limousine rates vary and are charged per hour, per mile, or both, with some minimums established.

Contacts Access Shuttle (☎ 619/282–1515 ⊕ www.accessshuttle.net). **San Diego Transit** (☎ 619/233–3004, 800/568–7097 TTY and TDD ⊕ transit.511sd.com). **Cloud 9 Shuttle/ SuperShuttle** (☎ 800/974–8885 ⊕ www.cloud9shuttle.com).

▌BOAT TRAVEL

Many hotels, marinas, and yacht clubs rent slips short-term. Call ahead, because available space is limited. The San Diego and Southwestern yacht clubs have reciprocal arrangements with other yacht clubs.

The San Diego Bay Ferry takes you between downtown and Coronado in a nostalgic, old-school ferry every hour from 9 am to 10 pm. The ride lasts about 15 minutes and costs $4.25 each way; bicycles are free. The Water Taxi is a great alternative for nighttime transit along San Diego Bay. It is on call daily from 9 to 9 (11 pm Friday and Saturday) and costs $7 each way.

Ferry Contacts San Diego Bay Ferry (☎ 800/442–7847 ⊕ www.flagshipsd.com). **Water Taxi** (☎ 619/235–8294 ⊕ www.flagsjpsd.com).

Marinas Best Western Island Palms Hotel & Marina (☎ 619/223–0301). **The Dana on Mission Bay** (☎ 619/222–6440). **Kona Kai Resort** (☎ 619/224–7547). **San Diego Marriott Hotel and Marina** (☎ 619/230–8955). **San Diego Yacht Club** (☎ 619/221–8400). **Southwestern Yacht Club** (☎ 619/222–0438).

CRUISE TRAVEL

Several cruise lines make San Diego a port of call. Holland America and Royal Caribbean use San Diego as a regular point of embarkation for seasonal cruises to Alaska, the Mexican Riviera, and the Panama Canal. Other lines, including Princess and Celebrity, originate repositioning cruises in San Diego throughout the year. The San Diego cruise-ship terminal is on the downtown waterfront, steps from the San Diego Maritime Museum and Midway Museum. The terminal is a short taxi ride from Balboa Park, Little Italy, and the Gaslamp Quarter. Fares between the cruise-ship terminal are $18 to Balboa Park, $15 to SeaWorld, and $12 to the Gaslamp Quarter.

Cruise Lines Celebrity (📞 800/647–2251 ⊕ www.celebritycruises.com). **Holland America** (📞 800/426–0327 ⊕ www.hollandamerica. com). **Princess Cruises** (📞 800/774-6237 ⊕ www.princess.com). **Royal Caribbean International** (📞 800/398–9819 ⊕ www.royalcaribbean.com).

▌BUS AND TROLLEY TRAVEL

Under the umbrella of the Metropolitan Transit System, there are two major transit agencies in the area: San Diego Transit and North County Transit District (NCTD). Day Tripper passes, available for 1 to 30 days and starting at $5, give unlimited rides on nonpremium regional buses and the San Diego Trolley. You can buy them from most trolley vending machines, at the downtown Transit Store, and at some hotels. A $14 Regional Plus Day Pass adds Coaster service and premium bus routes.

The bright-red trolleys of the San Diego Trolley light-rail system operate on three lines and serve downtown San Diego, Mission Valley, Old Town, South Bay, the U.S. border, and East County. The trolleys operate seven days a week from about 5 am to midnight, depending on the station, at intervals of about 15 minutes. The trolley system connects with San Diego Transit bus routes—connections are posted at each trolley station. Bicycle lockers are available at most stations and bikes are allowed on buses and trolleys though space is limited. Trolleys can get crowded during morning and evening rush hours. Schedules are posted at each stop; on-time performance is excellent.

NCTD bus routes connect with Coaster commuter train routes between Oceanside and the Santa Fe Depot in San Diego. They serve points from Del Mar North

to San Clemente, inland to Fallbrook, Pauma Valley, Valley Center, Ramona, and Escondido, with transfer points within the city of San Diego. NCTD also offers special express-bus service to Qualcomm Stadium for select major sporting events. The Sprinter light rail provides service between Oceanside and Escondido, with buses connecting to popular North County attractions.

San Diego Transit bus fares range from $2.25 to $5; North County Transit District bus fares are $1.75. You must have exact change in coins and/or bills. Pay upon boarding. Transfers are not included; the $5 day pass is the best option for most bus travel and can be purchased on board.

San Diego Trolley tickets cost $2.50 and are good for two hours, but for one-way travel only. Round-trip tickets are double the one-way fare.

Tickets are dispensed from self-service machines at each stop; exact fare in coins is recommended, although some machines accept bills in $1, $5, $10, and $20 denominations and credit cards. For trips on multiple buses and trolleys, buy a day pass good for unlimited use all day.

Bus and Trolley Information North County Transit District (📞 800/266–6883 ⊕ www.gonctd.com). **San Diego Transit** (📞 619/233–3004, 800/568–7097 TTY and TDD ⊕ transit.511sd.com). **Transit Store** (✉ 102 Broadway, Downtown 📞 619/234–1060).

▌CAR TRAVEL

A car is handy for San Diego's sprawling freeway system and for visiting the North County beaches, mountains, and Anza Borrego Desert. Driving around San Diego County is pretty simple: most major attractions are within a few miles of the Pacific Ocean. Interstate 5, which stretches from Canada to the Mexican border, bisects San Diego. Interstate 8 provides access from Yuma, Arizona, and points east. Drivers coming from the Los Angeles area, Nevada, and the mountain regions beyond can reach San Diego on I–15. During rush hour there are jams on I–5 and on I–15 between I–805 and Escondido.

There are border inspection stations along major highways in San Diego County. Travel with your driver's license, or passport if you're an international traveler, in case you're asked to pull into one.

PARKING

Meters downtown usually cost 50¢ to $1.25 an hour; enforcement is 8 am–6 pm every day but Sunday. ■TIP→ If you are headed to Horton Plaza, the mall validates for three hours with no purchase required. Be extra careful around rush hour, when certain on-street parking areas become tow-away zones. Violations in congested areas can cost you $25 or more. In the evening and during events downtown, parking spaces are hard to find.

Balboa Park and Mission Bay have huge free parking lots, and it's rare not to find a space, though it may seem as if you've parked miles from your destination. On game day at PETCO Park, expect to pay $17 or more for a short walk to the stadium, less for a longer one. Other downtown lots cost $5–$35 per day.

Old Town has large lots surrounding the transit center, but parking spaces are still hard to find. Parking is more of a problem in La Jolla and Coronado, where you generally need to rely on hard-to-find metered street spots or expensive by-the-hour parking lots.

ROAD CONDITIONS

Highways are generally in good condition in the San Diego area. From 6 to 8:30 am and 3:30 to 6 pm, traffic is particularly heavy on I–5, I–8, I–805, and I–15. Before venturing into the mountains, check on road conditions; mountain driving can be dangerous. Listen to radio traffic reports for information on the length of lines waiting to cross the border from Mexico. For roadside assistance, dial 511 from a mobile phone.

RENTAL CARS

In California you must be 21 to rent a car, and rates may be higher if you're under 25. Some agencies will not rent to those under 25; check when you book. Children up to age six or 60 pounds must be placed in safety or booster seats. For non–U.S. residents an international license is recommended but not required.

Rates fluctuate with seasons and demand, but generally begin at $39 a day and $250 a week for an economy car with air-conditioning, automatic transmission, and unlimited mileage. This doesn't include an 8.75% tax.

Most American car-rental companies prohibit drivers from taking rentals into Mexico. If you do take a rental to Mexico, you must get permission from the car-rental company and you should always carry your rental agreement with you.

Automobile Associations American Automobile Association (AAA) (☎ 315/197-5000 ⊕ www.aaa.com).

Local Rental Agencies Autorent Car Rental (☎ 619/692-3006 ⊕ www.autorentsd. com). **Fox Rent A Car** (☎ 619/692-0300 or 800/225-4369 ⊕ www.foxrentacar.com).

Major Rental Agencies Alamo (☎ 800/462-5266 ⊕ www.alamo.com). **Avis** (☎ 800/331-1212 ⊕ www.avis.com). **Budget** (☎ 800/527-0700 ⊕ www.budget. com). **Hertz** (☎ 800/654-3131 ⊕ www.hertz. com). **National Car Rental** (☎ 800/227-7368 ⊕ www.nationalcar.com).

CAR-RENTAL INSURANCE

If you don't have auto insurance, buy the collision- or loss-damage waiver (CDW or LDW) from the rental company. This eliminates your liability for damage to the car. Some credit cards offer CDW coverage, but it's usually supplemental to your own insurance and rarely covers SUVs, minivans, luxury models, and the like. If your coverage is secondary, you may still be liable for loss-of-use costs from the car-rental company (again, read the fine print). But no credit-card insurance is valid unless you use that card for *all* transactions, from reserving to paying the final bill.

U.S. rental companies sell CDWs and LDWs for about $15 to $25 a day; supplemental liability is usually more than $10 a day. Note that some states, including California, have capped the price of the CDW and LDW.

If you're driving into Mexico, you must purchase Mexican car insurance to protect yourself from theft and liability to third parties for property damage or bodily injury as a result of an accident. If you're involved in an accident in Mexico and don't have car insurance, you could be detained by the authorities until they can determine fault. They mean business. If you're at fault, you would be required to demonstrate financial responsibility to post bond and cover the estimated costs of the damage.

Sanborn's Insurance, which has been in business for more than 50 years, offers short-term auto coverage to those traveling south of the border. You can purchase a policy online in advance of your trip.

Insurance Contact Sanborn's Insurance (☎ *800/222–0158* ⊕ *www.sanbornsinsurance.com*).

▌ TAXI TRAVEL

Fares, including the ride back to the airport, vary among companies. If you are heading to the airport from a hotel, ask about the flat rate, which varies according to destination; otherwise you'll be charged by the mile (which works out to $15 or so from any downtown location). Taxi stands are at shopping centers and hotels; otherwise you must call and reserve a cab. The companies listed below don't serve all areas of San Diego County. If you're going somewhere other than downtown, ask if the company serves that area.

Taxi Companies Orange Cab (☎ *619/291–3333* ⊕ *www.orangecabsandiego.com*). **Silver Cabs** (☎ *619/280–5555*

⊕ *www.sandiegosilvercab.com*). **Yellow Cab** (☎ *619/444-4444* ⊕ *www.driveu.com*).

▌ TRAIN TRAVEL

Amtrak serves downtown San Diego's Santa Fe Depot with daily trains to and from Los Angeles, Santa Barbara, and San Luis Obispo. Connecting service to Oakland, Seattle, Chicago, Texas, Florida, and points beyond is available in Los Angeles. Amtrak trains stop in San Diego North County at Solana Beach and Oceanside. You can obtain Amtrak timetables at any Amtrak station, or by visiting the Amtrak Web site.

Coaster commuter trains, which run between Oceanside and San Diego Monday–Saturday, stop at the same stations as Amtrak as well as others. The frequency is about every half hour during the weekday rush hour, with four trains on Saturday (with additional Friday and Saturday night service in spring and summer). One-way fares are $4 to $5.50, depending on the distance traveled. The Oceanside, Carlsbad, and Solana Beach stations have beach access. The Sprinter runs between Oceanside and Escondido, with many stops along the way.

Metrolink operates high-speed rail service between the Oceanside Transit Center and Union Station in Los Angeles.

Information Amtrak (☎ *800/872–7245* ⊕ *www.amtrak.com*). **Coaster** (☎ *619/233-3004* ⊕ *www.sdcommute.com*). **Metrolink** (☎ *800/371–5465* ⊕ *www.metrolinktrains.com*).

ESSENTIALS

▌ CUSTOMS AND DUTIES

If you make a shopping trip to Mexico, keep receipts for all purchases. Upon reentering the country, be ready to show customs officials what you've bought. Pack purchases together in an easily accessible place. If you think a duty is incorrect, appeal the assessment. If you object to the way your clearance was handled, note the inspector's badge number. In either case, first ask to see a supervisor. If the problem isn't resolved, write to the appropriate authorities, beginning with the port director at your point of entry.

Customs officers operate at the San Ysidro border crossing, at San Diego International Airport, and in the bay at Shelter Island.

You're always allowed to bring goods of a certain value back home without having to pay any duty or import tax. But there's a limit on the amount of tobacco and liquor you can bring back duty-free. If the total value of your goods is more than the duty-free limit, you'll have to pay a tax (most often a flat percentage) on the value of everything beyond that limit.

U.S. Information U.S. Customs and Border Protection (⊕ www.cbp.gov).

▌ MONEY

With its mild climate and proximity to the ocean and mountains, it's no wonder that San Diego is a relatively expensive place to visit. Three-star rooms average between $200 and $280 per night in high season, but there is also a good variety of modest accommodations available. Meal prices compare to those in other large cities, and you can usually find excellent values by dining in smaller, family-run establishments. Admission to local attractions can cost anywhere from $10 to $70. Thankfully, relaxing on one of the public beaches or meandering through the parks and neighborhoods is free—and fun. ■TIP→ To save money on restaurants, spas, and boutiques, scour the coupon section at ⊕ www.sdreader.com.

ITEM	AVERAGE COST
Cup of Coffee	$2
Glass of Wine	$7
Sandwich	$8
One-Mile Taxi Ride	$2.70
Museum Admission	$12

Prices throughout this guide are given for adults. Substantially reduced fees are almost always available for children, students, and senior citizens. Many museums offer free admission one day of the month.

CREDIT CARDS

Throughout this guide, the following abbreviations are used: **AE**, American Express; **D**, Discover; **DC**, Diners Club; **MC**, MasterCard; and **V**, Visa.

TAXES

In San Diego County a sales tax of 8.75% is added to the price of all goods, except food purchased at a grocery store or as takeout from a restaurant. Hotel taxes are 6%–13%.

▌ PACKING

San Diego's casual lifestyle and year-round mild climate set the parameters for what to pack. You can leave formal clothes and cold-weather gear behind.

Plan on warm weather at any time of the year. Cottons, walking shorts, jeans, and T-shirts are the norm. Pack bathing suits and shorts regardless of the season. Few restaurants require a jacket and tie for men. Women may want to also bring something a little dressier than their sightseeing garb.

Evenings are cool, even in summer, so be sure to bring a sweater or a light jacket.

Rainfall in San Diego isn't usually heavy; you won't need a raincoat except in winter, and even then, an umbrella may suffice.

Be sure you have comfortable walking shoes. Even if you don't walk much at home, you will probably find yourself covering miles while sightseeing on your vacation. Also bring a pair of sandals or water shoes for the beach.

Sunglasses and sunscreen are a must in San Diego. Binoculars can also come in handy, especially if you're in town during whale-watching season, from December through March.

PASSPORTS AND VISAS

PASSPORTS

When traveling to Mexico by air, land, or sea you must have a passport that is valid for a minimum of six months from date of departure, regardless of how long you intend to stay in the country. U.S. passports are valid for 10 years. You must apply in person if you're getting a passport for the first time; if your previous passport was lost, stolen, or damaged; or if your previous passport has expired and was issued more than 15 years ago or when you were under 16. All children under 16 must appear in person to apply for or renew a passport.

Take special note if you're traveling with a child: it's no longer necessary for single parents, unaccompanied minors, widows/widowers, or parents with estranged partners to produce notarized letters or other supporting documentation for minors entering Mexico. Instead, each child must have his or her own passport. As with adults, the passport must be valid for at least six months from the date of departure.

When a minor is traveling alone, without a parent or legal guardian, all parents and guardians named on the child's birth certificate, adoption papers, or court documents must give signed and notarized authorization for the child to travel without them. It's advised that they also travel with a clear copy of the authorizing

parent or guardian's driver's license. Contact the Mexican Embassy (⊕ *www. embassyofmexico.org*) for additional information.

VISAS

A visa isn't required for U.S. tourists visiting Mexico for up to 90 days. However, tourists traveling beyond the border zone or entering Mexico by air must pay a fee (usually around $20) to obtain a tourist card, also known as an FMT, available from Mexican consulates, Mexican border crossing points, Mexican tourism offices, airports within the border zone, and most airlines serving Mexico. The fee for the tourist card is generally included in the price of a plane ticket for travelers arriving by air.

The tourist card is issued upon presentation of proof of citizenship, such as a U.S. passport or a U.S. birth certificate, plus photo ID, such as a driver's license. Tourist cards are issued for up to 90 days with a single entry, or if you present proof of sufficient funds, for 180 days with multiple entries.

Upon entering Mexico, retain and safeguard the traveler's copy of your tourist card; you must surrender it to Mexican immigration when you depart. Be sure to leave Mexico before your tourist card expires or you will be subject to a fine.

U.S. Passport Information U.S. Department of State (☎ *877/487–2778* ⊕ *www.travel.state. gov/passport*).

RESTROOMS

Major attractions and parks have public restrooms. In the downtown San Diego area, you can usually use the restrooms at major hotels and fast-food restaurants. The Bathroom Diaries is a Web site that's flush with unsanitized information on restrooms the world over—each one located, reviewed, and rated.

Find a Loo The Bathroom Diaries (⊕ *www.thebathroomdiaries.com*).

▌SAFETY

IN SAN DIEGO

San Diego is generally a safe place for travelers who observe all normal precautions. Dress inconspicuously, remove badges when leaving convention areas, and know the routes to your destination before you set out. At the beach, check with lifeguards about any unsafe conditions such as dangerous riptides or water pollution. The San Diego Convention & Visitors Bureau publishes a Visitor Safety Tips brochure listing normal precautions for many situations. It's available at the International Visitor Information Center.

IN MEXICO

There are no guarantees when it comes to traveling in Mexico. In recent years, drug-related crime has tarnished Tijuana's reputation as a tourist destination. Many U.S. authorities, including the State Department, have noted an increase in crime in recent years. Even police officers have been known to demand money during routine traffic stops. Be as prepared as possible: hide important travel documents and carry small amounts of cash for bribes. Stick to well-traveled areas and, if possible, travel with a friend or guide who knows the area. If you're determined to see Tijuana, consider taking one of the escorted bus tours that depart from San Diego.

Contacts San Diego Police Department (☎ 619/531–2000 ⊕ www.sandiego.gov/police). **San Diego Convention & Visitors Bureau International Visitor Information Center** (⊠ 1040⅓ W. Broadway, at Harbor Dr., Downtown ☎ 619/236–1212 ⊕ www.sandiego.org). **U.S. Department of State** (⊕ travel.state.gov).

▌TIPPING

TIPPING GUIDELINES FOR SAN DIEGO	
Bartender	$1 to $5 per round of drinks, depending on the number of drinks
Bellhop	$1 to $5 per bag, depending on the level of the hotel
Hotel Concierge	$5 or more, if he or she performs a service for you
Hotel Doorman	$1–$2 if he helps you get a cab
Hotel Maid	$1 to $3 a day (either daily or at the end of your stay, in cash)
Hotel Room-Service Waiter	$1–$2 per delivery, even if a service charge has been added
Porter at Airport or Train Station	$1 per bag
Skycap at Airport	$1 to $3 per bag checked
Taxi Driver	15%–20%, but round up the fare to the next dollar amount
Tour Guide	10% of the cost of the tour
Valet Parking Attendant	$1–$2, but only when you get your car
Waiter	15%–20%, with 20% being the norm at high-end restaurants; nothing additional if a service charge is added to the bill

▌TOURS

BIKE TOURS

Pedal your way around San Diego with the Bike Revolution. Secret San Diego, by Where You Want To Be Tours, offers walking tours as well as tours on bike and Segway.

Contacts Bike Revolution (☎ 619/564–4843 ⊕ www.sandiegobiketoursinc.com). **Secret San Diego** (☎ 619/917–6037 ⊕ www.wheretours.com).

BOAT TOURS

Flagship Cruises and Events and Hornblower Cruises & Events both operate one- and two-hour harbor cruises departing from the Broadway Pier. No reservations are necessary for the tours, which cost $20–$25; both companies also do dinner cruises ($67–$85) and brunch cruises. Whakapono Sailing Charter, at Mission Bay, has afternoon and evening cruises of the harbor and San Diego Bay aboard six-passenger sailing ships ($75 per person). These companies also operate during whale-watching season, from December to March. Other fishing boats that do whale watches in season include H&M Landing and Seaforth Boat Rentals.

Contacts H&M Landing (⌨ *619/222–1144* ⊕ *www.hmlanding.com*). **Hornblower Cruises & Events** (⌨ *619/234–8687 or 800/668–4322* ⊕ *www.hornblower.com*). **Flagship Cruises and Events** (⌨ *619/234–4111 or 800/442–7847* ⊕ *www.flagshipsd.com*). **Seaforth Boat Rentals** (⌨ *619/223–1681* ⊕ *www.seaforthboatrental.com*). **Whakapono Sailing Charter** (⌨ *800/659–0141* ⊕ *www.whakapono.us*).

BUS AND TROLLEY TOURS

Free two-hour bus tours of the downtown redevelopment area, including the Gaslamp Quarter, are conducted by the Centre City Development Corporation, the agency in charge of redevelopment. Tours take place on the first Saturday of the month at 10 am and leave from the agency's Downtown Information Center, in Horton Plaza. Advance reservations are necessary, as the tour may be canceled if there aren't enough passengers.

Gray Line San Diego provides narrated sightseeing tours, picking up passengers at many hotels; the selection includes daily morning city tours ($32 for adults); charter-group tours to the San Diego Zoo, Safari Park, SeaWorld, and LEGOLAND California, as well as trips to Tijuana, Rosarito, and Ensenada, may be arranged through Gray Line.

Old Town Trolley Tours takes you to 11 sites, including Old Town, Seaport Village, Horton Plaza and the Gaslamp Quarter, Coronado, Little Italy, and El Prado in Balboa Park. The tour is narrated, and for the price of the ticket ($34 for adults, $17 for children 4–12; under 4, free) you can get on and off as you please at any stop. The trolley leaves every 30 minutes, operates daily, and takes two hours to make a full loop.

DayTripper and Five Star Tours do one-day or multiple-day bus tours of attractions in Southern California and Baja Mexico. San Diego Scenic Tours does narrated tours of San Diego and Tijuana.

Contacts Centre City Development Corporation Downtown Information Center (⌨ *619/235–2222* ⊕ *www.ccdc.com*). **DayTripper** (⌨ *619/299–5777 or 800/679–8747* ⊕ *www.daytripper.com*). **Five Star Tours** (⌨ *619/232–5040* ⊕ *www.fivestartours.com*). **Gray Line San Diego** (⌨ *800/331–5077* ⊕ *www.sandiegograyline.com*). **Old Town Trolley Tours** (⌨ *619/298–8687* ⊕ *www.trolleytours.com*). **San Diego Scenic Tours** (⌨ *858/273–8687* ⊕ *www.sandiegoscenictours.com*).

GO CAR TOURS

These miniature talking cars offer the benefits of a guided tour, but taken at your own pace. Tour the city in a bright yellow two-seater, equipped with GPS navigation and accompanying narration. Go Cars Tours offers two routes: choose from Downtown, Balboa Park, Uptown, and Old Town or Point Loma, Cabrillo National Monument, and Ocean Beach. The tours can be driven straight through, or visitors can park and explore any of the sights en-route. Rentals are $49 for the first hour, $39 for the second hour, and $29 for the third through fifth hours. There is a maximum daily charge of 5 hours if you want to keep the car for the entire day.

Contacts Go Car Tours (⌨ *800/914–6227* ⊕ *www.gocartours.com*).

WALKING TOURS

Several fine walking tours are available on weekdays or weekends; upcoming walks are usually listed in the *San Diego Reader*.

Coronado Walking Tours offers an easy 90-minute stroll ($14; Tuesday, Thursday, Saturday at 11 am) through Coronado's historic district, with departures from the Glorietta Bay Inn. Make reservations.

On Saturday at 10 am and 11:30 am, Offshoot Tours conducts free, hour-long walks through Balboa Park that focus on history, palm trees, and desert vegetation.

Urban Safaris, led by longtime San Diego resident Patty Fares, are two-hour-long Saturday walks ($10) through interesting neighborhoods such as Hillcrest, Ocean Beach, and Point Loma. The tours, which always depart from a neighborhood coffeehouse, focus on art, history, and ethnic eateries. Reservations are required.

The Gaslamp Quarter Historical Foundation leads two-hour historical walking tours of the downtown historic district on Saturday at 11 am ($10).

Contacts Coronado Walking Tours (☎ 619/435–5993 ⊕ www.coronadowalkingtour.com). **Gaslamp Quarter Historical Foundation** (☎ 619/233–4692 ⊕ www.gaslampquarter.org). **Offshoot Tours** (☎ 619/239–0512 ⊕ www.balboapark.org). **Urban Safaris** (☎ 619/944–9255 ⊕ www.walkingtoursofsandiego.com).

∎ VISITOR INFORMATION

For general information and brochures before you go, contact the San Diego Convention & Visitors Bureau, which publishes the helpful *San Diego Visitors Planning Guide*. When you arrive, stop by one of the local visitor centers for general information.

Citywide Contacts San Diego Convention & Visitors Bureau (☎ 619/232–3101 ⊕ www.sandiego.org). **San Diego Convention & Visitors Bureau International Visitor Information Center** (✉ 1040⅓ W. Broadway, at Harbor Dr., Downtown ☎ 619/236–1212 ⊕ www.sandiego.org). **San Diego Visitor**

Information Center (☎ 800/827–9188 ⊕ www.infosandiego.com).

San Diego County Contacts Borrego Springs Chamber of Commerce and Visitor Center (☎ 760/767–5555 ⊕ www.borregospringschamber.org). **California Welcome Center Oceanside** (☎ 760/721–1101 or 800/350–7873 ⊕ www.oceansidechamber.com). **Carlsbad Convention & Visitors Bureau** (☎ 800/227–5722 ⊕ www.visitcarlsbad.com). **Coronado Visitor Center** (☎ 619/437–8788 ⊕ www.coronadovisitorcenter.com). **Encinitas Chamber of Commerce** (☎ 760/753–6041 ⊕ www.encinitaschamber.com). **Julian Chamber of Commerce** (☎ 760/765–1857 ⊕ www.julianca.com). **Promote La Jolla, Inc.** (☎ 858/454–5718 ⊕ www.lajollabythesea.com). **San Diego East Visitors Bureau** (☎ 800/463–0668 ⊕ www.visitsandiegoeast.com).

Statewide Contacts California Travel and Tourism Commission (☎ 916/444–4429 or 800/862–2543 ⊕ www.visitcalifornia.com).

INSPIRATION

Check out these books for further San Diego reading. The novel *Drift* by Jim Miller explores San Diego's boom time through the eyes of a college professor in the year 2000. *Leave Only Paw Prints: Dog Hikes in San Diego* offers myriad walking spots that are dog-friendly, along with smart travel tips for your furry friend. *San Diego Legends: Events, People and Places That Made History* goes beyond the typical history-book material to reveal little-known stories about San Diego.

San Diego has a rich film history, thanks to the city's unique geography and proximity to Los Angeles. Some of the better-known films made here include *Top Gun,*

Traffic, and *Almost Famous.* The bar scene in *Top Gun* was filmed at a local restaurant, Kansas City BBQ, on the corner of Kettner Boulevard and West Harbor Drive. And of course, don't forget to take *Anchorman* Ron Burgundy's advice, and "Stay classy, San Diego."

ONLINE RESOURCES

For a dining and entertainment guide to San Diego's most popular nightlife district, check out Gaslamp.org. Visit the HillQuest guide to Hillcrest, a historic neighborhood with a large number of gay and lesbian households. For insider tips from a local perspective, try Local Wally's San Diego Tourist Guide. For information on the birthplace of California, search the Old Town San Diego organization's site. Browse the Web site of San Diego's premier upscale lifestyle magazine, *Ranch and Coast. San Diego Magazine* also has a useful site. Search the site of Arts Tix for half-price show tickets. For a comprehensive listing of concerts, performances, and art exhibits, check out the local alternative paper *San Diego Reader.* For edgier arts and culture listings, pick up the *San Diego Citybeat* alt-weekly. The Visitors Guide section of the *San Diego Union-Tribune* is a great trip-planning tool.

Websites Gaslamp Info (⊕ *www.gaslamp. org*). **Hillcrest** (⊕ *www.hillquest.com*). **Local Wally** (⊕ *www.localwally.com*). **Old Town San Diego** (⊕ *www.oldtownsandiego.org*). *Ranch and Coast* (⊕ *www.ranchandcoast. com*). *San Diego Citybeat* (⊕ *www.sdcitybeat. com*). *San Diego Magazine* (⊕ *www. sandiegomagazine.com*). **San Diego Performs** (⊕ *www.sdartstix.com*). *San Diego Reader* (⊕ *www.sandiegoreader.com*). *San Diego Union-Tribune* (⊕ *www.signonsandiego.com*).

INDEX

PHOTO CREDITS

1, Irene Chan/Alamy. 2, San Diego CVB/Joanne DiBona. 5, Matthew Field/wikipedia.org. Chapter 1: Experience San Diego: 8-9, Brett Shoaf/Artistic Visuals. 10, Brett Shoaf/Artistic Visuals. 11 (left), San Diego CVB/Joanne DiBona. 11 (right), San Diego CVB. 12, Corbis. 13 (left), Doug Scott/age fotostock. 13 (right), Werner Bollmann/age fotostock. 14, Jeff Greenberg/age fotostock. 15 (left), Xiao Li/Shutterstock. 15 (right), John W. Warden/age fotostock. 18 (left), mlgb, Fodors.com member. 18 (top center), SuperStock/age fotostock. 18 (top and bottom right), San Diego CVB/Joanne DiBona. 19 (left and top center), San Diego CVB. 19 (bottom center), Epukas/wikipedia.org. 19 (right), SeaWorld San Diego. 20, Corbis. 21 (left), Paul M. Bowers. 21 (right), San Diego CVB. 22, Joelle Gould/iStockphoto. 23 (left), San Diego CVB. 23 (right) and 25, Corbis. 26, Steve Rabin/iStockphoto. 28, zoonabar/Flickr. 30, San Diego CVB. Chapter 2: Downtown: 31, Johnny Stockshooter/age fotostock. 33, Lowe Llaguna/Shutterstock. 34, Steve Snodgrass/Flickr. 36, Brett Shoaf/Artistic Visuals. 38, Robert Holmes. 41, Brett Shoaf/Artistic Visuals. Chapter 3: Balboa Park and San Diego Zoo: 43 and 45, Brett Shoaf/Artistic Visuals. 46 and 51, Brett Shoaf/Artistic Visuals. 55, Ambient Images/Alamy. 57 (top), Dreyer Peter/age fotostock. 57 (bottom), Epukas/wikipedia.org. 58, Robert Holmes. 59, Steve Snodgrass/Flickr. 60 (left and top center), fPat/Flickr. 60 (bottom center), Matthew Field/wikipedia.org. 60 (top right), Jim Epler/Flickr. 60 (bottom right), Philippe Renault/age fotostock. 61, lora_313/Flickr. 62 (left), Cburnett/wikipedia.org. 62 (right), Susann Parker/age fotostock. 63 (top), George Ostertag/age fotostock. 63 (bottom), Sally Brown/age fotostock. 64, John Elk III/Alamy. 67, Brett Shoaf/Artistic Visuals. Chapter 4: Old Town and Uptown: 69, Brett Shoaf/Artistic Visuals. 71, dichohecho/Flickr. 72-81, Brett Shoaf/Artistic Visuals. Chapter 5: Mission Bay, Beaches, and SeaWorld: 83, Brett Shoaf/Artistic Visuals. 85, SD Dirk/Flickr. 86 and 87 (top), SeaWorld San Diego. 87 (bottom), Robert Holmes. 88, San Diego CVB. 91, Brett Shoaf/Artistic Visuals. Chapter 6: La Jolla: 93, Brett Shoaf/Artistic Visuals. 95, Roger Isaacson. 96, Jason Pratt/Flickr. 99, Brett Shoaf/Artistic Visuals. 100, Philipp Scholz Rittermann. Chapter 7: Point Loma and Coronado: 103 and 105, Brett Shoaf/Artistic Visuals. 106, San Diego CVB. 107 (top), jamesbenet/iStockphoto. 107 (bottom)., Cass Greene/iStockphoto. 108, rkkwan, Fodors.com member. 112-13, Brett Shoaf/Artistic Visuals. Chapter 8: Where to Eat: 117, Lorena Whiteside. 118, Amy K. Fellows. 122, Lorena Whiteside. 123 (top), Cucina Urbana. 123 (bottom), Mister A's. 124, George's at the Cove. 125 (top), Michele Coulon Dessertier. 125 (bottom), Gary Payne Photography. 126, Tioli's Crazy Burger. 127 (top), David Eskra. 127 (bottom), Tioli's Crazy Burger.139, Brett Shoaf/Artistic Visuals. 144, Lorena Whiteside. 153, Tower 23 Hotel and JRDN. Chapter 9: Where to Stay: 173, Brett Shoaf/Artistic Visuals. 174, Hotel del Coronado. 181 (top), Hard Rock Hotel San Diego. 181 (bottom left), robjtak/Flickr. 181 (bottom right), Westgate Hotel. 184, Graham Blair. 187 (top), Courtyard San Diego Mission Valley/Hotel Circle. 187 (bottom left), Catamaran Resort Hotel and Spa. 187 (bottom right), Britt Scripps Inn. 191 (top), Lodge at Torrey Pines. 191 (bottom), Grande Colonial Hotel. 194 (top), San Diego CVB. 194 (bottom), Sue Gillingham. Chapter 10: Nightlife: 197, Tower 23 Hotel and JRDN. 198, Andaz San Diego. 202, Sandy Huffaker. 207, Brett Shoaf/Artistic Visuals. 211, Chris Woo. 215, Tower 23 Hotel and JRDN. Chapter 11: The Arts: 219, AlanHaynes.com/Alamy. 220, Lynn Susholtz. 222, Brett Shoaf/Artistic Visuals. 225, San Diego CVB. 227, J.T. MacMillan/Lamb's Players Theatre. Chapter 12: Beaches: 229 and 230, Brett Shoaf/Artistic Visuals. 231 (top), San Diego CVB. 231 (bottom), Dija/Shutterstock. 232, alysta/Shutterstock. 233 (top), Lowe Llaguno/Shutterstock. 233 (bottom), San Diego CVB. 234, Sebastien Burel/Shutterstock. 240 and 245, Brett Shoaf/Artistic Visuals. Chapter 13: Sports and the Outdoors: 247, Brett Shoaf/Artistic Visuals. 248, Sebastien Burel/Shutterstock. 249 (top), Janet Fullwood. 249 (bottom), Sebastien Burel/iStockphoto. 250, Stas Volik/Shutterstock. 253, Brett Shoaf/Artistic Visuals. 258, Sebastien Burel/Shutterstock. 262-63 and 266, Brett Shoaf/Artistic Visuals. 271, SD Dirk/Flickr. Chapter 14: Shopping: 273, Brett Shoaf/Artistic Visuals. 274, Paul M. Bowers. 275, Brett Shoaf/Artistic Visuals. 276, Old Town Trolleys of San Diego. 277, Lowe Llaguno/Shutterstock. 278, Paul M. Bowers. 283 and 288, Brett Shoaf/Artistic Visuals. 292, San Diego CVB/Joanne DiBona. 295, Richard Wong/ www.rwongphoto.com/Alamy. Chapter 15: North County and Environs: 297, Brett Shoaf/Artistic Visuals. 299 (top left), San Diego CVB. 299 (top right), Ken Bohn, San Diego Zoo. 299 (bottom), Alan Vernon/Flickr. 300, LEGOLAND California Resort. 301 (top), San Diego CVB/Joanne DiBona. 301 (bottom), San Diego CVB. 302, Robert Holmes. 303 (top and bottom), Ken Bohn, San Diego Zoo. 304, Brett Shoaf/Artistic Visuals. 305 (top), Rancho Valencia. 305 (bottom), La Costa Resort and Spa. 306, San Diego CVB. 313, Brett Shoaf/Artistic Visuals. 321, San Diego CVB/Joanne DiBona. 330, San Diego CVB. 337, Brett Shoaf/Artistic Visuals. 338, Ian Vaughan Productions. 340, San Diego CVB. 351, Brett Shoaf/Artistic Visuals. 355, Emmanuel LATTES / Alamy.

NOTES

NOTES

NOTES

NOTES